A. P. Chalkley

Diesel Engines for Land and Marine Work

With an introductionary Chapter by Dr. Rudolf Diesel

A. P. Chalkley

Diesel Engines for Land and Marine Work

With an introductionary Chapter by Dr. Rudolf Diesel

ISBN/EAN: 9783954274291
Erscheinungsjahr: 2014
Erscheinungsort: Bremen, Deutschland

© maritimepress in EHV Academicpress GmbH, Fahrenheitstr. 11, 28359 Bremen. Alle Rechte beim Verlag und bei den jeweiligen Lizenzgebern.

www.maritimepress.de | office@maritimepress.de

Bei diesem Titel handelt es sich um den Nachdruck eines historischen, lange vergriffenen Buches. Da elektronische Druckvorlagen für diese Titel nicht existieren, musste auf alte Vorlagen zurückgegriffen werden. Hieraus zwangsläufig resultierende Qualitätsverluste bitten wir zu entschuldigen.

A. P. Chalkley

Diesel Engines for Land and Marine Work

With an introductionary Chapter by Dr. Rudolf Diesel

DIESEL ENGINES
FOR
LAND AND MARINE WORK

By A. P. CHALKLEY

B.Sc. (Lond.), A.M.Inst.C.E., A.I.E.E.

WITH AN INTRODUCTORY CHAPTER BY THE LATE
DR. RUDOLF DIESEL

FOURTH EDITION, REVISED AND ENLARGED

NEW YORK
D. VAN NOSTRAND COMPANY
25 PARK PLACE
1916

PREFACE

THE interest which has been roused in this country over the Diesel motor in the last two years is remarkable for its spontaneity and its widespread character. The reason is not far to seek. The questions involved are not merely technical, but of far-reaching commercial importance, and hence are by no means limited in their discussion to the engineering community. The Author has kept this point in mind in dealing with the subject and has endeavoured to render the book suitable to all those who, for widely differing reasons, find it necessary to become acquainted with the Diesel engine, and it is with intent that certain elementary matters have been included to aid the non-technical reader. Hitherto, no book has been published dealing solely with this type of motor, but it is hardly necessary to say that the importance it has now attained is more than sufficient to warrant such an undertaking.

In science, it is sometimes possible, in taking a wide survey, to arrive at an approximate idea as to the probable future developments in any particular direction. The general adoption of Diesel engines on land is assured, and, as already there are some 300 vessels in service propelled by these machines, it would seem safe to predict that a large degree of success will be obtained at sea, particularly as the very desirable probationary period, necessary in any engineering development for the gathering of experience, is nearly at an end. Should the expectations which have been formed be but partially realized, the effect of the introduction of the Diesel motor would still perhaps be more important than that produced by any other recent invention in engineering science.

The Author has received much help from various manufacturers to whom reference is made in the text. To Dr. Ernst Müller he would also wish to express his indebtedness, and is particularly grateful for the kindness Dr. Diesel has shown him, and the interest he has taken in the preparation of the book.

A. P. CHALKLEY.

LONDON,
December, 1911.

PREFACE TO THE FOURTH EDITION

THE present volume represents the second complete revision since the work was first issued, both of which are rendered essential by the rapid strides that were made in design and construction of the Diesel engine, more particularly for marine work.

Whilst practice has become standardized to a certain extent in regard to the manufacture of motors of the stationary type, it is still felt that the application of the engine to marine work is in its infancy. It is, therefore, in the section of the book dealing with Diesel motors for ships' propulsion that the greatest additions have been made. The number of illustrations has been nearly doubled, and besides much descriptive matter dealing with engines of new types that have been built since the last edition was published, there is an additional chapter on the design of Diesel engines. Beyond this the whole of the text has been carefully revised, and considerable additions have been made in the body of the work.

In paying a respectful tribute to the memory of the late Dr. Diesel, whose friendship to me was more valued than he knew, I feel that his great satisfaction always was the fact that the work he had initiated was being carried on so eagerly and successfully throughout the whole world.

A. P. CHALKLEY.

LONDON,
October, 1914.

CONTENTS

	PAGE
INTRODUCTION .	1

CHAPTER I
GENERAL THEORY OF HEAT ENGINES, WITH SPECIAL REFERENCE TO DIESEL ENGINES   9

CHAPTER II
ACTION AND WORKING OF THE DIESEL ENGINE .   32

CHAPTER III
CONSTRUCTION OF THE DIESEL ENGINE   57

CHAPTER IV
INSTALLING AND RUNNING DIESEL ENGINES   125

CHAPTER V
TESTING DIESEL ENGINES   146

CHAPTER VI
DIESEL ENGINES FOR MARINE WORK   170

CONTENTS

CHAPTER VII

Construction of the Diesel Marine Engine . . . PAGE 206

CHAPTER VIII

The Design of Diesel Engines . . . 302

CHAPTER IX

The Future of the Diesel Engine . . . 336

Appendix . . . 345

Index . . . 365

LIST OF ILLUSTRATIONS

FIG.	TITLE	PAGE
1.	Isothermal and Adiabatic Curves	12
2.	Isothermal and Adiabatic Curves	12
3.	Constant Temperature Cycle Diagram	15
4.	Constant Volume Cycle Diagram	17
5.	Constant Pressure Cycle Diagram	19
6.	Diesel Cycle Diagram	21
7.	Typical Indicator Cards with various Diesel Engines	29
8.	Indicator Cards of Four-Cylinder 800 B.H.P. Sulzer Two-Cycle Marine Diesel Motor	30
9.	Simultaneous Indicator Cards for Six-Cylinder Four-Cycle Marine Diesel Engine	31
10.	Diagram showing action of Diesel Engine	34
11.	Diagram showing action of Diesel Engine	34
12.	Diagram showing action of Diesel Engine	34
13.	Two-Stroke Cycle Diagram	38
14.	General Arrangement Plan of Diesel Plant	60
15.	Ditto—Elevation	60
16.	Longitudinal Section of M.A.N. Diesel Engine *facing*	62
17.	Transverse Section of M.A.N. Diesel Engine ,,	62
18.	1,000 H.P. M.A.N. Diesel Engine ,,	62
19.	880 H.P. M.A.N. Diesel Engine	64
20.	Diagram showing Arrangement of Cams with Diesel Engine	66
21.	Fuel Inlet Valve, Lever and Cam	67
22.	Details of Fuel Inlet Valve (Carels' Type) *facing*	68
23.	Arrangement of Fuel Admission when using Tar Oil	69
24.	Details of Fuel Valve of Hick, Hargreaves Diesel Motor	70
25.	Arrangement of Jointed Valve Lever for easy dismantling	71

LIST OF ILLUSTRATIONS

FIG.	TITLE	PAGE
26.	Fuel Inlet Valve and Pulveriser	72
27.	Details of Fuel Inlet Valve of Deutz Engine	73
28.	Fuel Inlet Valve of Aktiebolaget Diesels Motorer Type	74
29.	Mouthpiece or Bottom Part of Pulveriser	75
30.	Diagram showing Action of Pulveriser	76
31.	Air Inlet and Exhaust Valves (in section)	77
32.	Details of Suction and Exhaust Valves of Carels' Four-Cycle Land Motor	78
33.	Exhaust Valve (section)	79
34.	Arrangement of Governor and Fuel Valve of Mirrlees, Bickerton & Day Type	80
35.	Fuel Pump (Willans & Robinson Type)	82
36.	Arrangement for Controlling Fuel and Injection Air	85
37.	Front Elevation of Mirrlees Diesel Engine . *facing*	85
38.	Side Elevation of Mirrlees Diesel Engine . ,,	85
39.	Deutz Three-Cylinder Vertical Engine	86
40.	Longitudinal Section of 80 H.P. Nederlandsche Fabriek Engine . *facing*	87
41.	Transverse Section of 80 H.P. Engine . ,,	87
42.	Plan of 80 H.P. Engine	88
43.	Arrangement of Air Inlet	89
44.	Section of Fuel Pump	90
45.	General Arrangement of Carels' Four-Stroke Stationary Motor with Horizontal Three-Stage Compressor *facing*	90
46.	Method of removing Piston in Nederlandsche Fabriek Engine	91
47.	Nederlandsche Fabriek Engine	92
48.	End Section of 600 B.H.P. Four-Cycle Engine	95
49.	Carels' Slow Speed Engine . *facing*	93
50.	Front Section of 600 B.H.P. High Speed Engine (Ned. Fab.) . *facing*	96
51.	200 H.P. Sulzer High-Speed Four-Cycle Stationary Engine . *facing*	96
52.	General Arrangement Plans of Two-Cylinder Hick, Hargreaves Motor, 16 in. diameter, 19 in. stroke, speed 250 r.p.m. . *facing*	96
53.	Burmeister & Wain High-Speed Diesel Engine ,,	98

LIST OF ILLUSTRATIONS

FIG.	TITLE		PAGE
54.	Carels' High Speed Engine	*facing*	98
55.	Sulzer High Speed Engine		99
56.	Section through High Speed Engine and Air Pump		101
57.	Details of M.A.N. Horizontal Engine	*facing*	102
58.	,, ,, ,, ,, ,,	,,	102
59.	800 B.H.P. Horizontal Diesel Engine	,,	104
60.	50 H.P. Deutz Diesel Engine		105
61.	Sulzer Two-Cycle 2,400 B.H.P. Engine	*facing*	108
62.	Outline Dimension Drawing of 2,400 B.H.P. Engine		109
63.	1,500 B.H.P. Sulzer Two-Cycle Engine with Port Scavenging		110
64.	Section through Cylinder of Sulzer Two-Cycle Motor, showing Auxiliary Scavenge Ports		111
65.	Details of Scavenge Valve of Carels' Two-Cycle Motor		112
66.	Carels' Two-Cycle Stationary Motor (New Type)	*facing*	114
67.	Plan of Carels' Two-Cycle Stationary Motor (New Type)	*facing*	114
68.	1,000 H.P. Two-Cycle Diesel Engine		114
69.	Elevation of Carels' Two-Stroke Stationary Motor (New Type)	*facing*	114
70.	Details of Scavenge Pump and Air Compressor for Carels' Two-Stroke Stationary Motor (New Type)	*facing*	114
71.	Carels' Two-Cycle Stationary Engine of 1,000 H.P.		114
72.	1,000 H.P. Krupp Two-Cycle Motor. Speed, 150 r.p.m.	*facing*	114
73.	Reavell Quadruplex Compressor		116
74.	Section of Quadruplex Compressor		117
75.	Reavell's Compressor	*facing*	119
76.	Section of Three-Stage Vertical Compressor for Diesel Engines		118
77.	General Arrangement of Compressor for Carels' 1,500 H.P. Two-Cycle Marine Engine	*facing*	121
78.	Marine Type Compressor	,,	122
79.	Diagram of Vickers' Solid Injection System		123
80.	Sketch showing Solid Injection Arrangement		124
81.	Outline Drawing of Sulzer Four-Cycle Engines (to correspond with Table of Dimensions)		127

LIST OF ILLUSTRATIONS

FIG.	TITLE	PAGE
82.	Curve showing Fuel Consumption	151
83.	Curve showing Fuel Consumption	156
84.	Engine-room Arrangement of Motor-ship equipped with a 2,000 H.P. Two-Cycle Engine . *facing*	182
85.	Details of one of the two Scavenge Pumps for 1,500 B.H.P. Carels' Type Marine Diesel Engine	188
86.	Diagram of Position of Valves and Piston in Two-Cycle Engine (to show working)	190
87.	Two-Cycle Engine with Scavenge Ports instead of Valves	191
88.	Auxiliary Compressor and Dynamo driven by Diesel Engine, installed in a Motor Ship	196
89.	Sulzer Auxiliary Ship's Set	197
90.	2,000 H.P. Single Cylinder Two-Cycle Double-Acting Diesel Engine . *facing*	205
91.	Sectional Elevation of Two-Cycle Sulzer Marine Engine	207
92.	General Arrangement of small vessel equipped with Sulzer Diesel Engine	208
93.	General Arrangement of Diesel Ship showing Auxiliaries	209
94.	General Arrangement Plan of Torpedo Boat with Sulzer Engines	211
95.	Ditto for Submarines	211
96.	Sulzer Direct Reversible Marine Diesel Engine; a type used for relatively small powers	213
97.	Sulzer Marine Engine. Front View	214
98.	Sulzer Marine Engine. Back View	215
99.	Arrangement of Scavenge Pump with Sulzer Engine	217
100.	Arrangement of Scavenging Ports	218
101.	600 B.H.P. Sulzer High-Speed Marine Diesel Engine	221
102.	Sulzer Marine Engine . *facing*	222
103.	Sulzer Two-Cycle Submarine Motor of 600 B.H.P.	222
104.	1,000 H.P. Carels' Diesel Marine Engine	224
105.	View of Engine-Room of M.S. *France* with two Schneider-Carels' Motors of 900 B.H.P. at 230 r.p.m.	226
106.	Scavenge Pump or Compressor for 900 H.P. Two-Cycle Engine at 230 r.p.m.	227
107.	1,500 B.H.P. Carels' Type Marine Motor: End View showing Scavenge Pump . *facing*	228

LIST OF ILLUSTRATIONS

FIG.	TITLE		PAGE
108.	Marine Diesel Engine, Carels' Type	facing	228
109.	Plan of 1,500 H.P. Carels' Marine Engine	,,	228
110.	Sectional Elevation of 1,500 H.P. Carels' Marine Motor (New Type)	facing	228
111.	1,800 B.H.P. Carels-Reichersteig Marine Diesel Engine. Speed, 90–100 r.p.m.	facing	228
112.	1,500 H.P. Carels-Tecklenborg Engine	,,	228
113.	800 H.P. Carels-Westgarth Engine		229
114.	End View of 800 H.P. Carels' Type Two-Cycle Marine Motor		231
115.	General Arrangement of Engine-room of Ship equipped with Aktiebolaget Diesels Motorer Engine	facing	232
116.	800 B.H.P. Polar Marine Engine		235
117.	Near View of Cam Shaft of 800 H.P. Polar Diesel Marine Engine		237
118.	850 B.H.P. Polar Two-Cycle Reversible Marine Diesel Engine		239
119.	Near View of Cylinders of Polar Marine Engine as installed		241
120.	650 B.H.P. Neptune Polar Marine Engine, built by Messrs. Swan, Hunter & Wigham Richardson	facing	241
121.	High-Speed Reversible Marine Polar Engine for Submarines and Yachts		242
122.	Polar Diesel Marine Engine		243
123.	Krupp Two-Cycle 1,000 B.H.P. Engine		245
124.	Diagram showing action of Cams for Krupp's Engine		246
125.	Section of 1,250 B.H.P. Krupp Engine		248
126.	1,250 B.H.P. Krupp Engine		249
127.	Tops of two 1,250 H.P. Krupp Two-Cycle Engines installed in Motor Ship		250
128.	Reversing Mechanism of Krupp Engine	facing	252
129.	1,250 B.H.P. Krupp Two-Cycle Marine Engine	,,	252
130.	Diagrammatic Representation of Nürnberg Two-Cycle Marine Engine, showing Scavenge Arrangements		253
131.	Diagram illustrating Method of Reversing Nürnberg Engine		255
132.	Sectional Illustrations of Nürnberg Marine Engine	facing	258

LIST OF ILLUSTRATIONS

FIG.	TITLE		PAGE
133.	End View of Nürnberg Engine.		259
134.	M.A.N. 900 H.P. Submarine Engine.		261
135.	Standard Nürnberg Marine Engine	*facing*	262
136.	850 B.H.P. Weser-Junkers Marine Diesel Engine	,,	262
137.	850 B.H.P. Weser-Junkers Marine Engine.	,,	262
138.	Tanner-Diesel Engine	*facing*	264
139.	Doxford Diesel Engine		266
140.	500 H.P. Engine for *Vulcanus*.	*facing*	268
141.	Engine-room of *Vulcanus*		269
142.	Werkspoor Engine of 250 B.H.P.		271
143.	Werkspoor 1,100 B.H.P. Diesel Motor	*facing*	272
144.	1,100 B.H.P. Werkspoor Engine		272
145.	Arrangement of Piston Cooling in Werkspoor 1,100 B.H.P. Marine Motor		273
146.	Section of Werkspoor 1,100 B.H.P. Four-Cycle Marine Motor		274
147.	Top View of two 1,100 B.H.P. Werkspoor Four-Cycle Engines in the Motor Ship *Emanuel Nobel*		276
148.	Gusto Two-Cycle Marine Motor		278
149.	Elevation and Section of Gusto Diesel Motor		279
150.	M.A.N. High-Speed Engine		282
151.	1,250 I.H.P. Burmeister & Wain Engine.	*facing*	283
152.	1,000 B.H.P. Burmeister & Wain Marine Diesel Engine		284
153.	Interior of Engine-room of Motor Ship with two Burmeister & Wain Diesel Engines		285
154.	Starting, Inlet and Fuel Valves of 2,000 I.H.P. Burmeister & Wain Marine Diesel Engine	*facing*	286
155.	Section of Six-Cylinder Burmeister & Wain 2,000 I.H.P. Marine Engine		288
156.	2,000 I.H.P. Burmeister & Wain Marine Diesel Engine, showing intermediate Shaft and Push Rods for operating the Valves		290
157.	Kolomna Diesel Engine		292
158.	Kolomna Diesel Engine		293
159.	100 H.P. Daimler Diesel Four-Cycle Reversible Marine Engine.		295
160.	Krupp Four-Cycle Marine Motor		297

LIST OF ILLUSTRATIONS

FIG.	TITLE	PAGE
161.	Junkers 100 H.P. Marine Motor	298
162.	150 H.P. Two-Cycle American Diesel Marine Engine	299
163.	150 H.P. Kind Two-Cycle Marine Diesel Engine	301
164.	Details of Cylinder Cover of Hick, Hargreaves Motor	304
165.	Details of Piston of Hick, Hargreaves Diesel Motor	307
166.	Compression Curves in Two-Stage Compressor	326
167.	Diagrammatic Representation of Two-Stage Compressor	328
168.	Diesel Engine Indicator Diagram with Valve Scavenging	331
169.	Diagram of Engine with Port Scavenging	332
170.	Sulzer Diesel Locomotive built for the Prussian State Railways	338
171.	Diagram illustrating Arrangement of Sulzer Diesel Locomotive	339
172.	Arrangement of Drive for Sulzer-Diesel Locomotive *facing*	340

1.\
2.\
3.\
4.\
5. Relative to Diesel's Patent Specification, and are referred to\
6. in the Appendix.\
7.\
8.\
9.\
10.

INTRODUCTION

By DR. RUDOLF DIESEL

VERY willingly do I accede to the Author's request to add an introduction to this book, because I am very glad that an attempt should thus be made to present the subject of the Diesel engine in a concise and well-ordered form, in view of the amount of scattered literature there is dealing with the question.

Since its first appearance about fourteen years ago, many thousands of Diesel engines have been installed in all kinds of factories in all industrial countries, and also in the remotest corners of the world; proof has thus been obtained that the motor, when properly installed, is a reliable machine, whose operation is as satisfactory as the best of other types of engine, and, in general, simpler, owing to the absence of all auxiliary plant, and because the fuel can be employed directly in the cylinder of the motor in its original natural condition, without any previous transformatory process.

In 1897, when after four years of difficult experimental work I completed the construction of the first commercially successful motor in the Augsburg Works, it was proclaimed by the numerous engineering and scientific committees and deputations from various countries, who tested the machine, that a higher heat efficiency was attained by it than with any other known heat engine. As a result of subsequent experience in practice, and the gradual improvement in the manufacture, still better results have been obtained, and at the present time the thermal efficiency the motor attains is up to about 48 per cent. and the effective efficiency in some cases up to nearly 35 per cent.

Technical knowledge and science are always progressing, and in later days these figures will be even further improved, but in the present state of our knowledge a higher efficiency cannot be reached by any process for changing heat into work; a further advance seems only possible by a new process of conversion, with an essentially novel method of operation which we to-day cannot conceive.

Therefore the Diesel motor is the engine which develops power from the fuel directly in the cylinder without any previous transformatory process, and in as efficient a manner as, according to the present state of science, seems possible; it is therefore the simplest and at the same time the most economical power machine.

These two conditions explain its success, which lies in the novel principle of its method of operation and not in constructional improvements or alterations to earlier engine types. Naturally the questions of construction, and the careful design of the details, are of considerable moment in a Diesel motor as in every engine; but they are not the cause of the great importance of this motor in the world's industry.

A further reason for this importance lies in the fact that the Diesel engine has destroyed the monopoly of coal, and has in the most general way solved the problem of the employment of liquid fuel for motive purposes. The Diesel motor has thus become in relation to liquid fuel, what the steam and gas engine are to coal, but in a simpler and more economical manner; it has by this means doubled the resources of man in the sphere of power development, and found employment for a product of nature which previously lay idle.

In consequence thereof the Diesel motor has had a far-reaching effect in the liquid fuel industry, which is now progressing in a way that could not previously be anticipated. I cannot here enlarge on this point, but it may in general be said that owing to the interest which the petroleum producers have taken in this important matter, new wells are being constantly opened out, and fresh developments inaugurated, and that from the latest geological researches it has been shown that there is probably as much, and perhaps more, liquid fuel than coal in the earth, and moreover in much more favourable and more widely distributed geographical positions.

That the undertakings dependent on the petroleum industry have been equally strongly influenced is shown by the marked development which in quite recent times has occurred in the oil transport trade, especially the great development in the number of tank vessels which themselves use the Diesel motor for propulsion.

But the influence of the Diesel engine on the world's industry does not end here. Already in the year 1899 I employed in my motor the by-products from the distillation of coal, and the manufacture of coke—tar or creosote oil— with the same success as with natural liquid fuel. The quality of these oils was however generally unsatisfactory for use in Diesel motors and subject to continual variations. Only recently the interested chemical industries have succeeded in getting the necessary quality, and to-day this product enters definitely into the sphere of influence of the Diesel motor.

It follows therefore that this engine has an important influence on the two further industries—gas and coke manufacture—from which the by-products have now become so important that a great movement is beginning in connexion with this question. It is impossible further to discuss this matter here, but one fact arises distinctly from this movement, namely, that the coal which appeared to be threatened by the competition of liquid fuels will, on the contrary, enter into a new and better era of utilization through the Diesel motor. Since tar oil can be employed three to five times more efficiently in the Diesel motor than coal in the steam engine, it follows that coal can be much more economically utilized when it is not burnt barbarously under boilers or grates, but converted into coke and tar by distillation. The coke is then employed in metallurgical work and for all heating purposes; the valuable products from the tar must be extracted and used in the chemical industries, while the tar oil, and its combustible derivatives, and under certain circumstances the atr itself, can be put to exceptionally favourable use in Diesel motors.

It is, therefore, of the greatest interest to employ the largest possible amount of coal in this refined and more economical manner, and thus both coal mining and the related chemical industry come within the influence of the Diesel motor, which is not inimical but most helpful to the development of the coal industry. The proper evolution of the fuel question which has already begun and is now progressing rapidly is as follows : on the one side use liquid fuel in Diesel motors, on the other side, gas fuel, also in the form of coke, in gas motors : solid fuel should not be employed at all for power production, but only in the refined form of coke for all other uses of heat in metallurgy and heating.

The liquid fuels already mentioned by no means exhaust the list of fuel which may be used for Diesel motors.

It is well known that lignite, whose production is about 10 per cent. of that of coal, leaves tar on dry distillation which when worked for pure paraffin leaves as a by-product the so-called paraffin oil. Not all kinds of lignite are suitable for this purpose, nevertheless so much of this oil is produced that up to now it has supplied, for instance in Germany, a very large proportion of the demand for liquid fuel for Diesel motors. Further there are to be considered other products available in smaller but noteworthy quantities such as shale oil, etc.; certain countries, as for instance France and Scotland, have large quantities of them and they are in use in many Diesel engine installations.

But it is not yet generally known that it is possible to use animal and vegetable oils direct in Diesel motors. In 1900 a small Diesel engine was exhibited at the Paris exhibition by the Otto Company which, on the suggestion of the French Government, was run on Arachide oil,[1] and operated so well that very few people were aware of the fact. The motor was built for ordinary oils, and without any

[1] Botanical name: Arachis hypogæa L.

INTRODUCTION

modification was run on vegetable oil. I have recently repeated these experiments on a large scale with full success and entire confirmation of the results formerly obtained. The French Government had in mind the utilization of the large quantities of arachide or ground nuts available in the African colonies and easy to cultivate, for, by this means, the colonies can be provided with power and industries, without the necessity of importing coal or liquid fuel.

Similar experiments have also been made in St. Petersburg with castor oil with equal success. Even animal oils, such as fish oil, have been tried with perfect success.

If at present the applicability of vegetable and animal oils to Diesel motors seems insignificant, it may develop in the course of time to reach an importance equal to that of natural liquid fuels and tar oil. Twelve years ago we were no more advanced with the tar oils than to-day is the case with the vegetable oils; and how important have they now become!

We cannot predict at present the rôle which these oils will have to play in the colonies in days to come. However, they give the certainty that motive power can be produced by the agricultural transformation of the heat of the sun, even when our total natural store of solid and liquid fuel will be exhausted.

Having now made a short survey of the importance of the Diesel motor to the world's industry in general, I would add a few words concerning its importance to England in particular. The following three facts must be kept in mind for consideration:—

1. England is an exclusively coal-producing country.
2. England is the greatest colonizing country in the world.
3. England is the greatest marine nation in the world.

(1) England possesses (at any rate up to now) no natural liquid fuel, and is a purely coal-producing country; owing to this fact the opinion has lately been frequently and strongly expressed that England has intrinsically no concern with the Diesel motor, and that it is against her most vital

interests to help in the more widespread adoption of this engine, since she would neglect her own wealth of coal and would render herself dependent on other countries by the employment of liquid fuel.

Both these statements are wrong and the reverse is true. It is in England's greatest interest that the coal-devouring steam engine should be replaced by the economical Diesel motor, and particularly so as by such a change, economies can be effected in her most important wealth, the coal—and the life of the mines prolonged ; further, because it improves in a most rational way the use of coal and the results of the allied chemical industries, in utilizing the coal in the refined manner previously mentioned ; finally, because by this method of utilizing the coal (that is through the employment of tar and tar oils in Diesel motors), England becomes free and independent of foreign countries for the supply of her liquid fuel.

(2) The extent to which England may help her colonies through the Diesel motor can, as yet, hardly be conceived ; even when using natural mineral oils alone, the Diesel motor is a machine essentially adapted for work in the colonies, as only from one-fourth to one-sixth part of the weight of fuel has to be transported to the colony and into the interior, as compared with a steam engine ; because in the colonies the freight charges for the fuel are generally the deciding factor in the profitableness of power plants. Further, because the transport of this liquid fuel is incomparably easier and more convenient than coal, and finally because the difficulties of running a boiler installation —particularly marked in the hinterland—put the steam plant out of question.

It may be mentioned in this connexion that a pipe line for crude petroleum 400 kilometres long will be laid from Matadi to Leopoldville on the Congo, by means of which this immense country will be provided with a constant source of liquid fuel, which will give its essential living element—the motive power—to agricultural and transport enterprises, and other industries about to be established.

INTRODUCTION

This wonderful example should be followed in the English colonies; it is unnecessary to follow the far-reaching effects of such a course on the prosperity of the colonies.

When it is remembered that, as previously mentioned, the Diesel motor can also run on vegetable oils, it is not difficult to see that this fact opens out a new prospect for the prosperity and industry of the colonies, a fact which is of greater importance to England than to any other country owing to the large number of its possessions. On this point and as quickly as possible the problem should be tackled; the Diesel motor can be driven by the colonies' own products, and thus in a great degree can aid in the development of the agriculture in the country in which it operates. This sounds to-day somewhat as a dream of the future, but I venture the prophecy with entire conviction that this method of the employment of the Diesel motor will in days to come attain great importance.

(3) Finally, England is the greatest marine power in the world.

When the first success of the Diesel motor as a marine engine became known in England last year; when it was realized that already a large number of small merchant and naval vessels were equipped with Diesel engines, and that progress was gradually being made on a larger scale; that already large American liners were to be propelled by Diesel motors, and at the same time a warship was in construction to be equipped with a very large Diesel engine; then there was much stir and some excitement throughout the country which is still fresh in the mind.

And rightly so! The reports of satisfactory sea voyages with Diesel motors under very bad weather conditions are becoming more numerous. The ships' captains who have Diesel motors in their ships certify to their great reliability and convenience of running, and figures are published showing the economy effected; it can no longer be doubted that in this direction the Diesel motor will create one of the greatest evolutions in modern industry.

That the greatest shipping nation in the world should derive no advantage from such a change would be simply impossible. England is bound, in the face of competition with other countries, to take full advantage of this new departure.

Finally, a few words on the manufacturing :—The Diesel motor must be constructed with extreme care, and the best materials employed in order that it may properly fulfil all its capabilities ; only the best and most completely equipped works can build it. Fourteen years ago there were very few factories which were able to undertake its construction, and it may be said that through the Diesel engine the manufacture of large machines has been raised to a higher level, in the same way as the manufacture of small machines has been brought on new lines by the automobile engine.

The Diesel motor is therefore not a cheap engine, and I would add a warning that the attempt should never be made to try to build it cheaply, by unfinished workmanship, particularly for export.

These fundamental conditions regarding the construction of the Diesel engine are no disadvantage, as has been frequently proved ; on the contrary they are precisely the reason of its strong position and form a guarantee of its worth.

MUNICH, DIESEL.
December, 1911.

CHAPTER I

GENERAL THEORY OF HEAT ENGINES WITH SPECIAL REFERENCE TO DIESEL ENGINES

EXPANSION OF GASES — ADIABATIC EXPANSION — ISOTHERMAL EXPANSION — WORKING CYCLES — THERMO-DYNAMIC CYCLES — CONSTANT TEMPERATURE CYCLE — CONSTANT VOLUME CYCLE — CONSTANT PRESSURE CYCLE — DIESEL ENGINE CYCLE — REASONS FOR THE HIGH EFFICIENCY OF THE DIESEL ENGINE.

Expansion of Gases.—Though it is unnecessary to go fully into any detail regarding the theory of heat engines, a general study of the laws governing the expansion of gases, and the theoretically and practically attainable efficiencies of motors working on gaseous fuel, is desirable in order to understand the action of the Diesel engine, and the reason for its higher efficiency than that of any other heat engine. The basis of the various formulae quoted in the following pages will be found in any text-book on heat engines, and elucidation is only given in this volume where it bears directly on the theory of the Diesel engine.

In a consideration of the expansion of gases with the consequent production of work there is always a definite relation, for the same weight of gas, between the volume, pressure, and temperature at any moment during the expansion, and this relation is given by the formula $PV = \eta T$ where P = absolute pressure in lb. per square foot.

$\quad$ V = Volume in cubic feet.

$\quad$ T = absolute temperature in degrees Fahrenheit.

$\quad$ η = constant.

and of course the same formula applies for other units (e.g. metric units), with a different value for η. The value of η varies with different gases, and it is in fact the difference between the specific heats of the gas at constant pressure, and at constant volume and may be expressed as

$$\eta = K_p - K_v$$

where K_p = Specific heat of gas at constant pressure.
K_v = Specific heat of gas at constant volume.
In the units given above, for air $K_p = 184 \cdot 7$ $K_v = 131 \cdot 4$ and $\eta = 53 \cdot 3$. In the formulae which follow, it will be seen that the ratio of the two specific heats is of importance and this ratio, i.e. $\dfrac{K_p}{K_v}$ is usually denoted by the symbol γ which for air is 1·405 and for other gases used in heat engines somewhat less, 1·32 being for instance a fair figure for lighting gas.

Since with all gases $PV = \eta T$, it is evident that for the same quantity of gas either the pressure, volume, or temperature, is determinate if the two other values be known, i.e. $\dfrac{P_1 V_1}{T_1} = \dfrac{P_2 V_2}{T_2}$ where P_1, V_1, and T_1, represent respectively the pressure, volume, and temperature of the gas in one state and P_2, V_2 and T_2 the pressure, volume, and temperature of the same weight of gas in another state.

For purposes of solving the problems of the behaviour of gases during expansion, there are two methods of expansion which are generally considered, neither of which however is exactly attained in actual heat engines. These are :—

1. Expansion at constant pressure.
2. Expansion in which the pressure and volume vary according to the formula $PV^n =$ constant

Under the heading (2) come the two special cases of expansion which are of the most importance in the theory of heat engines, namely (a) adiabatic expansion according to the formula $PV^\gamma =$ constant, and (b) isothermal expansion, according to the formula $PV =$ constant.

Adiabatic Expansion.—When a gas expands adiabatically no heat is lost or gained during the expansion, the whole of the heat being employed in doing external work, and it is evident at once that such can never be quite realized in practice. The relation between temperature and volume is important in considering the question of the efficiencies of the cycles on which the Diesel and other heat engines operate, and this relation may be arrived at as follows :—

For any gas $\dfrac{P_1 V_1}{T_1} = \dfrac{P_2 V_2}{T_2}$ hence $P_1 T_2 = P_2 T_1 \dfrac{V_2}{V_1}$ ....(1)

also $P_1 V_1^{\gamma} = P_2 V_2^{\gamma}$ hence $\dfrac{V_2}{V_1} = \dfrac{P_1^{\frac{1}{\gamma}}}{P_2^{\frac{1}{\gamma}}}$ ....(2)

Substituting (2) in (1) $P_1 T_2 = P_2 T_1 \times \dfrac{P_1^{\frac{1}{\gamma}}}{P_2^{\frac{1}{\gamma}}}$

or $\dfrac{T_2}{T_1} = \dfrac{P_2}{P_1} \times \dfrac{P_1^{\frac{1}{\gamma}}}{P_2^{\frac{1}{\gamma}}}$

which is $\dfrac{T_2}{T_1} = \dfrac{P_2^{1-\frac{1}{\gamma}}}{P_1^{1-\frac{1}{\gamma}}} = \left(\dfrac{P_2}{P_1}\right)^{\frac{\gamma-1}{\gamma}}$ ....(3)

and in a similar manner it may be shown that

$$\dfrac{T_2}{T_1} = \left(\dfrac{V_1}{V_2}\right)^{\gamma-1} \qquad \ldots\ldots\ldots\ldots(4)$$

Isothermal Expansion.—In isothermal expansion the temperature of the gas during the whole expansion remains unaltered, and hence the internal energy in the gas itself remains unaltered, and the heat given to the gas is equivalent to the external work done. In this expansion from the general formula $PV = \eta T$, since T is constant the pressure must vary inversely as the volume, and since the equation $PV = $ constant is that of an equilateral hyperbola, isothermal expansion is sometimes known as hyperbolic expansion.

The relation between isothermal and adiabatic expansion

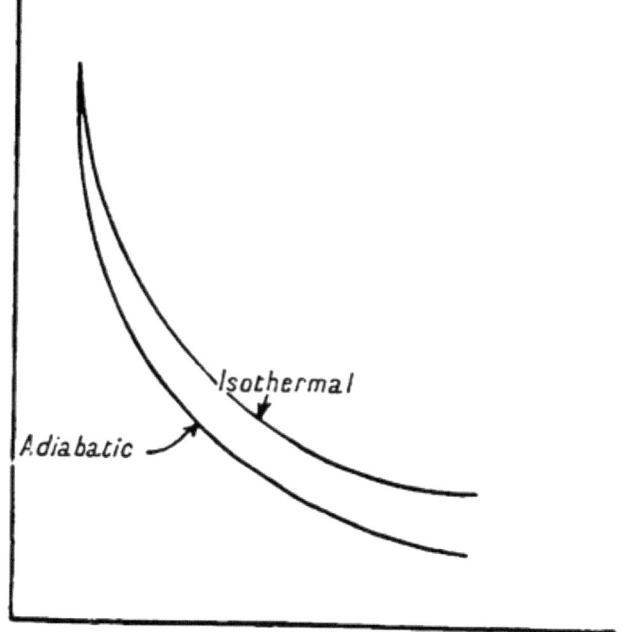

FIG. 1.—Isothermal and Adiabatic Curves.

curves is readily seen on a pressure volume diagram, *Fig.* 1, in which the isothermal is above the adiabatic line, and

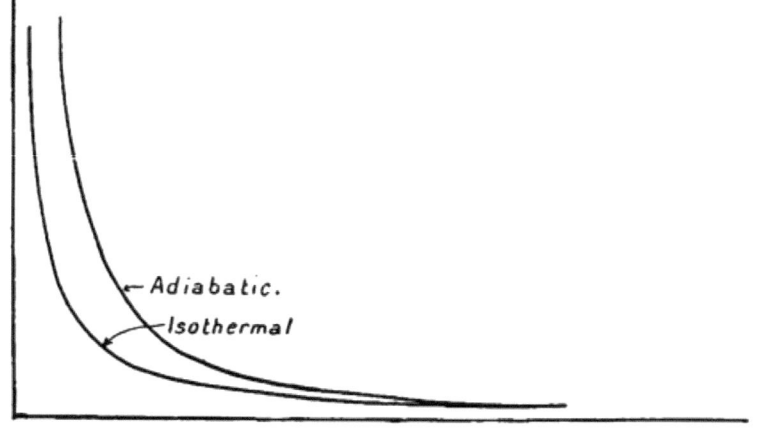

FIG. 2.—Isothermal and Adiabatic Curves.

Fig. 2 shows the same curves during compression in which the adiabatic is above the isothermal. During adiabatic compression the temperature after compression must rise, since

$$\frac{T_2}{T_1} = \left(\frac{P_2}{P_1}\right)^{\frac{\gamma-1}{\gamma}}$$ and this must be greater than 1.

It follows therefore that comparing adiabatic and isothermal compression a higher temperature may be reached with the former than with the latter (in which there is no rise of temperature), employing the same compression pressure, which is the reason of gas engines working with adiabatic compression rather than isothermal, since a high temperature is required with a minimum pressure.

Working Cycles.—All heat engines work through a mechanical cycle of operations, which is continually repeated, that most commonly employed being the four-stroke cycle, in which the working fluid passes through a complete series of operations in four strokes of the piston, or in two revolutions of the crank shaft. It is obvious that if it be possible to complete the cycle for an engine in two strokes instead of four, nearly double the power might be obtained from the same size of cylinder, and this fact has led to the introduction and wide adoption of gas engines working on a two-stroke cycle. As will be seen later, the two-stroke cycle Diesel engine has already made much headway and must of necessity be adopted for large powers, and the ultimate general employment of this type for the propulsion of very large ships no longer seems in doubt. In the two-stroke cycle engine, one stroke in two is a working stroke, as against one in four with the four-stroke cycle, and a still further advantage may be gained by the employment of the former type, and using also the double acting principle so that every stroke of the piston is a working stroke. The possibilities of this system in so far as it affects Diesel engines will be discussed later and need not to be further entered into here.

Thermo-Dynamic Cycles.—The principles upon which all heat engines theoretically work, may be divided up into three main divisions, according to the cycle of changes of state, through which the working fluid continually passes, these cycles being thermo-dynamic cycles in contradistinction to the mechanical cycles mentioned in the last paragraph. As a matter of fact no actual engine exactly follows along the lines of the theoretical machine, but these principles form a necessary and useful basis of comparison. They are :—

1. Constant temperature cycle.
2. Constant volume cycle.
3. Constant pressure cycle.

In engines in which the working fluid passes through one of these cycles, there is a certain efficiency which cannot be exceeded or indeed reached, and an examination of the maximum possible efficiency in each case will lead us to the points of difference between the Diesel and other heat motors.

Constant Temperature Cycle.—In this cycle all the heat is taken in from its source at a temperature which remains constant during the whole process, and the heat is rejected also at a constant temperature which is of course lower than the temperature at which the heat is received. All cycles can be illustrated diagrammatically by a closed series of curves drawn relative to two lines at right angles, the vertical line representing the pressure, and the horizontal line the volume of the gas at every stage of compression and expansion, and these curves are the indicator diagrams of perfect engines working on the various cycles. *Fig.* 3 represents the constant temperature cycle, the line OP denoting the pressures, and OV the volumes of the gas. bc represents the compression line in which the gas is compressed adiabatically from the point b where the volume is V_2, the pressure P_2, and the temperature T_1, to the point c, where the pressure is P_3 the volume V_3, and the temperature T_3. Heat is taken in from c to d, at constant temperature T_3, the pressure and volume at d, being P_4 and V_4 respectively. From d to a is adiabatic expansion, the pressure, volume, and temperature at a, being P_1, V_1, and T_1

respectively. From *a* to *b* heat is rejected at the constant temperature T_1, this completing the cycle.

The efficiency of an engine working on this cycle may be

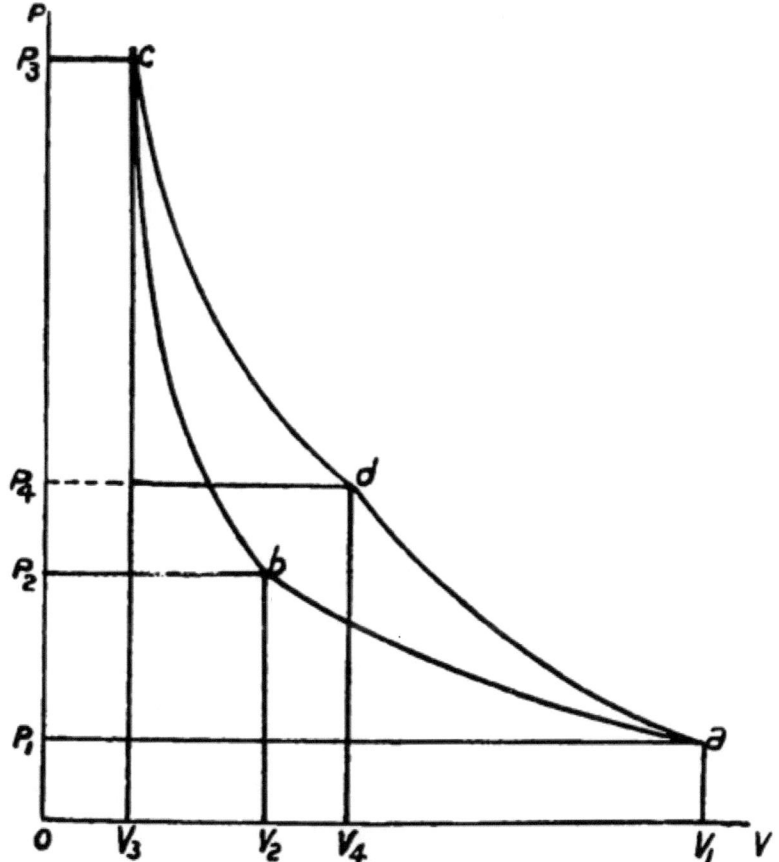

Fig. 3.—Constant Temperature Cycle Diagram.

readily expressed in terms of the top and bottom limits of temperature during the process. If

Q_3 = the heat taken in by the gas and
Q_1 = the heat rejected at the lowest temperature,

then $Q_3 - Q_1$ = the heat usefully employed in doing work, and the efficiency of the cycle is represented by the expression

$$n = \frac{Q_3 - Q_1}{Q_3}$$

As generally, $Q = wkT$, where w is the weight of gas and k its specific heat it follows that since neither w nor k vary during the cycle the quantity of heat is always directly proportional to the absolute temperature, or the efficiency of the cycle is

$$n = \frac{T_3 - T_1}{T_3}$$

This expression represents the efficiency of the constant temperature cycle, T_3 being the top temperature and T_1 the bottom temperature during the complete cycle.

No actual engine can have an efficiency so high as the ideal constant temperature engine, and an ordinarily efficient steam engine, working between limits of say 150 lb. per sq. inch pressure and 28 inches vacuum, or say 819° F. and 563°F. absolute temperatures, would, if a perfect machine, have an efficiency $\frac{819 - 563}{819} = 31 \cdot 3$ per cent. As a matter of fact steam engines are seldom more than half as economical as the ideal constant temperature engine, and hence an ordinary steam engine would have an actual efficiency of something under 16 per cent., and this may be compared with the possible efficiencies of gas and Diesel engines, deduced later.

Constant Volume Cycle.—An engine working on the constant volume cycle differs from one acting on the constant temperature cycle in that all the heat is taken in while the volume of the gas remains constant, and the heat is rejected under similar conditions. The cycle is shown in *Fig.* 4 in which as before OP represents pressures and OV volumes. Compression takes place adiabatically along the line ab, the pressure, volume, and temperature changing from P_1, V_1, and T_1 at a to P_2, V_2, and T_2 at b. Heat is then taken in at the constant volume V_2, the pressure rising to P_3, and the temperature to T_3. Next there is adiabatic expansion along the line cd till the volume is once more V_1, the pressure and temperature then being P_3 and T_3 and finally heat is rejected while the volume remains unaltered until the original pressure P_1 and temperature T_1 are attained.

To obtain the thermal efficiency of the ideal constant

volume engine let Q_2 = the heat taken in by the fluid,
and Q_3 = the heat rejected by the fluid.

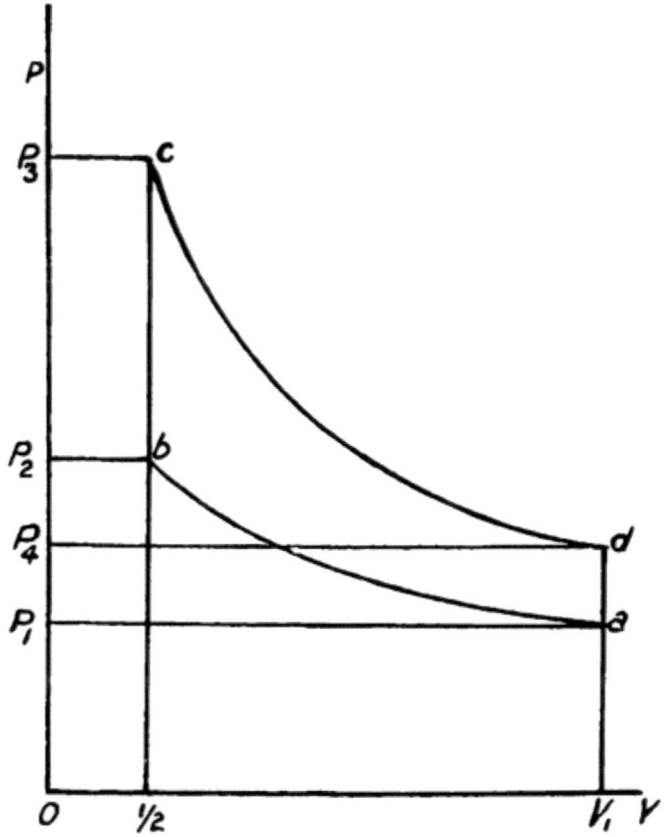

Fig. 4.—Constant Volume Cycle Diagram.

The heat usefully employed is $Q_2 - Q_3$ and the efficiency is $\dfrac{Q_2 - Q_3}{Q_2}$ or $1 - \dfrac{Q_3}{Q_2}$. Considering 1 lb. of gas to eliminate the question of weight—this remaining constant throughout the cycle—the quantity of heat taken in or rejected during a constant volume change is, generally, $Q = k_v (T_a - T_b)$ where T_a and T_b are the respective absolute temperatures before and after the change. Hence
$$Q_2 = k_v (T_3 - T_2)$$
$$Q_3 = k_v (T_4 - T_1)$$
from which it follows that the efficiency
$$n = 1 - \frac{T_4 - T_1}{T_3 - T_2}$$

From formula (4) page 11, with adiabatic expansion

$$\frac{T_4}{T_3} = \left(\frac{V_2}{V_1}\right)^{\gamma-1} = \frac{T_1}{T_2}$$

since the volume V_1 is constant during the change of temperature from T_4 to T_1 and the volume V_2 is constant during the change from T_2 to T_3

hence $\quad\dfrac{T_4 - T_1}{T_3 - T_2} = \dfrac{T_4}{T_3} = \dfrac{T_1}{T_2}$

that is $\quad n = 1 - \dfrac{T_4}{T_3}$

or from the above $\quad n = 1 - \left(\dfrac{V_2}{V_1}\right)^{\gamma-1}$

The ratio $\dfrac{V_1}{V_2}$ is usually called the compression ratio and is designated by r, so that the general formula for the efficiency of the constant volume cycle is

$$n = 1 - \frac{1}{r^{\gamma-1}}$$

Practically all gas engines work on a cycle closely approximating to the constant volume cycle.

Constant Pressure Cycle.—In this cycle all the heat is taken in at constant pressure, and the heat is also rejected at constant pressure, expansion and compression of the gas being adiabatic as before. *Fig.* 5 represents the constant pressure cycle on the pressure-volume basis.

Starting from b when the pressure, volume and temperature are respectively P_1, V_2, and T_2, the gas is compressed adiabatically to c where P_2 is the pressure, V_3 the volume and T_3 the temperature. Heat is taken in along the line cd at constant pressure P_2, the volume at d being V_4, and the temperature T_4. Adiabatic expansion next occurs along the line da, to a, where the pressure, volume, and temperature become P_1, V_1 and T_1 respectively. Heat is then rejected at constant pressure P_1, along the line ab to the starting point b where the original conditions prevail.

GENERAL THEORY OF HEAT ENGINES

As before let Q_2 = heat taken in by the fluid.
and Q_1 = heat rejected by the fluid.

The efficiency of the cycle is then $n = \dfrac{Q_2 - Q_1}{Q_2}$

and, considering 1 lb of gas $Q_2 = k_p (T_4 - T_3)$
and $Q_1 = k_p (T_1 - T_2)$.

The efficiency is therefore $n = 1 - \dfrac{T_1 - T_2}{T_4 - T_3}$

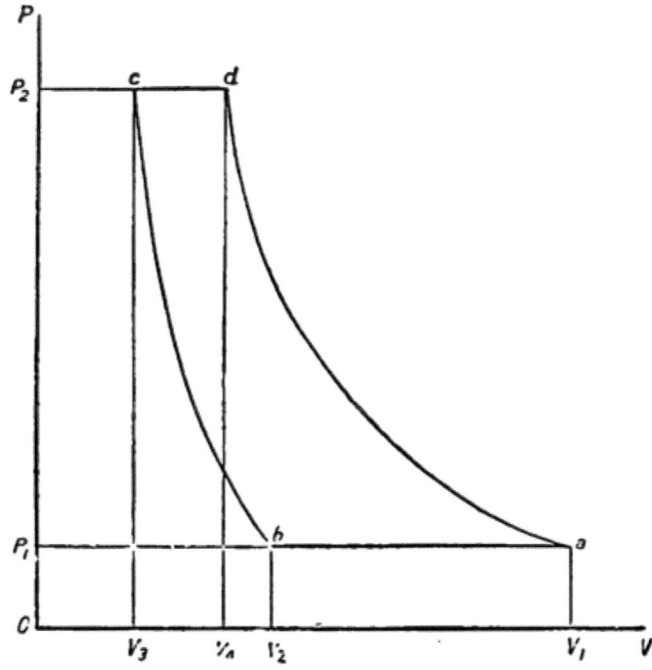

Fig. 5.—Constant Pressure Cycle Diagram.

Expansion along da and compression along bc are adiabatic so that, from formula (3) page 11.

$$\frac{T_1}{T_4} = \left(\frac{P_1}{P_2}\right)^{\frac{\gamma-1}{\gamma}} = \frac{T_2}{T_3}$$

From this $\dfrac{T_1}{T_4} = \dfrac{T_1 - T_2}{T_4 - T_3}$.

The efficiency is thus $n = 1 - \dfrac{T_1}{T_4} = 1 - \left(\dfrac{P_1}{P_2}\right)^{\frac{\gamma-1}{\gamma}}$

but with adiabatic expansion $\left(\dfrac{P_1}{P_2}\right)^{\frac{\gamma-1}{\gamma}} = \left(\dfrac{V_2}{V_1}\right)^{\gamma-1}$

and the efficiency may be expressed

$$n = 1 - \left(\frac{V_2}{V_1}\right)^{\gamma-1} = 1 - \frac{1}{r^{\gamma-1}}$$

which is the same expression as was obtained for the efficiency of the constant volume cycle, and in fact the efficiencies of the constant temperature, constant volume, and constant pressure cycles are identical.

It is at once apparent from the above results that whatever cycle of operations a heat engine works upon, the higher the compression ratio can be made, the less becomes the fraction $\frac{1}{r^{\gamma-1}}$ by which the possible efficiency is reduced below unity, and hence the greater becomes the efficiency of the engine if mechanical and other losses are not increased in the same proportion. It is for this reason that in all gas engines it is desirable to work with a high compression ratio. In internal combustion engines of the ordinary design, that is to say gas engines working on the constant volume cycle, the compression ratio is limited by the fact that during the suction stroke a mixture of air and gas is drawn into the cylinder and the mixture is compressed in the compression stroke. The pressure to which this compression may be carried, may not reach beyond a relatively low figure, since it must not approach the temperature of combustion of the mixture, for were it to reach this point, ignition would occur before the commencement of the working stroke, i.e. there would be pre-ignition. In the Diesel engine pure air alone is drawn into the cylinder and compressed, and the fuel is admitted *after* compression, so that very much higher compression pressures may be employed than with ordinary gas engines, there being of course absolutely no danger of pre-ignition. In actual working the compression ratio with Diesel engines is about 12, as against 6 or 7 with gas engines, which shows at once the possibilities of higher efficiencies with Diesel engines than with the usual type of internal combustion engines. This can be easily illustrated by working out the thermal efficiencies in the two cases with $r = 6$ and $r = 12$. In the first instance $n = \cdot 51$ while in the second $n = \cdot 63$, showing a gain of over 23 per cent. There are however other factors influencing the efficiency of the actual engines, and these can be better illustrated by an examination of the cycle of the Diesel engine as constructed.

Diesel Engine Cycle.—The complete cycle of operations of the Diesel engine will be fully discussed in the next

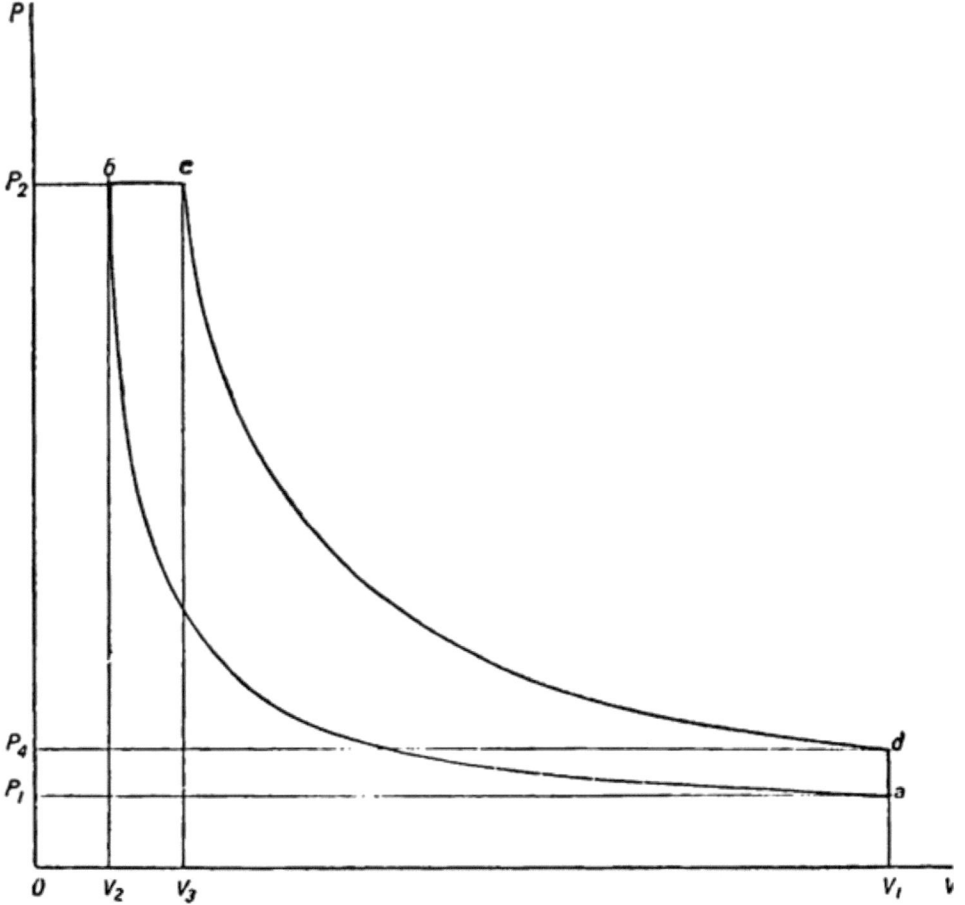

Fig. 6.—Diesel Cycle Diagram.

chapter, but for present purposes it is sufficient to explain that in the ordinary four-stroke engine as at present constructed, the cycle of operations is somewhat similar to constant pressure cycle, except that the rejection of heat to the exhaust is more nearly at constant volume than at constant pressure, and that the expansion and compression are not perfectly adiabatic which, of course, is impossible with any actual heat engine. *Fig. 6* represents fairly accurately the Diesel cycle on the usual pressure volume basis. Compression takes place adiabatically along *ab*, then heat is taken in at constant volume to the point *c*, after which there is adiabatic expansion to *d*, and rejection of heat to exhaust at constant volume to *a*. The pressures and volumes at the various stages are indicated on the diagram, while the temperatures correspond.

Let Q_2 = heat taken in by the fluid,
Q_1 = heat rejected to exhaust,

then the efficiency of the cycle is $n = \dfrac{Q_2 - Q_1}{Q_2}$, or $1 - \dfrac{Q_1}{Q_2}$.

Since the heat is taken in at constant pressure

$$Q_2 = k_p (T_3 - T_2)$$

and since heat is rejected at constant volume

$$Q_1 = k_v (T_4 - T_1).$$

From the general formula $\dfrac{PV}{T}$ = constant we have

$$\frac{P_2 V_3}{T_3} = \frac{P_2 V_2}{T_2} \text{ or } T_3 = T_2 \frac{V_3}{V_2} \text{ hence}$$

$$Q_2 = k_p T_2 \left(\frac{V_3}{V_2} - 1\right)$$

similarly $\qquad T_4 = T_1 \times \dfrac{P_4}{P_1}.$

From the general formula for adiabatic expansion PV^γ = constant it follows $P_1 = P_2 \left(\dfrac{V_2}{V_1}\right)^\gamma$ and $P_4 = P_2 \left(\dfrac{V_3}{V_1}\right)^\gamma$

and hence $\qquad T_4 = T_1 \left(\dfrac{P_4}{P_1}\right) = T_1 \left(\dfrac{V_3}{V_1}\right)^\gamma$

Substituting this value in the expression for Q_1

$$Q_1 = k_v T_1 \left\{\left(\frac{V_3}{V_2}\right)^\gamma - 1\right\}$$

GENERAL THEORY OF HEAT ENGINES

The expression $\dfrac{V_3}{V_2}$ is the ratio of the cut-off volume to the clearance volume and may be denoted by R. The efficiency of the Diesel cycle may then be expressed by substituting in the formula

$$n = 1 - \frac{Q_1}{Q_2} \text{ which then becomes}$$

$$n = 1 - \frac{k_v}{k_p} \frac{T_1}{T_2} \frac{(R^\gamma - 1)}{(R - 1)}$$

$$= 1 - \frac{T_1}{T_2} \times \frac{R^\gamma - 1}{\gamma(R - 1)}$$

Since the compression from a to b is adiabatic $\dfrac{T_1}{T_2} = \dfrac{1}{r^{\gamma-1}}$ as before, and the final expression for the efficiency of the Diesel engine is

$$n = 1 - \frac{1}{r^{\gamma-1}} \times \frac{R^\gamma - 1}{\gamma(R - 1)}$$

From this it would be seen that the cut-off ratio exercises an important influence on the thermal efficiency of a Diesel engine, this depending on the two variables, the compression ratio and the cut-off ratio.

The effect of the alteration of the cut-off can be shown by giving actual values to R and r. Taking the clearance volume as $\tfrac{1}{15}$ of the volume swept through by the piston, and the cut-off as $\tfrac{1}{10}$ which is common with Diesel engines and referring to *Fig. 6* we have

$$V_3 - V_2 = \frac{Vs}{10} \text{ and } V_2 = \frac{Vs}{15} \text{ and hence}$$

$$V_3 - \frac{Vs}{15} = \frac{Vs}{10} \text{ or } V_3 = \frac{Vs}{6} \text{ so that}$$

$$R = \frac{V_3}{V_2} = 2.5$$

Assuming that $r = 12$ and $\gamma = 1.405$ (which is somewhat higher than in actual engines) the thermal efficiency of the

Diesel cycle from the formula previously deduced, works out at ·56, whereas with the same values of r and γ but with $R = 1·5$ the efficiency becomes ·61.

In the above remarks it has been assumed that γ remains constant, which is, of course, the case for any particular mixture. In comparing the efficiencies of ordinary gas engines and Diesel engines it is to be noted however that the efficiency on any cycle becomes larger as γ is increased, which occurs when the gaseous mixture has a larger proportion of air, or as it is generally termed, is a leaner mixture. In Diesel engines the mixture is very much leaner than in gas engines, and hence this accounts to a certain extent for the greater economy of this type of engine.

Reasons for the High Efficiency of the Diesel Engine.—Summarizing the foregoing analysis it may briefly be said that the superior efficiency of the Diesel engine is due to several causes, the first being the successful employment of high compression pressures rendered possible by the fact that air alone is compressed in the cylinder and not a mixture of fuel and air in which the temperature of ignition always limits the compression pressure. In the second place, a leaner mixture may be employed than with gas engines, less weight of fuel is necessary, and the loss in the cooling water is correspondingly reduced. There are, moreover, further reasons which probably exercise an important influence, namely, the perfect combustion of the fuel due to the high pressure during the whole combustion period and mechanical advantages such as the efficient method of its injection. It is obvious that oil with a high flash point is very suitable for the Diesel engine, thus permitting of the cheapest crude residue oils being employed. On the other hand, a separate compressor is necessary to inject fuel with compressed air at a higher pressure than the compressed air in the cylinder, and this causes a slight loss of efficiency, usually about 6 per cent., which is, however, of no great import.

It must be distinctly remembered that the Diesel engine cycle itself does not account for the economy of the engine since, as a matter of fact, the constant pressure cycle is rather less efficient than that at constant volume, on which most gas engines work, provided the conditions are the same. In other words, for the same compression pressure the constant volume engine would be superior to the constant pressure engine, but for the reasons already given it is impossible that a gas engine should approach the conditions which are easily attained with the Diesel engine. The limits of pressure of the working fluid are fixed by the ultimate strengths of the materials of which the engine parts are constructed, and the Diesel cycle gives the maximum economy for these limits of pressure.

Though very much higher compression pressures (but not maximum pressures) are employed in the Diesel engine than in gas engines, the temperature at the end of combustion in the first case is very considerably below that in the second, since the period during which the burning of the fuel occurs is so long compared with the explosion in the gas engine cylinder, thus allowing the heat to be taken up to a greater extent by the jacket water. The combustion in the Diesel engine is however by no means isothermal, and the temperature rises a good deal after the injection of the fuel and also to a slight extent after the fuel valve is closed, but allowing for this the important fact remains that in Diesel engines, in spite of high pressures, the temperatures are less.

The following table gives the actual consumption in British Thermal Units per B.H.P. hour for various types of engines, namely, non-condensing and condensing steam engines, turbines using superheated steam, suction gas engines, and Diesel engines. The figures quoted represent generally the limiting results obtained in practice, and the efficiencies are also given based on the heat equivalent of one H.P. hour which is $\dfrac{33000 \times 60}{778} = 2545$ B.Th.U. The corresponding ranges of pressure are also added.

Type of Engine.	Range of Pressure lbs. per sq. inch.	B.Th.U. per B.H.P. Hour.	Efficiency per cent.
Non-condensing steam engines . . .	—	30,000 to 38,000	8·4 to 6·6
Condensing steam engines and turbines using superheated steam. . . .	160 to 220	17,000 to 25,000	15 to 10
Suction gas engines .	300 to 370	11,000 to 14,000	23 to 18
Diesel engines .	500 to 600	7,500 to 8,000	34 to 32

Two-cycle Diesel engines are about 2 per cent. less efficient than the four-cycle slow speed type, and all the efficiencies refer to the engines running under full load condition being of course lower with smaller outputs.

These figures are all the effective efficiencies, but the thermal efficiencies are very much higher—the efficiency for Diesel engines being, for instance, from 42 to 48 per cent.

Practical Diesel Engine Cards.—Needless to say, the actual indicator cards obtained from Diesel engines in practice are by no means identical with the ideal diagram given on page 21. At the same time by very careful adjustment of the engine, it is possible to obtain a very good card showing quite a prolonged combustion at constant pressure, although this is usually only possible at full load. The maximum pressure attained after the compression stroke is generally between 450 and 500 lb. per sq. inch, 470 lb. per sq. inch being an ordinary figure. In two-cycle motors it is frequently less than this, although in some cases it is exceeded, particularly for instance in a Junkers motor, for reasons which will be understood from the description of this engine later. Considerable improvement may sometimes be effected in the card by an alteration of the lift of the fuel valve. In general this is between three and four mm., although the actual lift due to the knocker of the cam may be considerably in excess of this in order to allow a reasonable clearance between the knocker and the roller of the fuel valve lever. The amount of clearance to be allowed depends upon the accuracy with which the motor has been designed, and the experience gained in operation. and in some cases it is as much as 3 to 4 mm., and in others not much greater than $\frac{1}{2}$ mm.

The following table gives the actual setting of the valves of one of the cylinders in an engine of the four-cycle type running at 300 r.p.m. developing 300 B.H.P. and having four cylinders. The dimensions of the cylinders were 380 mm. bore and 420 mm. stroke.

Fuel valve opens per cent. before upper dead centre	0·7
Lift fuel mm.	3·1
Fuel valve closes per cent. after upper dead centre	8
Starting valve opens per cent. after upper dead centre	2
Stroke of starting valve mm.	5
Starting valve closes per cent. after upper dead centre	38
Play between roller and cam (s.v. closed) mm.	0·2
Air suction valve opens per cent. after upper dead centre	6
Stroke of air suction valve mm.	30
Air suction valve closes per cent. after upper dead centre	8
Play between roller and cam (air suction v. closed) mm.	0·2
Exhaust valve opens per cent. before lower dead centre	25
Stroke of exhaust valve mm.	29·8
Exhaust valve closes per cent. after upper dead centre	3
Play between roller and cam (e.v. closed) mm.	0·4
Fuel nozzle, bore of flame disc mm.	4·2
Diameter of holes in atomiser plates mm.	2
Distance apart of holes in atomiser plates	3
Diameter of fuel test valve mm.	1·1
Compression space in working cylinder mm.	21·3
Liner to be placed in connecting rod at top end	2·5

In a two-cycle marine engine of the Sulzer type with port scavenging having four cylinders 310 mm. bore and with 450 mm. stroke, running at 280 r.p.m., the following were the lifts of the fuel valve :—

LIFTS OF FUEL VALVE FOR TWO-CYCLE 380 H.P. MOTOR.

	MINIMUM LIFT.				MAXIMUM LIFT.			
	Angle of Lead.	Angle open after dead centre.	Per cent. stroke duration.	Lift of Valve. mm.	Angle of Lead.	Angle open after dead centre.	Per cent. stroke duration.	Lift of Valve. mm.
Ahead	3° 38′	23° 30′	4·94	1·5	10° 13′	43° 41′	16·24	5
Astern	4° 18′	24° 44′	5·46	1·75	10° 5′	43° 13′	15·94	5

In the descriptions of various Diesel engines given later, it is explained that in some types a fuel pump is provided for each cylinder, whereas in other engines there is only one fuel pump for perhaps four or six cylinders. In stationary engine practice, it is still more common to use only one pump and supply the fuel to a distributing box from which pipes are taken to the various fuel valves of the cylinders, but for marine work, especially for two-cycle engines, most builders prefer to employ one fuel pump for each cylinder. In cases, however, where one fuel pump has to supply a number of cylinders it is especially important to ascertain by means of indicator cards that all the cylinders are doing approximately the same amount of work, otherwise it is easy for one to become much overloaded, even though the whole engine itself is only developing the normal output. The set of cards given in *Fig.* 9 are taken simultaneously upon a six-cylinder four-cycle engine of 1,500 I.H.P., and in this case one fuel pump supplies all the cylinders. It will be seen that even though the variation is not great it is quite well marked.

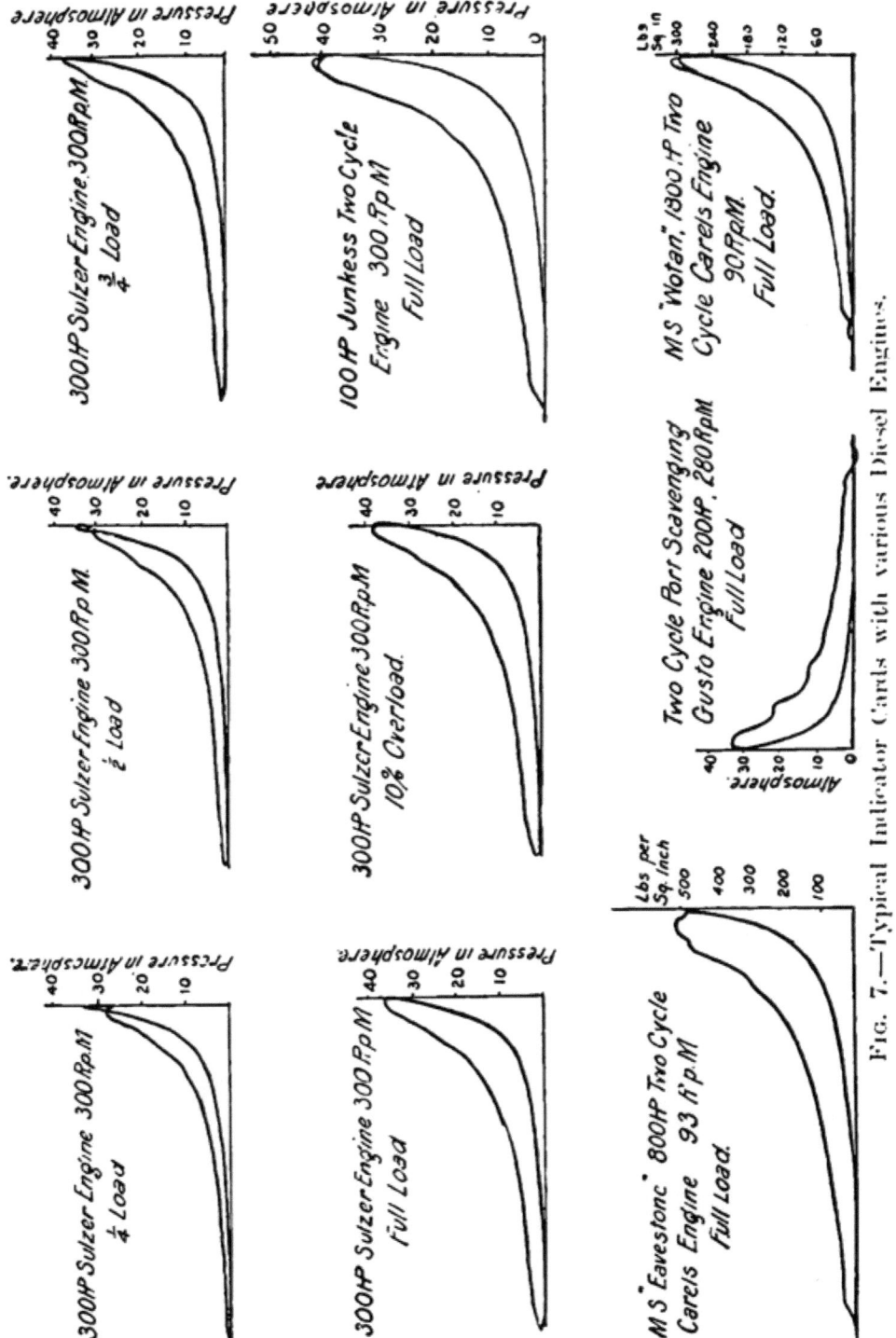

Fig. 7.—Typical Indicator Cards with various Diesel Engines.

FIG. 8.—Indicator Cards of Four-Cylinder 800 B.H.P. Sulzer Two-Cycle Marine Diesel Motor.

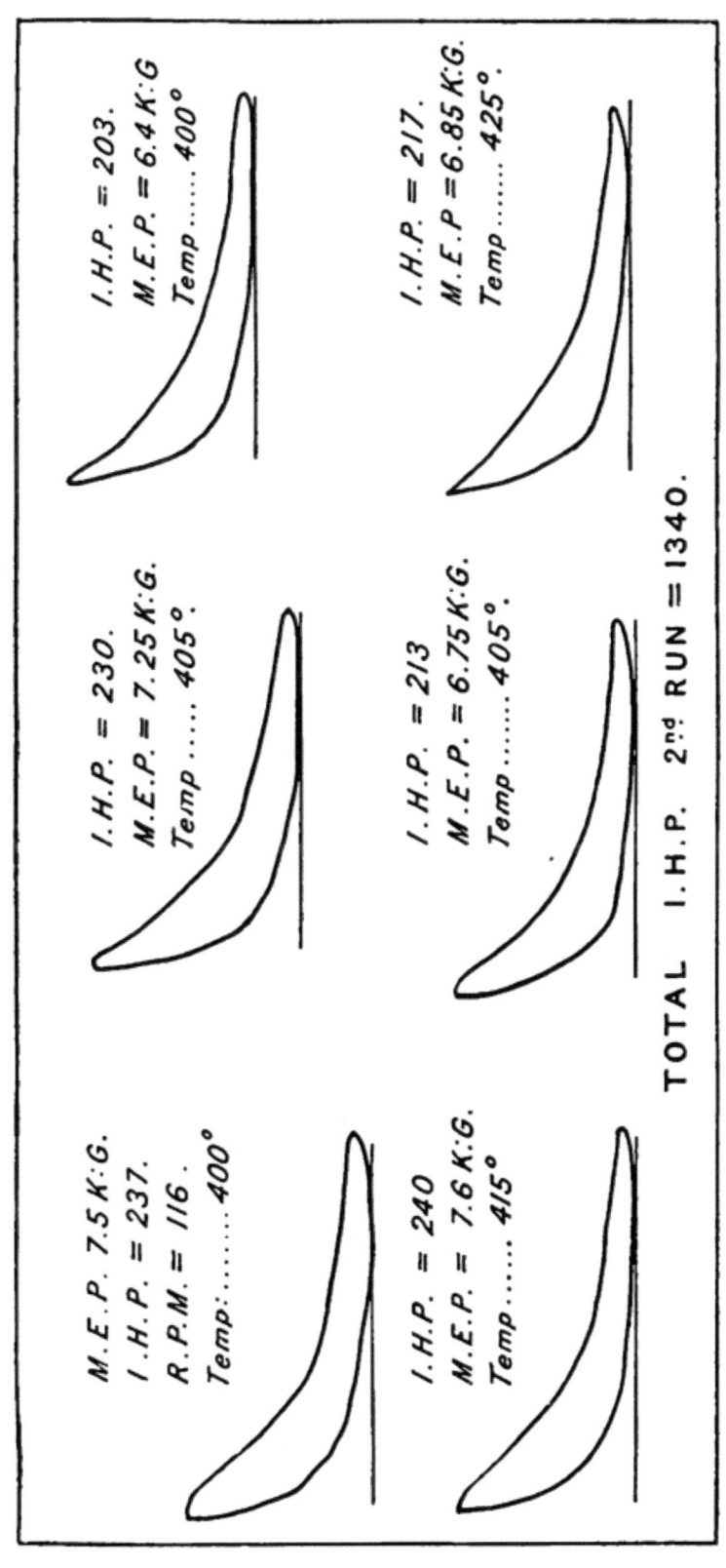

Fig. 9.—Simultaneous Indicator Cards from Six-Cylinder Four-Cycle Marine Diesel Engine.

TOTAL I.H.P. 2nd RUN = 1340.

CHAPTER II

ACTION AND WORKING OF THE DIESEL ENGINE

FOUR-CYCLE ENGINE — TWO-CYCLE ENGINE — TWO-CYCLE DOUBLE ACTING ENGINE—HORIZONTAL ENGINE—HIGH SPEED VERTICAL ENGINE—RELATIVE ADVANTAGES OF THE VARIOUS TYPES OF ENGINE—LIMITING POWER OF DIESEL ENGINES—WEIGHTS OF DIESEL ENGINES—FUEL FOR DIESEL ENGINES.

THE essential difference between the Diesel engine and practically all other motors working with gaseous or liquid fuel, is that it is in reality an internal *combustion* engine in contradistinction to other gas and oil engines which are, strictly speaking, internal *explosion* engines.

Four-stroke Cycle Engine.—In four-stroke cycle gas engines of the ordinary explosion type a mixture of gas and air is drawn into the cylinder during the suction stroke, and compressed in the following stroke, the mixed gases being then exploded by external means (i.e. by ignition) in the third stroke, which is the working stroke of the cycle. The method of operation of the Diesel engine as has been partially explained in the last chapter, is on quite a different principle, and is as follows for a motor working on the four-stroke cycle, considering a vertical engine of the usual type :—

1. In the first downward stroke of the piston air is sucked into the engine cylinder direct from the atmosphere through a slotted cylinder, and thence through the main air inlet valve on the top of the cylinder. At the end of the stroke the cylinder is full of pure air at practically atmospheric pressure, ready for the compression stroke.

2. In the next stroke the air is compressed to the required pressure, usually about 500 lb. per sq. inch, while the temperature rises to between 1,000° F. and 1,100° F., all the valves of course being closed during this action. In this compression period a certain amount of negative work has to be done, detracting somewhat from the efficiency of the cycle, but as the compression is very approximately adiabatic, nearly all the work is returned.

3. During the early portion of the third and working stroke the fuel oil is injected into the cylinder above the piston by a blast of air at a higher pressure than that in the cylinder (about 800 lb. per sq. inch) through a special form of needle valve. Combustion takes place during this period as the temperature of the compressed air in the cylinder is above the burning point of the oil fuel. The duration of this part of the stroke depends on the setting of the valves, but cut-off usually occurs not later than one-tenth of the stroke at full load. After cut-off when the fuel inlet valve closes, combustion continues for a short period, expansion then occurs and work is done on the piston for the rest of the stroke. Just before the piston reaches the end of its travel the exhaust valve begins to open, and the pressure drops off rapidly, since it is obvious that to carry expansion to anything like its full extent would necessitate inordinately large cylinders.

4. In the final stroke the exhaust valve remains open and the burnt gases are expelled from the cylinder into the exhaust pipe, and the cycle of operations begins once more, the cylinder being ready to receive a further charge of air on the next out stroke of the piston.

*Fig.*10 shows an indicator card of an actual Diesel engine, ab representing the first or suction stroke in which the air is drawn in, bc the compression of the air more or less adiabatically, cd the combustion of the fuel during the admission portion of the next stroke, and de the following expansion of the mixture until the exhaust valve opens at e when for the remainder of the stroke ef, the pressure falls more rapidly as some of the gases are expelled; fa represents the final stroke in which all the products of combustion are exhausted through the exhaust valve.

Diesel's original proposal was to build an engine working practically on the constant temperature cycle, and though the engines as now made work in a manner somewhat different from that which the inventor first intended, the reprint

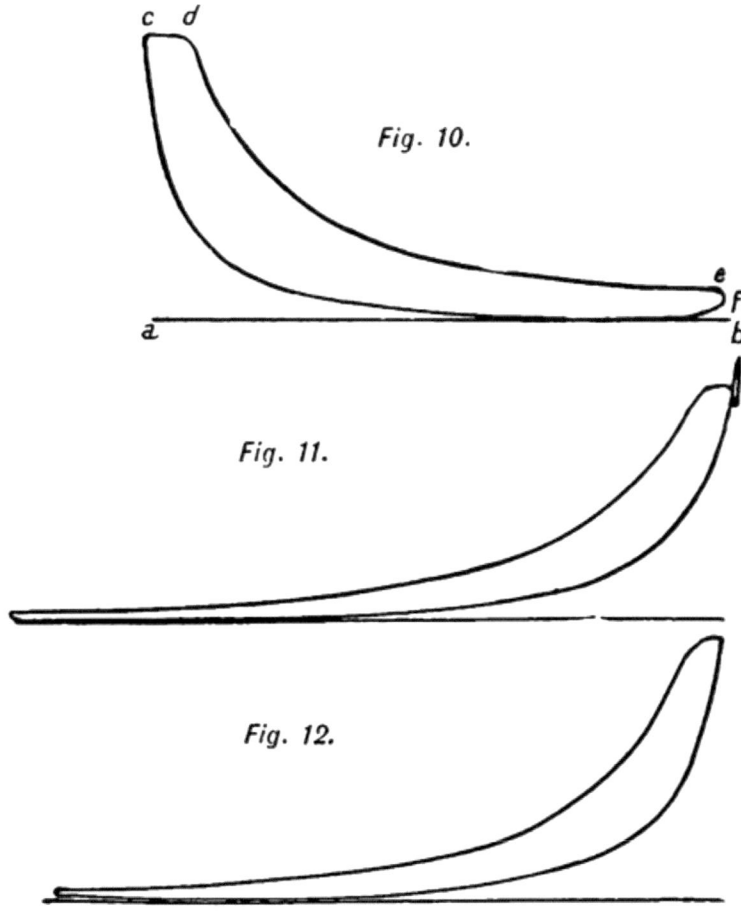

Diagram showing action of Diesel Engine.

of the patent specification in the Appendix of this volume will prove interesting both as an historical document, and as indicating the objects which Diesel had in view with his earliest engines.

As has been seen by the diagram and description of the action of actual Diesel engines, the combustion line of the cycle, which was originally intended to be isothermal, is, in reality, a constant pressure line and, as a matter of fact, by no means an isothermal, as the temperature rises to a considerable extent during the burning of the fuel, and probably for a short period after cut off. This type of combustion was also intended and realized by Diesel and is described in his second patent.

It is very important, however, to note from a practical point of view, that the duration of the combustion is considerable, and hence there is much greater time to get rid of the heat by the jacket water than in gas engines, where the explosion is instantaneous and the temperature must of necessity rise very rapidly. It follows, therefore, that for the same *maximum* pressures in the cylinders of a gas engine and a Diesel engine the temperature rise in the first case would be much higher than in the latter, and it is to be remembered that these maximum pressures are not very different, but that in the gas engine the highest point is not reached during compression, but only after ignition of the mixture. Since a Diesel engine may work with much higher compression pressures than a gas engine, and yet not be subjected to such high temperatures, this points to the fact already well established that greater powers may be obtained per cylinder than with the ordinary types of internal combustion engines, though there are, however, other factors governing this matter.

It is obvious from the description previously given that the Diesel engine is not a self-starting motor any more than other internal combustion engines, and the invariable method of running up the machine is by the employment of compressed air which is admitted to the cylinder through a separate starting valve in the cylinder cover, arranged so that it cannot be in operation at the same time as the fuel inlet valve. The engine is barred round until the crank is well over the dead centre and it runs as an air engine until it has attained sufficient speed to take up its work as an oil engine, which it does after two or three revolutions. A supply of compressed air is therefore necessary both for starting the engine, and for the blast for fuel injection into the cylinder when the engine is running. The usual arrangement is to provide three cylindrical air reservoirs of quite small dimensions, two for starting (one as a standby) and one for injection blast, and the supply is maintained by an air compressor driven off the engine itself, of such capacity as to easily deliver all the air needed at the required pressure. All the valves are arranged in the cylinder cover with the vertical type engine which has hitherto been almost universal, although the horizontal type is now being manufactured by some firms on a large scale. There are thus in a single cylinder four-cycle engine four valves, the fuel inlet, the air inlet, the exhaust, and the starting valves. Each of these is operated separately by a lever whose motion is obtained from a cam on a cam shaft, which is driven through spur gearing and a vertical shaft, from the crank shaft. All the valves are kept on their seats by strong springs. It is evident that by a simple adjustment of any of the cams, the valves can readily be set to suit the requirements of the engine, and, of course, in a multi-cylinder engine, but one starting valve is essential (though more are sometimes fitted) since the motor is run up on one cylinder, and the remaining cylinders are then only provided with fuel inlet, air inlet, and exhaust valves. *Fig.* 11, an indicator card of a 250 B.H.P. engine, shows how readily any defect in the adjustment of the valves can be seen, as it is evident from this card that ignition occurs too late due to the fuel inlet valve not opening early enough. *Fig.* 12 is an indicator card taken on the same cylinder after adjusting the valve, which shows by the horizontal combustion line at top pressure that the fuel is admitted at the right moment.

The air compressor is arranged in different ways by various makers of Diesel engines, some preferring to drive it by a link off the connecting rod, while others have the piston or pistons of the compressor driven by eccentrics on the shaft. Usually two or three stage compressors are employed, particularly with large engines, and in marine installations, a separate auxiliary air compressor driven by a Diesel engine or other motor is absolutely essential. The regulation of the engine is effected in many ways, but the general principle usually consists in simply regulating the amount of oil admitted to the cylinder via a small feed pump actuated from eccentrics on the governor shaft. This method is obviously more efficient than that most usually adopted in gas engines where the hit and miss principle is employed, though, of course, many other efficacious methods are now used in the more modern engines.

Full details of the construction of various types of Diesel engines will be given in the next chapter, and need not be further discussed here.

Two-Cycle Engine.—For many years after its inception the Diesel engine was constructed solely of the four-cycle single acting type, but of late much progress has been made in the manufacture of an engine working on the two-stroke cycle. The general action of such an engine is as follows :—

1. Consider the piston at the end of its stroke in its bottom position. The cylinder is full of air at nearly atmospheric pressure, and this is compressed during the first or upward stroke of the cycle to the usual top compression pressure of 500 lb. per sq. inch, as in the second stroke of the four-stroke cycle.

2. During the second stroke, combustion, expansion, expulsion of the burnt gases to the exhaust and the filling of the cylinder with fresh air are the operations which have to be effected. Fuel is sprayed into the cylinder during the early portion of the stroke, through the inlet valve, by compressed air as before. This valve then closes and expansion occurs while the piston passes through about another 75 per cent. of its stroke, at which point the exhaust opens and the products of combustion begin to pass out. Air under a pressure of about 4 to 8 lb. per sq. inch then enters the cylinder through a separate valve or port in the cylinder, being supplied from a so-called scavenge pump, which is quite separate from the air compressor for the provision of fuel ignition and starting air supply, the necessity of which is apparent. All the exhaust gases are thus forced out through

the exhaust ports, and at the end of the stroke the cylinder is left full of pure air with all the valves closed, ready for the first stroke of the next cycle.

The diagram for this cycle does not differ materially from that for the four-stroke cycle as is seen in *Fig.* 13, which illustrates the two-stroke cycle. *cd* represents the combustion of fuel, *de* the expansion until *e*, when the exhaust ports begin to open, the rapid fall of pressure to *f*, along *ef*, being notable, and during the process of exhaust the cylinder

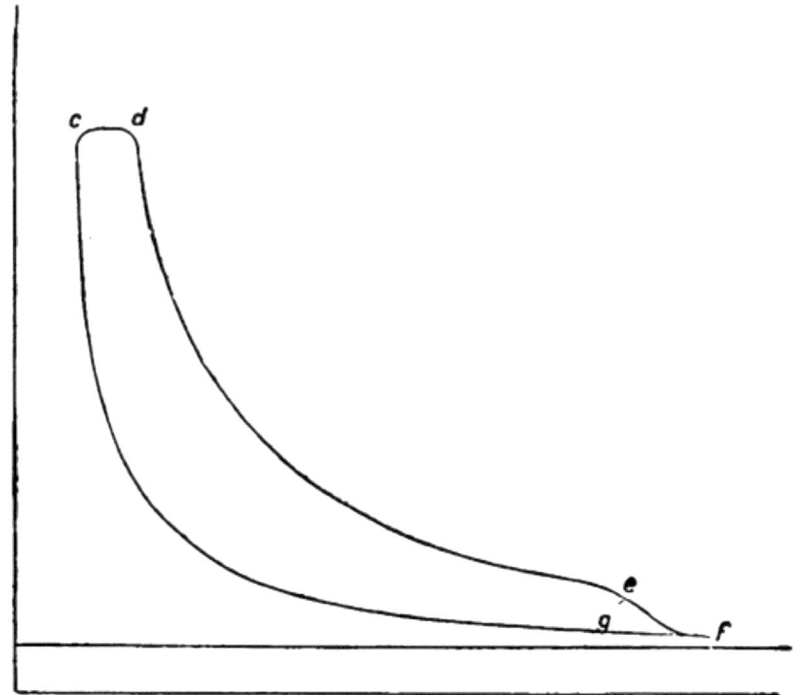

Fig. 13.—Two-stroke Cycle Diagram.

is filled with air from the scavenge pump. There is no longer a horizontal line representing the entrance of the air at atmospheric pressure as in the four-stroke diagram, since all the air is admitted at a pressure above atmospheric. The admission of air continues along *fg* to the predetermined point *g*, after which compression takes place. The scavenge valve or port opens slightly after the exhaust port, so that the pressure has already dropped to some extent before the admission of the scavenge air.

As far as constructional details go, the two-stroke cycle

engine differs from the four-stroke type in the arrangement of valves, and the provision of a scavenge pump in the former case. Otherwise the engines are identical. In large engines this pump is usually placed in line with the engine cylinders, and its piston driven through a connecting rod off an extension of the crank shaft, while in other cases it is worked by levers off the connecting rod.

The scavenge pumps are designed to deliver air at a pressure of 4 to 8 lb. per sq. inch, but this depends to a large extent on the size and type of the scavenge valves. There is no atmospheric air inlet valve, and the scavenge air may be admitted either through valves in the cover of the cylinder or through ports near the bottom of the cylinder. The exhaust ports are in any case arranged vertically, extending in the cylinder walls from the bottom of the piston stroke, a distance of about 15 per cent. of the stroke.

Two-Cycle Double Acting Engine.—In this cycle, each stroke is a working stroke, and the action may be understood by considering each cylinder as two separate cylinders with the same central exhaust ports serving for each cylinder, and separate inlet valves at the top and bottom. The cylinder has of necessity to be considerably longer than with the single acting type, and the piston is rather less than half its length. The action is as follows:—

Consider the piston in its bottom position when it is fully uncovering the exhaust valves in the centre, and the space above the piston is full of pure air which has been injected by the scavenge pump, while below the piston in the cylinder is the air which has been compressed to a high pressure in the last downward stroke. The upward stroke is then a combination of the two strokes in the two-cycle single acting engine already described. Above the piston, the air is compressed, while below the piston there is first fuel injection and combustion, then expansion, and finally opening of the scavenge valves, admission of scavenge air and the consequent expulsion of the burnt gases to the exhaust through the exhaust ports which are uncovered as before, as the piston reaches the end of its stroke.

Horizontal Engine.—Although Diesel himself built a horizontal type of engine in the early days of development, up to within a year or two ago all Diesel engines were constructed for commercial purposes of the vertical type. Recently, however, an engine of the horizontal type has been perfected, which may possess advantages in certain cases, where, for instance, the available head room is limited and floor space is of secondary importance, since the horizontal machine is much lower, but occupies a greater superficial area than the vertical type. This engine is made both single and double acting, and differs in no essential details from the vertical engine as far as its general method of working is concerned. The fuel inlet valve is arranged horizontally on the end of the cylinder, while the air inlet, and the exhaust or scavenge valves as the case may be, are fitted on the top side or bottom of the cylinder, all being actuated by rolling levers, operated by cams or eccentrics on a horizontal shaft somewhat as in the usual type of horizontal gas engine, the shaft being driven through gearing from the crank shaft. The compressor is ordinarily coupled to the crank shaft direct, and may be of the two or three stage type —generally the former. This engine possesses the advantage of easy accessibility of all the parts for cleaning and repair, less pressure on the bedplate and foundations, and has a rather lower initial cost than a vertical engine.

High Speed Vertical Engines.—For land work, which comprises chiefly dynamo driving for electrical work, a high speed engine possesses advantages over a low speed one, inasmuch as it reduces the size, cost, and weight of the dynamo, while its own size and weight are also minimized. The usual speed of the ordinary vertical four-cycle slow speed Diesel engine varies from about 150 to 250 revolutions per minute according to the power, but the high speed type, which is now built by a large number of firms, runs at speeds ranging from 180 to 350 revolutions per minute, or more. The principle of this machine is precisely the same as the slow speed type, but all parts are usually enclosed, and forced lubrication, with a pressure of 50 to 70 lb. per sq. inch, is adopted. The crank chamber is entirely sealed up, and has inspection doors, as in a steam engine of the high speed vertical type, while the cam shaft and cams generally run in an enclosed oil bath. The advantages claimed for the high speed engine, are, beyond any saving in connexion with its drive, the reduced space and weight, the lesser height, and a reduction in capital cost.

Relative Advantages of the Various Types of Engine.—Engineering design and construction is invariably a matter of compromise, and it is difficult or impossible to lay down general laws to be always followed, since in many individual cases, there are considerations which modify what might in the ordinary way be thought the most suitable and efficient arrangement. The following remarks regarding the applications of the several types of engines should therefore only be taken as applying in such instances where no special considerations are likely to render departures from the usual practice advisable or necessary.

The largest experience has been gained in Diesel engines of the slow speed, four-stroke type, and their efficiency must inevitably be slightly higher than that of any other, whilst the absolute reliability and low running cost have been abundantly proved during the last fifteen years. These facts alone will for a long time render the application of this type most general, and for engines of small and moderate powers it is difficult to see the reasons which would render it advisable to displace them for stationary work, except in cases where the space or height available is very limited. The tendency of late years is to employ larger engines, a tendency which will probably be more accentuated in the future, and from this point of view the question assumes a rather different aspect. The maximum power which it is advisable to develop in a four-cycle engine is relatively small, and as to multiply the number of cylinders beyond six or eight as a maximum would render the engine unwieldy, there comes a limiting point in the output of the machine, when it is no longer desirable to employ the four-cycle principle, and when this is reached it is well to sacrifice the small difference in efficiency between the two types for greater convenience of operation. Most manufacturers make their standard engines of the four-stroke type up to about 700 H.P. to 1,000 H.P., above which power the two-stroke single acting machine is adopted. Pursuing this line of argument further it might be deduced that for the very largest engines, the two-stroke double acting machine is the ultimate evolution, but this is apparently not necessarily the case. Two-cycle single acting Diesel engines have already been constructed, developing 1,200 H.P. per cylinder, and there would seem to be no insuperable difficulty in reaching 2,000 H.P. for a single cylinder, so that from the mere question of obtaining a large output the double acting principle is not essential. As has been explained, there are certain difficulties to contend with in the double acting type, such as the question of cooling the piston and piston rods, and the liability of trouble with the piston rod stuffing boxes, which have certainly been satisfactorily overcome by some manufacturers, but have nevertheless to be seriously considered, and must be recognized in deciding on the relative advantages of the machine. There is also the point that such large scavenge cylinders are required as to nullify partially the advantage gained by the double acting engine in the saving in space occupied by the engine. It is possible that for very large powers for stationary work, horizontal double acting engines will be employed.

In the two-cycle single acting engine, the power obtained per cylinder is theoretically double that of the four cycle, while when double acting, still greater powers can be developed, and, of course, the engine is lighter for the same power. The theoretical proportions do not quite coincide with those which obtain in practice, owing to the impossibility of the efficient employment of the whole of the cylinder volume in two-cycle engines. This is brought about by the necessity for exhaust and possibly scavenge ports in the cylinder walls and in any comparison between the two-cycle and four-cycle types it may be taken generally that only 75 to 80 per cent. of the cylinder volume is actually usefully employed. Other things being equal it would seem advisable to adopt the two-cycle type, and preferably engines working on the double acting principle, but there are however many considerations affecting the matter. A two-cycle engine can never be quite so efficient as one working on the four-cycle principle, for the reason that the entrance of the scavenge air does not permit of the most efficient expansion, and there is, of course, a further loss of power in driving the scavenge pump; it may be taken as a general rule that the two-cycle engine is 5 or 7 per cent. less efficient than four cycle, which is quite sufficient to render the employment of the latter advisable, unless the space available for the engine is limited, since, of course, the four-cycle engine is much larger than the two cycle.

Considering now the question of Diesel marine engines, the four-cycle machine will probably be replaced for very large vessels in spite of its high efficiency. Several four-stroke cycle engines have been built for marine work up to 1,500 H.P., but that this practice will continue for very large powers is far from likely, and it has probably only been adopted since so much experience has been obtained with this type and it was desired to lessen as far as possible what might be termed the experimental nature of the installation.

For marine work there are two very important reasons which render the two-cycle engine preferable to the four-cycle, the first being the lesser space required and the reduction in weight, while the second is the greater ease with which it is possible to reverse engines working on this cycle, compared with the more complicated mechanism and comparative difficulty encountered with four-cycle engines. There is a still further point in favour of two-cycle engines for marine work, namely, that there are no actual exhaust valves on this type, but only ports which are cleared out by scavenge air every revolution; hence they do not so readily become foul, and require less cleaning.

Practically the only parts in a four-cycle Diesel engine which require attention are the exhaust and fuel valves, and these should, if possible, be cleaned out once a fortnight, though if care be taken that the exhaust is always clear and not smoky, the exhaust valve may be in operation as long as six months without cleaning. Frequent cleaning is usually inconvenient with vessels making long voyages, though various means can be devised for overcoming the difficulty, such as an arrangement for shutting off the cylinders separately and taking out the fuel valve while the engine is still running, which method has, in fact, been actually employed. But it is naturally preferable to avoid the necessity of cleaning at all since any interference with running machinery is to be deprecated. For powers up to 1,500 B.H.P. or 2,000 B.H.P., however, there is no doubt still a wide field for the four-cycle engine, in spite of its disability as regards weight, cost and complication, and this fact has been amply demonstrated by the success which has attended the various vessels now in commission, propelled by four-cycle Diesel engines.

The question resolves itself mainly into whether the double acting or the single acting two-stroke engine should be employed for large powers, and it should be mentioned that many firms constructing Diesel engines are at present averse to the double acting principle, although engines of this type are now running satisfactorily. Larger powers may be obtained per cylinder, and in fact the number of actual working cylinders will, generally speaking, be only one-half that required with the single acting engine for the same power and turning moment. The chief objection is that there is always a certain liability of danger with the stuffing boxes of the piston rods, which is sometimes experienced with double acting gas engines, and the trouble is likely to be more acute with Diesel engines owing to greater combined temperatures and pressures, and more inequality in the pressures. The double acting machine is in some ways more complicated than the single acting, and though this is not a certain preventative against its success, simplicity is to be desired for marine engines, and the questions of reliability, accessibility of parts, and ease of repairs must be carefully attended to, in any design which is to meet with

ACTION AND WORKING OF THE DIESEL ENGINE 45

the approval of the marine engineer. With double acting engines large scavenge pumps are required, and indeed compare in size with the dimensions of the working cylinders, so that the saving in space and weight is not so great as might at first sight be expected. Moreover, greater care has to be taken with regard to the cooling of the pistons, piston rods, exhaust ports, etc.

With a double acting engine it is impossible to arrange the fuel admission in the centre at the bottom of the cylinder owing to the piston rod passing through, while in the horizontal type the piston rod is sometimes arranged to pass through the cylinder at the back end in order that the weight of the piston may be supported. This leads to the necessity for admitting the fuel eccentrically, which is probably not such an efficient method, and moreover renders the valve gear considerably less simple, and the valves at the bottom are not easy to get at for overhaul and repairs. If, in the vertical type, fuel is admitted in the centre at the top and eccentrically at the bottom, this causes a different distribution of pressure on the piston on the up and down stroke respectively and has to be allowed for in the design. Another point which to some extent places the double acting engine at a disadvantage, is the fact that the clearance space between the piston and cylinder cover is equally important at each end, and it is of course impossible to adjust both ends by the means adopted in the single acting engine—namely by the insertion or removal of a liner at the back of the big end bearing—and some special arrangement has to be adopted.

As a matter of fact there is little reason to suppose that either the single or double acting engine should be adopted to the exclusion of the other, though if as large powers as are necessary can be obtained in cylinders working on the single acting principle, the main object of the double acting type is destroyed. Evidently there are many matters affecting the choice of type for marine work, quite apart from mere theoretical considerations, and the only safe statement in connexion with marine work is that the widespread adoption of the two-cycle type is extremely probable once the experimental stage is passed, which must continue for a few years, but whether the single acting or double acting engine will find general favour is a problem which future experience alone can solve.

Engine Speeds.—It was at one time thought that the speeds of Diesel engines to give maximum economy must be slightly higher than was desirable from the point of view of propeller efficiency, particularly for the slow cargo vessel for which this motor is peculiarly applicable. It would seem, however, from recent practical experience that there is very little reason to anticipate that the Diesel motor will suffer much, if at all, in this direction in comparison with steam engines, although many of the earlier motor ships have been equipped with motors running at a speed considerably in excess of corresponding steam engines.

The difference in any case is not of great importance from the point of view of actual overall fuel consumption, but at the same time it is desirable for many reasons that the Diesel motor should conform as far as reasonable with existing marine practice. Engines of even as low a power as 800 H.P. are now designed to run at 100 revolutions per minute and below, and recent motors of 2,000 H.P. have been designed for a normal speed of 90 revolutions per minute for vessels of about 10 to 12 knots. It has also been found practicable to run these engines at a minimum of 25 to 30 per cent. of the normal speed or even less, which is sufficient flexibility for most practical purposes.

The Diesel engine therefore satisfies all the requirements as far as speed is concerned, but nevertheless in certain cases a gear reduction has been employed, in some instances a mechanical or hydraulic gear, and in at least one case, an electric transmission system, utilizing high-speed stationary Diesel engines.

Limiting Power of Diesel Engines.—One of the chief difficulties met with in the development of the internal combustion engine was the trouble in producing a satisfactory motor of large power without a multiplicity of cylinders. The necessity for such machines led to the introduction of the two-cycle and the double acting gas engines, chiefly for use with blast furnace gas, and the experience gained has been utilized to the full by manufacturers of Diesel engines. Gas engines of various types are now built up to 4,000 B.H.P. with single cylinders of 1,000 B.H.P. each, and with these machines no insuperable difficulties are encountered in construction or operation. There are several reasons why motors working on the Diesel cycle should be capable of developing larger powers per cylinder than gas engines operating on the constant volume cycle. As will have been noticed from an examination of the indicator cards of a Diesel engine, the mean effective pressure exerted on the piston is far higher than in a gas engine, the average being about 100 to 110, and in some cases even 125 lb. per sq. inch. against 60 to 70 lb. per sq. inch with gas engines. For equal cylinder volumes a Diesel engine will thus give a higher power than a gas engine. The temperature rise has probably the most important influence in limiting the size of engine cylinders and, as has been seen, this is less with Diesel than with gas engines, while the clearance volume in the former is also well below that of the latter, being some 6 to 8 per cent. against 25 per cent. or more with four-cycle engines, though the proportion does not quite hold in larger powers, and with the two-cycle type. It is difficult at the present time to say exactly what is the maximum power that could safely be developed in a single cylinder of a Diesel engine, and the point cannot be satisfactorily settled until further experience has been gained. The piston diameter cannot be very largely increased owing to the high compression pressure and the consequently excessive resultant pressures on the connecting rod and crank, while with very large cylinder diameters the question of efficiently cooling the piston rod becomes somewhat troublesome.

The point is chiefly of importance in connexion with the marine engine, since it is safe to say that Diesel engines of the stationary type can now be built up to any power that may be reasonably required. In view of the experience already gained with large engines the opinion of designers is that no insuperable difficulties will be encountered in building Diesel engines developing 2,000 H.P. per cylinder working on the two-cycle, single acting principle, or 4,000 H.P. for double acting machines; as a matter of fact, two three-cylinder, double acting, two-cycle engines of more than 8,000 H.P. each have already been built and run satisfactorily, one of the engines developing nearly 2,800 H.P. per cylinder. Engines, therefore, of 15,000 to 20,000 H.P. are quite within the bounds of immediate possibility. In all probability engines of nearly 4,000 H.P. per cylinder will be built within a short time which would allow the highest powers at present required to be obtained.

Weights of Diesel Engines.—One point of great interest in connexion with a comparison between the various types of Diesel engines is the weights of the different motors, referring for the moment to stationary engines, since marine engines are dealt with separately in the section on marine Diesel motors. Economy in weight is advantageous in various directions, not the least being that it allows of considerable reduction in cost which has always been of great moment in oil engines of the high compression type.

The following tables which give actual weights of some of the M.A.N. engines, do not apply generally to all designs, but the variations are not large and the figures are sufficiently accurate for comparisons. Horizontal motors are lighter than those of the vertical type and vertical two-cycle engines do not shew quite so favourably as the horizontal ones, although nearly so. The weights given are sufficient to show how it is possible to manufacture a two-cycle Diesel motor at a price of from £6 to £8 per B.H.P., whereas the four-cycle type costs nearly £10 per B.H.P. even in the larger sizes.

Weights of Four-Cylinder Diesel Motors.

Cylinder Diam. Inches.	Piston Stroke. Inches.	Revs. per Min.	B.H.P.	Weight. Lbs.	Lbs. per B.H.P.	Type.
13·6	19·3	195	200	65,560	328	4-cycle vertical single-acting.
17·7	24·9	175	400	118,880	299	Ditto
21·0	29·1	167	600	187,000	312	Ditto
25·2	35·4	150	1,000	339,900	340	Ditto
23·0	31·4	150	1,200	308,000	257	4-cycle horizontal double-acting
29·0	39·4	125	2,000	479,600	240	Ditto
36·0	51·0	94	3,000	785,400	262	Ditto
39·4	55·0	94	4,000	913,000	228	Ditto
16·9	25·1	187	400	110,000	275	4-cycle horizontal single-acting
18·9	27·5	167	500	145,200	290	Ditto
20·0	29·1	167	600	165,000	275	Ditto
21·0	30·6	167	700	189,200	270	Ditto
19·6	29·5	167	1,000	154,000	154	2-cycle horizontal single-acting
24·3	31·4	150	1,500	242,000	161	Ditto
26·3	35·4	150	2,000	330,000	165	Ditto

Fuel for Diesel Engines.—Speaking generally, it may be said that practically any kind of oil can be employed with Diesel engines. The chief among those at present produced and obtainable in large quantities are the natural oils from the oil wells now productive in all parts of the world, and the oils resulting from the distillation of coal and brown coal or lignite. There has been some question as to whether the increasing employment of the Diesel engine will not result in a shortage of supply of oil and a consequent increase of price, which would at once diminish the great advantage of economy now possessed by this motor. When, however, it is considered that the world's output of oil from the wells is in the neighbourhood of fifty million tons annually and that this figure is rising rapidly it is difficult to imagine that this anticipation will be in any way fulfilled. At the present time all the Diesel engines extant consume only quite a minute proportion of the world's supply, and moreover it is the general opinion of geologists that there are vast oil-fields in many parts of the globe which have not yet been exploited, and that the supply from these is wellnigh unlimited. It seems therefore that in the future, by the very fact of the wide demand for crude oils, the production will largely increase and the tendency of the price of oil will be to drop rather than to rise. There seems little doubt that the occurrence of oil is about as widespread as coal, and hence any large permanent increase in the cost of the former is less likely than in the latter. There will be, and have been, temporary and artificial fluctuations in the price owing to the conditions under which oil is marketed, but too much importance should not be laid on this point, although it may at times detrimentally affect the development of Diesel engines.

There is, however, this fact to be remembered, that most of the countries in which machinery is most largely required —namely, in many parts of Europe—are not oil-producing lands, and hence are dependent on their supply of natural oil from outside sources. This is a matter of no great importance in Great Britain and other countries such as Belgium, Denmark and Sweden, where there is no duty on imported oil, but makes a vast difference in Germany, France, Italy and Spain where the duty is high, this being particularly the case in the two first named, and in France it is such as wellnigh to prohibit the use of Diesel engines running on crude oils.

The matter can be well explained by a statement of the price of residue oil which at present obtains. Its approximate value near the oilfields is 15s. to 25s. per ton, and delivered at a European port it should be about 45s. to 60s. per ton. In Germany the duty is about 36s. per ton, or nearly equivalent to the actual value of the oil, which renders the fuel cost of a Diesel engine running on natural oil much higher than it is in this country. For this reason much attention has been paid in Germany and elsewhere to the question of employing other oils, and those produced by the distillation of coal, and lignite or brown coal, of which large quantities are available, are being much used. The lignite oils are in every way suitable for Diesel engines and have been employed for many years, but the price of these oils again is high (75 marks per ton) and very little saving is effected as compared with the imported residue oils.

The oil from the distillation of coal is very much more largely produced in Germany than lignite oil, nearly twice the amount being available for sale at a price of less than 40s. per ton. The difficulty originally experienced in the use of this coal tar oil for Diesel engines was its high flash point, which is about 400° Fahr. or over, and with the ordinary construction this would necessitate a considerably higher compression pressure in the cylinder for its ignition than the residue oil with a flash point of under 200° Fahr. In order to avoid this high compression an arrangement has now been generally adopted which has proved in every way satisfactory, of injecting a small amount of crude oil into the cylinder through the pulveriser immediately before, or simultaneously with, the main charge of coal tar oil, the quantity usually admitted being from 5 to 10 per cent. of the total weight of fuel. Even this is not always necessary if pre-heating is adopted.

Combustion takes place with the fuel first injected, and the resultant temperature is sufficient to ignite the oil of higher flash point when it enters without any higher compression pressure being necessary. The same fuel valve may be used for both injections and is suitable without any alteration for all other oils. This arrangement has worked very successfully and is now very widely adopted. The calorific value of coal tar oil is about 16,000 B.Th.U. per lb. as against 18,000 to 19,000 B.Th.U. of the crude or residual oils, and the consumption in a Diesel engine of moderate power at full load is slightly higher than with the natural oils, in the inverse proportion of the respective calorific values, being usually about 0·45 lb. per B.H.P. hour for engines of moderate power.

The oil which is utilized for Diesel engines in this country and in all oil-producing countries, or countries in which there is no duty levied, is the so-called crude or residual oil. This is obtained by the distillation of the oil from the well, the lighter bodied oils, benzine and lighting petroleum coming over first and leaving a residual oil. Its specific gravity is usually between ·85 and ·92, and owing to its high flash point it is quite unsuited for lamp oil or for use in most explosion engines, such as petrol motors, though useful for such engines as the Brons and Bolinder.

Whilst the question of the price of fuel oil for Diesel engines is one of very great importance, it will never affect the prosperity of the Diesel engine industry in a vital degree, however high it may rise, since, as shown later, the fuel economy with this type of motor is not its sole claim for consideration.

A very large number of different oils are now employed for the operation of Diesel engines, among which may be mentioned the crude oil from Texas and Tarakan, and the residual oil from numerous other countries. Californian oil, Roumanian oil and that from the Galician fields have been commonly utilized for a number of years, while recently, owing to the enormous supplies which are now available from Mexico, the Mexican oil has also been used. Trinidad oil is now upon the market, as is that from Persia, so that there is a wide choice.

There is not much to say as regards their composition, since practically all of them are entirely suitable for the Diesel engine of every type. The only point to note is that those which have an asphalt base are liable to leave a considerable amount of ash on the valves, and are therefore not quite so good as the others which are not from an asphalt base. The Mexican oil is perhaps one of the worst in this direction. As regards the question of sulphur, which many people considered a serious and detrimental constituent in oil for Diesel engines, it has now been shown by a large number of experiments that its real effect (even when it is present in the oil to the extent of 4 or 5 per cent.) is practically negligible. This arises mainly from the fact that there is no moisture present in the Diesel engine cylinder, and that without moisture no liquid sulphuric acid is formed, which is the main cause of trouble due to the presence of sulphur. So clearly is this view now held, that the Admiralty specification for oil has been altered to suit the new ideas upon the subject. The specific gravity of most oils which are used in Diesel engines varies between 0·9 and 0·97; the flash-point is generally from 220° to 250° Fahr.

Further interesting details with regard to the employment of fuel oil for Diesel engines may be obtained from Dr. Sommer's book dealing with the subject, *Petroleum as a Source of Power on Ships*, from which the following table is extracted :—

	S.P.G.	Bé.	Gross Heating Value by Experiment.		Per cent.
			Cals.	B.T.U's.	
Roumanian gas oil	0·871	31·9	10,712	19,282	100
Admiralty fuel.	0·907	24·25	10,696	19,253	99·8
Roumanian fuel	0·927	20·95	10,557	19,003	98·5
Roumanian residuum	0·928	20·8	10,558	19,004	98·5
Trinidad crude oil	0·945	18·05	10,200	18,360	95·2
Roumanian residuum	0·946	17·9	10,510	18,918	98·1
Tarakan crude oil	0·948	17·6	10,487	18,877	97·8
Trinidad residuum	0·964	15·5	10,224	18,405	95·4

The British Admiralty issues a specification for fuel

oil which has comparatively recently been modified, and now stands as follows:—

"*Quality*:—The oil fuel supplied shall consist of liquid hydrocarbons, and may be either (*a*) shale oil or (*b*) petroleum as may be required, or (*c*) a distillate or a residual product of petroleum, and shall comply with the Admiralty requirements as regards flash-point, fluidity at low temperatures, percentage of sulphur, presence of water, acidity, and freedom from impurities.

"The flash-point shall not be lower than 175° Fahr., close test (Abel or Pensky-Matens). (This compares with a flash-point of 200° Fahr. in 1910.)

"The proportion of sulphur contained in the oil shall not exceed 3·00 per cent. (as against 0·75 in 1910).

"The oil fuel supplied shall be as free as possible from acid, and in any case the quantity of acid must not exceed 0·05 per cent., calculated as oleic acid when tested by shaking up the oil with distilled water, and determining by titration with deci-normal alkali the amount of acid extracted by the water, methyl orange being used as indicator. (In 1910 it was required that the oil should be free from acidity.)

"The quantity of water delivered with the oil shall not exceed 0·5 per cent.

"The viscosity of the oil supplied shall not exceed 2,000 secs. for an outflow of 50 cubic centimetres at a temperature of 32° Fahr., as determined by Sir Boverton Redwood's standard viscometer (Admiralty type for testing oil fuel).

"The oil supplied shall be free from earthy, carbonaceous, or fibrous matter, or other impurities which are likely to choke the burners.

"The oil shall, if required by the inspecting officer, be strained by being pumped on discharge from the tanks, or tank steamer, through filters of wire gauze having 16 meshes to the inch.

"The quality and kind of oil supplied shall be fully described. The original source from which the oil has been obtained shall be stated in detail, as well as the treatment to which it has been subjected and the place at which it has been treated. The ratio which the oil supplied bears to the original crude oil should also be stated as a percentage."

In view of the widespread employment of tar oil in Germany, and its probable utilization in this country in the future on a much larger scale, the specification of this tar oil which is supplied by a large company in Germany is worthy of quotation.

Specification of Tar Oil Suitable for Diesel Engines. (From the German Tar Production Syndicate of Essen-Ruhr.)—(1) Tar-oils should not contain more than a trace of constituents insoluble in xylol. The test on this is performed as follows:—25 grammes (0·88 ounce av.) of oil are mixed with 25 grammes (1·525 cub. inch) of xylol shaken and filtered. The filter-paper before being used is dried and weighed, and after filtration has taken place it is thoroughly washed with hot xylol. After redrying the weight should not be increased by more than 0·1 gramme.

(2) The water contents should not exceed 1 per cent. The testing of the water contents is made by the well-known xylol method.

(3) The residue of the coke should not exceed 3 per cent.

(4) When performing the boiling analysis, at least 60 per cent. by volume of the oil should be distilled on heating up to 300° C. The boiling and analysis should be carried out according to the rule laid down by the Syndicate.

(5) The minimum calorific power must not be less than 8,800 cal. per kg. (15,800 B.T.U.'s per lb.). For oils of less calorific power, the purchaser has the right of deducting 2 per cent. off the net price of the delivered oil for each cal. below this minimum.

(6) The flash-point, as determined in an open crucible by Von Holde's method for lubricating oils, must not be below 65° C.

(7) The oil must be quite fluid at 15° C. The purchaser has not the right to reject oils on the ground that emulsions appear after five minutes' stirring when the oil is cooled to 8°.

Purchasers should be urged to fit their oil-storing tanks and oil pipes with warming arrangements to redissolve emulsions caused by the temperature falling below 15° C.

(8) If emulsion has been caused by the cooling of the oils in the tank during transport, the purchaser must redissolve them by means of this apparatus.

Insoluble residues may be deducted from the weight of oil supplied.

CHAPTER III

CONSTRUCTION OF THE DIESEL ENGINE

GENERAL REMARKS—FOUR-CYCLE SINGLE ACTING ENGINE; GENERAL ARRANGEMENT—STARTING AND RUNNING—DESCRIPTION OF FOUR-CYCLE ENGINE—VALVES AND CAMS—REGULATION OF THE ENGINE—TYPES OF FOUR-CYCLE ENGINES—HIGH SPEED ENGINE—HORIZONTAL ENGINE—TWO-CYCLE ENGINE—AIR COMPRESSORS FOR DIESEL ENGINES—SOLID INJECTION MOTORS.

General Remarks.—In the manufacture of Diesel engines there is one point which must be most strongly kept in view, this being that greater care has to be taken in their construction than with ordinary steam engines. A properly designed and well-built Diesel engine has no superior, for reliability and simplicity of operation. but it is essential that the materials employed should be well selected, the work should be of the best. and the greatest precision should be exercised in the fitting of the valves and gear, and other mechanism. It might be thought that these matters need no emphasis, but the difference in the running of an engine under working conditions, which has been built as a Diesel engine should be, and one which has been constructed with no more care than is given to a similar steam engine is so material that no excuse need be made for enlarging on this point.

It is a well-known axiom in the manufacture of internal combustion engines that in the attention to details of design and construction lies the difference between success and failure; and this is peculiarly applicable to the Diesel engine, whose satisfactory running depends so entirely on the high compression pressure in the cylinder.

Practically all manufacturers of Diesel engines now make them in standard sizes and types, which is rendered comparatively easy by the fact that the larger machines have two, three, four, or more cylinders of the smaller standard type. By this means some of the chief manufacturers have as many as fifty standard stationary machines of the four-cycle type from 10 H.P. to 1,000 H.P. based on some fifteen standard single-cylinder engines ranging from 10 H.P. to 250 H.P. Some of the engines have the same power with a different number of cylinders, but it is possible with this range to have some thirty-five differently rated engines, though there are only fifteen actual standards. This point of standardization is of the utmost importance as regards reduction in cost of construction, interchangeability of parts between different engines, and reduction of spare gear in complete installations, particularly when engines of different powers are employed; these advantages will be readily appreciated by all who have had experience with the operation of large plants. It is doubtful if in any other construction this matter has received such attention, and if, as should be the case, all the important portions of the engine are made most carefully to gauge, any part of the mechanism may be taken from one engine and fitted on to another of the same class. Most manufacturers claim that this is possible with all their engines, and some of them make a point of interchanging the parts of several engines when on the test bed, to prove the point.

Four-Cycle Single Acting Engine.—*Figs.* 14 *and* 15 show, diagrammatically, in plan and elevation, the general arrangement of a vertical single-cylinder Diesel engine of the ordinary type with all the necessary accessories. The cylinder K is cast with the engine frame of the A type, being secured to the bed-plate B by long bolts. The cylinder cover K_1 is of massive construction separate from the main cylinder and frame casting, and contains all the valves, of which there are four. A is the starting valve, connected by piping to the starting vessels C_2 and C_3; D is the exhaust valve through which the exhaust gases pass from the cylinder into the exhaust pipe E and thence to the silencer F (often placed below ground level), to which is attached the long pipe G for the escape of the gases to the atmosphere; H is the air suction inlet valve by which air is drawn into the cylinder from the engine-room through the inlet pipe J of special construction; X is the fuel inlet valve and pulveriser, the function of which is to admit fuel to the cylinder at the right moment and in the form of a fine spray. The oil reaches the fuel valve from the fuel pump L, whose action is controlled by the governor, the fuel pump chamber being a small reservoir into which the oil gravitates from the fuel filter M. The fuel pipe is also arranged that it may take its supply from another small cylindrical vessel N which usually contains paraffin, since it is an advantage to run the engine for a few minutes every day on paraffin, which is most helpful in cleaning the cylinder and valves. The fuel filter itself is connected by a pipe from a larger oil reservoir O, fixed at a rather higher level, and it is convenient to have this reservoir of such size as will contain several days' supply. The main oil tanks containing perhaps several months' supply are commonly fixed underground and the oil is pumped up into the reservoir as required by a small pump which may be driven in any convenient manner. The cooling water circulation is arranged so that the water enters the jacket through a pipe at the bottom and leaves at the top from the cylinder cover. This pipe is usually broken, the water flowing into an open funnel, this forming a ready means of ascertaining that there is no stoppage in the circulation. In some cases, however, water is expensive and a cooling tower is installed so that the supply may be used continuously, and in this event the circuit is usually a closed one; it is preferable wherever possible to employ open circuit piping, and in any case a thermometer should be fixed on each cylinder to indicate the temperature of the cooling water. Referring to *Figs.* 14 *and* 15 again, P

represents the air compressor shown as being driven off the engine crank shaft (though there are various other methods), and delivering air at the high pressure needed for fuel injection and starting the engine into the air reservoir C_1 containing the air for the injection of the fuel. All the air vessels C_1, C_2 and C_3 are connected by air piping and valves so that the pressure in any one may be lowered by abstracting from either of the others; of the two reservoirs C_2 and C_3 one may be considered as a spare to the other. During the running of the engine, the only air used is, of course, that necessary for the fuel injection and hence the com-

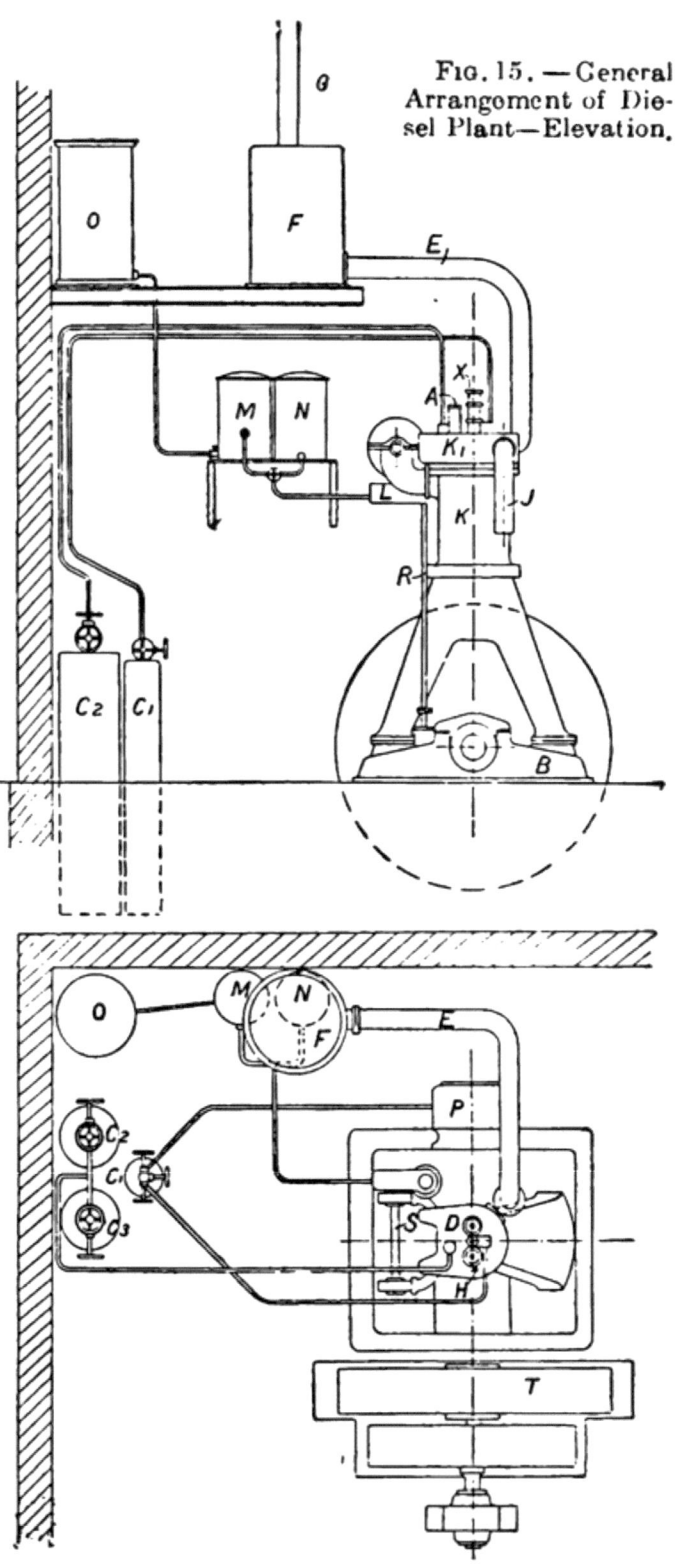

Fig. 15.—General Arrangement of Diesel Plant—Elevation.

Fig. 14.—General Arrangement Plan of Diesel Plant.

pressor delivers its air directly into the reservoir C_1, the valves being regulated to suit the required pressure, but at the same time the starting vessels are replenished so that there is always an efficient supply for re-starting the engine. The vertical governor shaft R shown in the figures is driven through worm gearing off the crank shaft, and this through further gearing drives the horizontal cam shaft S, supported between two bearings mounted on the cylinder casting, and on which are all the cams for operating the various valves in the cylinder cover. The governor shaft also actuates the fuel pump L and the governor, the combined action of which regulates the speed of rotation of the engine. The cams and valve levers which they control are not shown in *Figs* 14 *and* 15 but the valves are in the relative positions most commonly adopted as being best suited for the arrangement of the four cams on the cam shaft. The exhaust and air suction inlet valves are on the outside (longitudinally), while the fuel and starting valves are close together, the object being to have their levers interconnected so that it is impossible for the two valves to be open at the same time. The fuel valve is, of course, in the centre of the cylinder cover, and thus allows the oil to enter centrally and give an equal distribution of pressure over the piston during combustion.

A third outer bearing, separate from the engine bed-plate is always provided, with the flywheel T, mounted between this and the inner crank shaft bearing. Diesel engines are never constructed as two bearing machines with an overhung flywheel.

Starting and Running.—The starting and running of the engine is as follows: The starting lever on the engine is put in the starting position, that is, so that the lever actuating the fuel valve is out of operation and the fuel valve remains closed, whilst the lever actuating the starting valve on the cylinder is in its working position, that is, it is moved by its cam on the cam shaft as it revolves and thus opens the starting valve. The engine is barred round till it is just over the dead centre, the fuel valve is pumped up by hand to ensure the oil piping is full of oil, and the air blast valve on the reservoir C_1 is opened so that there is a supply of high pressure air on the fuel valve when it is ready to open. The valve on the starting reservoir which is to be used is then opened and the engine starts up as a compressed air engine. It is allowed to make two or three revolutions when the starting handle is moved so that the lever operating the starting valve on the engine is no longer moved by its cam, and the valve thus remains closed, while the same operation brings the fuel valve lever into working position, and thus opens the fuel valve as the cam operating it, comes round. The arrangement is such that when the starting handle is in the starting position the lever operating the fuel valve is held well out of the range of its cam on the cam shaft, while when the starting lever is pushed back to the running position the lever operating the starting valve is similarly held away from its cam.

Description of Four-Cycle Single Acting Engine.—*Figs* 16 *and* 17 show longitudinal and transverse sectional elevations of a single-cylinder Diesel engine of the ordinary slow speed four-cycle single acting type as constructed by the Maschinenfabrik Augsburg Nürnberg A.G. All the four valves are arranged in the cylinder head, the air inlet suction valve E and the exhaust valve A being similar. These are of the mushroom type, opening downwards directly into the cylinder, and they are kept on their seats by strong springs, the pressure on which may be regulated if required. The outlet from the exhaust valve is connected by piping to the silencer, while to the air suction inlet is coupled a pipe through which the air is drawn from the atmosphere. This consists virtually of a closed cylinder with a number of very narrow longitudinal slits arranged usually in two sections as shown, and by this means the access of dust is prevented, while the noise due to the rush of the incoming air is reduced to a minimum. The fuel valve and pulveriser, B—perhaps the most important detail of the engine—is fixed directly in the centre of the

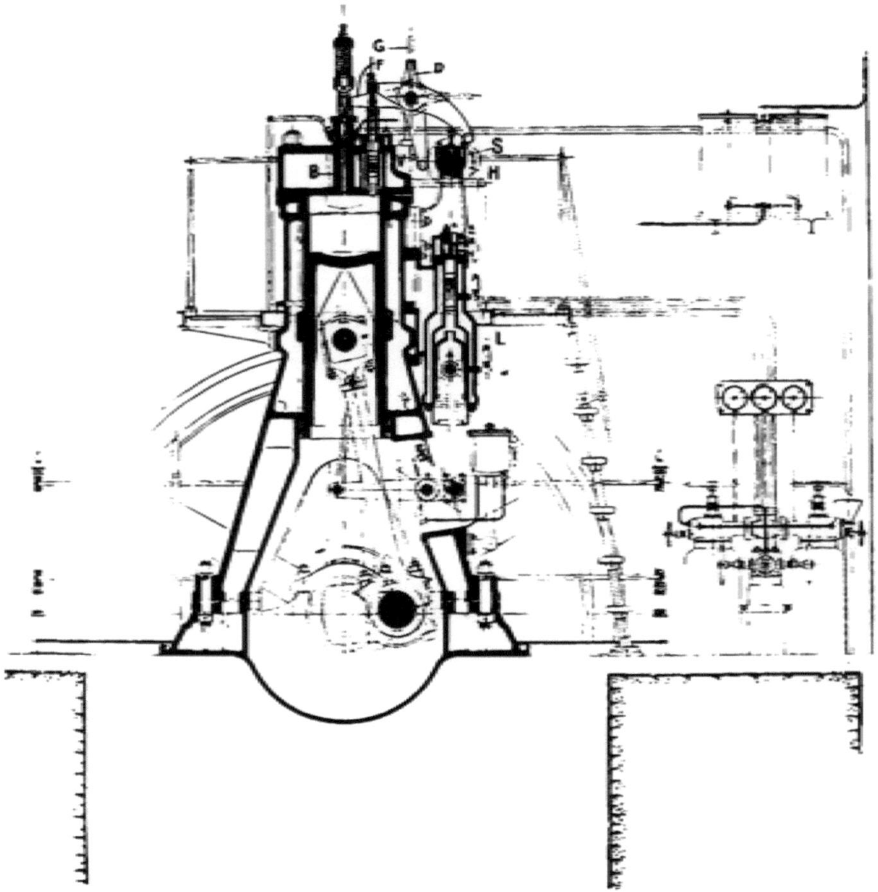

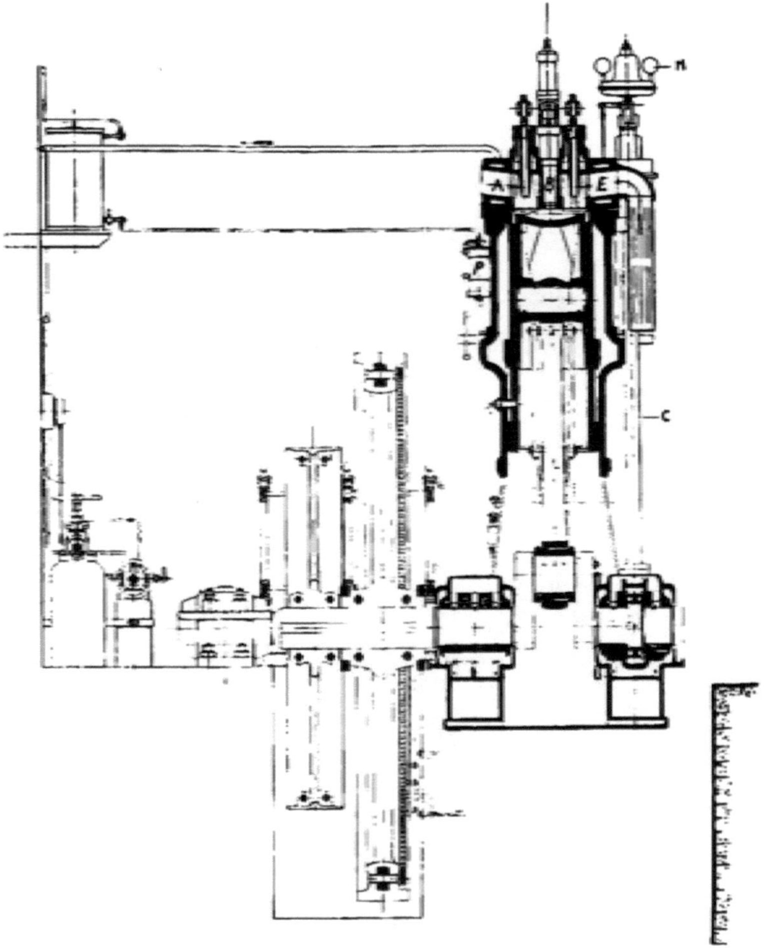

Fig. 16.—Longitudinal Section of M.A.N. Diesel Engine.

Fig. 17.—Transverse Section of M.A.N. Diesel Engine.

[To face page 62.

Fig. 18.—1,000 H.P. Four Cycle Augsburg Engine. [To face page 62.

cylinder, and is likewise contained in the cylinder head, the needle being held in position by an adjustable spring. The starting valve V is fixed as close as is practicable to the fuel valve, and is of somewhat similar type in this design to the exhaust and suction valves, except that it is much smaller. The cam shaft H is supported between two bearings on brackets bolted to the cylinder casting, one of these brackets being seen in *Fig* 17. This shaft carries the four cams S in *Fig.* 17. The valve levers which are actuated by the several cams are pivoted on a spindle supported by two small standards fixed to the cylinder head, the starting valve cam lever D, and the fuel valve lever F being seen in *Fig.* 17. The vertical governor spindle C which operates the cam shaft, the fuel valve pump, the governor, and in some machines the small lubricating pumps, is driven off the main crank shaft by a worm drive, running in oil and provided with a coupling near the bed-plate to facilitate removal and inspection. The gear box contains the spur wheels through which rotation is given to the cam shaft at half the speed of the engine shaft. The governor M is of the ordinary type, and regulates the speed of the engine by controlling the amount of fuel admitted to the cylinder in a manner described later. The cylinder liner is separate from the main casting, both of which are usually of cast iron, and ample space is left for the water jacket, the cooling water entering the bottom of the cylinder and leaving at the top of the cylinder cover, through the delivery pipe P. In some engines the exhaust pipe and the exhaust valve are also water jacketed, this adding slightly to the efficiency of the machine. It is essential in any case that the cover should be well cooled, in order to prevent the valves becoming overheated, and it is made of massive construction, being secured to the cylinder by eight studs of ample size. The piston is usually of the cast-iron trunk type, slightly dished at the top, and is particularly long in order to provide a good bearing surface to reduce the pressure due to the obliquity of the piston rod. It is always fitted

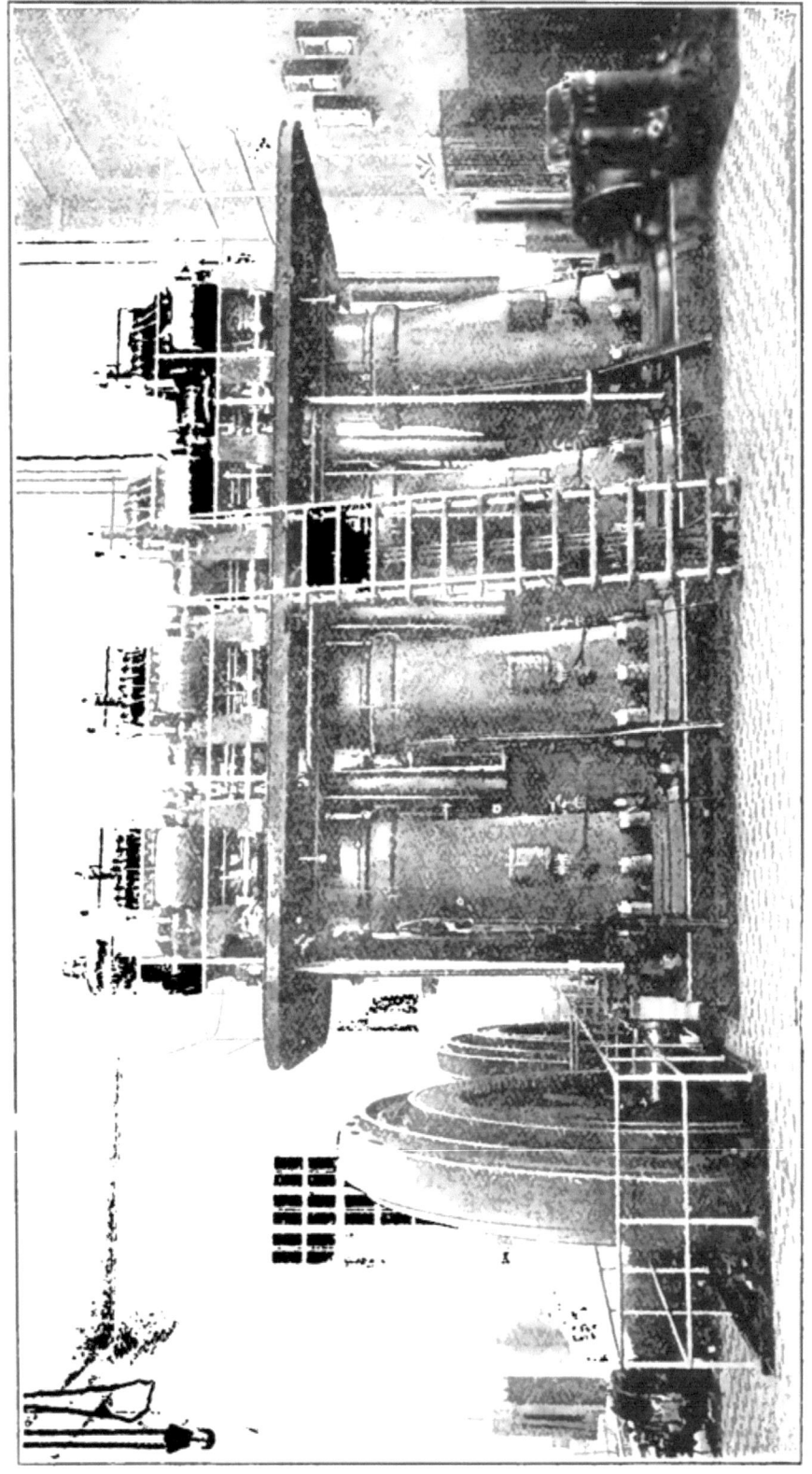

Fig. 19.—880 H.P. M.A.N. Diesel Engine.

with six to eight Ramsbottom rings to secure tightness, and lubrication is effected through a small pipe, which communicates with the cylinder liner near the centre, and delivers into an annular space in it, provided with a number of very small holes piercing the liner and giving access of the oil to the piston. The connecting rod brasses are made adjustable in the usual way to take up wear, and are well lubricated. The air compressor L in this machine is driven off the connecting rod by link levers, the compressor cylinder being bolted to the front of the engine cylinder, though this method is by no means generally adopted, the drive often being arranged directly off the crank shaft at the end of the machine remote from the flywheel, with the cylinders fixed to the bed-plate. The compressor shown in *Figs.* 16 *and* 17 is of the two-stage type, as employed for small machines, and the cylinder is also water cooled, the same water being used as for the engine cylinder jacket, or by-passed from the main supply as may be desired. The compressed air from the compressor is delivered direct into the air injection blast reservoir through copper piping. An illustration of two M.A.N. four-cycle engines is shown in *Figs.* 18 *and* 19, the first being of 1,000 H.P. and the second of 880 H.P.

Valves and Cams.—The action of the various cams may be examined at this point, this being a matter of importance, as the exact time of the opening of the valves, relative to the position of the piston, and the duration of this opening is controlled entirely by the cams which operate the valves through intermediary levers. The position of the cams relative to each other is thus an important point, and is best explained by a diagrammatic representation of them. In *Fig.* 20 the fuel valve cam is indicated by A, the exhaust valve cam by B, the air suction valve by C, and the starting valve cam by D. In a four-cycle engine each valve must be open once in two revolutions, and the cam shaft must necessarily rotate at half the speed of the crank shaft. In the diagrams, therefore, one revolution of the crank shaft is represented by a semicircle or 180°, while during one stroke of the piston each cam makes a quarter of a revolution. The vertical and horizontal diameters in *Fig.* 20 therefore represent top and bottom dead centres of the crank, the vertical lines being taken as top dead centres and the horizontal ones as the bottom dead centres. The arrangement of the cam is now easily understood. The fuel cam opens the fuel valve just previous to the piston reaching the end of its up stroke, thus giving pre-admisson to the extent of perhaps 1 per cent. of the stroke or less, depending on the speed of the engine. The valve is then held open for the required period,

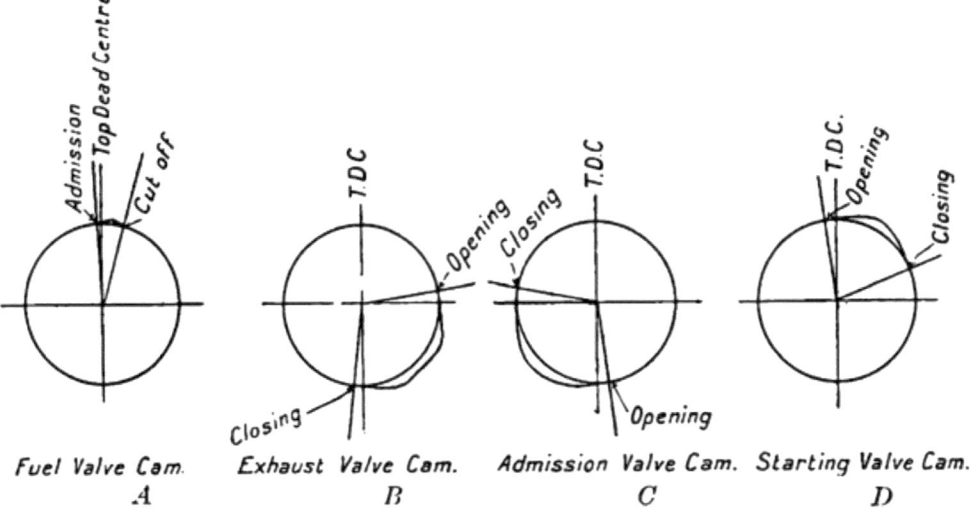

Fig. 20.—Diagram showing Arrangement of Cams with Diesel Engine.

the total amount of the opening being through an angle of 8 or 10 per cent. The exhaust valve cam similarly opens slightly before the end of the working stroke, remains open during the whole of the next or exhaust stroke, and closes just after the top dead centre is reached. Air admission commences through the air suction valve just before the end of the exhaust stroke, and the valve is kept open during the next stroke, and closes immediately after the crank passes the bottom dead centre. The starting valve cam is arranged to open the valve just before the top dead centre is reached, and to close it some considerable time before the end of the stroke. All the cams are arranged so that the

CONSTRUCTION OF THE DIESEL ENGINE

valve opens very slightly during the first moment of contact of the cam with the lever, after which the valve opens

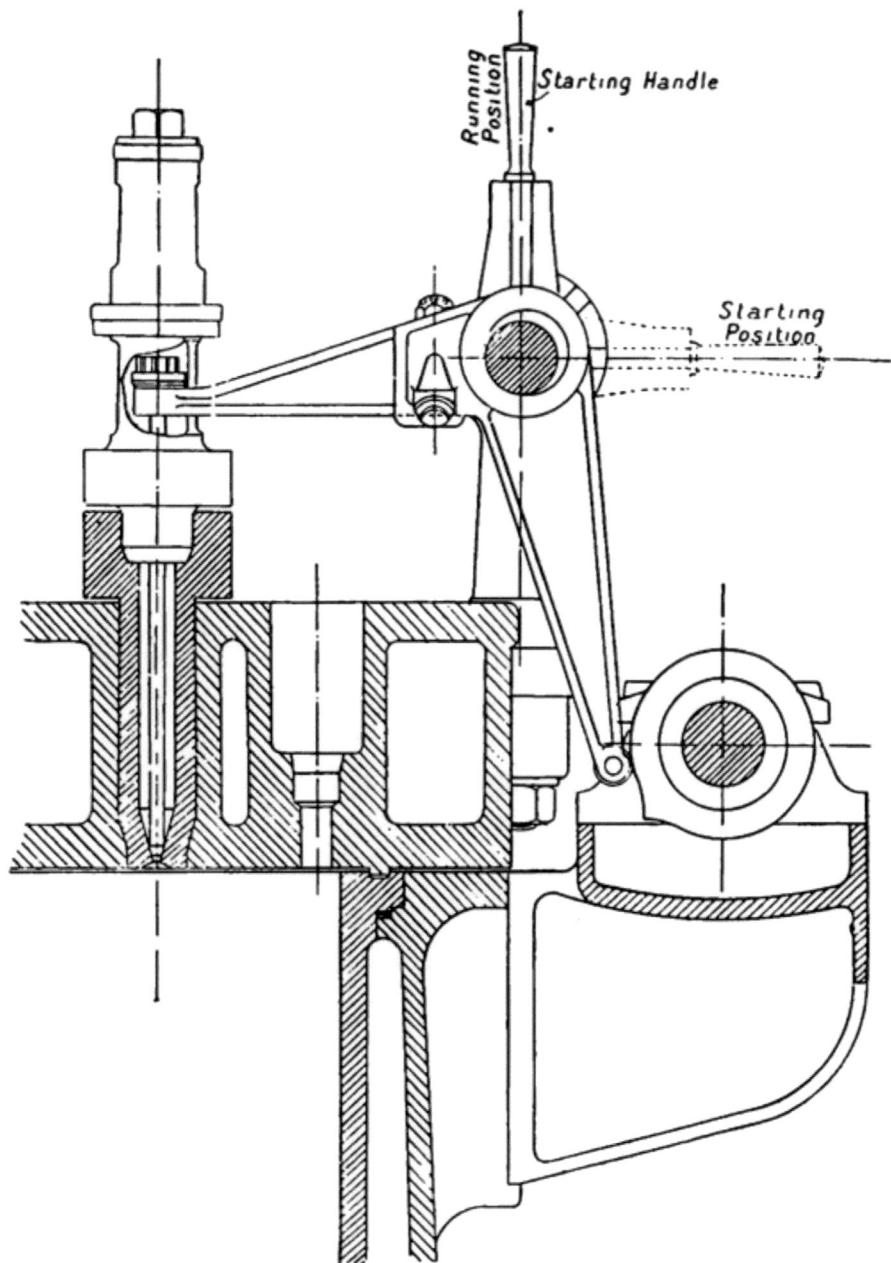

Fig. 21.—Fuel Inlet Valve, Lever and Cam.

rapidly to its full extent, and closes in the same manner, so that in the actual operation a very quick admission and cut off is obtained. The diagram does not show the cams in their actual relative positions, as if this were so all the levers would have to be arranged parallel with each other and the valves open in the same direction; usually, in the actual engine, the exhaust, air suction, and starting valves all open inwards to the cylinder, whilst the fuel inlet valve opens outwards, and the lever actuating it has therefore to be set at a different angle from the other levers.

The general arrangement of the fuel inlet valve with the cam and lever for its operation is shown in *Fig.* 21. When the nose of the cam comes in contact with the valve lever, this is forced outwards and the valve is opened against the pressure of a spring, which normally keeps the valve on its seat, the amount of the opening being extremely small. *Fig.* 21 also shows the starting handle which when in the horizontal position causes the starting valve lever to come in contact with the nose of its cam as the cam shaft rotates, while the fuel valve lever is held clear of its cam at the same time. When the starting handle is in the vertical position the starting valve lever is clear of its cam, and the fuel valve lever then comes into operation. It is a great convenience if the lever is so constructed that there is a joint between the spindle on which it is pivoted and the valve spindle, since this joint can then readily be broken and the valve easily removed. This arrangement, though not universal, is now adopted by a large number of makers, and the design employed by Messrs. Sulzer Bros. is shown in *Fig.* 25.

Fig. 26 shows a detail drawing, partly diagrammatic, of the type of fuel inlet valve and pulveriser most commonly employed with Diesel engines, though there are slight differences with engines of various makes. The oil from the fuel pump enters through the pipe A, the amount being regulated by the action of the governor on the pump to suit the load on the engine. The oil flows down the small cylindrical hole B and enters the annular space C through D near the bottom of the needle valve E, ground to an angle of about

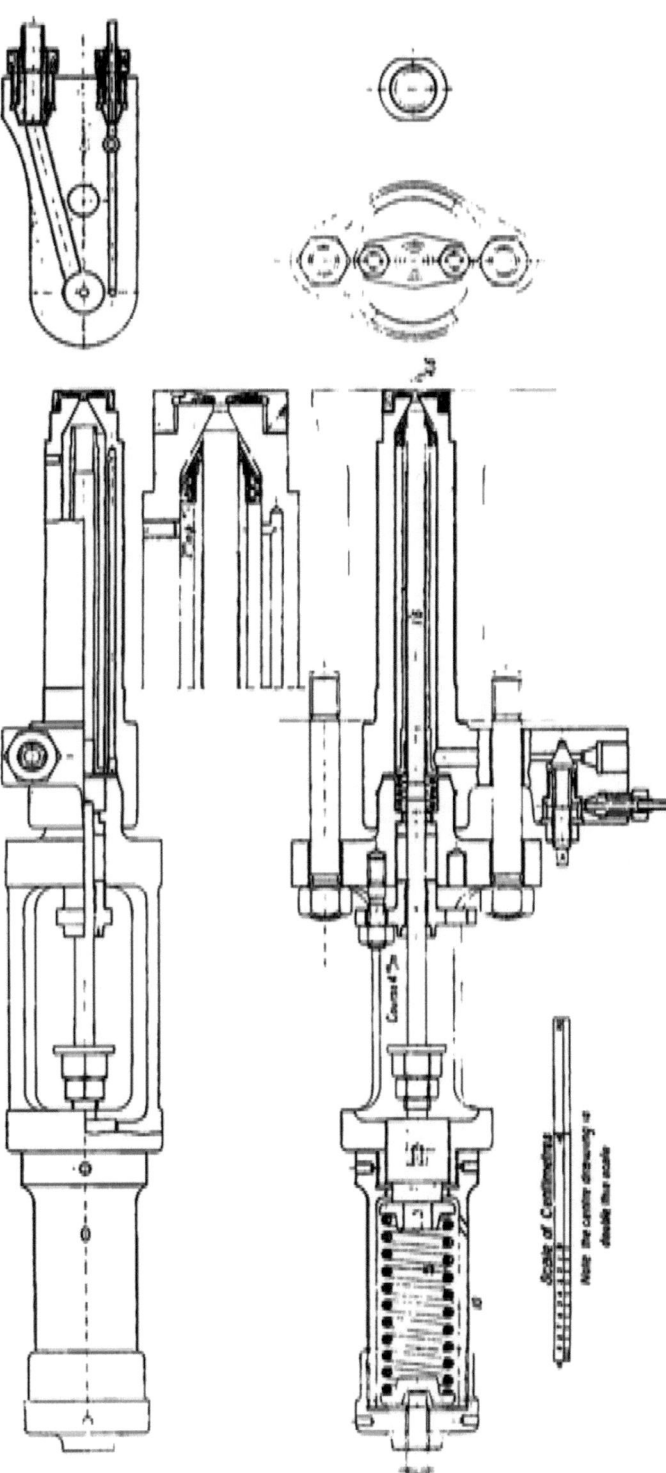

Fig. 22.—Details of Fuel Inlet Valve (Vickers Type).

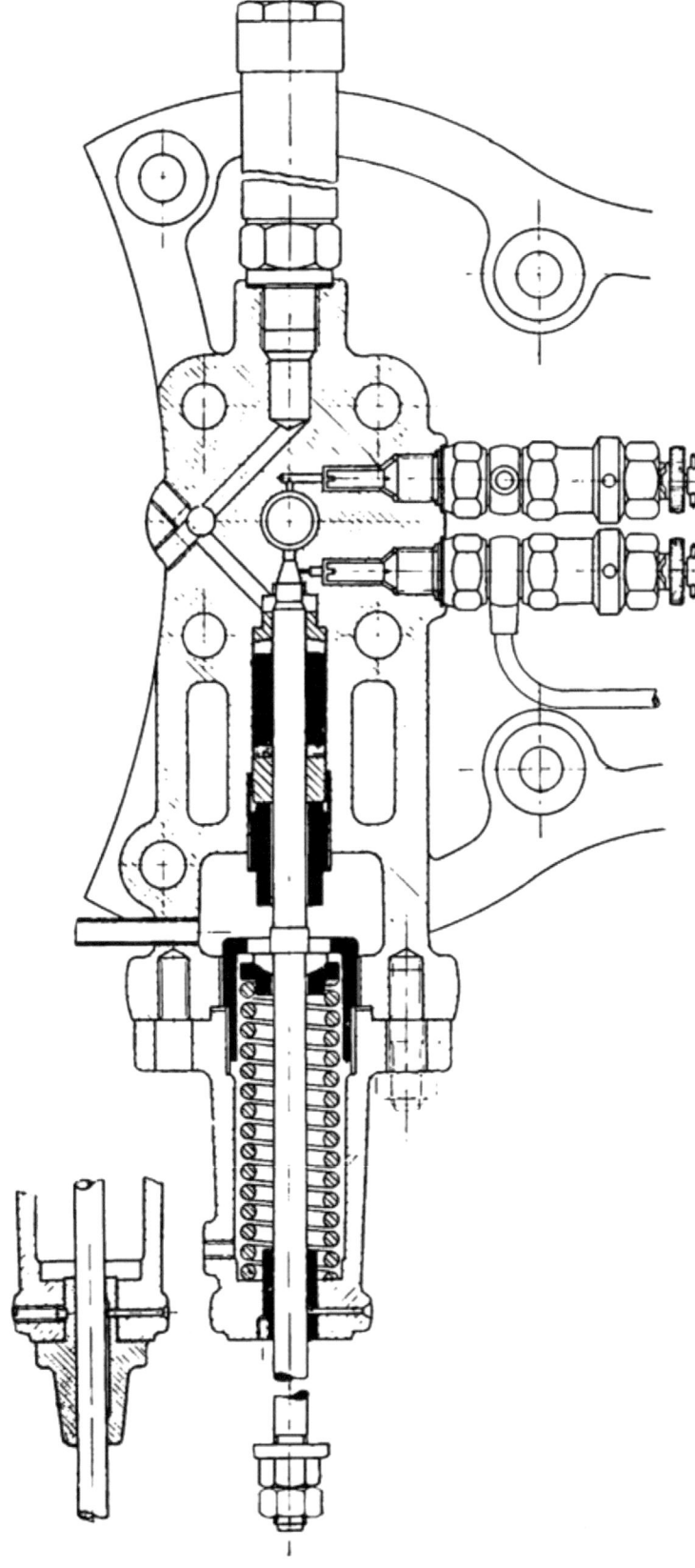

Fig. 23.—Arrangement of Fuel Admission when using Tar Oil.

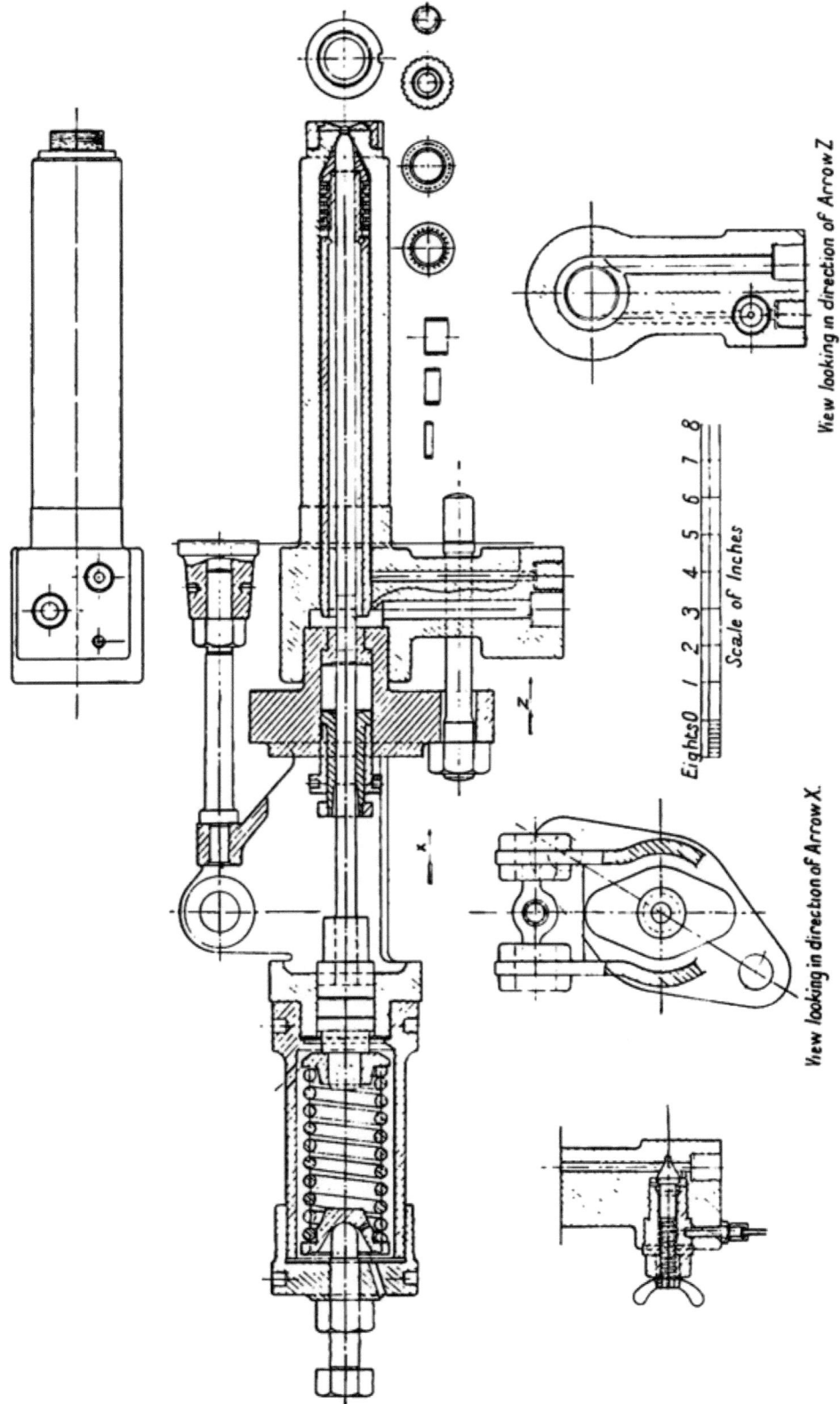

FIG. 24.—Details of Fuel Valve of Hick, Hargreaves Diesel Motor.

CONSTRUCTION OF THE DIESEL ENGINE 71

30°, just above the pulverising or spraying arrangement. For this purpose there are four metal rings F, each containing a large number (twenty or more) of small holes usually one-tenth to one-sixteenth of an inch in diameter. The holes in the plates or rings are staggered as shown in the figure, so that the oil may not be blown directly through them, and between the plates are very small bands G. Below

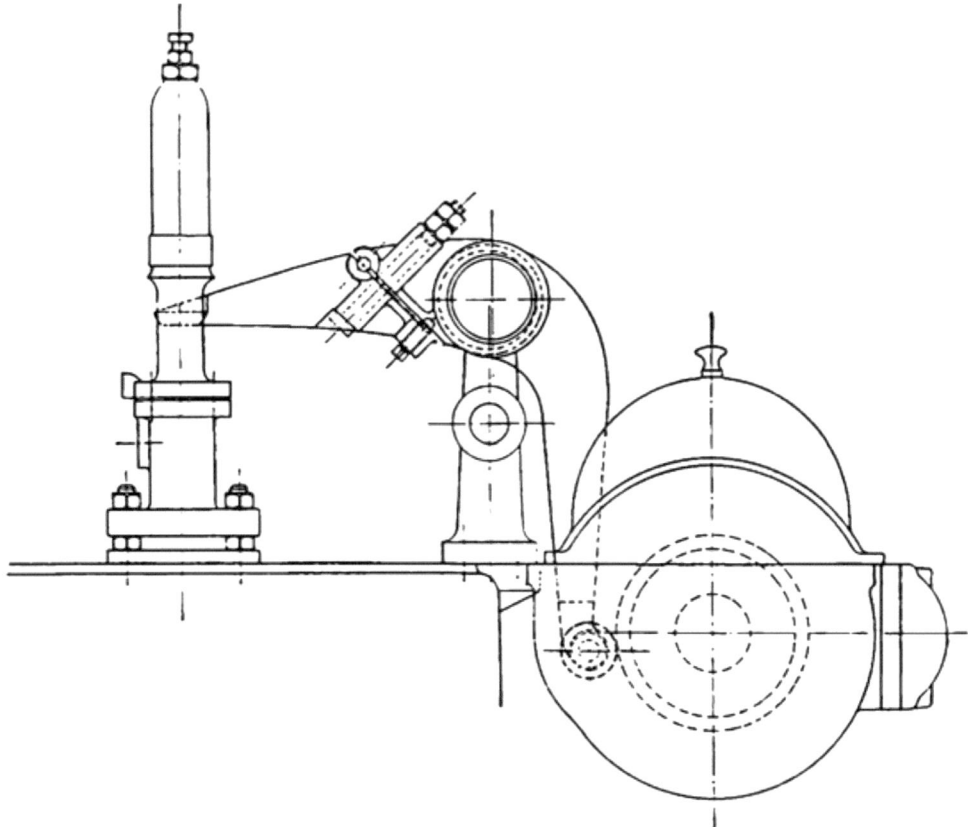

FIG. 25.—Jointed Valve Lever.

the rings is a conically-shaped piece, in the periphery of which is about the same number of channels as there are holes in the rings, and these channels, which may be from one-sixteenth to one-twentieth of an inch deep, form a series of nozzles, through which the fuel has to pass, after getting through the holes in the rings. It then enters the cylinder by the expanding orifice, which is made of steel, the guides for the needle valve being of cast iron. The annular space C is always in direct connexion with the injection air reservoir as soon as the valve on the reservoir is opened, and the air enters the space near the top through another pipe and a cylindrical hole in the same casting as that for the

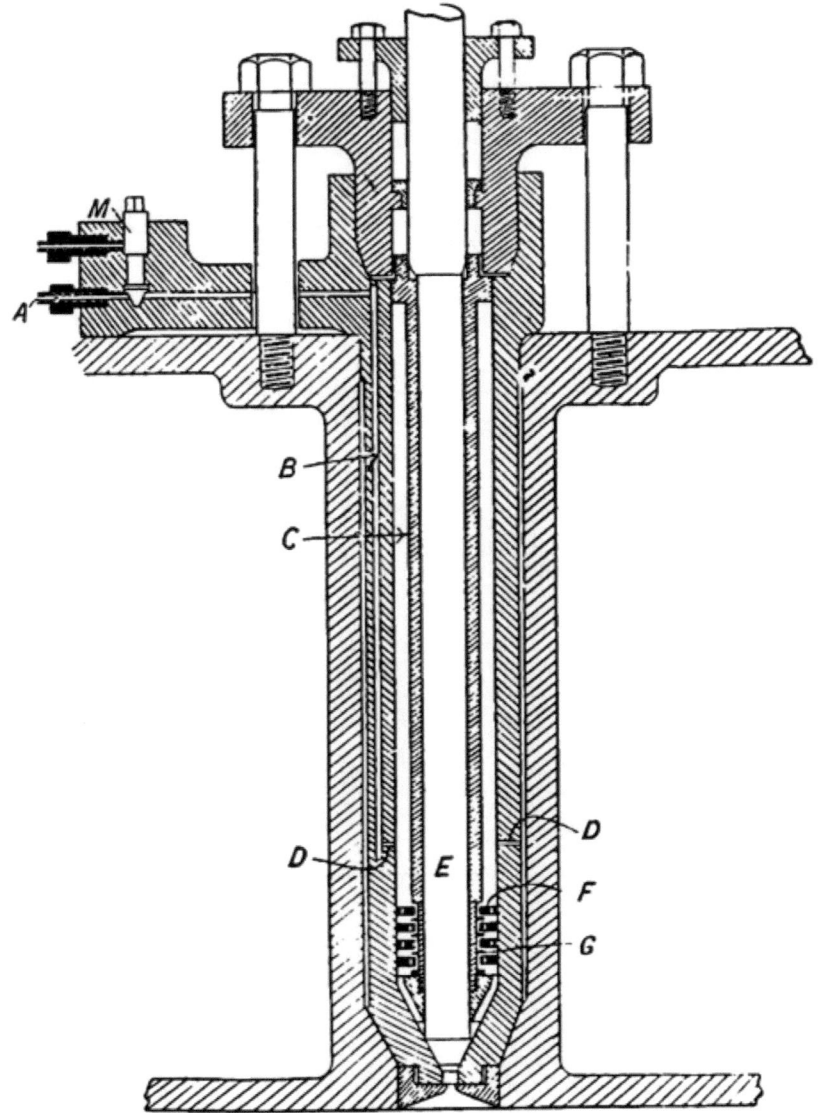

Fig. 26.—Fuel Inlet Valve and Pulveriser.

fuel inlet. The space C is thus always subjected to the high pressure of the injection air, and immediately the needle valve lifts, the fuel is forced through the pulveriser by the air in the form of a very fine spray, and combustion at once takes place. A small cock *M* is provided having connexion with the inlet pipe and serves the purpose of a test

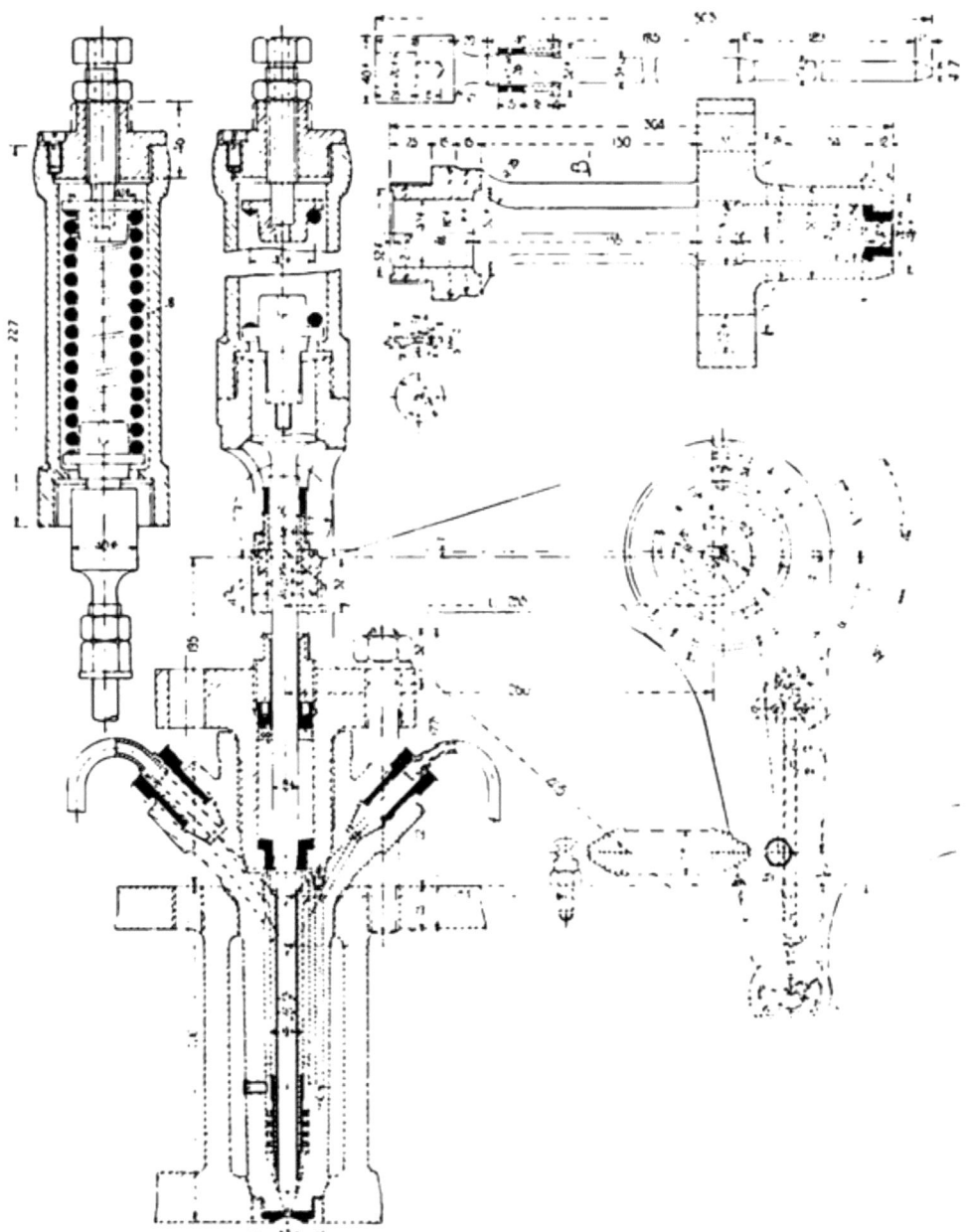

Fig. 27. — Details of Fuel Inlet Valve of Deutz Engine.

cock and an overflow. The oil may be pumped up by hand before starting the engine, and by opening the cock *M* it can be seen at once if the flow of oil is uninterrupted. The

74 DIESEL ENGINES FOR LAND AND MARINE WORK

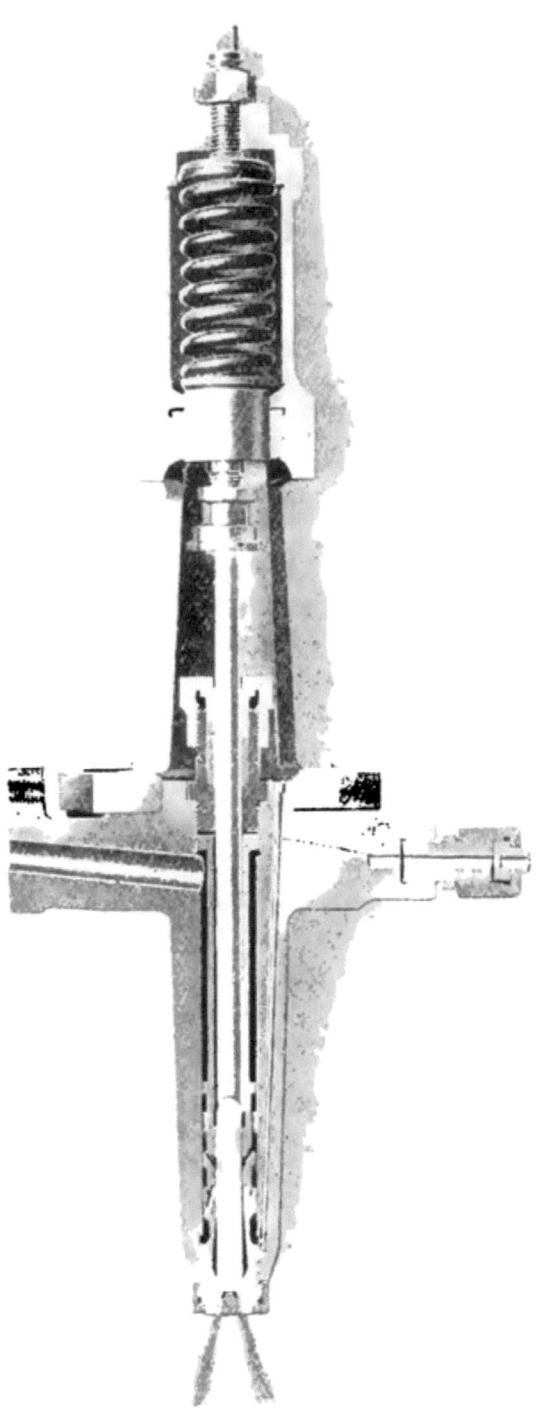

Fig. 28.—Fuel Inlet Valve of Aktiebolaget Diesels Motorer Type.

method of fixing the valve guides in position, and the arrangement of the stuffing box, will be understood from the figure. By removing the valve lever, the valve can readily be taken out and examined, and as is seen in *Fig.* 21, the compression of the spring can be altered as required. It might be expected that different pulverisers would be required when different fuels are employed, but as a matter of fact it is found that the same pulveriser will operate quite satisfactorily for grades of fuel of very different viscosity, and they are constructed to be suitable for the thickest oils,

Fig. 29.— Mouthpiece or Bottom Part of Pulveriser.

and no trouble is then experienced with less viscous fuels.

The type of pulveriser and fuel inlet valve adopted by the A. B. Diesels Motorer of Stockholm differs somewhat from the usual construction, and is said to give very efficient results. This is illustrated in *Figs.* 28 *and* 29, and the method of operation is shown in *Fig.* 30. The oil enters the annular space at the bottom from the fuel pumps in the usual way, position 1 (*Fig.* 30) showing the amount left immediately after the injection into the cylinder. In position 2 the oil has been pumped up from the fuel pump, while in position 3 the fuel valve has lifted, and the oil is being injected into the cylinder. The blast of air forces the oil through specially shaped passages, which are usually curved, or of irregular form, and the mixture is given a spiral motion, the heavier particles of oil being thrown against the sides of the passage so that complete pulverisation takes place. The pulveriser is entirely cleared of oil with each injection, which in reversible marine engines is a considerable advantage, and it

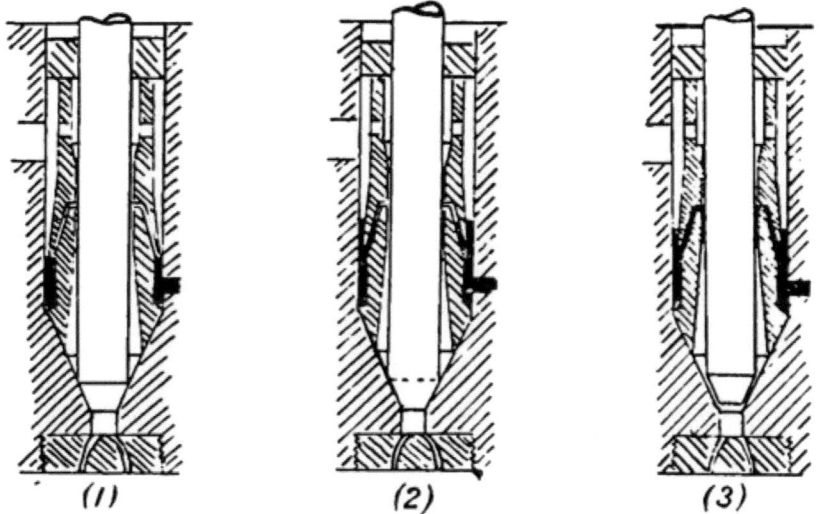

Fig. 30.—Diagram showing Action of Pulveriser.

necessitates that the exact amount of oil delivered by the pump is injected into the working cylinder.

The general arrangement with the ordinary type of Diesel engine of the fuel valve, exhaust and air suction valves in the cylinder cover is shown in *Fig.* 31, while *Fig.* 33 gives a section through the exhaust valve and cam shaft showing the operation of the valve. It will be noticed from the illustrations that the removal of the valves can be carried out very expeditiously in all cases. In some engines, notably those constructed in America, the fuel inlet valve is arranged horizontally on the side of the cylinder head, which projects well over the cylinder, and the exhaust valve and admission valve are also fitted into this projection, the exhaust valve in the top and the admission valve underneath.

Regulation of the Engine.— The same method of governing the speed of Diesel engines of the land type with varying

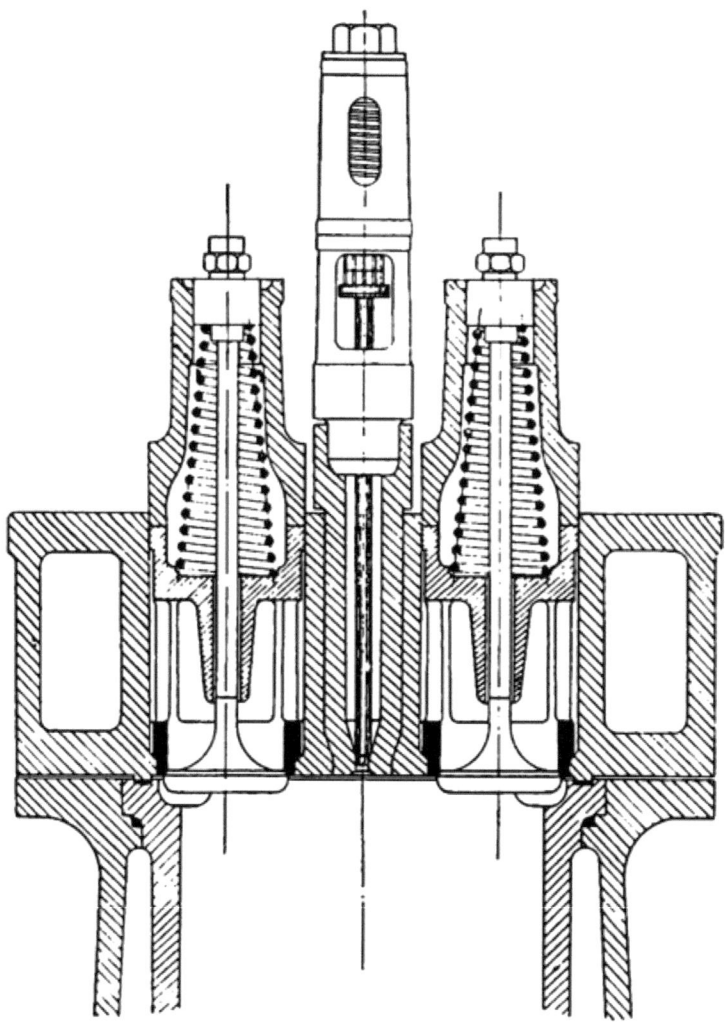

Fig. 31.—Air Inlet and Exhaust Valves (in section).

load is adopted by practically all the chief manufacturers, there being naturally some differences in constructional detail. The control is effected entirely by regulation of the amount of oil admitted into the cylinder through the fuel inlet valve, and hence no alteration in the stroke or the dura-

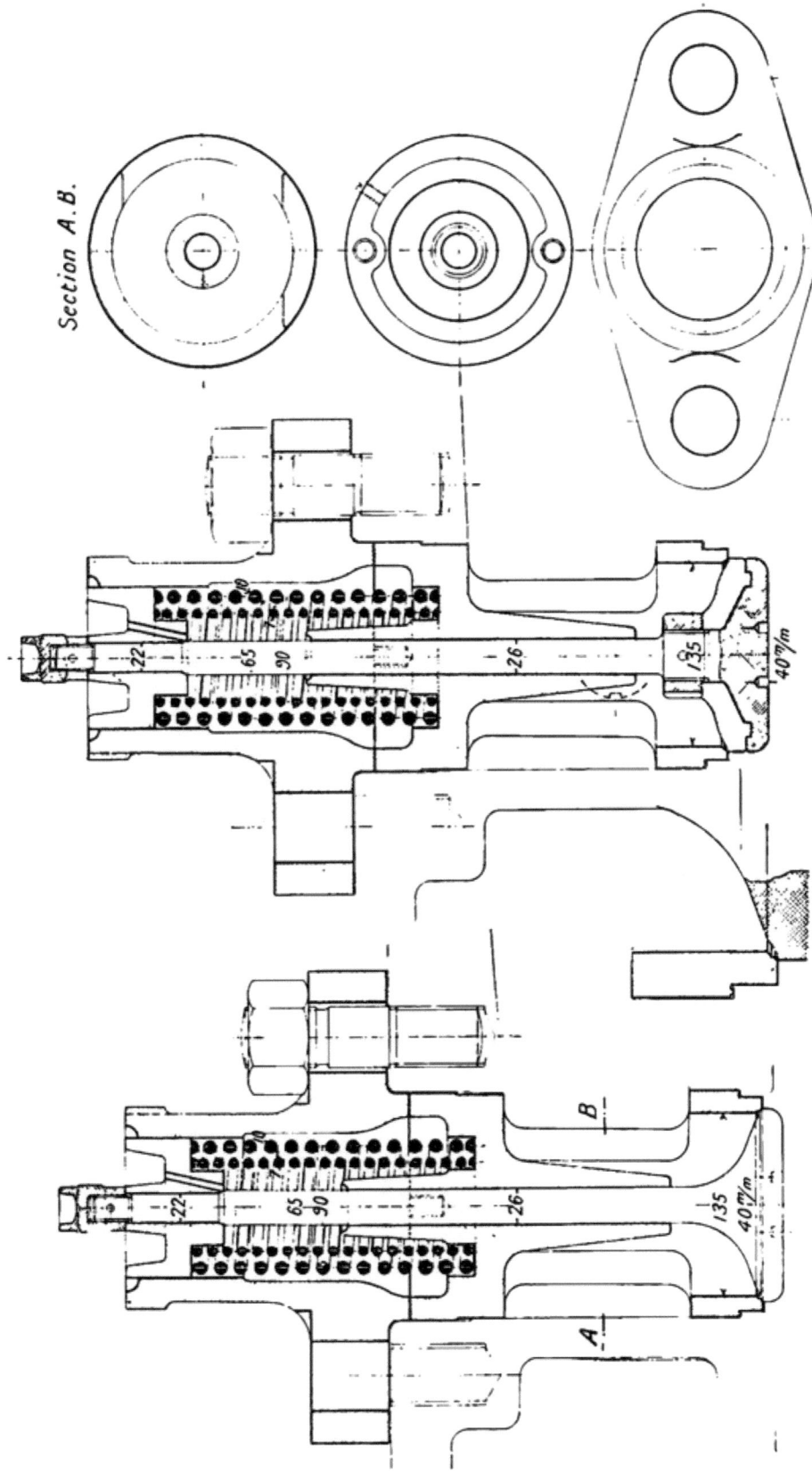

FIG. 32.—Details of Suction and Exhaust Valves of Carels' Four-Cycle Land Motor.

tion of the opening of this valve is required, which would be the necessary means of governing if the fuel supply were not varied; the latter method is obviously more convenient from many points of view, particularly inasmuch as the

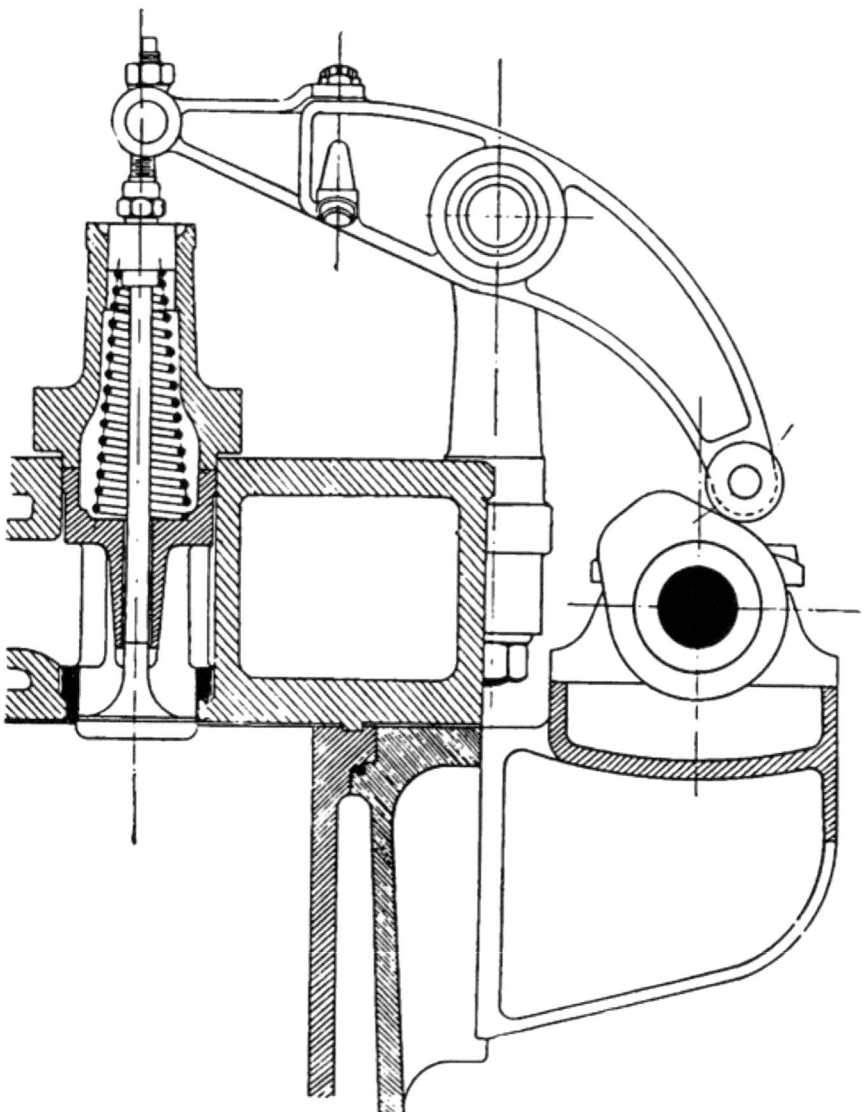

Fig. 33.— Exhaust Valve (section).

valves may be set and never touched once the engine has been put to work. A small fuel pump is provided which pumps the oil to the fuel valve through a connecting delivery pipe. The oil is drawn into the pump cylinder on the up

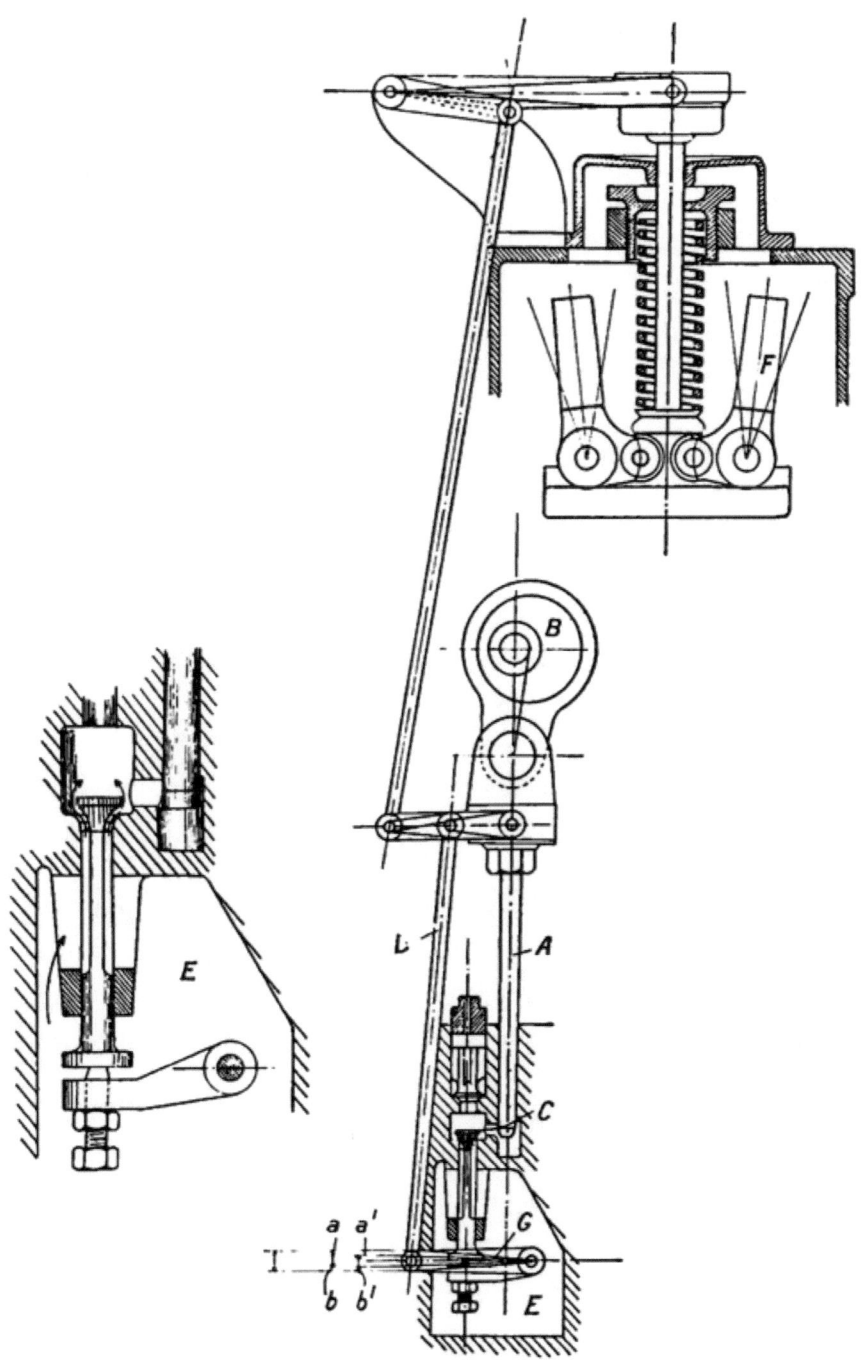

Fig. 34.—Arrangement of Governor and Fuel Valve of Mirrlees, Bickerton & Day Type.

stroke of the pump plunger, through a small valve, and on the down stroke this valve remains open for a short period, after which all the oil is pumped into the cylinder. The period during which the suction valve remains open in the down stroke of the plunger of the pump, is controlled by the governor, so that if the speed rises too high the suction valve is held open for a longer time, and less oil is delivered to the engine cylinder, whereas if the speed is low the suction valve closes almost immediately at the beginning of the down stroke of the plunger, and most of the oil drawn in during the suction stroke is pumped into the cylinder during the delivery stroke. In multi-cylinder engines some makers prefer to have a separate fuel pump for each cylinder, whilst others employ only one pump for supplying all the cylinders, though this is perhaps on the whole not quite so satisfactory, but is, of course, simpler.

Fig. 34 shows diagrammatically the arrangement adopted by Messrs. Mirrlees, Bickerton & Day, Ltd., for governing the supply of fuel to the cylinder. A is the plunger of the fuel pump, which obtains its motion from an eccentric on the cam shaft or vertical intermediate shaft of the engine. On the up stroke of the plunger, oil is drawn in through the suction valve C, which is opened by the motion of the rod D, attached to a link in the crosshead of the fuel pump. The action of the suction valve is more clearly seen in the illustration to the left of *Fig.* 34, the oil being drawn from the chamber E in the direction of the arrows. During the down stroke of the plunger the oil which has been drawn in is forced up through the fuel delivery pipe to the fuel inlet valve so long as the suction valve remains closed, but while this latter is open no oil can be delivered, all being forced back into the chamber E. The action of the pump can now be explained in relation to the governor F, which is of the Hartnell type. When the speed of the engine rises, the governor balls or weights spring outwards to the positions as indicated by the centre lines, and by means of the link mechanism shown, the rod D, actuating the suction valve, is raised till the centre of the pin on which the lever G turns, reaches the level a, and the stroke of D is then $a\,b$ instead of $a'b'$ when the governor balls are "in." The suction valve is thus held open for a longer period of the down stroke of the plunger A, and less oil is therefore delivered to the engine cylinder, and the speed drops, when the governor balls move inwards and the lever G returns to its normal stroke.

In the type of fuel pump employed by the Maschinenfabrik Augsburg-Nürnberg, the pump plunger is actuated

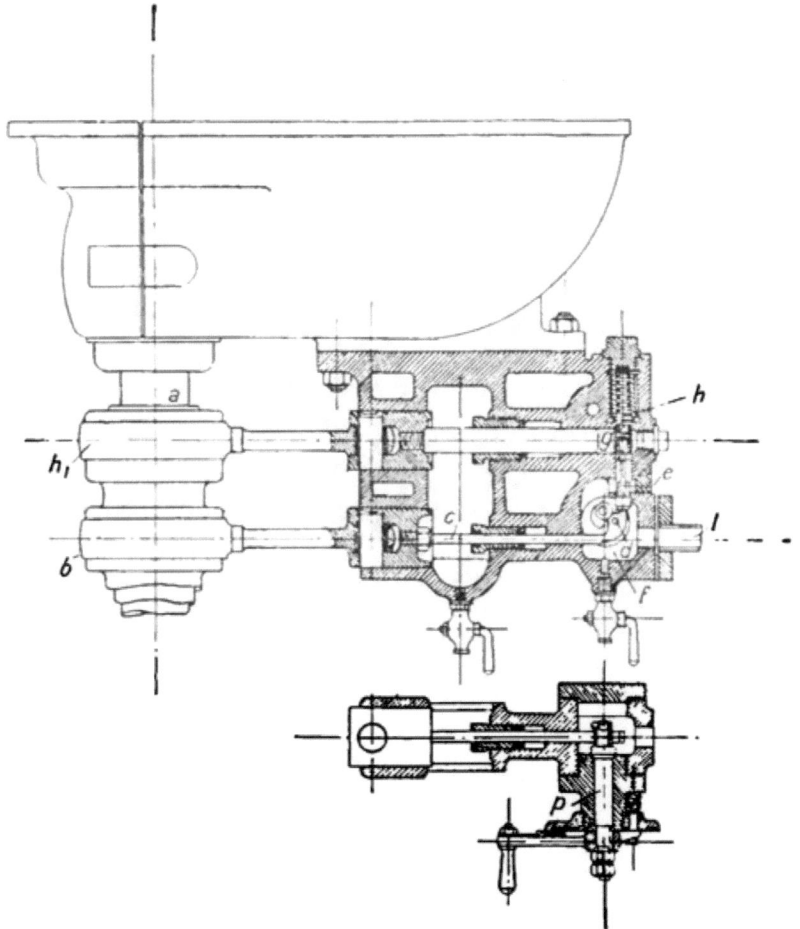

Fig. 35.—Fuel Pump (Willans & Robinson Type).

by an eccentric on the motion shaft as before, and the suction valve is opened by a finger piece attached to a vertical lever, which derives its up and down motion from another lever attached to the pump rod and pivoted eccentrically to the spindle driving it. The spindle has a small crank fixed to it, to which is attached a vertical rod, actuated by the governor mechanism, and when the speed of the engine falls so that the governor balls move inwards, this rod is depressed, and the small crank turned through an angle, thus causing the rod operating the suction valve to hold it open for a shorter period than the normal. More oil is then delivered to the fuel inlet valve and the engine speed rises.

The level of the oil in the oil chamber is maintained constant by a float, and a pipe from this chamber is connected directly with the supply from the fuel filters. The fuel pump casing is usually fixed to the cylinder about the middle, and the plunger has a vertical motion from the eccentric on the horizontal cam shaft, while the governor lever is attached to the governor sleeve on the vertical governor shaft of the engine.

Fig. 35 shows the design of fuel pump and governor adopted by Messrs. Willans & Robinson, Ltd., for their standard engines, this being of the horizontal type. The vertical governor shaft a, which also drives the cam shaft through bevel gearing, is driven off the crank shaft of the engine by worm gearing, and has fixed to it the governor casing. The governor consists of weights attached to a central sleeve, the effect being that any outward or inward motion of the weights due to variation of speed of the engine, causes an angular motion to the loose sleeve, carrying the eccentric b which operates the small rod c. The movement of this rod gives an angular motion to the crank piece d, which in turn raises the oil suction valve e off its seat and admits oil from the chamber f into the plunger cylinder g, the plunger itself being driven from an eccentric h_1 on the governor shaft. The fuel inlet from the filters is seen at l. On the outward stroke of the plunger if the suction valve is closed, the oil is delivered past the valve h, which is opened against a spring, and the oil flows through the outlet pipe to the fuel inlet valve of the engine cylinder. The action of the governor, except for its mechanism, is similar to that already described. If the engine speed rises and the weights move outwards the sleeve carrying the suction valve rod eccentric is turned through a small angle. The stroke of the rod is then such as to keep the suction valve open during a greater portion of the outward stroke of the plunger, so that less oil is delivered through the outlet pipe, and hence the speed of the engine falls, and the eccentric regains its normal position. The spindle p may be turned by hand, and this allows for three positions of the spindle. In the normal or running position both the suction and delivery valves are quite free : in the second position the suction valve is closed, the fuel supply thus being cut off from the engine, which must then stop, while in the third position the suction valve still remains closed and the delivery valve is opened, so that any oil in the pipes between the pump and the fuel inlet valve runs back into the plunger cylinder. By this means the oil is prevented from being pumped in excess in the fuel chamber at starting, and if a separate fuel pump be provided with each cylinder, one cylinder may be readily cut out of operation. The pressure on the governor springs may be altered by means of the arrangement shown, and hence the running speed of the engine can be varied within reasonable limits.

It is not usual, in the smaller sizes of Diesel engines, to employ any other form of governing other than by altering the amount of fuel injected into the cylinders, according to the load, by means of one of the methods previously described. In the larger engines, it is desirable for the amount of injection air to be independently controlled, and also the period of admission for the fuel and air, which is not generally arranged for in stationary motors.

This is, however, accomplished in one of the designs of Messrs. Sulzer, as illustrated in *Fig.* 36, and it is useful for engines which have to be run in parallel with steam engines, gas engines or water turbines, and where there are sudden and substantial variations of load. Referring to the illustration, the governor r influences, according to its position, all the factors on which the desired output depends, i.e., the quantity of fuel injected, the volume and pressure of the air necessary for injecting and pulverizing the fuel, as well as the period of admission of the fuel valve,

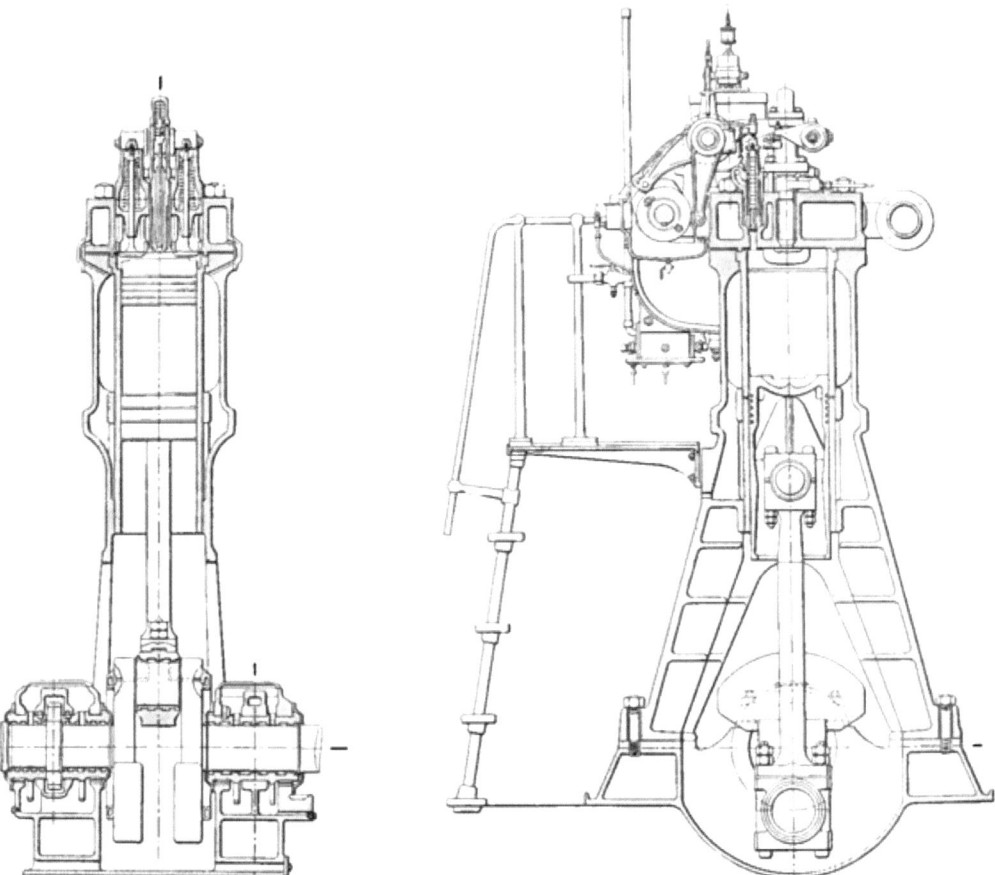

Fig. 37.—Front Elevation of Mirrlees Diesel Engine.

Fig. 38.—Side Elevation of Mirrlees Diesel Engine.

in accordance with the quantities of air and fuel. The quantity of the fuel and the volume and pressure of injection air are adjusted from the governor by direct action, since the power for carrying out the movements is small. The quantity of injection air depends on the position of the piston valve d, which is inserted in the suction pipe of the first stage of the injection air pump. The control of the admission period of the fuel valve, however, requires some effort, owing to the resistance of the valves, which cannot conveniently be exercised by the governor direct. For this purpose, a small servo-motor S is employed, which is operated by the variation of pressure effected in any stage of the injection air pump. Referring to the illustration, the pressure existing between the first stage l and the second stage k of the injection pump is used for the purpose, the servo-motor being connected by the pipe u.

Types of Four-Cycle Engine.—*Figs.* 37 *and* 38 show vertical front and side sectional elevations of the standard Diesel engine constructed by Messrs. Mirrlees, Bickerton & Day, Ltd. The usual long piston is employed, and the head is slightly dished and ribbed to add to its strength. The weight, however, of the piston is not excessive, as its thickness is considerably reduced below the gudgeon pin, which is hollow and is fixed to the piston by two studs screwed in from below. The big and small end bearings are lined with white metal, and the former is of the box type, and has distance pieces in it so that the length of the connecting rod

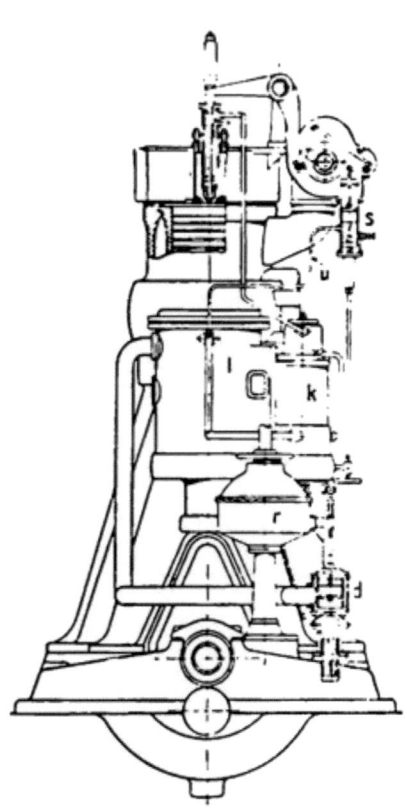

Fig. 36.— Arrangement for controlling Fuel and Injection Air.

86   DIESEL ENGINES FOR LAND AND MARINE WORK

may be varied, which besides taking up wear allows for variation of the clearance between the piston and cylinder,

Fig. 39.—Deutz Three-Cylinder Vertical Engine.

and hence is useful for varying the compression of the engine. A two stage vertical air compressor is used, driven direct off

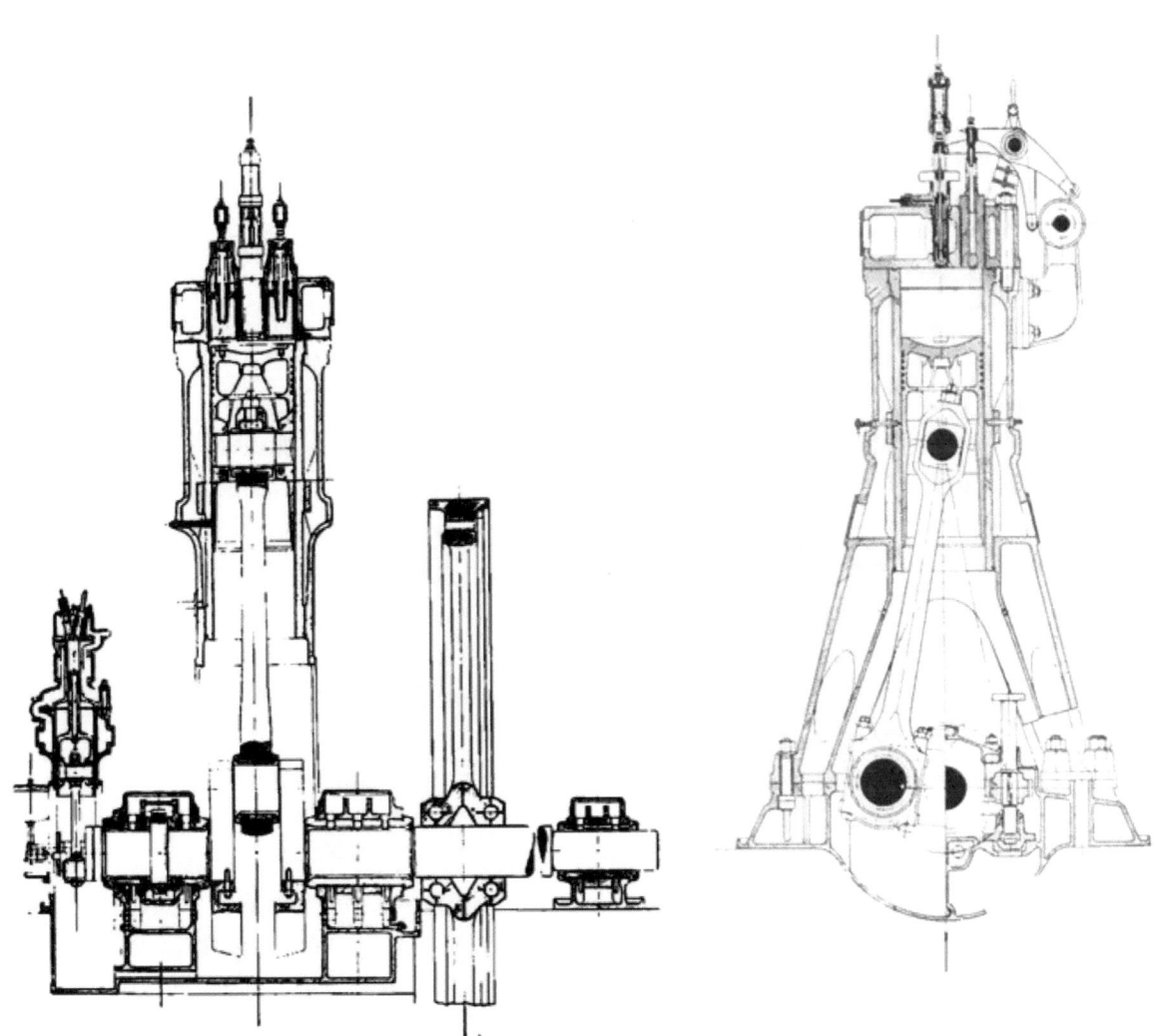

the end of the crank shaft, the high pressure cylinder being directly above the low pressure, and an intercooler for reducing the temperature of the air between the two stages is provided.

A longitudinal and transverse section of the standard slow speed type of single cylinder engine, manufactured by the Nederlandsche Fabrick of Amsterdam, are given in *Figs.* 40 *and* 41 respectively. The general arrangement does not differ in any marked degree from the designs already described, except that the air pump for the injection and starting air is mounted on the end of the engine on an extension of the bed-plate, and is driven by an overhung crank, the compressor being of the two stage type with intercooling between the stages. The piston is of the trunk type, made of high-grade cast iron, as is also the cylinder liner, a special mixture as usual being employed for the cylinder head, in view of the high pressures to which it is subjected. A small lubricating pump and oil reservoir are provided in the compressor end of the engine, seen in *Fig.* 40 and also in *Fig.* 42, which is a plan of the engine, and shows the general arrangement of the valves in the cylinder head, and the cam shaft, cams and valve levers operating them. The cam shaft is driven in the usual way at half the speed of the engine, by means of spur gearing through a vertical spindle, itself driven off the crank shaft by a worm drive. *Fig.* 43 shows the air inlet valve with its cam and valve lever, and also the by-pass through which the cooling water passes from the cylinder jacket to the cylinder head. In *Fig.* 44 a detailed section is given of the governor and fuel pump in their relation to the overhead cam-shaft. The principle of the action of the fuel pump and the regulation of the speed of the engine is the same as that generally adopted with Diesel engines— namely, the control of the period of opening of the suction valve of the fuel pump. If owing to increase of speed the governor balls spring outwards, the governor sleeve, to which the pivoted arms carrying the balls are attached, is lowered, carrying with it the horizontal lever seen in the illustrations. This lever is attached at one

88 DIESEL ENGINES FOR LAND AND MARINE WORK

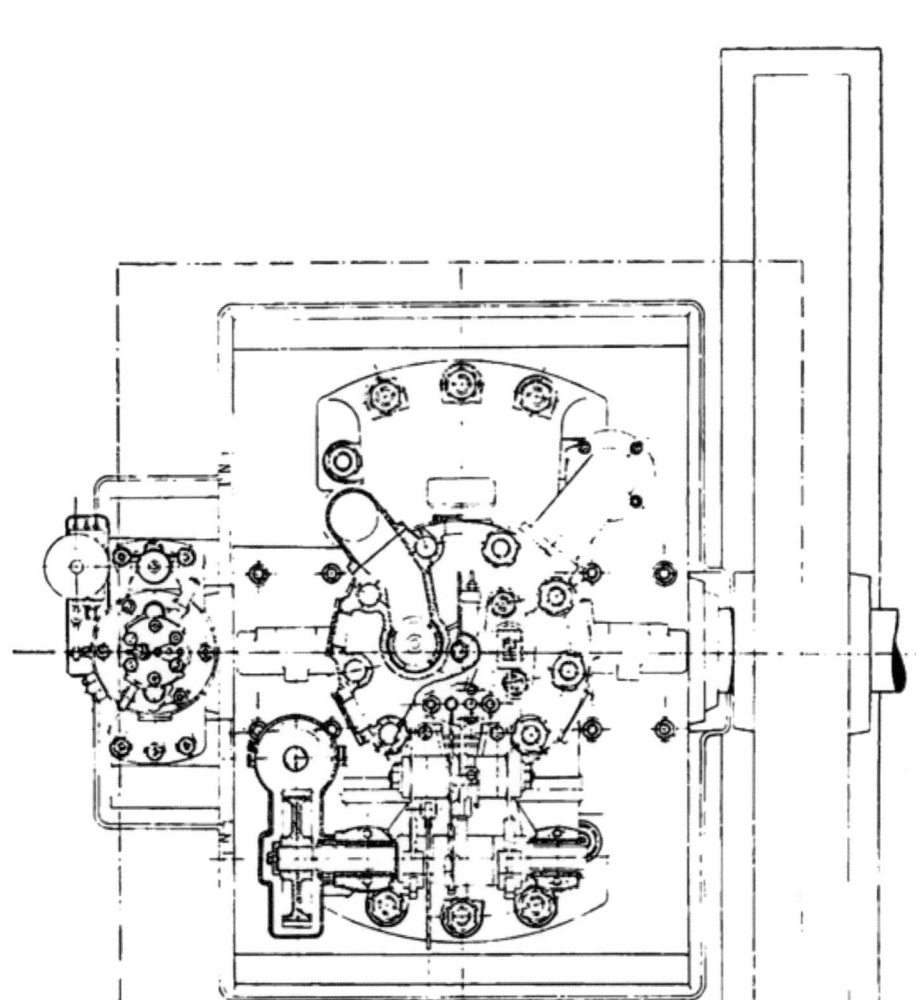

Fig. 42.—Plan of 80 H.P. Engine.

end to a piston moving in a dash pot to prevent too rapid motion, and at the other end is connected by a short link to the rod controlling the opening of the suction inlet valve of the fuel pump. The plunger of the pump is driven by an eccentric off the vertical governor shaft, and this eccentric by means of a link attached to the eccentric rod, also gives a regular oscillating motion to the suction valve operating rod previously mentioned and so opens and closes the valve. When the horizontal lever on the governor sleeve is depressed by the opening out of the governor balls due to the increased engine speed, the link connecting it to the suction valve operating rod becomes straightened out, and it is moved to the right so that the period of opening of the suction valve during the forward stroke of the plunger is increased; less oil is consequently delivered through the outlet valve of the pump to the fuel inlet valve of the engine, and the speed of the motor falls until it reaches the normal, when the governor resumes its ordinary running position.

In this engine a safety valve is fitted in the cylinder head to

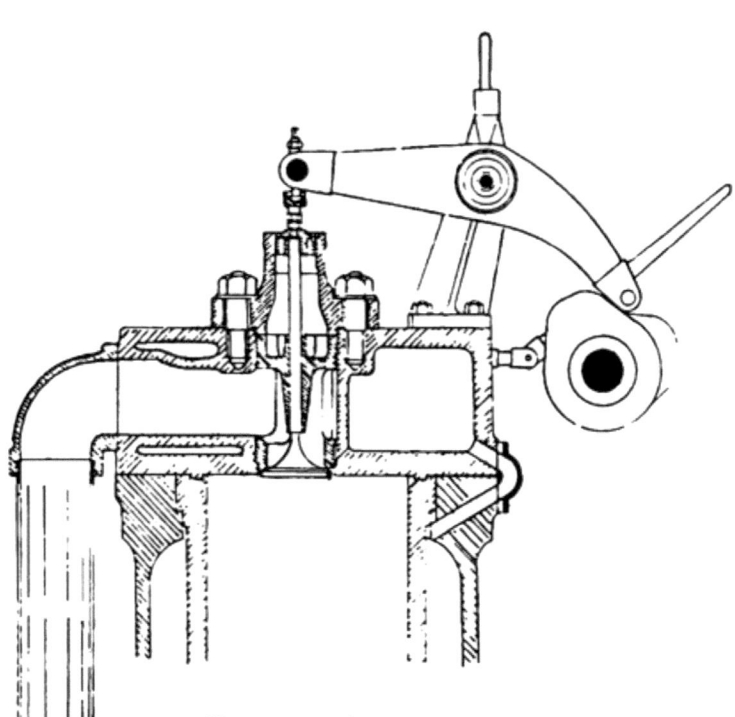

Fig. 43.—Arrangement of Air Inlet.

prevent danger arising through any excess of pressure in the cylinder, and this valve may be operated by hand, by the lever seen in *Fig.* 43 and in the plan view *Fig.* 42. All the valves are provided with inserted cages for ease in removing, while the jackets have large mud holes for purposes of cleaning, which is frequently of great advantage where engines are cooled with dirty water, as is occasionally necessary.

With the ordinary type of Diesel engine, the piston has to be taken out from the top, which necessitates removing

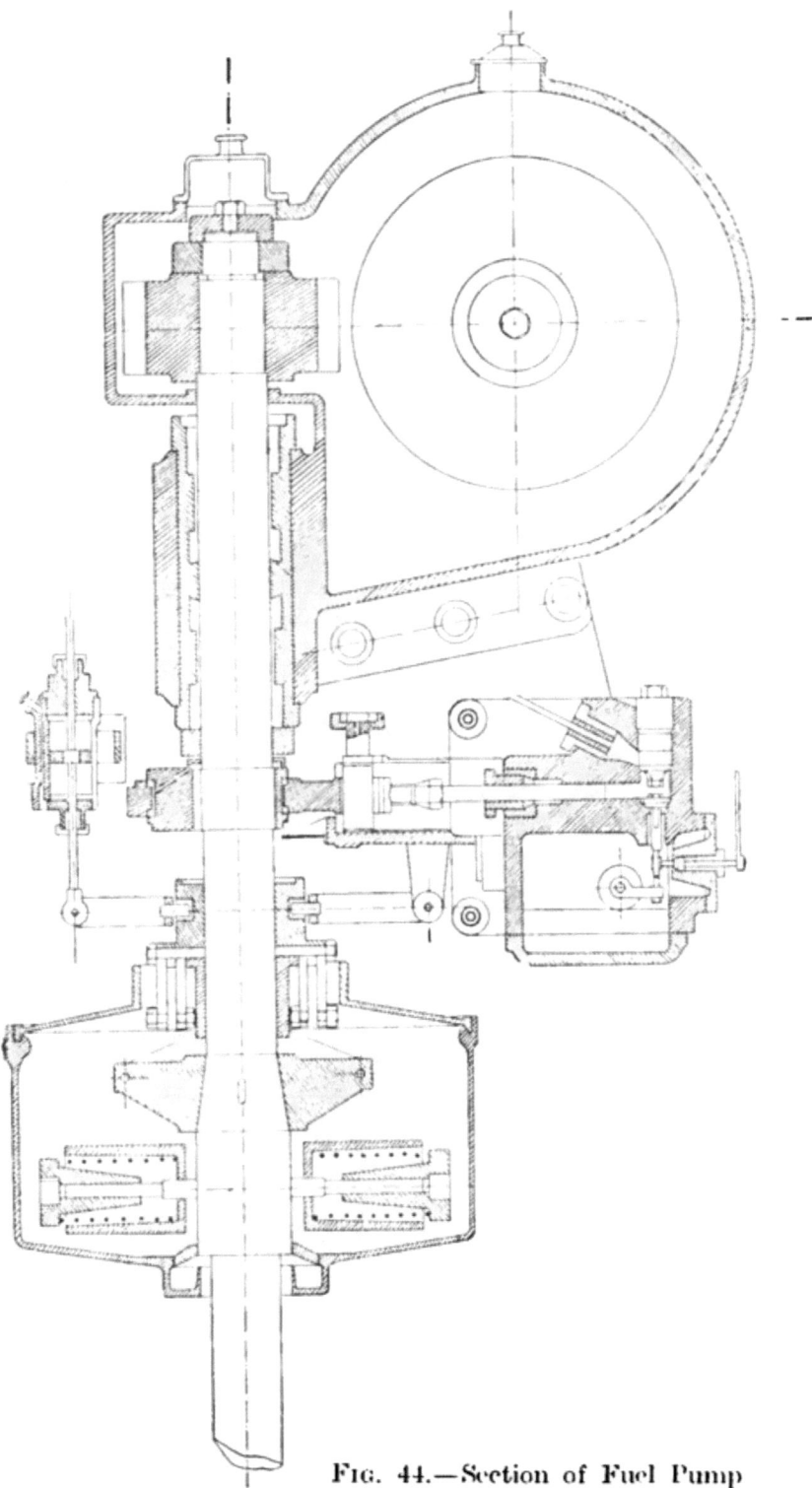

Fig. 44.—Section of Fuel Pump

all the valve levers and lifting the cylinder top. In the more recent construction of the engines of the Nederlandsche

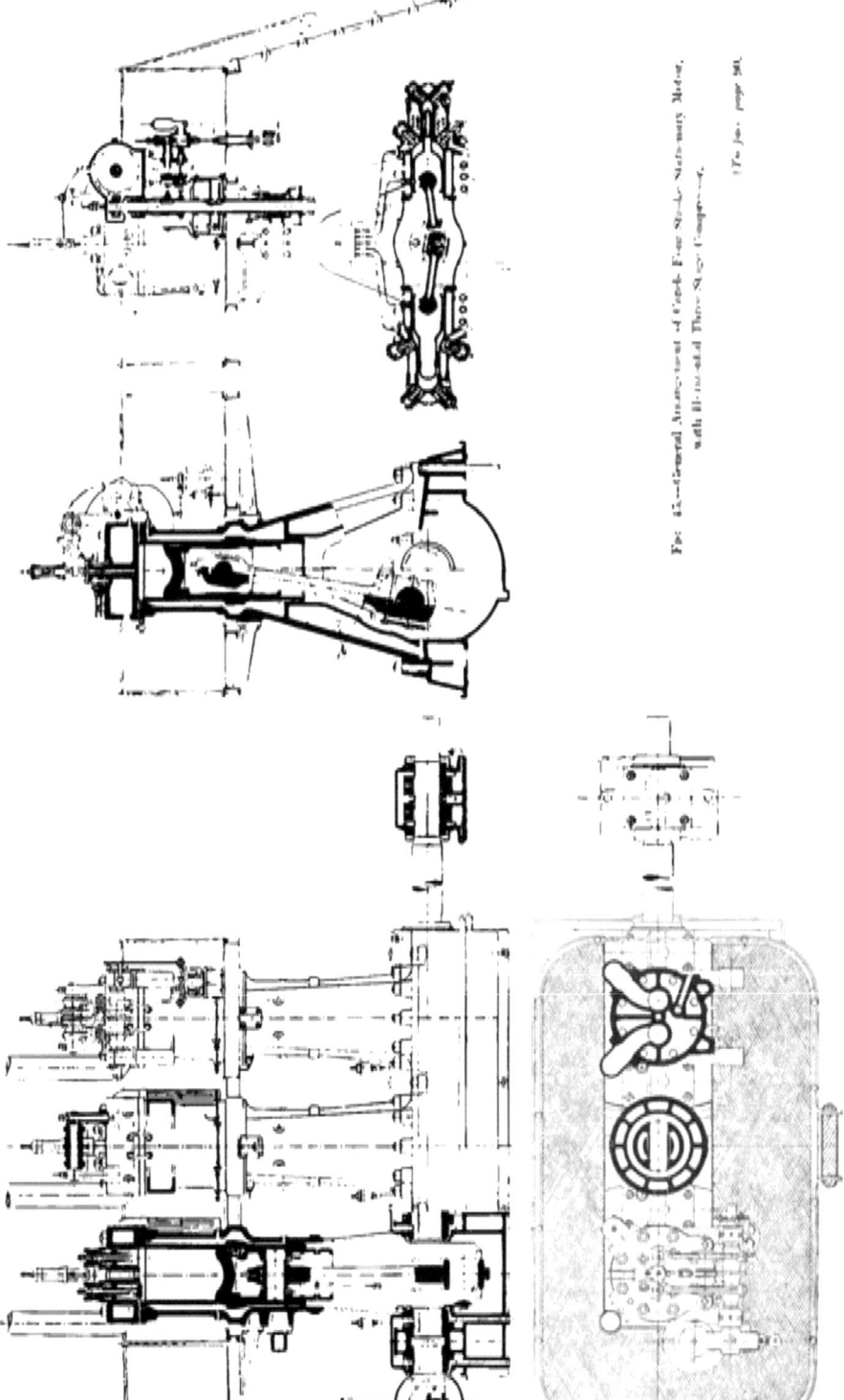

Fig. 44.—General Arrangement of 6-cycle Four Stroke Stationary Motor, with Bi-sected Three-Step Compressor.

[To face page 98.]

CONSTRUCTION OF THE DIESEL ENGINE

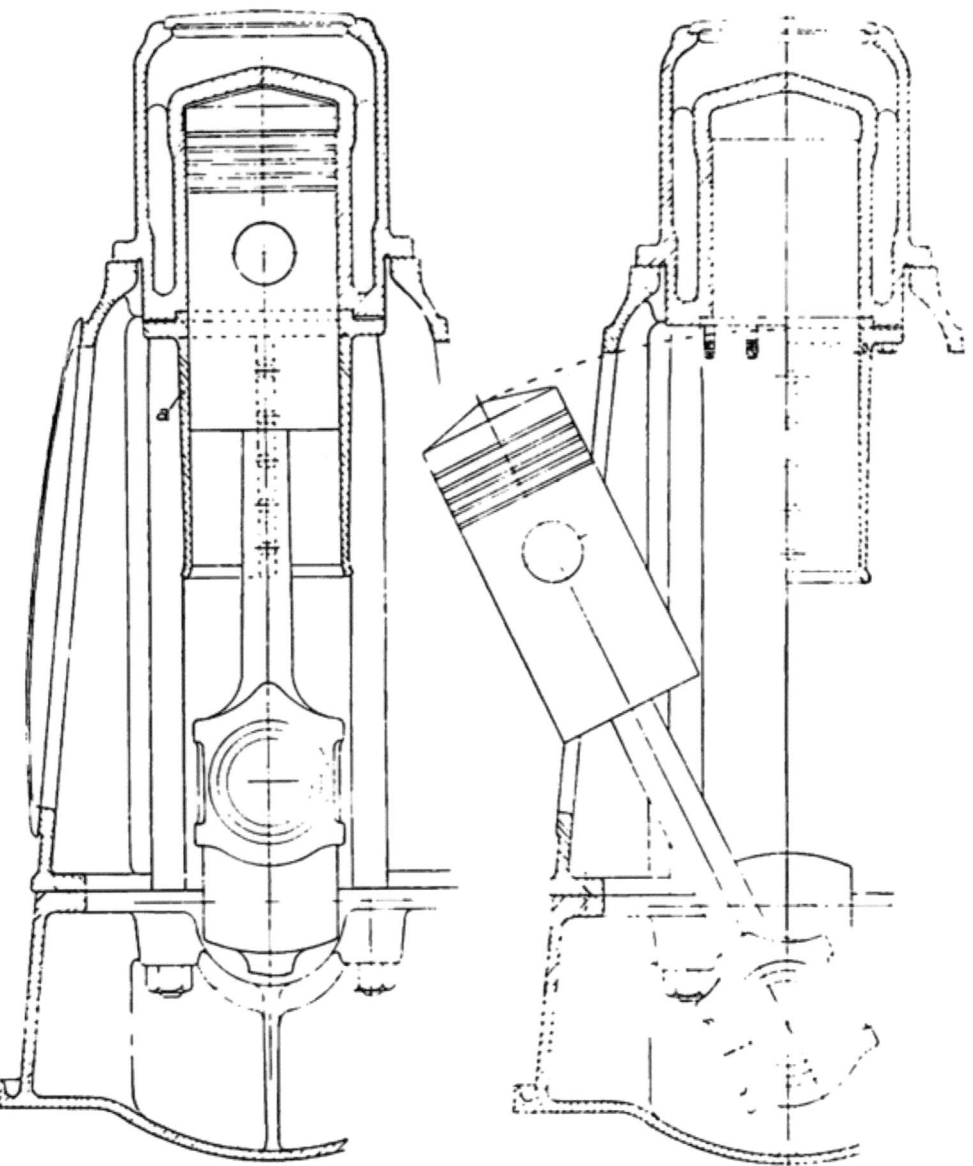

Fig. 46.—Method of removing Piston in Nederlandsche Fabriek Engine.

Fabriek, an arrangement has been adopted by means of which the piston can be taken out from the bottom without interfering with the valves at all. This is illustrated in *Fig. 46* and is applicable to the type of motor in which the trunk piston is adopted. The bottom half of the cylinder consists of an extended liner bolted on the upper half, and when the piston is lowered and the portion *a* of the liner removed, it can be swung forward in the manner shown. *Fig. 47* shows

92 DIESEL ENGINES FOR LAND AND MARINE WORK

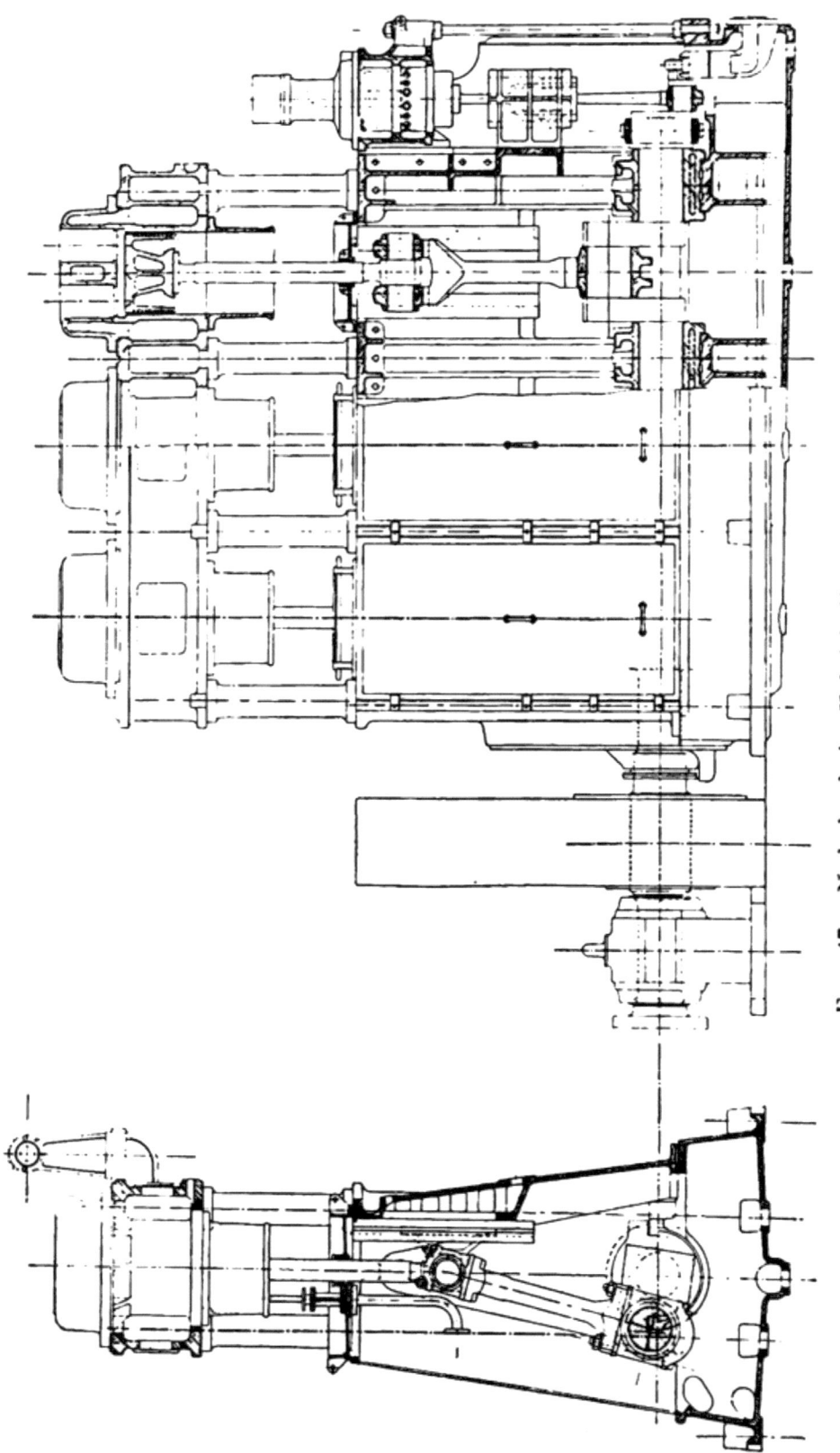

Fig. 47.—Nederlandsche Fabrieck Engine.

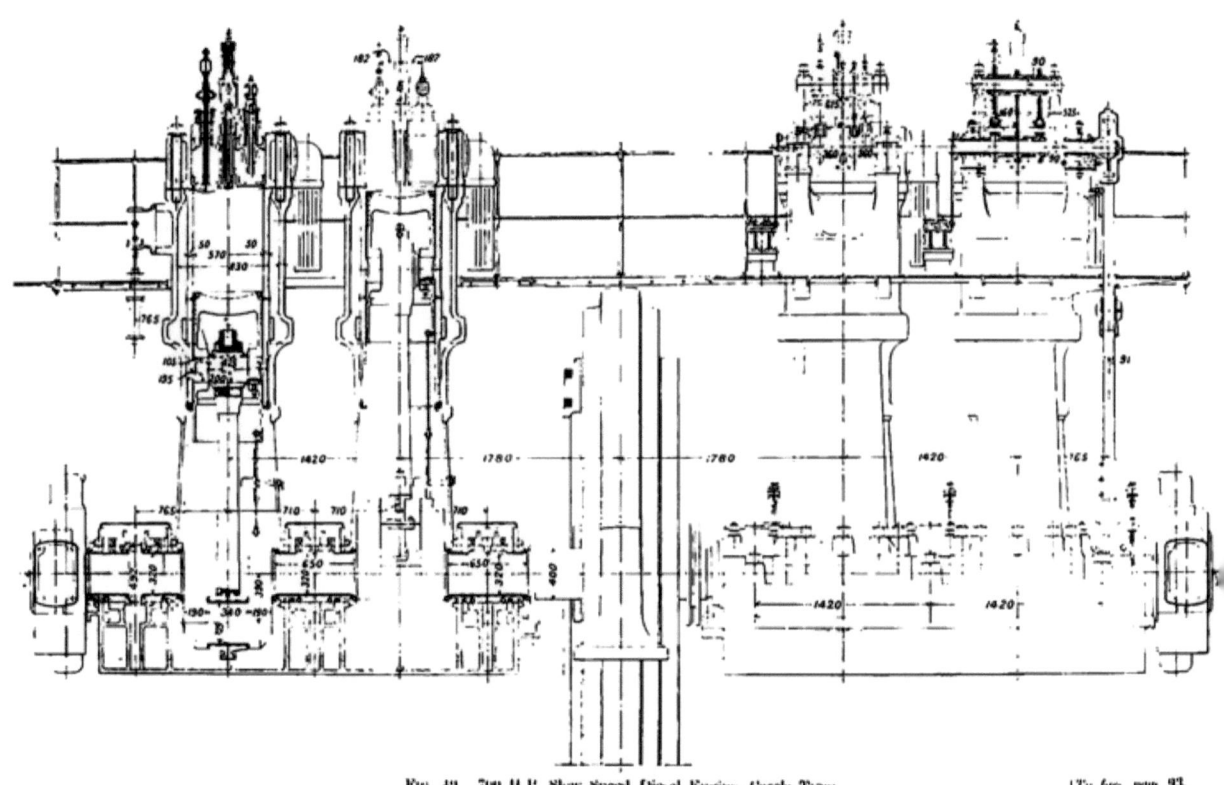

Fig. 49.—700 H.P. Slow Speed Diesel Engine, Carels Type.

the latest design of three cylinder stationary engine adopted by this firm, in which a connecting rod and crosshead are employed, the same arrangement of removable extended liner being used. In this engine there is a two-stage vertical compressor mounted on the end of the bed-plate in line with the working cylinders, and driven direct off the crank shaft.

In *Fig.* 49 a dimensioned drawing is given of a four-cylinder four-cycle slow speed engine of Messrs. Carels' construction. The motor illustrated is one of 700 B.H.P., running at 150 r.p.m., arranged for dynamo driving, with a generator in the centre and two cylinders on each side. Two air compressors of the Reavell type are provided—one at each end. The diameter of the cylinders is 570 mm. and the stroke 780 mm., and even for this relatively high power the trunk piston is retained.

High Speed Engines.— As has been explained in Chapter II, there are certain advantages attaching to engines of the high speed type, and for special purposes they will probably be widely adopted in the future. The high speed machine is, of course, eminently adapted for direct driving of dynamos, and though it is hardly probable that it will come into general use for this purpose, its employment for many purposes is likely to be very extensive, since saving in weight and space is often of great importance, while the reduced cost of installation is always a point to be considered. As a matter of fact, high speed Diesel engines direct coupled to dynamos have for some time past been installed on battleships. Some details of the size, power and speed of high speed engines are given in Chapter IV, but in many cases these speeds are exceeded, and engines of 300 H.P. running at 400 revolutions per minute are common, while the type constructed by Messrs. Mirrlees, Bickerton & Day, Ltd., for British battleships consisting of a 120 H.P. engine coupled to the dynamo runs at 400 revolutions per minute. With larger powers the same speed of rotation is employed, being about double that of the ordinary land type.

The high speed types of engine built by this firm is made in the following sizes, all at 400 revolutions per minute :—

3 Cylinder engine.		45 B.H.P.
3	,,	90
4	,,	120
6	,,	180
6	,,	240
6	,,	300

The chief feature of the construction of the high speed engine lies in the fact that practically all the moving parts are totally enclosed, and very efficient splash lubrication is effected, and a smooth operation of the machine is obtained. The bed-plate is usually of the flat-bottomed box pattern and has bolted on to it the crank casing, which is totally enclosed and provided with as many inspection covers on each side as there are cranks. All the outer cylinder walls are bolted on to the crank casing, instead of being cast in one with the framing as is the case with low speed engines.

In *Figs.* 51 to 56 inclusive are given drawings of high speed engines built by various firms, from which it will be seen that there is not any very marked difference between the several types. In each case they are totally enclosed and provided throughout with forced lubrication, which is of course an essential feature in motors running at relatively high speed. It should, however, be pointed out an engine rotating at say 350 revolutions per minute does not necessarily imply that the piston speed is correspondingly in excess of that in the slow running type, for the difference is in fact not usually very great. It follows from this that a larger number of cylinders is usually adopted for the same power in a high speed engine, whilst the ratio of stroke to bore is much diminished, being usually in the neighbourhood of unity or slightly over. This does not give the maximum efficiency, but in cases where it is desirable to employ the high speed engine its advantages are usually

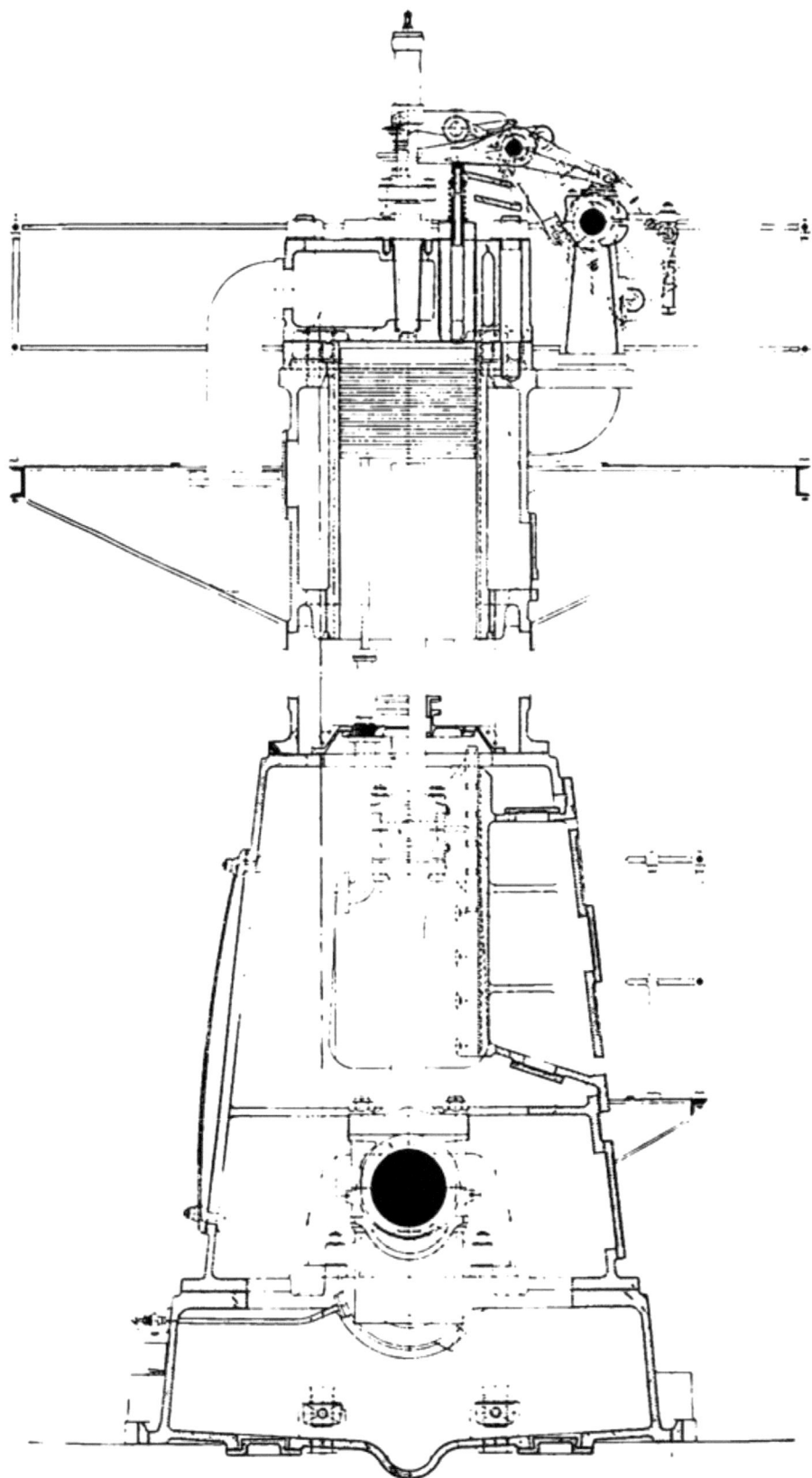

Fig. 48.—End Section of 600 B.H.P. Four-Cycle Engine.

such as to counterbalance any slight increase in fuel consumption.

The large high speed type of engine manufactured by the Nederlandsche Fabriek offers some important points of difference from that of the usual construction. *Fig. 50* shows a front section of a 600 B.H.P. engine built by this firm, to run at 215 revolutions per minute. It is of the usual four-stroke type, with four cylinders, the two inner having the cranks set at 180° with the outer pair. A single air pump is employed, mounted on the end of the bed-plate, being of the vertical two stage type, and driven direct off the crank shaft. A trunk piston is not used, but there is a crosshead and a short connecting rod, and though the length of the piston is diminished, since it no longer has to be of the usual bearing surface, the engine is necessarily somewhat higher than the ordinary trunk piston type. The crosshead has two bearing surfaces, and the guides are bolted on to the engine framing, and a forked connecting rod end is employed, as shown in the illustration. All the main bearings are water-cooled, as is also the piston, which is an unusual feature in a four-cycle engine, cooling with this type of engine usually being adopted for cylinders of more than 100 H.P. The arrangement for the piston cooling is clearly indicated in *Fig. 50*. The piston rod itself is hollow and is secured to the piston, which is also hollow, through a flange wrought on the piston rod, fixing studs being arranged in the piston body. Two small pipes are connected to the water spaces in the piston, and these slide up and down within two long tubes which are connected with the supply and delivery pipes for the cooling water. Both these tubes are of course provided with stuffing boxes, and although the water is under slight pressure no leakage takes place. The water outlet for the cooling water for the crank shaft bearings delivers into a cup in front of the engine at the bottom, and as there is a separate cup for each bearing there is no occasion for trouble with any of the bearings, since the temperature can be readily ascertained and varied as required. Forced lubrication is

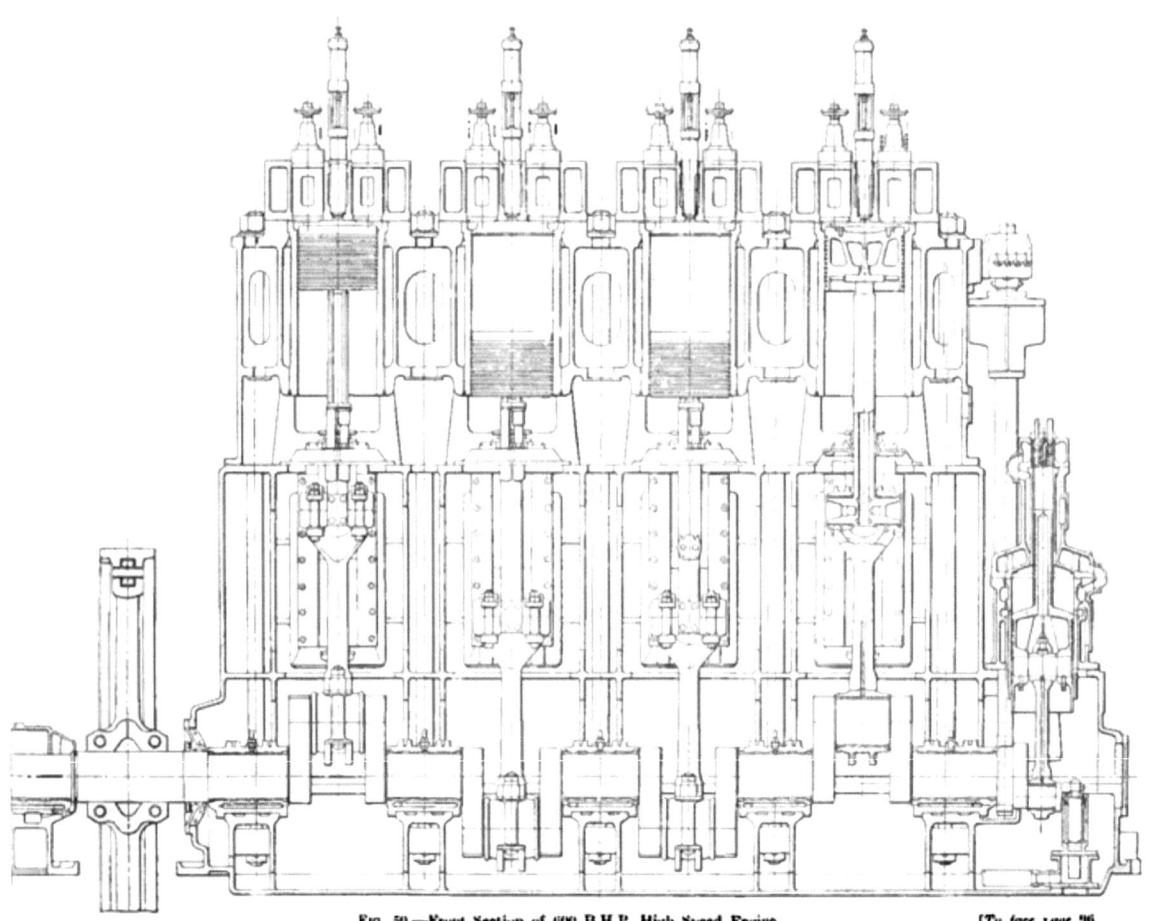

FIG. 50.—Front Section of 600 B.H.P. High Speed Engine. [To face page 96.

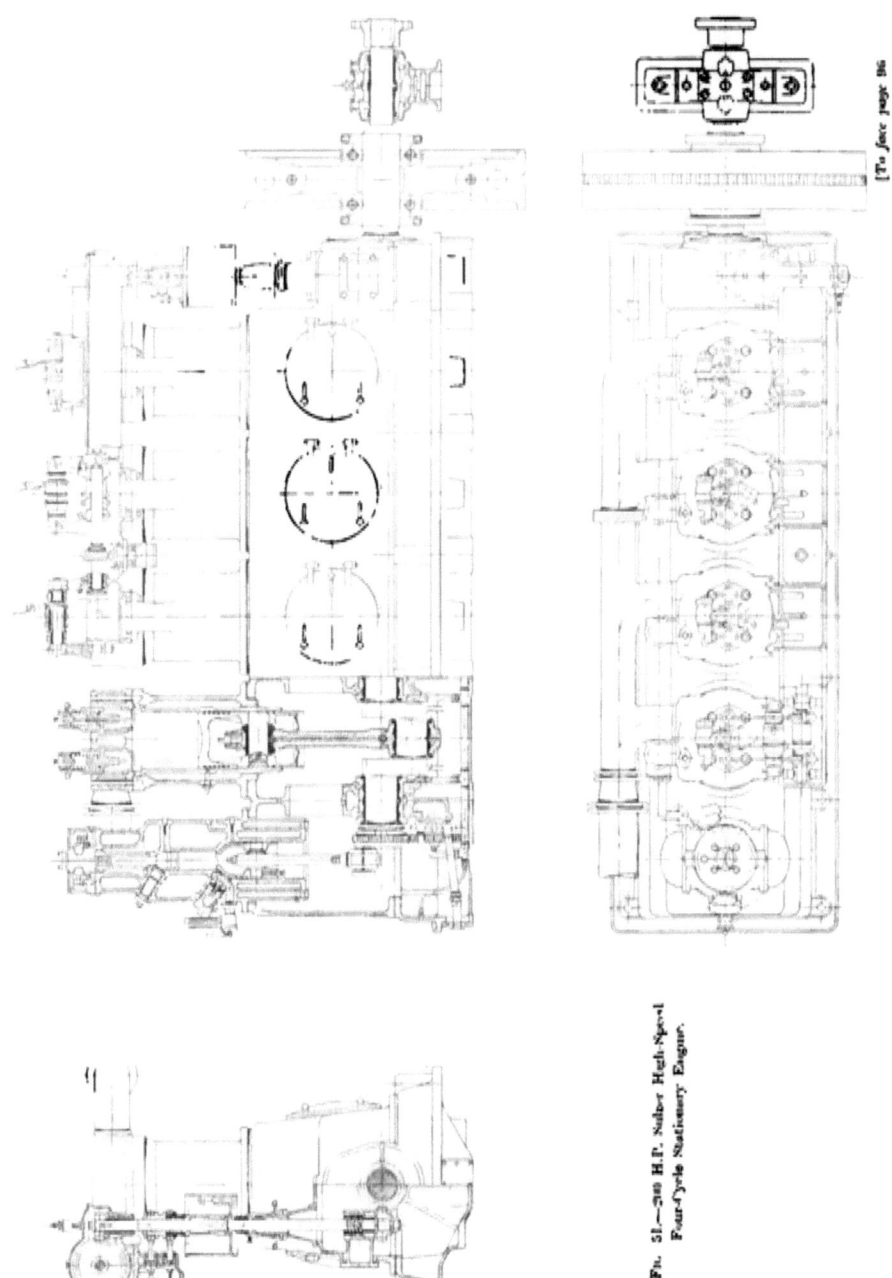

Fig. 51.—240 H.P. Sulzer High-Speed Four-Cycle Stationary Engine.

[To face page 86.

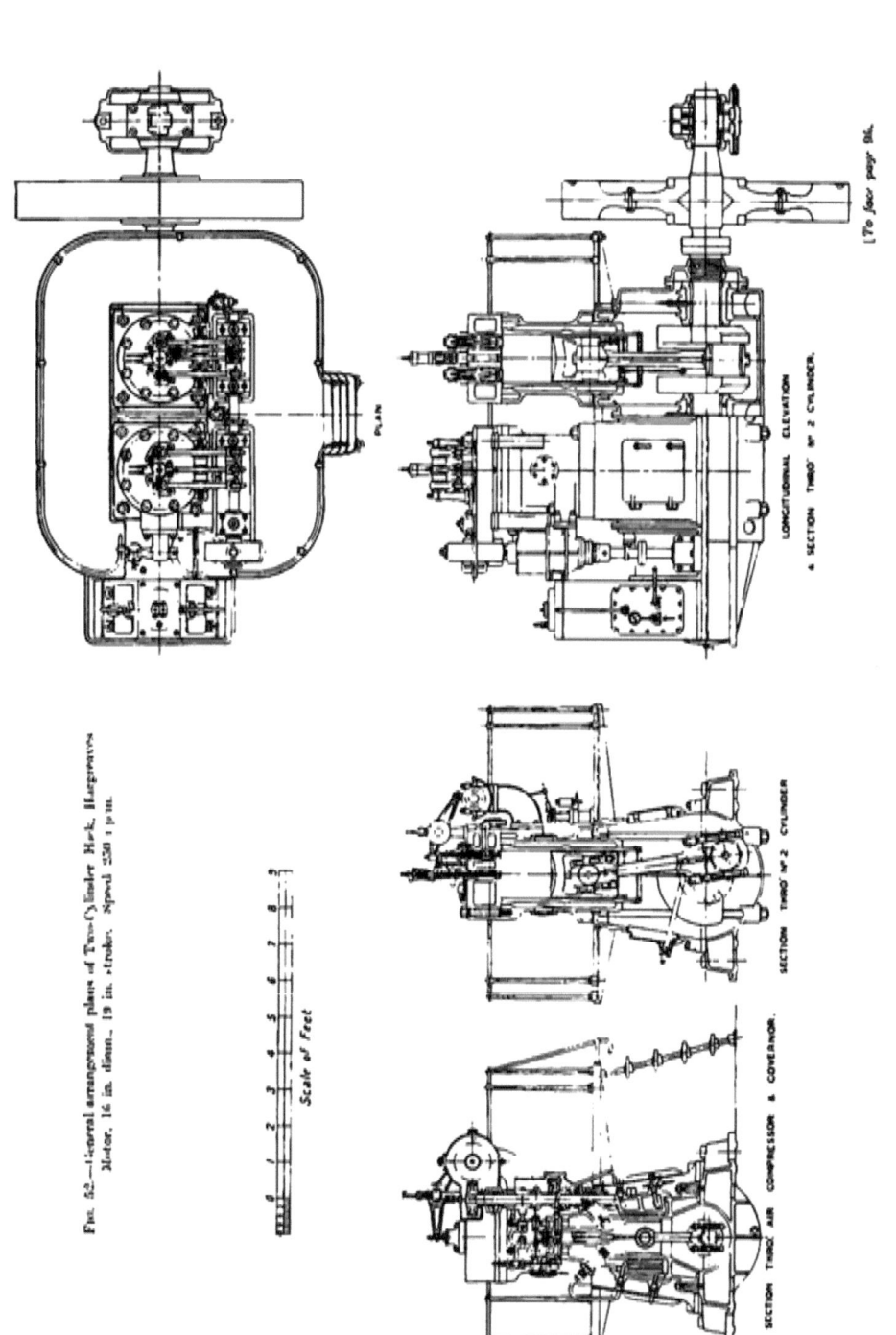

Fig. 52.—General arrangement plans of Two-Cylinder Hurd, Hargreaves Motor, 16 in. diam., 19 in. stroke. Speed 250 r.p.m.

[To face page 96.

adopted for all the main shaft bearings, as well as for the connecting rod bearings, and these latter are very accessible —more so, of course, than in engines in which a trunk piston is employed.

The engine is constructed with a box frame, the cylinders which are cast together being supported directly on the frame, while further strength is given by means of long vertical bolts which attach the cylinders rigidly to the bed-plate. With a four-cylinder engine there are ten of these bolts —five at the front and five at the back. The crank chamber is entirely enclosed, a hinged door being provided in front of each connecting rod, and the piston rods pass through the stuffing boxes in the box frame, so that the connecting rod small end bearing is in a cool atmosphere away from the heat of the cylinder.

One of the main variations in construction from the ordinary engine is the use of eccentrics for operating the valve levers instead of the cams, which are so commonly employed, the object being to diminish noise and increase the smoothness of running. The engine is constructed with a horizontal cam shaft driven in the usual way off the main crank shaft, but in place of cams, it has fixed on to it eccentrics. The eccentric rods are attached at the ends to horizontal levers pivoted eccentrically on a horizontal spindle, and these levers thus receive an up and down motion. At the opposite end to that at which they are connected to the eccentric rods, the valve rods operating the valves rest upon them, and hence the motion of the eccentric is transmitted to the valves, which open in the usual way. For the starting valve, which of course is only in operation for a few seconds, the ordinary cam and valve lever are employed. The governor is arranged on the vertical shaft driving the horizontal eccentric spindle, and regulates the speed of the engine by controlling the duration of the opening of the suction valve of the fuel pump during the delivery stroke, and thus regulating the amount of oil admitted to the cylinder. The construction of the pump and governor is similar to that described previously, and four fuel pumps are used with a single pump chamber.

Engines of this type are hardly high speed in the ordinary sense, inasmuch as they run only about 30 per cent. faster than the usual stationary engine. They are standardized from about 200 B.H.P. up to 1,000 B.H.P. with speeds varying between 275 and 200 revolutions per minute. Under 300 H.P. the engines are made frequently of the three-cylinder type, but above that power, and sometimes below, four cylinders are always used. The weight per B.H.P. is remarkably constant for all sizes, being somewhere in the neighbourhood of 280 lb. per B.H.P. including all accessories. The approximate overall dimensions of the engine illustrated are 6 ft. 8 in. by 27 ft. 6 in. floor space and 12 ft. 6 in. in height.

The high speed engine has of late been coming more into general use, particularly for driving electrical generators, centrifugal pumps, etc., and has led the chief manufacturers to take up its construction for powers up to about 1,000 H.P. As now developed, its cost may roughly be taken as 20 per cent. less than the corresponding slow speed engine, its weight some 25 per cent. less, whilst as regards the question of upkeep, the difference, so far as present experience goes, does not seem to be considerable.

In *Figs.* 51, 55 *and* 56 the high speed four-cycle Sulzer engine is shown, the type being similar for all sizes from 150 to 1,000 B.H.P. The four-cylinder construction is usually adopted, with a vertical three-stage injection air pump mounted on the end of the engine, and driven off the crank shaft direct from an overhung crank. The engine, which runs at 300 r.p.m. for 200 H.P., and 220 r.p.m. for 800 H.P., is totally enclosed, and forced lubrication is adopted throughout. The oil is forced through the different bearings by a pump driven off the engine, and flows back into the crank chamber, being drawn from the bottom by means of another pump through a filter and an oil cooler. The consumption of lubricating oil is slightly higher than with a low speed engine, being in the neighbourhood of ·015 to ·02 lb. per B.H.P.

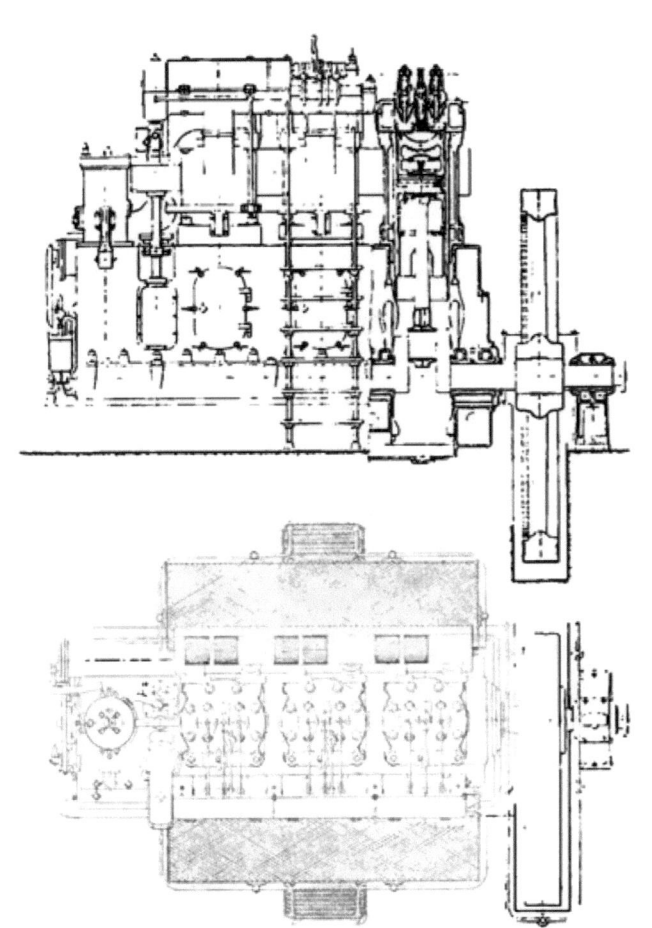
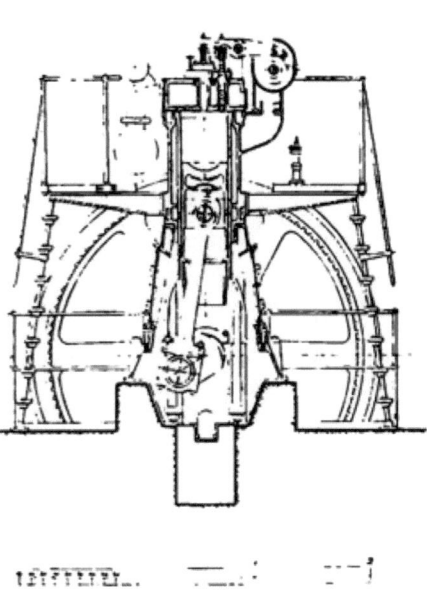

FIG. 53.—Burmeister & Wain High-Speed Diesel Engine.

[*To face page 96.*

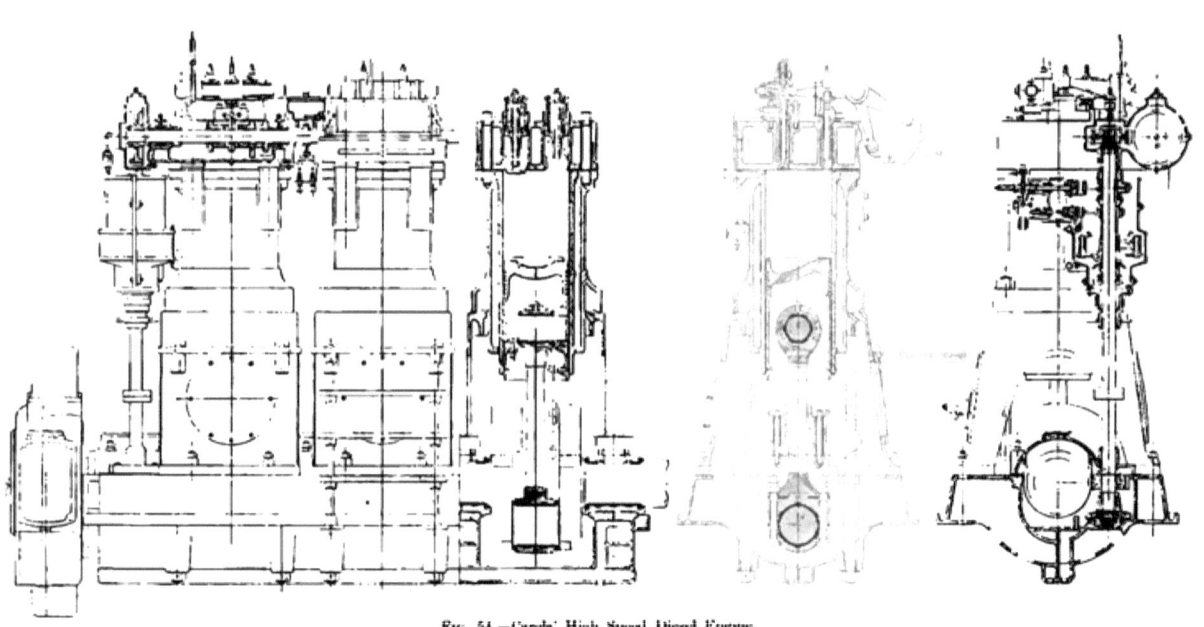

Fig. 54.—Carels' High Speed Diesel Engine.

CONSTRUCTION OF THE DIESEL ENGINE

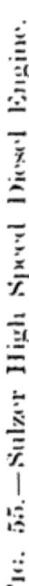

Fig. 55.—Sulzer High Speed Diesel Engine.

hour as against ·01 to ·015 lb. The fuel oil consumption is also slightly in excess of the slow speed motor to the extent of some 5 or 10 per cent.

The cams which control the fuel valve levers have steel inserted pieces, and the other cams are arranged to have large bearing surfaces. All the cams run in an oil bath, and the noise is reduced to a minimum, being in fact less than with a slow speed engine.

The design of the high speed motor of Messrs. Carels' construction is somewhat similar, and is shown in section in *Fig.* 54.

Horizontal Engine.—At present the construction of the horizontal Diesel engine has only been taken up to a comparatively small extent, and this type is something of an innovation, inasmuch as the Diesel motor has from its earliest development been considered essentially a vertical engine. There is this to be said in favour of the horizontal type, that in the past ten years such a wide experience has been obtained with large horizontal gas engines, and hence advantage can be taken of the knowledge gained with these machines, and such knowledge can be well utilized in the design and construction of Diesel engines of the same type, since both types are so-called internal combustion engines and present many similarities. Though naturally more floor space is required for a horizontal engine, much less height is needed for the installation and dismantling, and it has to be remembered that the pistons on Diesel engines of the ordinary type have to be drawn out from the top, and this point must not be lost sight of in estimating the necessary height of the engine room. Among the advantages offered by the horizontal engine are a reduction of the pressure on the foundations due to the greater surface, and practically a complete absence of vibration, though it must be said that the vibration with vertical engines is very small. With a horizontal engine the piston can be more readily removed than in the vertical type, since in a single acting engine by disconnecting the connecting rod, the piston can be drawn out of the cylinder from the crank end,

CONSTRUCTION OF THE DIESEL ENGINE

leaving all the valve gear untouched. The connecting rod is made of greater length relative to the crank than in vertical engines (six times instead of five) in order to reduce the pressure on the bottom of the cylinder due to the obliquity of the connecting rod, and as of course is the case in all horizontal engines, the pressure on the top side of the cylinder is partially counteracted by the weight of the crank and connecting rod, which is not the case in vertical motors.

The horizontal Diesel engine is made as a four or two cycle machine, and for large sizes the double acting principle is employed. For engines under 200 B.H.P. a single cylinder is usually employed, and for larger sizes, two cylinders are fixed side by side, with the flywheel at one end of the crank shaft. For still greater powers two sets of two cylinder engines are employed with the flywheel between, while for the largest machines and with double acting engines a twin tandem arrangement is adopted, and for dynamo driving the generator is between the two pairs of engines. The four-cycle type may be constructed in one, two, or four cylinders, but the two-cycle machine is only built in two or four cylinders.

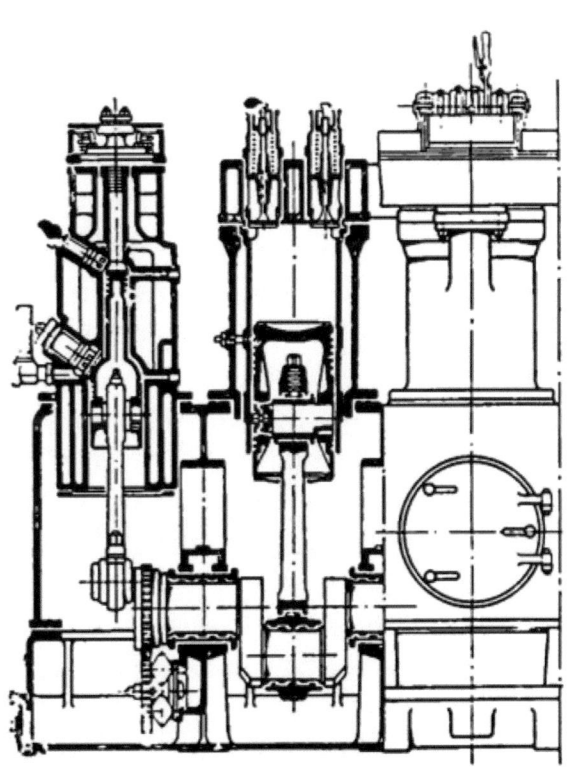

FIG. 56.—Section through High Speed Engine and Air Pump.

The bed-plate of the horizontal engine is of the box pattern, the outer cylinder covers being cast in one with it, though generally bolted on in the case of the two-cycle engines. The cylinder liners are removable, and are constructed of close-grained cast iron. As with vertical engines, the cylinder head which contains some of the valves is bolted on to the main cylinder casting, but the arrangement of valves differs considerably from that adopted with the vertical type. In the four-cycle type the fuel inlet valve is horizontal and in the centre of the cylinder head, while the starting valve for admitting compressed air is arranged close to the fuel valve. The exhaust valve is at the bottom of the cylinder head, while the air suction inlet valve is at the top, both of these valves being, of course, vertical. In the two-cycle engine ports are adopted, uncovered by the movement of the piston, and both the exhaust and air admission valves of the four-cycle machine are utilized as scavenge valves, through which the air from the scavenge pump enters the cylinder. The cam shaft for operating the valves is horizontal, driven off the crank shaft by worm gearing, as in the established practice for gas engines. The exhaust and air admission valves (or the scavenge valves in a two-cycle engine) are actuated by a single eccentric on the cam shaft, this being possible since they are symmetrically placed, and in two-cylinder engines but one cam shaft and eccentric are usually employed, the valves of the second cylinder remote from the cam shaft being operated by a connecting lever between the two valves. For the working of the fuel inlet valves a small subsidiary shaft is driven off the cam shaft through gearing, at right angles to it, and an eccentric on this small shaft actuates the inlet valve direct. In the double acting machines, in order that the piston rod may not be subjected to the highest temperature, the fuel is injected on each side of the piston in pockets which are formed between the cylinder cover, the valve and the piston. This method is exceedingly helpful in avoiding trouble with the stuffing boxes.

The governor is mounted on a vertical governor shaft driven off the crank shaft, and its action is the same as that already described for vertical engines in which regulation

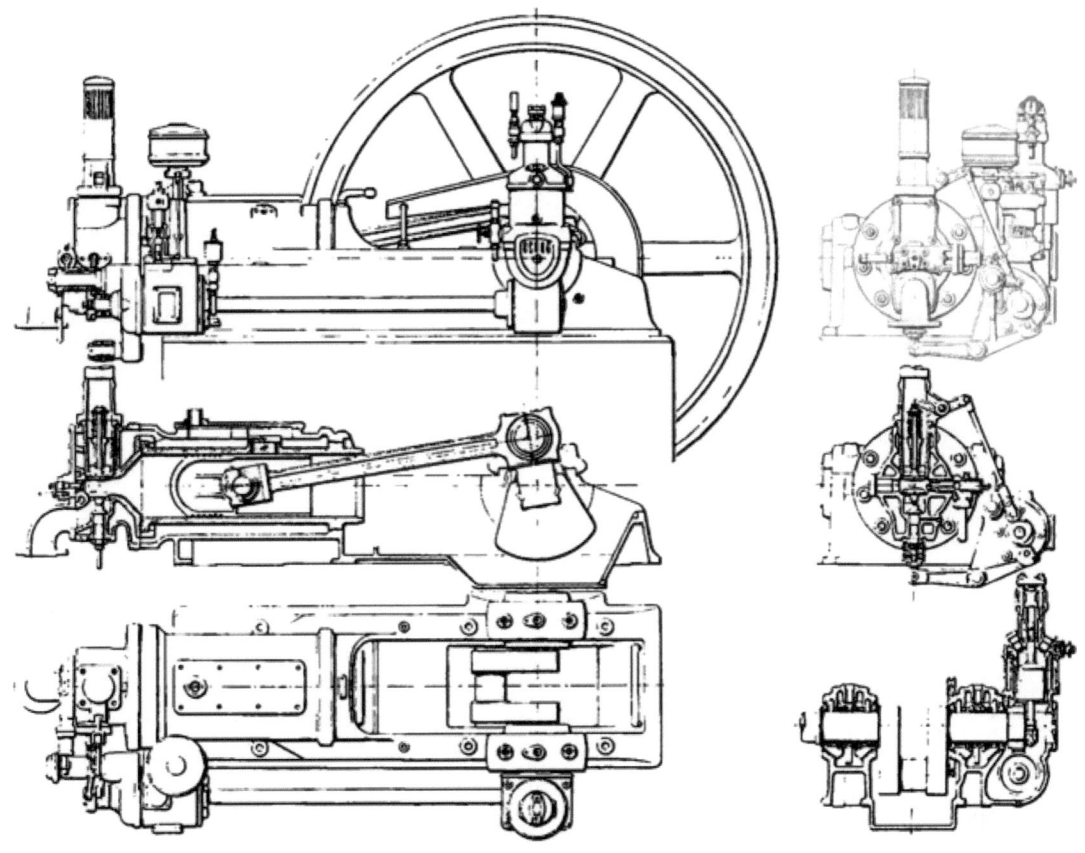

Figs. 57 and 58.—Details of M.A.N. Horizontal Engine.

[To face page 102

installed in the Städiches Elektrizitätswerk, Halle a. Saale. The cylinder diameter of the engine is 650 millimetres and the stroke 900, while the speed at the normal output of 1,800 H.P. is 150 revolutions per minute. Further engines of this type have been constructed, most working on tar oil with paraffin as ignition oil; *Figs.* 57 and 58 give details of a standard M.A.N. horizontal engine, and *Fig.* 59 shows one of 800 H.P.

The Deutz Horizontal Engine.—The horizontal engine built by the Gasmotorenfabrik Deutz is in many important respects a different type from that previously described. It is, however, not made in large sizes and has been mainly developed for cylinders up to about 50 H.P. It may incidentally be mentioned that with such small powers in this country (Great Britain) the Diesel engine has not found general favour owing to the success which has been attained with the hot-bulb motor, since the cost of installation of the Diesel type is generally in excess of that of the other design, and the difference in fuel consumption in such small sizes is usually scarcely sufficient to warrant the extra cost involved. On the Continent, however, very large numbers of these small horizontal engines are manufactured and sold, and practically all those which are employed in Germany run on tar oil, which, as mentioned elsewhere, can be obtained at a relatively low price.

In main construction the engine follows somewhat along the lines of accepted horizontal gas engine practice. The cylinder jacket and bed-plate are in one piece, and the horizontal cam shaft is driven through gearing off the crank shaft. From the illustration of the engine which is given in *Fig.* 60 it will be noticed that the suction air valve is vertical with a silencer above it, whilst the exhaust valve is immediately below this suction valve. The fuel inlet valve is horizontal and is arranged in the centre of the cylinder cover, which also contains the two valves previously mentioned and the starting air valve, which is on the side of the cover. Naturally, this construction, and indeed any form of horizontal engine, does not give the most perfect

Fig. 20.—800 B.H.P. Horizontal Diesel Engine.

Fig. 60. 50 H.P. Deutz Diesel Engine.

combustion chamber for a Diesel engine, but from the results which are attained, viz. a consumption of about ·45 lb. of oil per B.H.P. hour, it appears that the effect is not serious.

The arrangement of the air compressor is interesting inasmuch as it is of the vertical two-stage type driven by a small crank from the end of the crank shaft through worm gearing. The cooler is concentric with the pump barrels, and an interesting modification in this motor from other types lies in the fact that the air for injection is delivered direct to the fuel valve from the high pressure cylinder, no injection air reservoir being provided. The reason for this is explained later. For starting purposes it is, of course, necessary to have compressed air, and in this case the pressure is under 200 lb. per sq. inch, the diminished pressure being compensated by an increased opening of the starting air valve.

A special arrangement of fuel pump and fuel valve is provided, the method adopted being to pump the fuel to the valve just at the moment when it is opening so that it is injected direct by the compressed air. The governing of the amount of oil pumped into the cylinder through the injection valve is carried out by controlling the delivery from the fuel pump, which is arranged with an overflow by-pass instead of the suction valve as is common with most types of Diesel motors. When tar oil is utilized with this engine there is a small auxiliary pump and a separate inlet to the fuel valve, by means of which the ignition oil, such as gas oil, is pumped direct into the fuel pump chamber and thus into the combustion chamber before the tar oil.

Two-Cycle Engine.—Exclusive of exceptional circumstances it may be taken that for powers up to 600 or 700 B.H.P. the four-cycle single acting engine will be employed for land work, and above that power the two-cycle engine will be frequently adopted, or in certain cases the double acting two or four-cycle type. In four-cycle engines of large powers the engine frame, bed-plate, and flywheel become so heavy as to render them unwieldy, and the main disadvantage of the two-cycle motor—namely the necessity of a scavenge pump—becomes of less relative importance than is the case with smaller engines, when the slight extra complication of the two-cycle engine is undesirable. The difference in construction and external appearance between the two and four cycle engines is small, and is chiefly marked by the addition of the air scavenging pump or pumps commonly mounted on the end of the bed-plate, though in some types of engine it is arranged underground beneath the bed-plate. The speed of two-cycle engines, which are seldom made in sizes of less than 500 H.P. and are usually 700 H.P. and upwards, is from about 180 to 150 revolutions per minute or rather less. The exhaust valves of the four-cycle engine are replaced by ports at the bottom of the cylinders, uncovered by the piston as it moves outwards, and this is in itself a simplification of the construction. In present designs of this type of motor, the scavenging air is admitted through valves in the cylinder cover, operated from the horizontal cam shaft in the usual way, but as is the case with marine engines, it is probable that an arrangement in which ports are employed will be generally adopted in the future. Such a method is already being used by Messrs. Sulzer, and the exhaust ports are arranged on one side of the cylinder, while the scavenge ports are on the other side. In large engines, and particularly with marine engines, not only is the admission of fuel controlled for varying the power of the engine, but the admission of scavenge air to the working cylinders is automatically limited with decreasing load, as if this were not done, there would be a considerable excess of air and consequently inefficient operation.

Fig. 61 shows a two-cycle single acting four-cylinder Diesel motor of Messrs. Sulzer's construction. It is of 2,400 B.H.P. and is employed for dynamo driving in a central electric station in France. There are two scavenge cylinders on the end of the bed-plate driven direct off the crank shaft, while the three-stage air compressors, of which there are also two, are arranged, the low pressure stages below, the middle and high pressure stages behind the scavenge pumps. The latter stages are driven by means of rocking levers. The ordinary open type A frame is adopted and the cylinder body and the frame are cast in one piece in each cylinder and provided with a liner as with four-cycle engine, while the usual trunk piston is adopted. Each cylinder is provided with a starting lever and valve so that the engine may be run up in almost any position, this being a necessity in view of the size of the motor. The horizontal cam shaft is totally enclosed, and all the cams run in oil, the operation of the engine being therefore particularly silent. The cooling water outlet pipes are clearly seen in front of the engine, there being one for each cylinder, delivering into an open funnel so that the flow is visible, and the temperature can be readily measured. The pistons are also water cooled, and the outlet water flows into the same funnel as the jacket water, and is delivered thence into the main delivery pipe. *Fig.* 62 shows an outline plan, front elevation and side elevation, of the engine with overall dimensions, from which it is seen that the overall length is 42 ft. 4 in. inclusive of the flywheel. There are two silencers placed underground, and the main exhaust pipe from the engine to the silencer is also below the engine room floor, the exhaust gasses from each cylinder being delivered into this main pipe by a separate pipe seen in *Fig.* 61.

There has recently been a tendency to construct the large two-cycle engines for stationary work exactly similar to the marine type except for the reversing gear—a tendency much to be commended. In the engines of 4,000 B.H.P. which Messrs. Sulzer are building, this procedure has been adopted, and in general design such motors are the same as the marine engines described later in detail.

In the 4,000 B.H.P. type there are six cylinders, each of 30 in. diameter and 40 in. stroke, the speed of rotation for full load being 132 revolutions per minute. Two scavenge pumps are arranged at the end of the engine, driven direct off the crank shaft, and between these cylinders, also driven

[*To face page* 108.

Fig. 61.—Sulzer Two-Cycle 2,460 B.H.P. Engine.

[To face page 108.

CONSTRUCTION OF THE DIESEL ENGINE

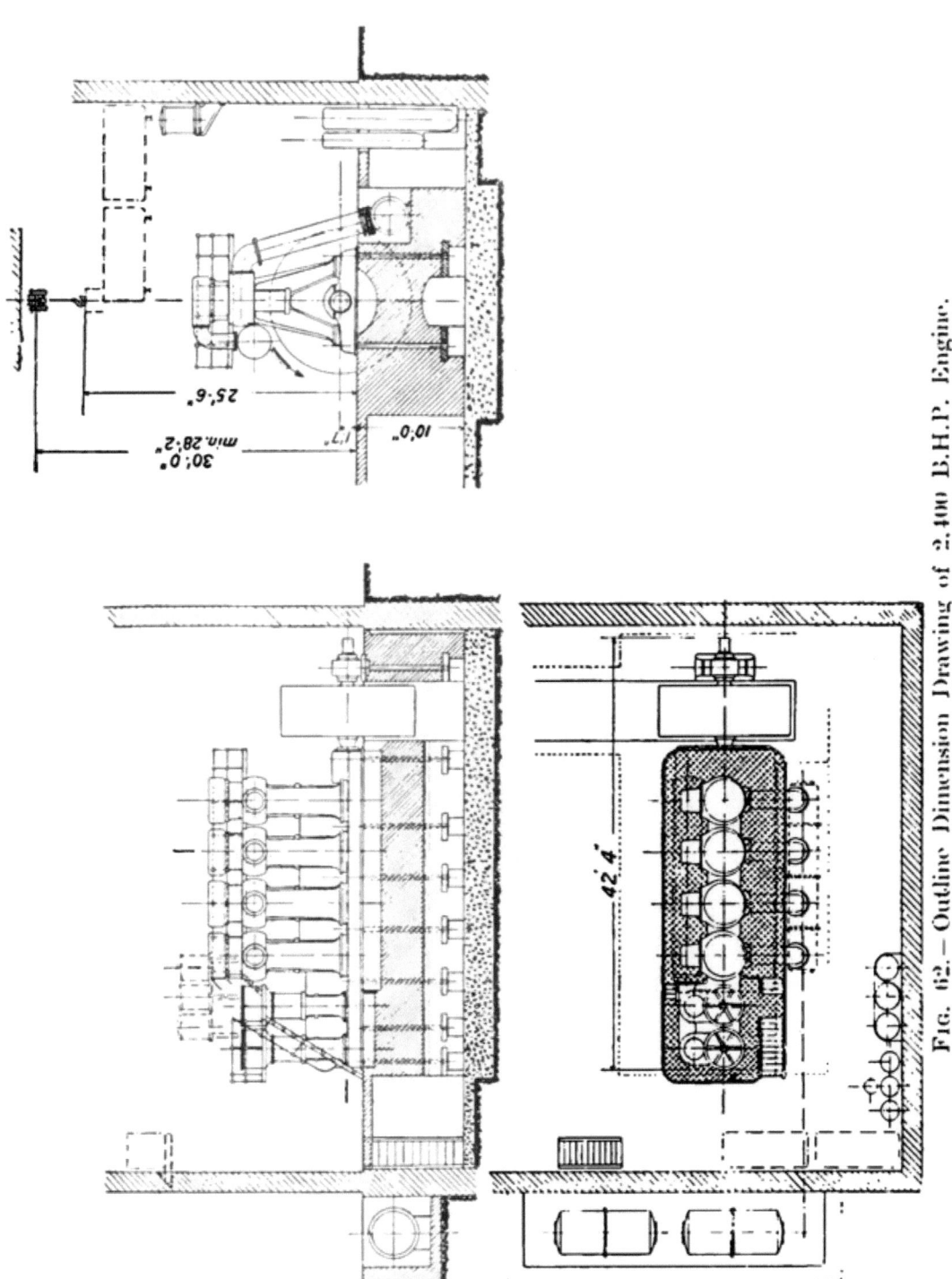

Fig. 62.—Outline Dimension Drawing of 2,400 B.H.P. Engine.

direct off the crank shaft, are the high and intermediate pressure stages of the fuel injection pump. The crossheads

CONSTRUCTION OF THE DIESEL ENGINE 111

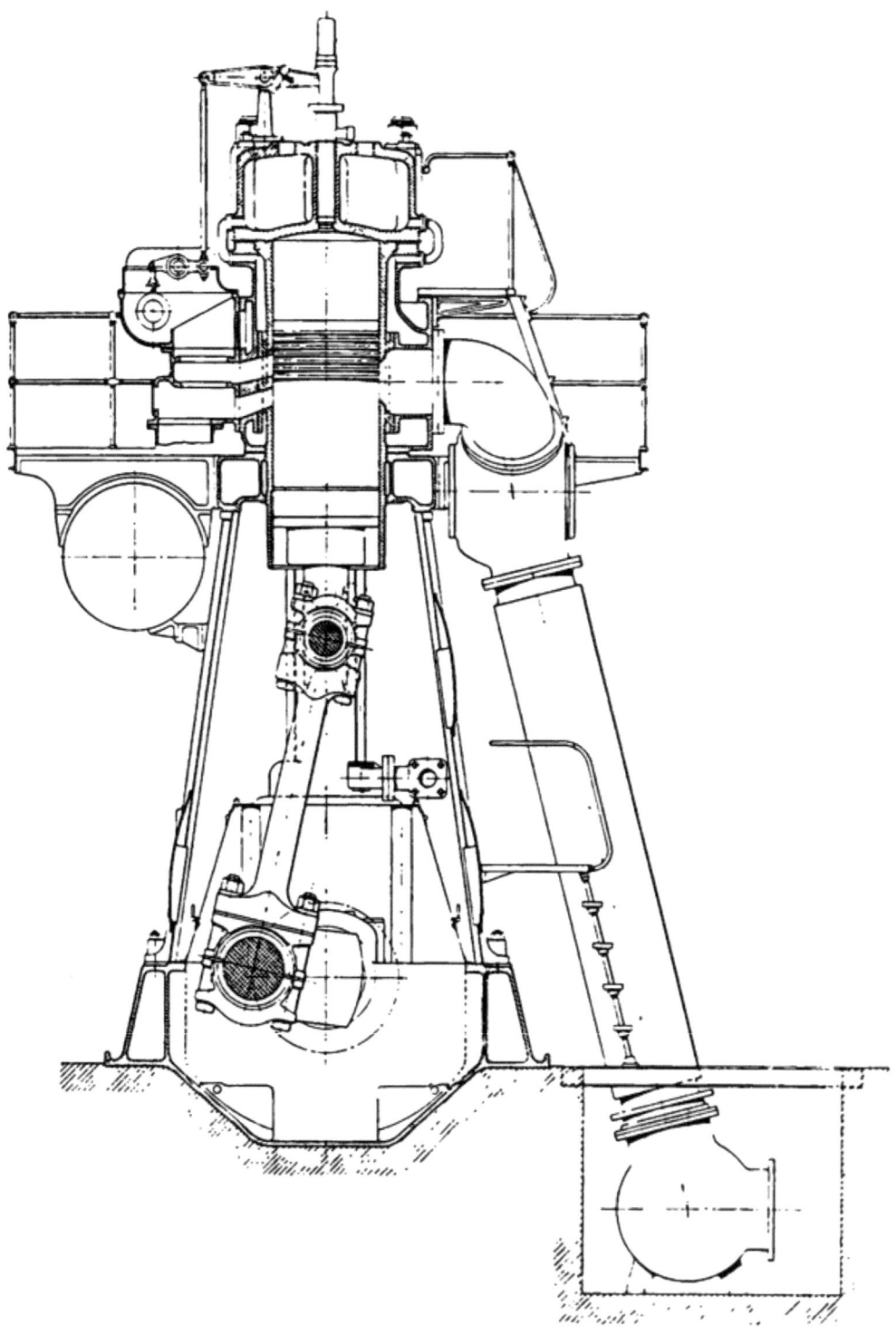

Fig. 64.—Section through Cylinder of Sulzer Two-Cycle Motor, showing auxiliary scavenge ports.

112 DIESEL ENGINES FOR LAND AND MARINE WORK

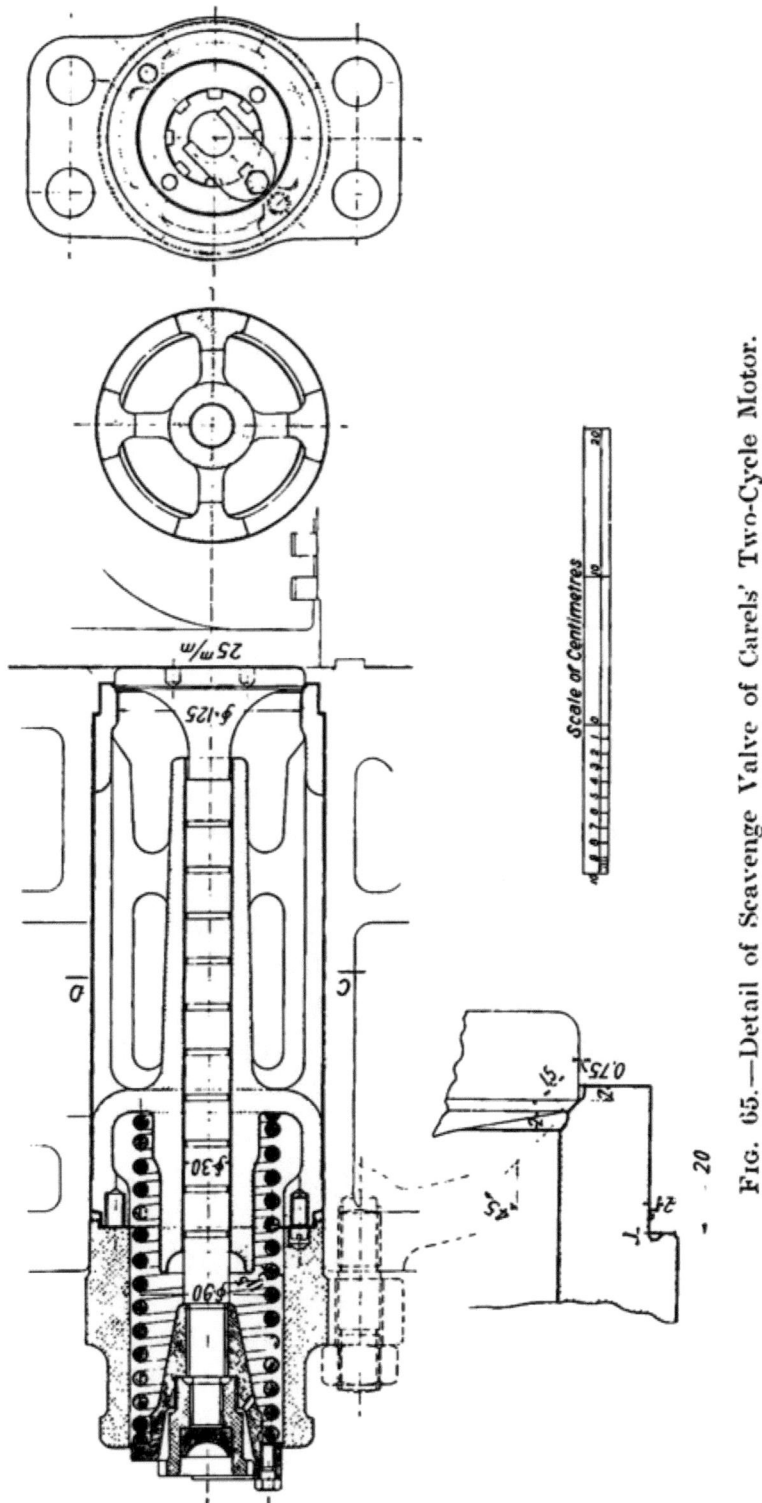

Fig. 65.—Detail of Scavenge Valve of Carels' Two-Cycle Motor.

of the scavenge pump are arranged as the two low pressure stages of the injection air compressor.

The method of scavenging is identical with that employed in the marine engines and described later. Scavenge valves in the cylinder head are dispensed with, ports being provided at the bottom of the cylinder, uncovered by the piston, whilst auxiliary valve-controlled air-ports are also arranged just above the main ports. Only three of the cylinders have starting valves, and in each case there are two valves in the cylinder head, whilst each cylinder has one fuel inlet valve. No other valves are required.

An important feature of the engine and one which is much adopted in various marine designs, is that the cylinder is supported by steel columns and not by a cast-iron frame. The cylinder liner itself is quite free to move downward during expansion, which is a necessary safeguard in large cylinders.

The weight of this engine complete is some 470 tons, and its length about 55 ft.

A similar principle is followed in the design adopted by Messrs. Carels in their large two-cycle engines, which are built up to 2,500 H.P. in six cylinders. *Fig.* 68 shows a 1,000 B.H.P. stationary engine of four cylinders of the standard two-cycle type, running at 125 revolutions per minute. Except that no reversing mechanism is provided, and the scavenge pump is driven direct off the crank shaft instead of by means of rocking levers off the crossheads, the motor is almost identical with the Carels marine engine which is described later.

The motor is of the open type, somewhat resembling a steam engine in appearance, and the trunk piston has been dispensed with in favour of the crosshead and connecting rod —a step which seems advisable for motors of large power. The cylinders are supported on " A " frames, and a Reavell three-stage air compressor (not seen in the illustration) is employed, driven direct off the crank shaft in the usual manner.

There is much to be said in favour of arranging the scavenge pump on the end of the bed-plate, instead of by levers as in the marine type ; in the latter the method is objected to by

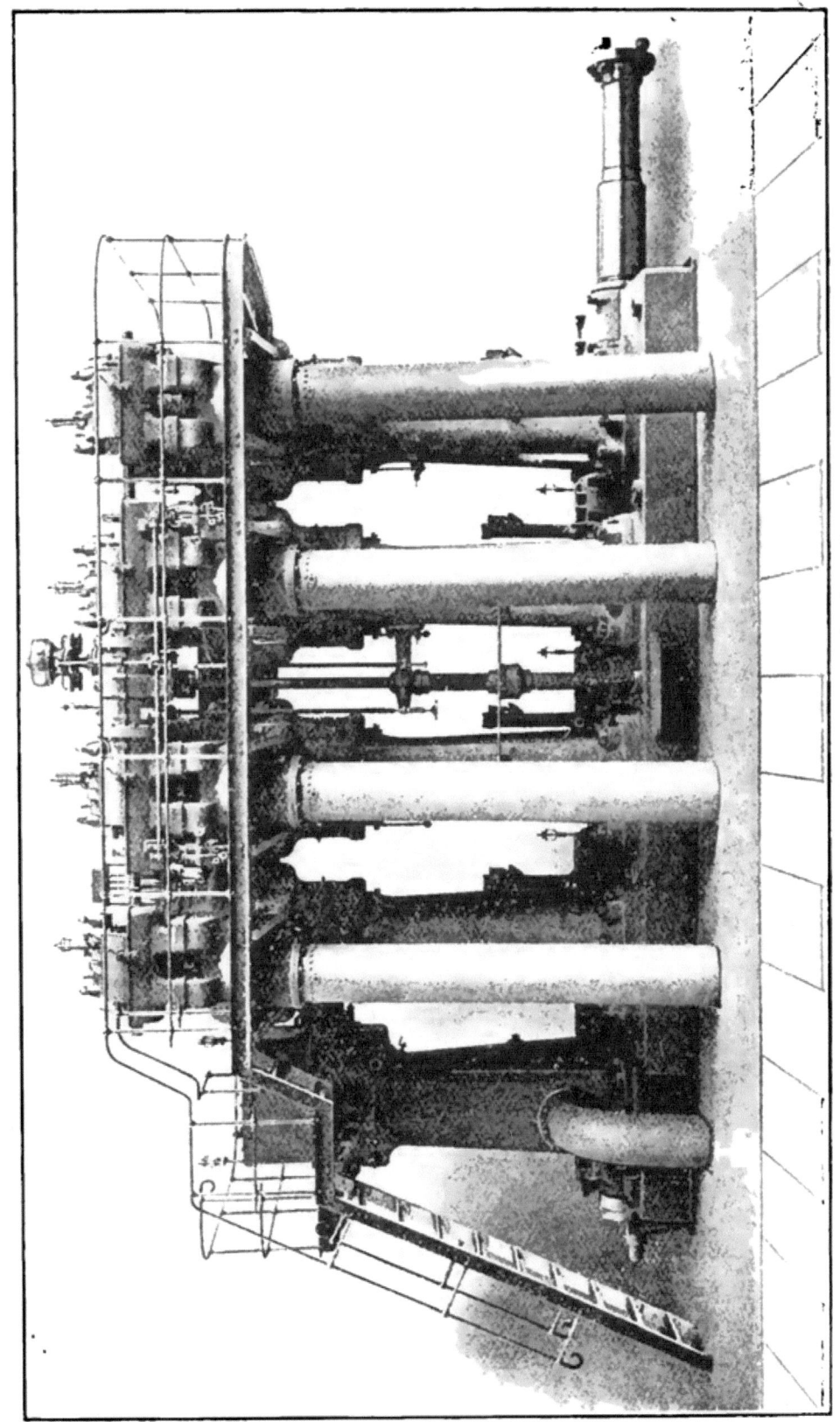

Fig. 68.—1,000 H.P. Two-Cycle Diesel Engine.

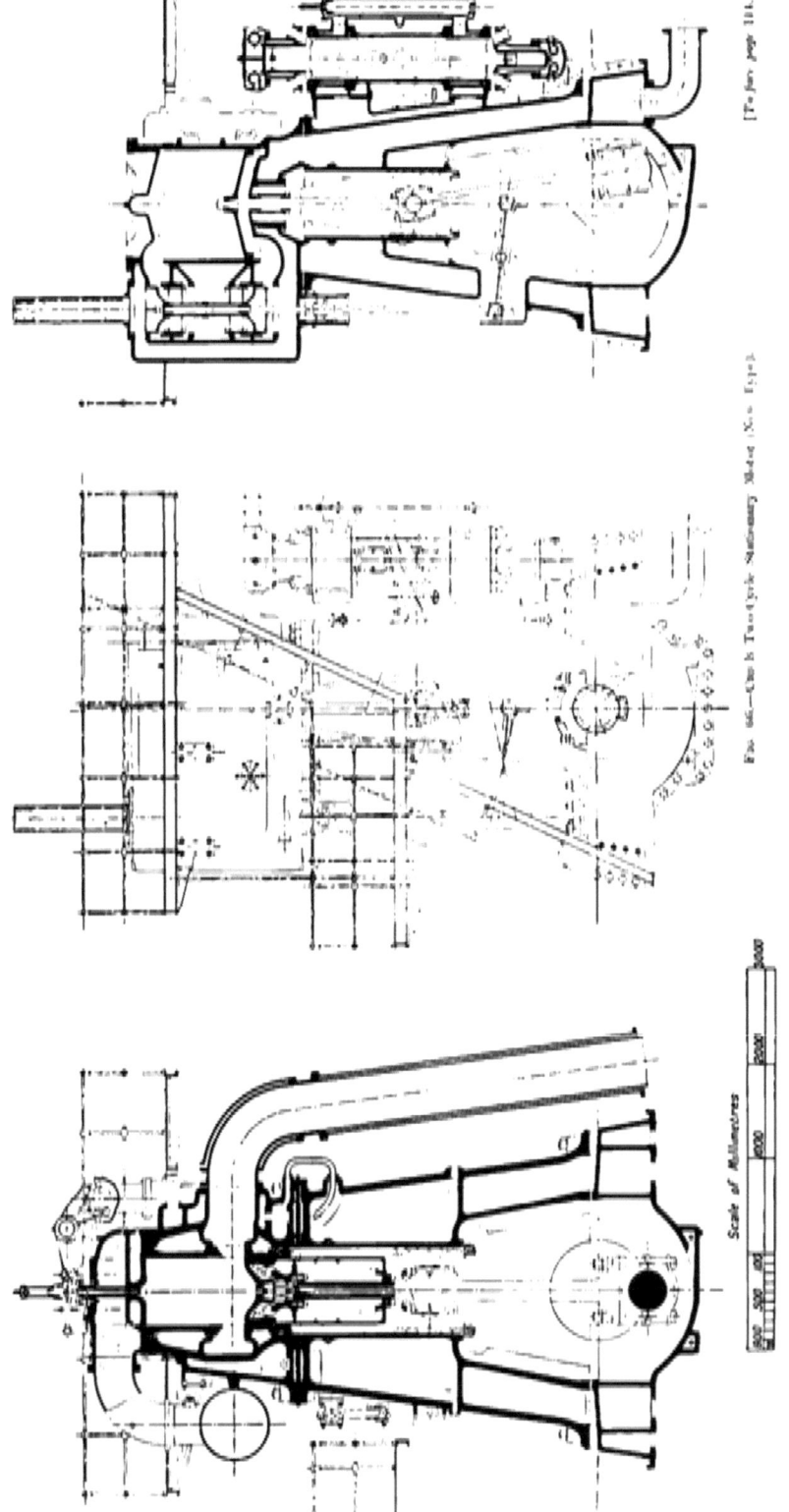

Fig. 66.—Clerk Two-cycle Stationary Motor (New Type).

[To face page 114.

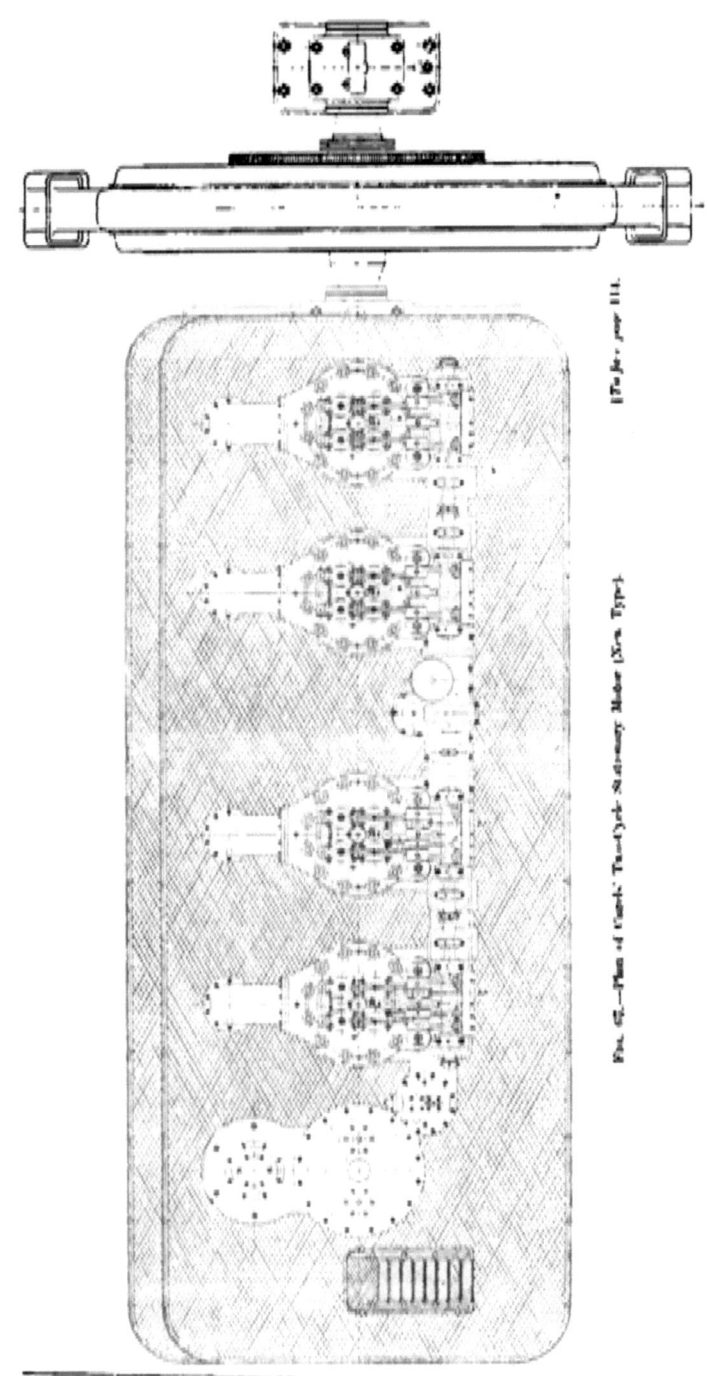

Fig. 6.—Plan of Cock's Two-Cycle Stationary Motor (New Type).

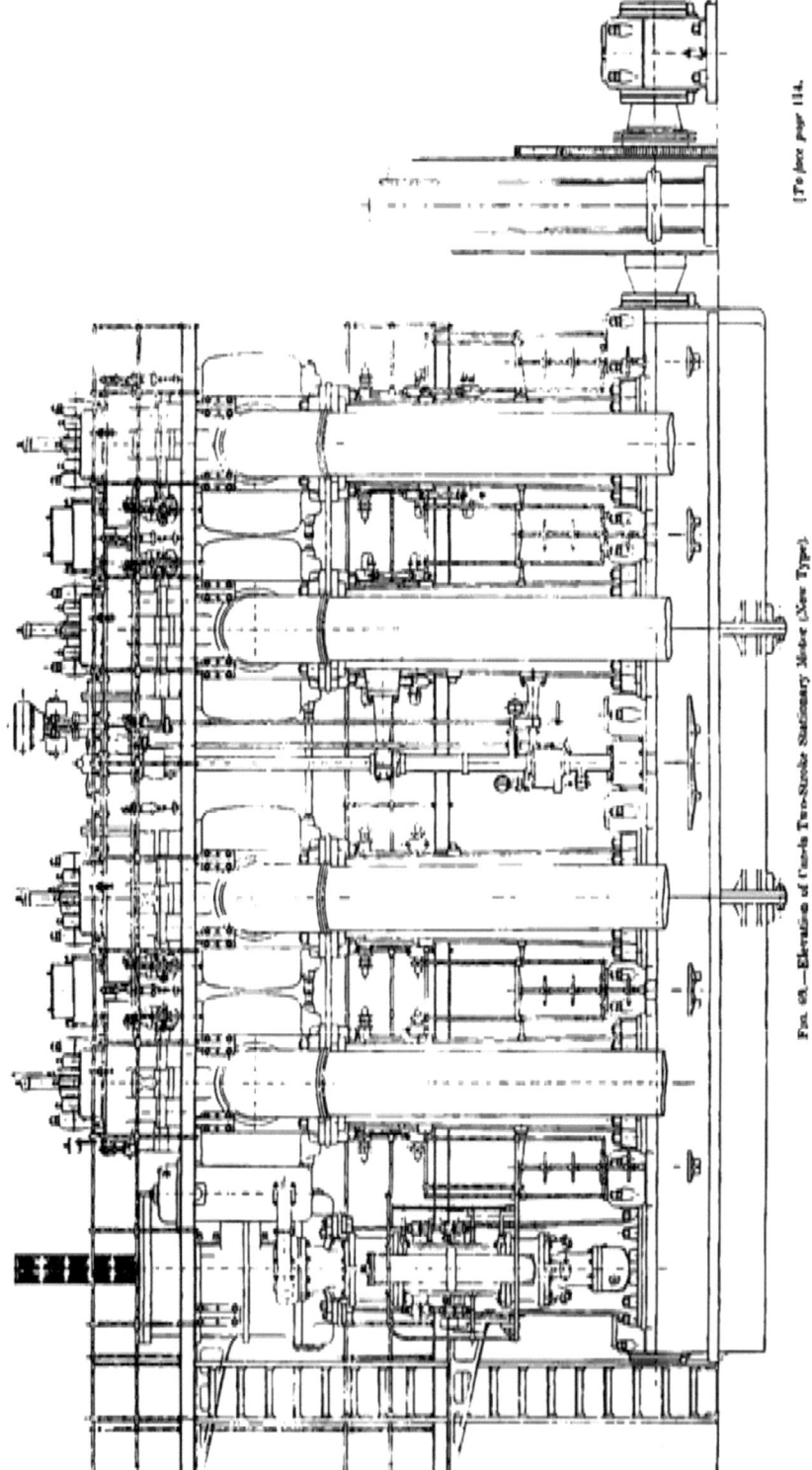

Fig. 63.—Elevation of Carels Two-Stroke Stationary Motor (New Type).

[To face page 114.]

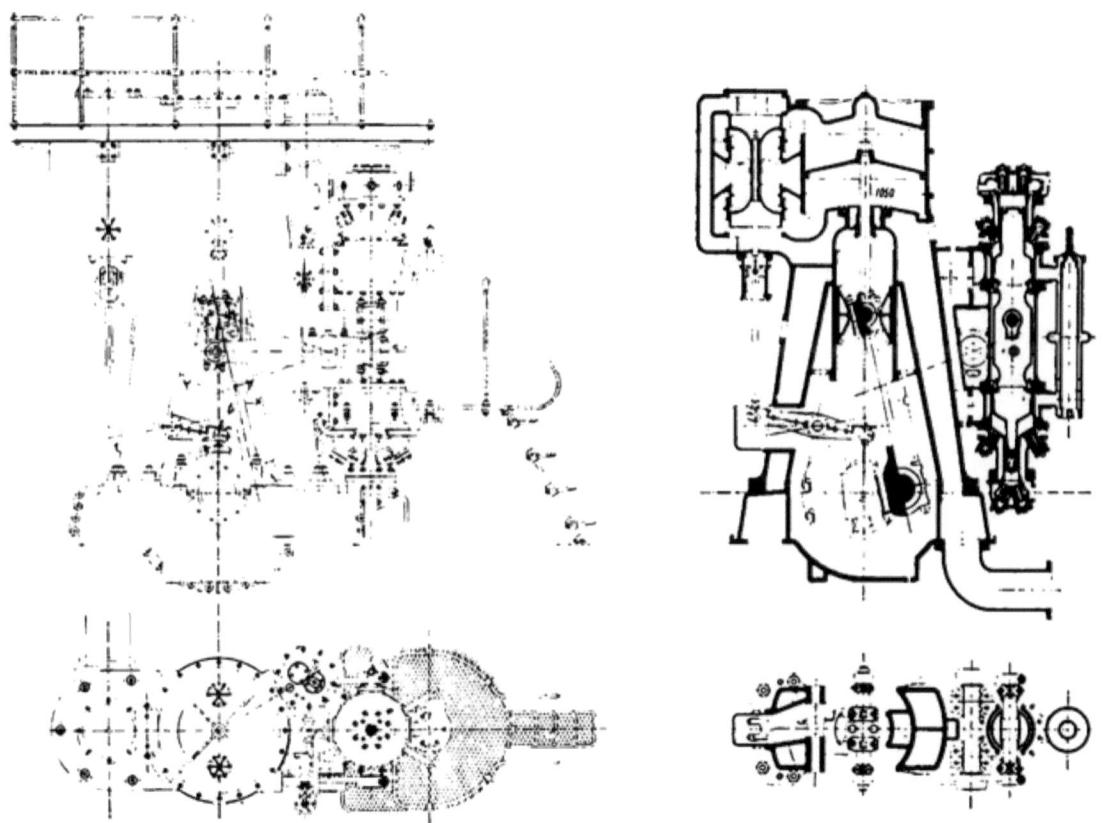

Fig. 70.—Details of Scavenge Pump and Air Compressor for Carels Two-Stroke Stationary Motor (New Type).

[To face page 114.

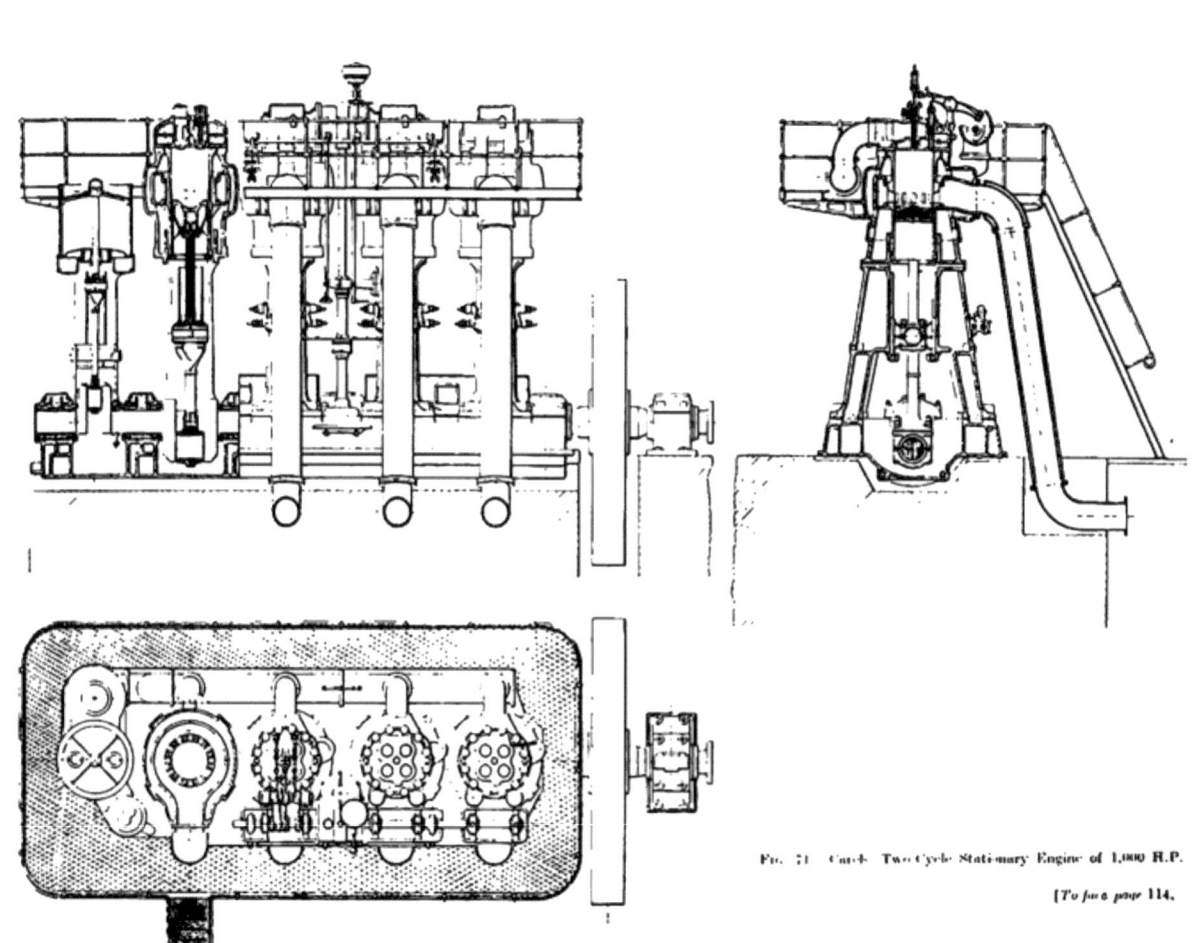

Fig. 71.—Oechelhäuser Two-Cycle Stationary Engine of 1,000 H.P.

[To face page 114.

Fig. 72.—1,000 H.P. Krupp Two-Cycle Motor. Speed 150 r.p.m. [*To face page* 114.

some makers owing to the increase in length of the engine, as there is generally more available space at the side, and moreover the engine cannot be made so symmetrical, which is a point of some importance in considering the spare parts—for instance, the crank shaft can be made in two equal portions. This is not possible with a design in which the scavenge pump is mounted on the end of the engine.

In common with all the present two-cycle Carels designs, valves are utilized for scavenging, fitted in the cylinder cover, two or four being adopted.

Figs. 66 to 71 show the most recent type of Carels' two-cycle engines, the main modification being in the air compressors.

Air Compressors for Diesel Engines.—The air compressors for the supply of injection air and for starting purposes, are very important features of the Diesel engines, and as the power absorbed by them is practically a dead loss from a commercial standpoint, a large amount of care has been bestowed upon their design to render them as economical and efficient as possible, more particularly as such high pressures as nearly 1,000 lb. per sq. inch have to be obtained. Air compressors for Diesel engines may roughly be divided into two classes: (1) the vertical type driven either by levers off the connecting rod, or direct from the crank shaft at one end of the engine; and (2) those of the Reavell or similar type, in which all the pistons are driven from eccentrics on the end of the crank shaft. Owing to the high pressure, single stage compressors are seldom used, the common type being either two stage or three stage compressors.

In the Diesel engine of some of the German types a separate compressor is often provided for each cylinder. The air is drawn from the atmosphere into the low pressure cylinder, and after being compressed by the piston, it passes into a receiver, and thence to the high pressure cylinder. Here it is further compressed and is delivered through a valve to the air reservoirs. There are two suction valves which open outwards and allow air to enter the cylinder through small passages, being returned through the same ports after compression and delivered to the receiver through outlet valves which open inwards. The cylinders and receiver are well water jacketed as the temperature of the air naturally rises considerably during compression.

Fig. 73.—Reavell Quadruplex Compressor.

The well-known Quadruplex form of single stage "Reavell" compressor has been suitably modified and used very largely by different makers of Diesel engines. Its general appearance for Diesel engines of the land type is shown by the illustration *Fig.* 73 and the two sections in *Fig.* 74.

CONSTRUCTION OF THE DIESEL ENGINE 117

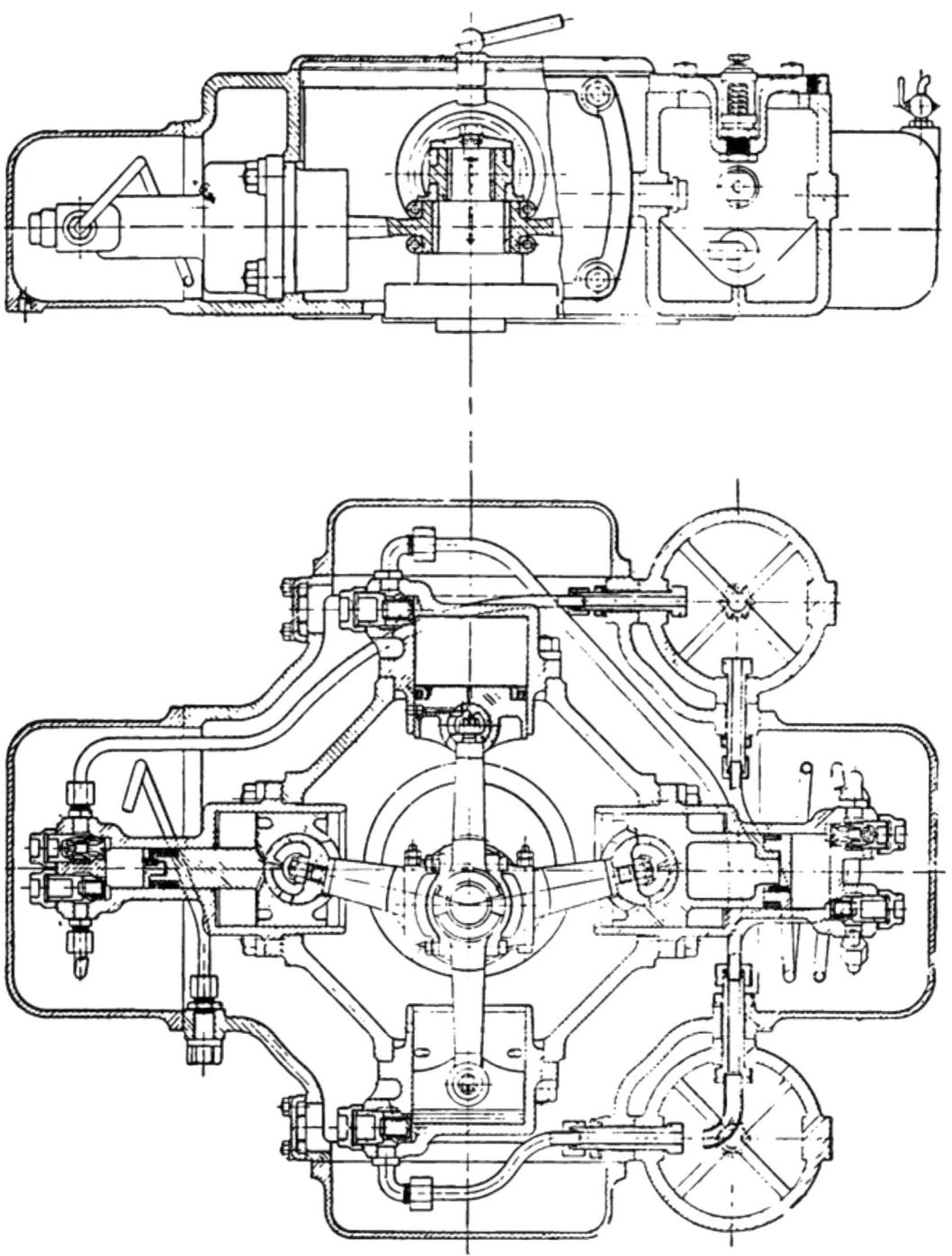

In these machines the compressing of the air is carried out in three stages, which is found to give better results than with the two stage compressors used in earlier Diesel engines.

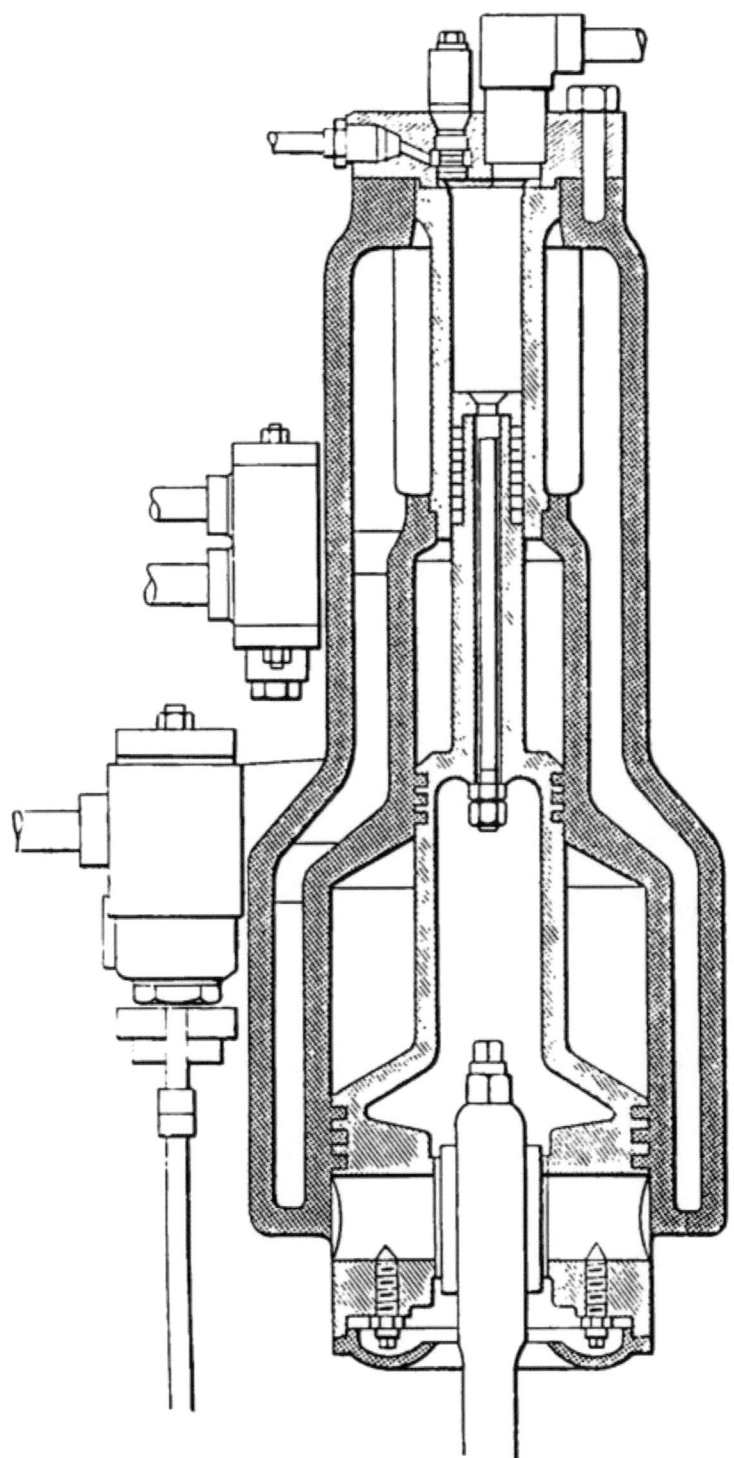

Fig. 76.—Section of Three-Stage Vertical Compressor for Diesel Engines.

The two horizontal cylinders seen in the illustrations are both low pressure cylinders, so that at each stroke of the

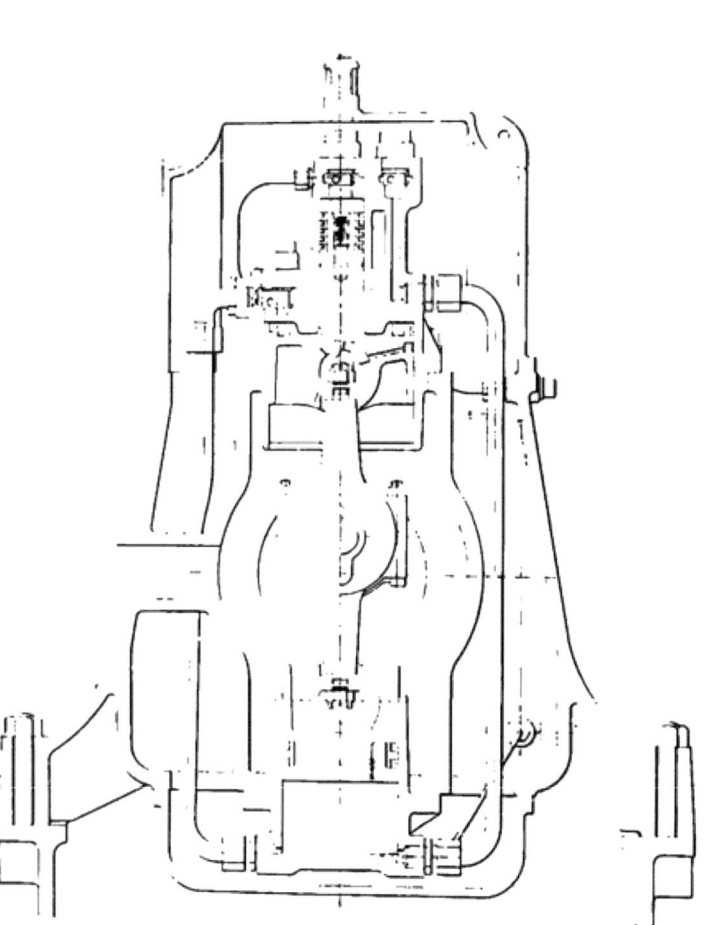
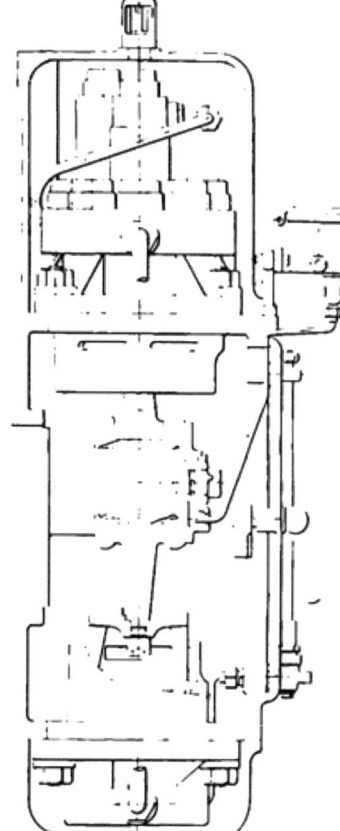

Fig. 75.—Reavell's Compressor.

[To face page 119.

CONSTRUCTION OF THE DIESEL ENGINE

engine low pressure air is passed over into the intermediate cylinder. The air is admitted into the crank chamber of the compressor, whence it passes through ports in the gudgeon and piston during the suction stroke, so that the cylinders are filled with air at atmospheric pressure, without the attenuation due to the use of suction valves.

On the delivery stroke the ports referred to are closed by the swing of the connecting rod, which moves the ports in the gudgeon away from the ports in the piston, and thus the air is compressed and delivered through the delivery valve and cooled by means of the coil seen in *Fig.* 74 and then delivered into a second chamber or purge pot, from which again any moisture which is separated out can be blown off.

The air then passes through another pipe to the high pressure cylinder placed at the top of the machine, which contains suction and delivery valves interchangeable with those on the intermediate cylinder. After the final stage of compression in this cylinder, the air is passed through the coiled pipe shown, to the delivery bonnet, whence it passes to the air storage bottles, which supply the Diesel engine.

Machines of this type are made in standard sizes for Diesel engines from about 100 H.P. at medium speed up to the large sizes.

The whole of the compressing cylinders being arranged in a symmetrical form of casing, it is possible to bolt this casing directly to the end of the bed-plate of the Diesel engine, so that no extra bearing is required for the compressor. The crankpin for driving the connecting rods and pistons is simply attached direct to the end of the standard crank shaft of the Diesel engine by means of studs, or any other simple manner, the crank disc of course being carefully spigoted to a recess in the shaft, so as to form a register and insure correct alignment.

Fig. 75 shows a type of vertical three stage compressor made by Messrs. Reavell & Co. for high speed Diesel engines. It embodies a novel feature in its construction, as the valves in the intermediate cylinder, both for suction and delivery, are altogether omitted.

As will be seen by the illustration, all of the cylinders are placed vertically, the low pressure and high pressure cylinders being above the crankpin and in tandem with each other, while the intermediate cylinder is below the crankpin. The same provision for the admission of air in the low pressure cylinder through the gudgeon ports, already described for the Quadruplex compressor, is made use of for this new vertical type, thus omitting the suction valves. Delivery valves are provided on the low pressure, from which a suitable design of pipe connexions leads the air to the bottom of the intermediate cylinder and onwards from the intermediate cylinder up to the suction valve on the high pressure cylinder.

By suitably proportioning the volumes of these pipes and the volume of the intermediate cylinder, the air during the second stage of compression is pushed backwards into the pipe leading to the high pressure cylinder, and cooling takes place during the very act of compression, which enhances the efficiency.

During the next stroke, the pressure behind the intermediate piston falls as the air expands, until the low pressure delivery valves open again and the next charge of air is passed over from the low pressure. On the succeeding compression stroke of the intermediate cylinder, the air passed over from the low pressure cylinder, together with the air which remains in the intercooler pipe connexion, is again compressed. At the same time the high pressure cylinder is performing its suction stroke, so that the increasing intermediate pressure rapidly reaches a point when the suction valve on the high pressure opens and some of the intermediate air is passed over into the high pressure cylinder. This, during the next stroke, is compressed by the high pressure plunger and delivered; and the cycle is repeated.

In other respects the compressor is the same as Messrs. Reavell's Quadruplex compressor, that is to say, it has no

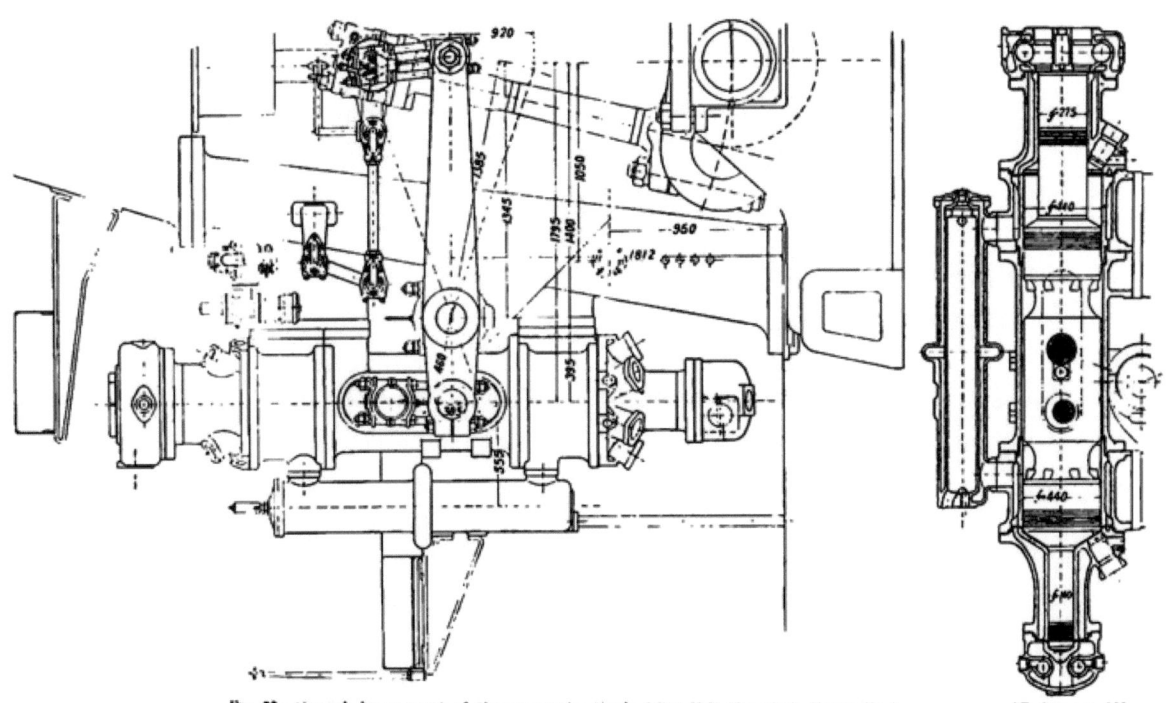

Fig. 77.—General Arrangement of Compressor for Carels 1,500 H.P. Two-Cycle Marine Engine. [To face page 121.

bearings and the crankpin is attached to the end of the shaft in just the same way.

For small and very high pressure engines this vertical compressor is attached direct to the bearers which also carry the engine, brackets being cast on the sides of the compressor for this purpose. For larger engines a segmental facing is provided on the back of the compressor casing, attached directly to a similar facing on the engine bed.

The advantage of this type of machine is that all valves below the centre line of the compressor are entirely done away with, and this not only simplifies the machine and improves its efficiency, but also makes periodical overhauling quite an easy matter. It will be seen that the only valves requiring attention are rendered accessible by lifting the top water bonnet, which uncovers both low pressure and the high pressure cylinders, and in all these compressors the whole of the valves and caps are completely surrounded with water, which experience has shown will obviate the trouble arising from the gumming up of valves due to the heating of the air.

For marine work a somewhat similar quadruplex compressor is employed, there being two modifications in the construction. A section of this marine type is shown on *Fig.* 78, and in comparing this with the sectional illustration of the land type of compressor, it will be noticed that the guide of the intermediate cylinder is removed and the valves are placed in pockets on the side of the cylinder instead of at the bottom. The omission of the guide is rendered possible owing to the increased dimensions of these larger compressors for marine work, and the alteration in the position of the valves enables a flat bottom to be provided for the compressor casing and makes it easy to place the casing directly on the tank tops in the ship or the engine seatings, in the same way as the bed of the Diesel engine itself.

As the compressor must be capable of compressing its air satisfactorily, whether the engine is running ahead or astern, the gudgeon inlet for the first stage air, which is adopted in the land type of compressor already described, is here replaced by ordinary suction valves, which obtain their air from a port leading into the crank chamber.

In *Fig.* 77 are given details of a Carels compressor for a 1,500 H.P. motor, driven by means of levers from the crosshead of the engine.

Solid Injection for Diesel Engines.—When the first experiments were first being made on Diesel engines by Dr. Diesel, it was attempted to carry out the cycle of operations simply by forcing the fuel into the combustion chamber under pressure from a pump. This was found to be unsatisfactory and was entirely abandoned. It was not until recently that any actual progress was made in the direction of solid injection for Diesel engines, and at the present time motors working on this principle are built only by Messrs. Vickers for submarine engines.

The advantages of the abolition of the air compressor for injecting air are obvious, particularly as it is found that in high-speed engines the air compressor represents one of the auxiliaries most liable to cause trouble, and even with the ordinary slow-speed marine engine, air compressors often need special attention. It must be remembered, however, that compressed air is necessary for starting purposes on most engines, whilst it is also required for other purposes on board ship. In motors for submarines this does not invariably apply, as starting may be accomplished by means of the electric motor which is installed for propelling the submarine when under water. Reversing may be carried out in the same way, that is to say, the astern power being provided only by the electric motors. Naturally this is not in all respects satisfactory, but for the purpose is not altogether unsuitable for submarines as at present constructed, although when larger sizes become common, direct reversibility will be a necessity.

Solid injection is now being employed with a large number of engines installed in British submarines, and has on the whole proved extremely satisfactory. In these vessels, however, a comparatively light oil is commonly employed, and although experiment seems to have demonstrated the

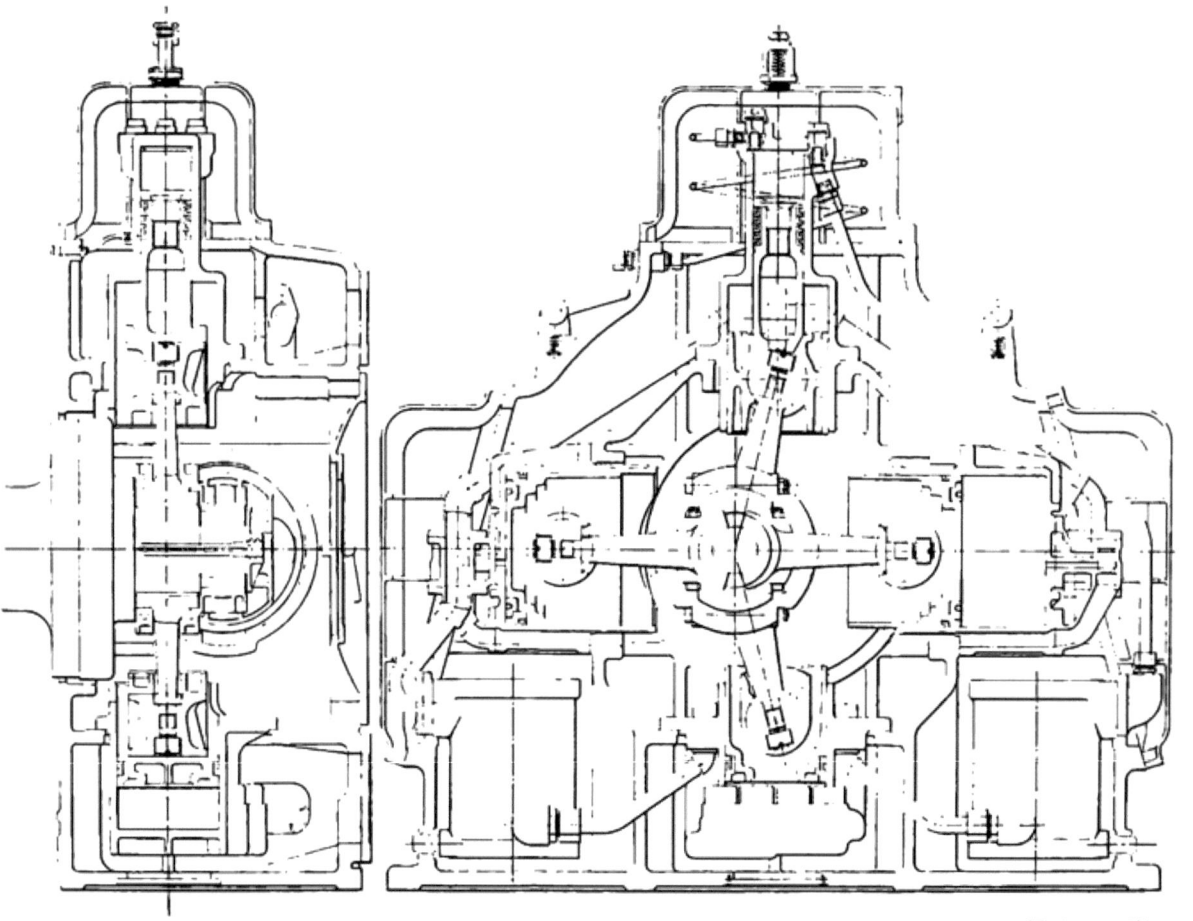

FIG. 74.—Marine Type Compressor.

possibility of utilizing the heaviest oil, including the Texas oil and tar oil, no commercial application has yet been made. It is hardly probable that the combustion with solid injection can be so satisfactory as with the employment of compressed air for the purpose, but on the other hand, the power required to drive the compressor is eliminated, which is a matter of seven to ten per cent. in many Diesel engines. As a heat engine, however, the motor with solid injection is not so efficient as the pure Diesel type with air injection, so that the advantage obtained

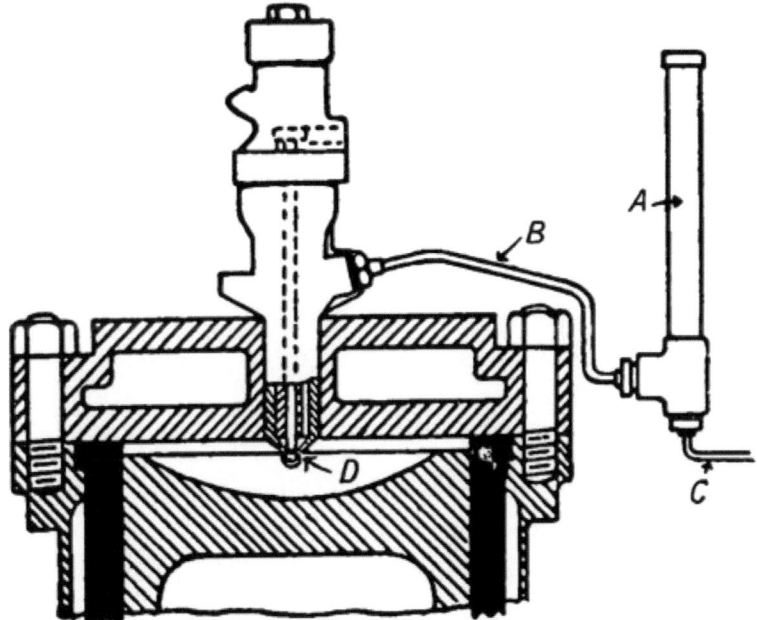

Fig. 79.—Diagram of Vickers' Solid Injection System.

by the abolition of the air compressor is to a certain extent counteracted. On the whole, the fuel consumption with this type is approximately the same as the ordinary engine using air injection.

The principle of the arrangement for solid injection is shown in *Figs.* 79 *and* 80, these being, of course, diagrammatic in every respect. The main idea is that oil should be pumped into a tube with collapsible walls which expand under the high pressure, the oil entering the tube, and on the opening of the fuel valve the walls collapse, forcing the oil under high pressure through the fuel valve into the combustion chamber.

In *Fig.* 79 *C* represents the pipe supplying oil from the oil pump, while *A* is the pressure tube referred to. *B* is the pipe leading to the injection valve which is shown in

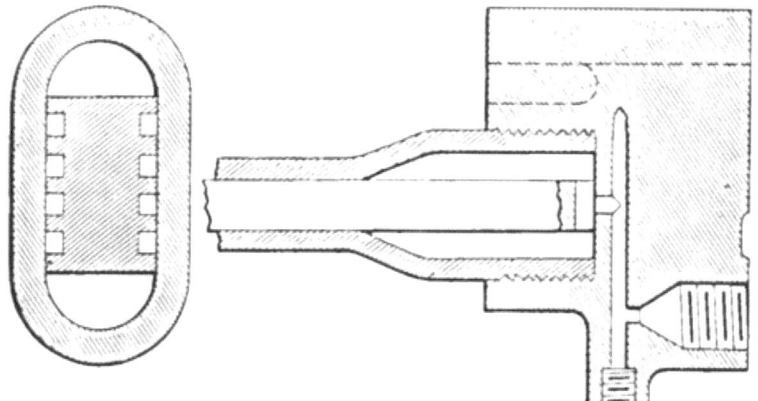

Fig. 80.—Sketch showing Solid Injection Arrangement.

the diagram at *D*. The pressure tube is usually made elliptical, and is forced into a cylindrical shape for the oil under pressure, which may be as much as 2,000 lb. to the sq. inch or perhaps more. There is a distance piece within this collapsible tube in order to prevent it collapsing to too great an extent.

This arrangement has hitherto been applied on a commercial scale to four-cycle engines, though others of the two-cycle type are under construction. It is also likely to be adapted for mercantile work, that is to say for marine motors of the four-cycle type running at normal speeds of revolution of 100 to 150 r.p.m.

CHAPTER IV

INSTALLING AND RUNNING DIESEL ENGINES

GENERAL REMARKS—SPACE OCCUPIED AND GENERAL DIMENSIONS—STARTING UP THE ENGINE—MANAGEMENT OF DIESEL ENGINES—COST OF OPERATION OF DIESEL ENGINES.

General Remarks.—The Diesel engine is perhaps the most scientifically designed motor in existence, and for that reason all its parts have to be constructed with great exactitude. From this point of view it may be considered as a delicate machine, and up to the time when the engine is actually put to work no emphasis is too strong as to the necessity of the utmost care to be taken, though after it is once in operation it becomes a machine of the greatest reliability, needing, on the whole, less care and attendance than a steam engine or gas engine. The installation of a Diesel engine therefore should be carried out with the same precision as its construction, and not be accompanied by the careless manipulation which is customary with steam plants. Above all, dust of any sort must be prevented from access to the essential working parts of the engine, particularly the fuel valve, which is very sensitive to any minute particles, owing to the restricted inlet passages for the air and fuel.

The foundations required are relatively heavy, as is the case with all vertical engines, but owing to the evenness of combustion and the absence of shock from the explosion of mixed gases, there is less vibration than with a gas engine of similar type. The depth to which it is necessary to carry the foundations depends of course to some extent on the nature of the subsoil, as it is essential to reach a firm basis. Holes are left in the concrete while the foundation is being built up, for the foundation bolts, either by means of boxes or pipes of ample size, which are withdrawn when the foundation is set. The bolts are thus put in when the engine is being installed, and in the usual arrangement an arched tunnel is left under the foundation so that a man may have access from the flywheel pit for tightening up all the bolts when the bed-plate is fixed in its exact position ready for grouting up. It is desirable, particularly where engines are installed in existing buildings when the vibration of the engine might possibly be transmitted through the walls, to keep the engine foundations well clear of the foundations and footings of the walls. In cases where two, three or four engines are erected in a somewhat confined space, which frequently happens in installations in the basements of large buildings, a good plan is to make a through foundation upon which all the engines are placed, and this is a method that has frequently been adopted.

The third outer bearing is always separate from the bed-plate, and this has to be carefully lined up with the other bearings, and the crank shaft is dropped in and all the bearings scraped till it is perfectly true, this being necessary even though the engine has already been running on the test bed, as there are bound to be variations when it is actually installed. The crank shaft is lifted out and replaced after the bottom half of the flywheel is lowered in the pit, and the erection of the rest of the engine is a straightforward matter, particularly so, as in the case of multicylinder engines, all parts of the different cylinders being interchangeable. The two starting vessels, and the air injection vessel, being commonly some six or seven feet high, are usually let into the floor three or four feet so that all the valves are at a convenient height for operation by the driver.

Space Occupied and General Dimensions.—The space required for a Diesel engine installation with all

INSTALLING AND RUNNING DIESEL ENGINES

accessories is much less than for a complete gas or steam plant. The following table (Table I) gives the approximate space necessary with Sulzer Diesel engines, of the standard four-cycle slow speed type, the dimensions referring to the outline drawing *Fig.* 81. Many of the measurements can be reduced if it is essential, owing to limitations of the engine-room, and with engines of the high speed type all the dimensions become somewhat less.

Table II gives measurements and weights of standard four-cycle engines built by the Maschinenfabrik Augsburg-Nürnburg, while Table III gives data relating to engines of the high speed type.

The engines given in the tables by no means exhaust the total number of standard machines. Each firm has its own standards, but of these there are so many that it is almost always possible to choose a standard engine whatever be the power required.

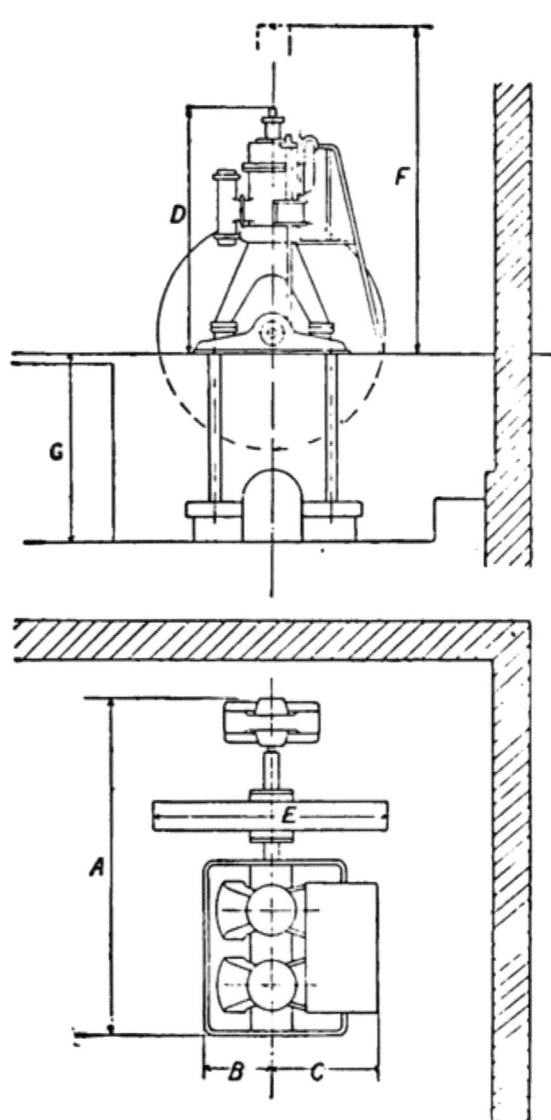

FIG. 81.—Outline Drawing of Sulzer Four-Cycle Engines (to correspond with Table of Dimensions).

TABLE I. (See Fig. 81.)

	Single Cylinder Engines.			Two Cylinder Engines.				Three Cylinder Engines.				
B.H.P.	25	50	65	60	80	100	130	200	300	400	500	600
	ft. in.	ft. in.	ft. in.	ft. in.	ft. in.	ft. in.	ft. in.	ft. in.	ft. in.	ft. in.	ft. in.	ft. in.
A	8 0	11 0	13 3	11 4	13 0	13 11	16 5	18 4	20 0	24 0	26 3	28 2
B	2 2	2 9	3 1	2 5	2 7	2 9	3 1	3 1	3 11	4 3	4 7	4 11
C	3 3	4 9	5 1	3 10	4 5	4 9	5 1	5 1	6 7	7 3	7 10	9 2
D	7 5	10 0	11 6	8 4	8 8	10 0	11 6	11 6	12 6	13 1	14 5	16 7
E	7 6	9 2	9 10	8 2	8 10	9 2	9 10	9 10	11 0	11 10	12 6	13 1
F	10 2	13 7	14 11	11 4	12 4	13 7	14 11	14 11	19 0	20 10	22 6	24 7
G	4 11	7 3	7 10	5 11	6 7	7 3	7 10	7 10	8 10	9 2	9 6	9 10

TABLE II. (M.A.N. ENGINES.)

	Single Cylinder Engines.				Two Cylinder Engines.				Three Cylinder Engines.				Four Cylinder Engines.			
B.H.P.	25	70	150	220	100	160	250	440	250	375	450	660	300	500	600	880
Revolutions per minute.	205	160	155	150	170	160	155	150	175	155	155	150	175	155	155	150
	ft. in.	ft. in.	ft. in.	ft. in.	ft. in.	ft. in.	ft. in.	ft. in.	ft. in.	ft. in.	ft. in.	ft. in.	ft. in.	ft. in.	ft. in.	ft. in.
Diameter of flywheel	8 2	8 10	10 12	8 14	1 10	2 11	2 12	1 14	2 11	2 12	2 12	7 14	7 10	10 12	2 12	7 14 7
Overall Dimensions { At right angles to the shaft	9 10 12	6 14	5 17	5 11	10 12	10 13	9 17	4 12	6 13	1 14	1 15	9 12	10 12	2 13	1 15 9
Parallel to the shaft	8 4 12	2 15	9 19	0 13	9 16	5 19	0 25	3 21	0 23	8 25	7 30	3 24	0 28	2 30	6 34 8
Height	8 6 12	2 16	5 18	4 10	10 12	10 14	9 18	4 12	9 14	9 16	5 18	1 12	2 14	9 16	5 18 0
Height desired for erection	13 6 19	1 27	2 29	7 17	1 21	8 25	5 30	3 21	8 25	6 27	10 30	3 19	4 25	7 27	0 30 2
Depth of foundations.	7 3 9	6 12	5 14	1 8	10 10	10 12	2 14	9 10	12	2 13	11 14	9 10 12	2 13	2 14 9
Approximate nett weight tons	6·5	19	41·5	61·5	24	37·5	57	100	51	76·5	93	135	51·5	91·5	114	171

TABLE III. (High Speed Engines.)

	Three Cylinder Engines.					Four Cylinder Engines.					
B.H.P.	105	180	360	510	700	140	240	400	500	760	950
Revolutions per minute	340	270	225	200	175	340	270	240	200	175	175
	ft. in.	ft. in.	ft. in.	ft. in.	ft. in.	ft. in.	ft. in.	ft. in.	ft. in.	ft. in.	ft. in.
Diameter of fly-wheel	5 3	6 7	8 10	10 6	12 6	5 3	6 7	8 10	10 6	12 2	12 6
Width of bed-plate	3 7	4 3	5 11	6 11	7 10	3 7	4 5	5 7	6 7	7 5	7 10
Overall length	13 1	14 9	21 8	24 3	28 10	15 5	18 4	23 4	26 11	31 6	33 6
Total height	7 3	8 6	11 6	13 1	15 5	7 3	8 10	11 2	12 6	14 5	15 5
Overall width	6 7	7 10	10 2	11 10	13 9	6 7	7 10	10 2	11 10	13 5	13 9
Depth of foundation	5 7	6 7	9 2	10 10	13 1	5 7	6 11	8 6	10 2	11 10	13 1
Height desired for erection	10 6	12 6	17 5	20 4	24 3	10 6	13 5	16 5	19 0	23 0	24 3

with all internal combustion engines the water supply is one of the first considerations, and needs to be carefully watched. Thermometers are usually provided giving the temperatures of the jacket water in each of the cylinders, and the supply of water can be separately regulated by means of cocks for each cylinder. The thermometers however are more necessary with a closed pipe circulation than with the ordinary arrangement where the flow of water can be seen, and this latter method is to be preferred where circumstances permit. As the supply of water is separate in each cylinder jacket, being arranged by branch pipes off the main supply pipe, and delivering into a common outlet pipe for all the cylinders, it is quite possible if there be an obstruction in one pipe for the water to be entirely cut off one cylinder without interrupting the main flow. The only indication in this event with the closed circuit system is a rise in the temperature of the jacket of the cylinder so obstructed, but with the open flow arrangement the stoppage is at once noted by the driver. The temperature of the cooling water as it leaves the jacket is best kept in the neighbourhood of 120° Fahr. in temperate climates, though it is perfectly safe to allow it to rise to as much as 180° Fahr. for a prolonged period. In Diesel engines of the ordinary design, the heat carried away by the jacket water is usually between 20 and 25 per cent. of the calorific value of the fuel, or some 60 per cent. of the heat actually converted into useful work reckoned as indicated horse power developed by the engine. One H.P. hour is equivalent to $\frac{33000 \times 60}{778} = 2,544$ B.Th.Us. per hour, so that the heat abstracted by the jacket water may be taken as $2,544 \times \cdot 6$ or about 1,500 B.Th.Us. per hour. Allowing a temperature rise in the water of 60° F. the quantity required per hour per I.H.P. developed by the engine should be about 25 lb. or $2\frac{1}{2}$ gallons per I.H.P. hour, and the allowance usually made is 4 gallons per B.H.P. hour, which from the above figures is an ample supply and is indeed never exceeded. Generally the quantity is considerably less and is frequently under 3 gallons per B.H.P. hour at full load.

The perfect combustion of the fuel oil in the cylinder prevents the valves from becoming very dirty, but if the machine is run for a considerable period without cleaning the combustion is not so good, the exhaust becomes smoky and the exhaust valve gets foul more quickly. In any case it is preferable to clean this valve regularly and as frequently as possible, though where careful attention is paid to the operation of the engine and no smoking of the exhaust allowed, it is quite feasible and satisfactory to clean it only two or three times a year. In most cases it is convenient to take out the exhaust valves about once a fortnight, and as the whole valve and seating may be quickly removed and as quickly replaced by a spare valve and seating the time lost during the operation is very small. The valve can then be cleaned at leisure and put back when the spare one is taken out at the end of the next fortnight. Such frequent cleaning is by no means absolutely essential for the satisfactory operation of the engine, but as in most installations it does not cause the least inconvenience, it is to be recommended. It is, however, of more importance that the fuel valve should be cleaned regularly, and certainly once every fortnight if possible, while the valves of the fuel pumps should also be overhauled at the same time and cleaned with oil and, if necessary, ground on their seats. Such attention, which takes very little time, materially reduces the running costs, and frequently minimizes the cost for repairs.

Owing to the high pressure of compression it is essential that all valves and joints subjected to the pressure should be perfectly tight and free from leakage. Leakage may occur through any of the valves, through the joint between the cylinder head and cylinder, or past the piston, and of course would also be apparent in the event of a crack developing in the cylinder. The effect of such leakage, which is also a trouble with most other internal combustion engines, is to prevent the necessary high temperature corresponding to the top compression pressure being reached, and hence combustion of the fuel is in such cases incomplete.

It is evident that this state of affairs will render it difficult for the engine to maintain its full power, since leakage is a pure loss of power, but with a liberally designed compressor it is always possible to overcome the difficulty by raising the pressure of the air used to inject the fuel into the cylinder, though this necessarily lowers the efficiency of the engine, and must only be looked upon as a temporary measure. The exhaust valve is generally the most liable to leak as it is subjected to the severest conditions, but with frequent cleaning not much trouble is likely to be experienced. In any case a very short time spent in grinding the valve upon its seat will soon render it tight. Leakage past the fuel inlet valve occasionally takes place, resulting in too early ignition, with a corresponding drop of efficiency, as may be readily seen on an indicator diagram, besides causing a knock on the engine; and it is a good plan, in order to avoid this, to test the valve at the same time as it is cleaned, that is about once a fortnight. In the event of leakage the valve should be ground in, but occasionally it is a result of a loose valve spindle, as very little play is allowable.

Great care should be taken at all times when handling the fuel valve, as any neglect of this valve may result in considerable diminution of the efficiency of the motor, even though it does not have a more serious effect. The needle (*E, Fig.* 26) should work easily in the glands and also in its guide above the lever where it enters into the spring casing, and it should be gently handled when taken out, as if bent in a slight degree it is liable to work badly.

The adjustment of the needle is usually arranged by means of a lock nut at the top where it screws into or is otherwise connected to the spring spindle above. The lock nut should be marked so that it is always set back at the same position as previously, when the needle is taken apart, and when required the length of the needle can easily be varied by setting the lock nut at a different angle, so that very minute alterations may be made.

If the bottom of the needle becomes damaged by any means and a cut or mark of any sort is caused, the surface should be carefully rubbed with sandpaper, to make it smooth, though usually it is sufficient to clean with oil. If the face of the needle has been altered at any time, the opening of the valve must be adjusted before running the engine, this being done first by admitting some compressed air to the injection pipe from the air reservoir, whose valve however is immediately closed. The engine is then barred round very slowly, and the exhaust valve held open by hand. At the moment when the fuel inlet valve is lifted off its seating by the cam and valve lever, the air can be heard issuing from the exhaust valve, and the timing of the opening can be properly adjusted by altering the lock nut previously mentioned, so that the lifting of the valve occurs at the exact moment required, namely, just before the crank reaches its top dead centre in its direction of rotation, or in other words just before the piston reaches the top of its stroke.

All the parts of the pulveriser should be cleaned with paraffin and a small brush, so that all the holes and channels should be quite free. It will not be found necessary to renew the packing for the needle at very frequent intervals, provided it is well packed in the first instance, tallow string packing being preferable to any special composition.

Occasionally it happens that the needle shows a tendency to stick to the seat, which may be caused by bad combustion and consequent smokiness, due to an overload, or possibly to the cylinder cover becoming hot, owing to poor or insufficient circulation of cooling water, and in this latter case the cooling space in the cylinder cover should at once be cleaned out. The same effect may also be produced by the injection air carrying with it small particles of matter, caused by too liberal lubrication of the compressor, some of the oil being forced into the reservoir and thence to the fuel valve.

It is not often that any trouble occurs with leakage past the piston, as particular care is taken in the construction of the rings, but it may happen that one or more of them becomes cracked or broken, when, of course, replacement is necessary, this being the most troublesome repair that is likely to have to be made on a Diesel engine in the ordinary course of running. The two top rings are subjected to the greatest heat and are the most liable to stick, and hence great care is taken in fitting them. Very little clearance is allowed between the piston and cylinder cover—only about one-third of that usually permitted with most other internal combustion engines on account of the high compression pressure—and should this be diminished to an appreciable extent by wear, the piston rod must be lengthened by the insertion of a liner of the requisite thickness on the top side of the crank pin bearing. This is not a common trouble, and is perhaps the least likely reason of imperfect combustion, and a knock on the engine is more likely to arise from a wrong setting of the cam operating the fuel inlet valve and causing it to open too early, while another possibility is end play in the top or bottom end connecting rod bearing. The latter defect is generally due to the bearing being wrongly fitted in the first instance, and does not often develop after the engine has been put to work.

In any engine, springs may always be expected to be some source of trouble, and it is necessary to have at least one and preferably more spare sets for every spring on the machine. As a matter of fact, a broken spring seldom has any serious effect, and engines often run a considerable time without the breakage being noticed, and in any case a broken spring can be replaced in a very short time.

With the long pistons which are always employed with Diesel engines the obliquity of the connecting rod seems to have little tendency to wear the cylinder liner oval to any extent, and an 80 H.P. engine which the author gauged after running some eight years showed that the cylinder was true within two thousandths of an inch. With the excellence of the design and manufacture of the air compressors employed for Diesel engines, in spite of the heavy duty they are called upon to perform, no special precautions need be taken in their operation. The possible troubles are those common to all machinery of this class, namely breaking of piston rings, and the springs, but such occurrences are rare.

The lubrication of the parts of a Diesel engine needs no more than ordinary attention, but as the quantity of fuel oil used is so small, the amount of lubricating oil employed appears to be relatively large, and it is indeed an item in the cost of running quite comparable with the fuel cost, hence the supply should be well regulated. The small fuel pumps which are provided are arranged so that the quantity delivered from the oil reservoir may be varied within a wide range, and the difference in the consumption with careful attention is well worth consideration. With large engines the oil which collects in the crank chamber is generally freed from water by being passed through a filter and used over again. As an outside figure it may be taken that the consumption of good lubricating oil with a 250 B.H.P. engine is about 1 gallon for four hours' running; being lower for slow speed than high speed engines, but of course if the oil is filtered the total cost should not be debited against the engine. It is very desirable, especially in the case of multi-cylinder engines, to take indicator cards at not too widely spaced intervals to ascertain that each cylinder is doing its proper amount of work, since it is quite possible to throw a considerable overload on one or more of the cylinders which could be avoided in a few minutes were the fact known, by altering the test cocks. Moreover, in installations in which the engine is employed for a drive where the power is intermittent (as for instance a mill, or shafting of any sort), by the addition of machines, the driving engine may become overloaded without the fact being apparent, and though a Diesel engine will readily take a 10 or 15 per cent. overload for two or three hours, it is inadvisable to allow this continually, and it is a point of real economy in such cases to provide additional power.

Cost of Operation of Diesel Engines.—It is, of course, always difficult and sometimes misleading to institute direct comparisons between different types of engines without a particular knowledge of all the conditions prevailing, but it is at the same time possible to take a general view of the advantages to be derived in certain common cases, more especially as there is at the present time a large amount of data relating to actual results which cannot be refuted. At sea, as is shown later, there may be many reasons for the employment of Diesel or other oil engines apart from the question of economy, but on land that is not the case, and, speaking generally, the success of the Diesel engine for this work must depend entirely on the reduction in *total* running costs it can show in comparison with steam and gas engines. The question is obviously not merely one of fuel economy, since there are a host of other considerations which come into play, and were it solely a matter of the cost of the oil consumed, in comparison with the cost of the coal used with gas and steam engine plant, the adoption of the Diesel engine would of necessity become almost universal. Capital cost, however, must always be an important consideration, and this also exercises a considerable effect upon the annual running costs owing to the necessary allowance which has to be made for interest and depreciation on the plant, and as at the present time a Diesel engine is dearer than either a steam engine with boiler and accessories, or a suction gas plant, this point puts the former at a certain disadvantage, though the difference is relatively small. In all new installations, and also frequently in additions to existing ones, the question of space occupied by the plant becomes of importance inasmuch as suitable buildings have to be constructed for the accommodation, and where the land is of high value, which is often the case, the expense involved in acquiring this makes the question an even more urgent one. In this matter the Diesel engine has the advantage, since it is much smaller for the same power than a steam or gas plant, and in many instances where additional power is required, and extension of premises is impossible, the question of the type of engine to be employed solves itself automatically in favour of the Diesel motor.

Though on land, reliability of operation is not usually of the same vital importance as at sea owing to spare power commonly being available, it frequently happens that perfect freedom from any possibility of breakdown is the deciding factor, and that a stoppage of but a few hours' duration may nullify the whole advantage of very much decreased running costs. It is for this reason that new types of machinery are so long in finding general adoption in spite of the undoubted economies they are capable of effecting until they have passed through long periods of satisfactory operation. After the wide experience of the last sixteen years with Diesel engines this point can no longer be said to weigh against them, and it is now admitted that in reliability they are quite equal to the best class of steam engine, and rather superior to gas engines. There is further the important point to be remembered that a Diesel engine is practically self-contained, whereas with the gas and steam engines there are the producer and boiler respectively to be considered as possible sources of failure, besides some auxiliaries which are unnecessary with Diesel engines. The next point which has to be considered is the cost of attendance and repairs, and it is well known that this item may easily reach a figure comparable with the fuel bill. This question is really dependent on the last, and the fact that the Diesel engine is a reliable and simple machine naturally reacts on the amount which has to be expended annually on wages, renewals, etc., which is relatively small, and may with safety be put at not more than three-quarters of that allowed for steam and gas engines. In fact this figure is very conservative, as may be understood when it is remembered that stokers for the boilers or producers may be dispensed with entirely, and it has generally been found that two-thirds is a more relative estimate. The amount to be apportioned in any estimate for renewals and repairs is always difficult to determine, as there are such wide variations, but there are many actual instances where this cost is but a few pounds per annum for large Diesel engines. There are certain advantages which should not be lost sight of in any comparison between engine types, but which cannot readily be expressed in money value, though their importance is great. There is the question of standby losses which always enters into consideration, and may cause a large addition to fuel costs, more particularly in the case of steam engines, and to a lesser extent with gas engines, that is to say, losses produced in the generating portion of the plant (the boiler or gas producer) when the engine itself is not running. In a Diesel engine these are, of course, absolutely non-existent, since the machine may be started up at a moment's notice immediately it is required. Another point of importance is the fact that in the large majority of installations, engines, during the greater portion of their operation, run at a comparatively low load factor, that is to say, generate a power much below their normal (and consequently most efficient) output. In a steam engine the efficiency falls very considerably with a decrease of the load, and in a gas engine the variation is very marked though not so serious. In a Diesel engine, on the other hand, the difference per B.H.P. hour at full load and at half or even quarter is relatively small, as may be seen from the following figures of consumption which most manufacturers guarantee with cylinders of 80 H.P. and upwards.

·42 lb. per B.H.P. hour at full load.
·45 ,, ,, ,, ,, three-quarters load.
·50 ,, ,, ,, ,, half load.
·51 ,, ,, ,, ,, quarter load.

The following figures which are given regarding the running costs of Diesel engines must not be taken too definitely as applying to every case, but they give a fair idea of what may be expected in ordinary installations. The size of the plant naturally makes some considerable difference, though not so much as with other engines for reasons given above, while the nearer the annual load factor approaches unity the lower becomes the cost of running per B.H.P. hour.

Considering an engine of 200 B.H.P. running for 300 days in the year an average of 15 hours per day at a load factor throughout of 60 per cent., the number of B.H.P. hours per annum would be $300 \times 15 \times 200 \times \cdot 6 = 540,000$. The fuel consumption may be taken at 0·5 lb. per B.H.P. hour, which from the guarantee figures given above is a high estimate, and with the price of crude petroleum at 45s. per ton the cost of fuel would be $£ \dfrac{\cdot 5 \times 540,000}{2,240} \times 2\frac{1}{4}$ = £270 per annum. The wages for the attendants would be about £200, while general maintenance and repairs may be estimated at £50, and waste, water, stores and sundries at another £20. Good lubricating oil for Diesel engines can be purchased at 1s. 3d. per gallon, and the quantity consumed by such an engine, assuming that it is not filtered and used over again, would be in the neighbourhood of 2 to 3 gallons per day, according to the care exercised by the attendant, and the annual cost may be put at £50. The cost of a Diesel engine, including erection, foundations and setting to work, varies at the present time from £8 to £11 per B.H.P., being dependent on the size, type (high or low speed, two or four cycle), the cost of foundations, accessibility of site, and other considerations, but for the purposes of estimate may be taken as £10 per B.H.P., or £2,000 for the engine in question. Making the usual allowance of 10 per cent. for interest and depreciation on the plant, an amount of £200 per annum has to be added to the yearly running costs, which may then be summarized as follows :—

Estimate of Annual Working Costs of 200 B.H.P. Diesel Engine Running 4,500 Hours

	Total £	Per B.H.P. hr. pence.
Fuel oil at 45s. per ton	270	0·12
Wages for attendants	200	0·089
Maintenance and repairs	50	0·022
Waste, water, stores, etc	20	0·009
Lubricating oil	50	0·022
Interest and depreciation on plant	200	0·089
Total	£790	0·351d.

Omitting interest and depreciation, the working costs aggregate to £590 per annum or 0·26d. per B.H.P. hour, and this figure may be relied upon as likely to cover by far the larger number of cases met with in ordinary practice, while in big installations an overall cost of 0·25d. per B.H.P. hour, including interest and depreciation charges, may be assumed as correct. In four installations with which the author is familiar, in none of which does the annual load factor rise above 30 per cent., the yearly working costs, excluding interest and depreciation, amount respectively to 0·26d., 0·31d., 0·21d. and 0·23d. per B.H.P. hour, or an average of 0·25d. for the four plants, the period over which the costs were reckoned being in no case less than six months.

Although in the matter of economy the Diesel engine shews more particularly to advantage in the smaller sizes, that is to say, up to about 1,500 B.H.P., now that the manufacture of very large engines has become a practical proposition, it is interesting to note how motors up to 4,000 B.H.P. can be shewn to compare favourably with the most efficient modern steam turbines.

The following data are based upon an actual case and refer to an installation of 2,500 K.W. units, considering Diesel engines in the one case and steam turbines in the other. The Diesel motor is of the two-cycle single-acting type, running at a normal speed for this size of about 130 revolutions per minute. The estimates are based on a year's working assuming an actual running period of 6,000 hours per annum, and an average load on the generator of 2,000 K.W. The cost of fuel oil is taken at 50s. per ton, and of coal at 15s. per ton.

Considering first the capital costs, and omitting switchboard and cables, etc., although the Diesel set is more expensive, there is a substantial saving in the cost of buildings, and the figures work out as follows—

	£
2,500 K.W. Diesel generating set with all necessary accessories	25,000
Engine room, foundations, etc., including cost of site	5,000
Total cost of Diesel plant	30,000
2,500 K.W. Turbo-generator with condensing plant, boilers and accessories	13,000
Engine and boiler house, foundations, chimney, etc., including cost of site	13,000
Total cost of steam plant	26,000

The approximate annual running costs in the two cases are as under:—

Diesel Set.—The consumption of oil with a Diesel motor of this size is about 0·45 lb. per B.H.P. hour, or with an alternator of ordinary efficiency about 0·66 lb. per K.W. hour. The lubricating oil, which is admittedly an expensive factor with Diesel engines, may be taken at 0·01 lb. per K.W. hour, although the builders would probably guarantee a lower figure if necessary. The cost of suitable oil is about 1s. 6d. per gallon.

With regard to cooling water a good deal depends on the circumstances, but in the case in question, sea water was available at a total cost of $\frac{1}{2}d$. per 1,000 gallons. The amount required is about 6 gallons per K.W. hour, but for piston cooling, fresh water is necessary, about 1$\frac{1}{2}$ gallons per K.W. hour being the quantity. This would of course be recooled in a cooling tower, and only the usual 10 per cent. make up losses need be reckoned upon.

Calculating on this basis, the total cost becomes:—

	£
Cost of fuel $= \dfrac{2{,}000 \times 6{,}000 \times \cdot 66 \times 2'5}{2{,}240} =$	8,850
Cost of attendance; four men and one foreman at an average of £2 per week	520
Water for jackets and pistons	200
Lubricating oil, etc.	1,000
Repairs and maintenance at 1 per cent.	250
Interest and depreciation at 10 per cent.	2,500
	£13,320

Steam Plant.—A steam turbo-generating set of 2,500 K.W. has a consumption of 15 lb. of steam (superheated) per K.W. hour, or allowing 30 per cent. stand-by losses, and an evaporation of 7 lb. of steam per pound of coal, the quantity of coal per K.W. hour at an average load of 2,000 K.W., is 2·8, which is 5,600 lb. per hour, or 15,000 tons per annum.

The amount of condensing water necessary is some 150,000 gallons per hour, or 900 million gallons per annum, for which the total cost of pumping may be taken at ½d. per 1,000 gallons as before. The following gives the overall estimate:—

	£
Cost of coal = 15,000 tons at 15s.	11,250
Cost of attendance; 6 men and 1 foreman at an average of £2 per week.	730
Condensing and feed water	2,000
Lubricating oil, etc.	250
Repairs and Maintenance at 1 per cent.	135
Interest and depreciation at 10 per cent.	1,350
	£15,715

The saving with the Diesel set thus amounts to about £2,400 or more than 15 per cent., and it will be noticed that no allowance has been made for depreciation of buildings, which item would greatly favour the Diesel equipment.

The respective costs per K.W. hour are $0.314\,d.$ for the steam plant, and $0.26\,d.$ for the Diesel driven set.

CHAPTER V

TESTING DIESEL ENGINES

OBJECT OF TESTING—TEST ON 200 B.H.P. DIESEL ENGINE—TEST ON 300 B.H.P. HIGH SPEED MARINE ENGINE—TEST ON 500 B.H.P. ENGINE—TEST ON HIGH SPEED DIESEL ENGINE.

Object of Testing.—The working of Diesel engines is so regular, and the efficiency is such a predetermined factor, that, generally speaking, such elaborate tests of fuel consumption as are usual with steam plants, are not essential, and there is very seldom any question of the guarantee being exceeded. The majority of Diesel engines supplied for land work are for the purpose of driving dynamos, either direct or through a belt, and hence most tests are made on the combined set, when, as with steam dynamo plants, it is convenient to express the fuel consumption in pounds per kilowatt hour. The efficiency of the dynamo is readily obtained separately, so that the actual brake horse power of the engine is at once determined, and hence a test on a direct coupled set is in every way satisfactory, and is more convenient than a brake test, especially for large engines. Though the main object of all engine testing from a commercial point of view must be to obtain the actual cost of running the machine at its various loads, or in other words the amount of fuel it consumes per H.P. hour, much other useful and interesting information may be obtained. The calorific value of the fuel oil used in Diesel engines differs very considerably, and though this has little effect from the commercial aspect, since the oil of lower heating value is generally cheaper, and thus though more oil may be used the cost is approximately the same. An ordinarily complete test on a Diesel engine should aim at producing the following results: The normal output, and overload capacity of the engine; the fuel consumption per I.H.P. and per B.H.P. hour at various loads; the mechanical efficiency; the quantity of cooling water required with a desirable rise of temperature (usually 60° F.); and the heat account to determine the respective amounts of heat, (1) converted to useful work, (2) carried away in the jacket water, and (3) dispelled in the exhaust gases.

The amount of lubricating oil is of importance, but this can hardly be obtained with any degree of accuracy in a short test and is best noted over a week's run; as a Diesel engine uses much more oil when starting up than in ordinary operation, the amount should never be gauged from a trial on the testing bed. The instruments and appliances necessary for such a test are neither elaborate nor expensive. The fuel consumed may be measured by weight or by volume provided its specific gravity be accurately determined. The temperatures of the jacket waters for each cylinder (in a multi-cylinder engine) are obtained from thermometers, placed in thermometer pockets, one in each cylinder head just at the water-outlet, and a common thermometer for all cylinders in the supply pipe to give the temperature of the inlet water. The temperature of the exhaust gases is registered on a high reading thermometer fixed in the exhaust pipe as near the cylinders as possible, and all these thermometers, except for the exhaust gases and the inlet cooling water, are employed under ordinary working conditions and need not be special for the test. The weight of the jacket cooling water can be conveniently found by delivering it alternately into measuring tanks of known capacity as with the common arrangement for estimating the quantity of condensed water from a steam engine, or the feed water entering the boiler in a steam engine or boiler test respectively. Indicator cards have to be taken frequently and simultaneously off each cylinder, which is provided with indicator cocks and operating gear for this purpose. The indicators employed may be of the ordinary Crosby or similar type and indicator pistons and springs are commonly used in which a pressure of about 400 lb. per sq. inch is represented by a compression of 1 inch, a common arrangement with Continental engines being one in which a pressure of 1 kilogram per sq. centimetre gives a movement of the indicator pencil of 0·8 millimetre. The calorific value of the oil has to be obtained, and this may be done in a special calorimeter in which combustion takes place with oxygen under high pressure. The calorific value may also be determined by analysis of the fuel into its three main constituents, carbon, hydrogen and sulphur—the oxygen and nitrogen being negligible quantities—and multiplying the weight of each of these elements by the respective known calorific values of each element, and adding to obtain the resultant calorific value, though this method is not perfectly satisfactory. The figures for carbon, hydrogen, and sulphur are respectively about 15,540, 52,000, and 4,500 B.Th.Us. per pound. The heat passing away in the exhaust gases can be determined from a knowledge of the weight of exhaust gas, its specific heat at constant pressure and the excess of temperature over that of the atmosphere.

Let t = the difference in temperature between the exhaust gases and the atmosphere.

V = volume swept through by the piston in cubic feet in one stroke.

w = weight of one cubic foot of air at atmospheric pressure and temperature.

K_p = specific heat of air at constant pressure.

W = weight of fuel consumed per revolution of the engine.

The weight of fuel and air entering the cylinder (for a single cylinder four-cycle engine) per revolution is $\frac{1}{2} Vw + W$, and hence the heat rejected to the exhaust is $(\frac{1}{2} Vw + W) K_p t$ B.Th.U. per revolution of the engine. This method, though giving a sufficiently accurate result for most purposes is not exact because the temperature of the air when the cylinder is full is above the atmospheric temperature to a degree which cannot be easily determined. If closer results are required an analysis of the exhaust gases must be made by collecting samples and testing them in an Orsat or similar apparatus. From the relative quantities of nitrogen and oxygen in the exhaust gases, the excess of air admitted to the engine over that required for combustion may be obtained. From the analysis of the oil the weight of air needed for complete combustion may be obtained from the equivalent combining weights of air (or rather the oxygen in it) with carbon, hydrogen, and sulphur. By multiplying the weight so obtained by the ratio of the air drawn into the cylinder to that used during combustion the actual weight of air taken into the cylinder per pound of oil is obtained, and the remaining calculations are as before.

Diesel engines run so regularly and with so little variation in any way, that comparatively short tests are quite satisfactory and reliable so long as frequent readings are taken to enable reasonable checks to be made against personal errors in measurements. Indicator cards should be taken every five minutes or quarter-hour, dependent on the duration of the trial, and as mentioned before, these are to be taken on all the cylinders of an engine simultaneously, even if this necessitates two or more operators, since it is, of course, impossible to rely on all the engines doing equal work or that the indicated power does not vary in the short interval of time elapsing while a man taking the indicator cards moves from one cock to another. The power developed by the dynamo is ascertained in the usual manner with a tested ammeter and voltmeter, and the work done in driving the air compressor may be obtained, if desired, by taking indicator cards of the pump cylinders, and if the compressors are separately driven, as is sometimes the case, the power absorbed by the motor has also to be noted.

In the following pages descriptions and results of tests on Diesel engines by well-known authorities are given, and these may well be taken as a basis in conducting similar tests. Some of them were made with varying loads on the engine, and trials under such conditions are frequently necessary, and in any case valuable, as most plants operate for a comparative large proportion of their life at less than the full load, and hence the results on normal load do not always represent the working conditions of the engine.

Test on a 200 B.H.P. Diesel Engine.—This test was made by Herrn Chr. Eberle, and described in a paper read before the Bayerischer Revisions Verein, on a 200 B.H.P. Diesel four-cycle slow speed single acting engine of two cylinders coupled direct to a continuous current generator. The test was made under working conditions after the engine had been installed. The diameter of the cylinder is 430 mm. (16·9 inches) and the piston stroke 680 mm. (26·8 inches), while the normal speed of rotation is 160 revolutions per minute. The engine is provided with a flywheel on each side of the cylinders; and there are two two-stage air compressors, one driven off each connecting rod. The consumption of fuel was obtained by employing an open reservoir connected by piping to the fuel pump, the test being started at the moment the oil in the reservoir reached a definite point as indicated by a gauge glass. The oil in the reservoir was kept up to its original level by replenishing from a small can, containing a known weight of oil, and tests were rejected if any of the intermediate readings varied by more than 2 per cent. The power developed by the cylinders was obtained by taking frequent indicator cards, and cards were also obtained from the air compressors. The speed was noted every minute, and the pressure in the compressors was taken. The oil fuel was tested and found to have a calorific value of 9,813 calories, which corresponds to 17,660 B.Th.U., and the specific gravity of the oil was 0·893. In Table IV the chief figures and deduced data are given, but as the quantity of cooling water was not measured, a detailed heat account could not be obtained, though the exhaust gases were analysed in an Orsat apparatus. It is to be noticed that the speed of the engine varied between 164·5 and 159·9 from no load to overload, a difference of only 2·8 per cent., the respective indicated powers being 46·4 and 298·4 I.H.P.

At normal full load the final pressure in the air pump cylinder from the diagrams was 61 atmospheres, and the combined indicated H.P. for the two cylinders of one pump was 6·82 I.H.P. or 13·64 I.H.P. for the two pumps, assuming them to be doing equal work. The temperature of the exhaust gases varies considerably with the load, being 131° C. at no load and 466° C. when the engine is developing its

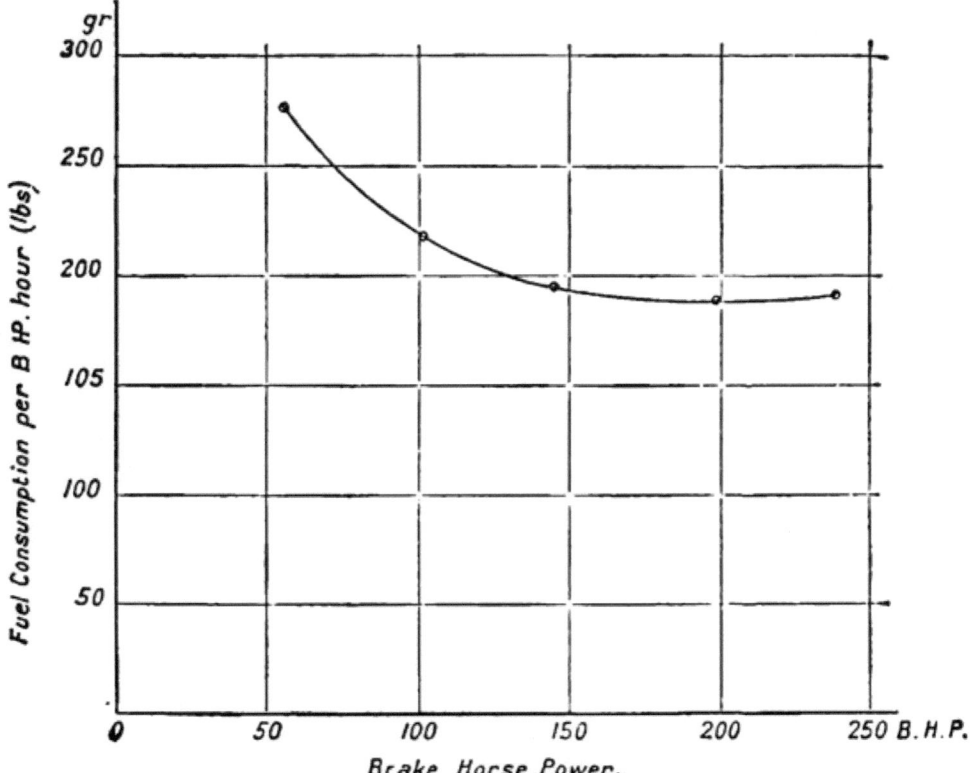

Fig. 82.—Curve showing Fuel Consumption.

maximum power. The consumption of fuel at the various loads is shown graphically in *Fig.* 82, the difference from half-load to full load being comparatively small. As showing the constancy of the fuel consumption with Diesel engines, four machines of similar type and construction were tested together, when it was found that the respective amounts of oil used per B.H.P. hour were 185·0, 189·9, 189·7 and 190·4 grams.

Test on 300 B.H.P. High Speed Marine Engine.—
This test was carried out by Herrn. Chr. Eberle, on a 300

TABLE IV.

			No Load.	Quarter Full Load.	Half Full Load.	Three-quarter full Load.	Normal Full Load.	Overload.
1	Duration of test	min.	81.9	55.5	82.0	87.5	67.5	27.5
2	Revolutions per minute		164.5	163.5	162.9	162.0	160.2	159.9
3	Compression pressure in air pump —							
4	(a) High pressure cylinder	atmos.	39.8	42.0	46.0	52.3	60.1	62.0
	(b) Low pressure cylinder		0.5	4.2	4.9	5.4	6.4	7.0
5	Indicated H.P. (a) A cylinder	I.H.P.	23.2	54.9	79.6	103.6	130.4	151.0
6	(b) B cylinder	„	20.2	54.7	75.2	101.1	130.8	147.4
7	(c) Total I.H.P.	„	46.4	109.6	154.8	204.7	261.2	298.4
8	Indicated H.P. of air pump (a) High pressure cylinder	„	—	—	—	—	3.43	—
9	(b) Low pressure cylinder	„	—	—	—	—	3.39	—
10	(c) Total	„	—	—	—	—	6.82	—
11	(d) Total for two pumps	„	—	34.4	67.2	98	13.64	153.2
12	Output of Dynamo	K.W.	—	46.7	91.3	133.1	132.4	216.5
13	„ „	E.H.P.	—	85.5	90.5	91	180.1	91
14	Efficiency of dynamo	per cent.	—	54.6	100.9	146.3	91	237.9
15	Brake horse power of Engine = $\frac{\text{E.H.P. of Dynamo}}{\text{efficiency of dynamo}}$	B.H.P.	—	—	—	—	197.9	—
16	Mechanical efficiency = $\frac{\text{I.H.P.}-\text{I.H.P. of compressors}}{\text{B.H.P. of engine}}$	per cent.	—	—	—	—	79.9	—
17	Oil consumption (a) Total	gms.	10,000	14,000	30,000	42,000	42,000	21,000
18	(b) Per B.H.P. hour	„	—	277.2	217.6	196.0	188.6	192.6
19	(c) Per B.H.P. hour reckoned for oil of 10,000 calories	„	—	271.9	213.5	193.5	185	188.9
20	(d) Per I.H.P. hour	„	157.8	138.1	141.8	140.4	142.9	153.5
21	(e) Per I.H.P. hour	„	154.8	135.5	139.1	137.7	140.2	150.6
22	Cooling water temperature (a) Inlet	°C.	9.0	8.9	8.7	8.7	9.0	9.0
23	(b) Outlet from cylinder A (average)	°C.	51.7	46.9	55.7	55.6	55.7	55.5
24	Exhaust gases (a) Temperature	°C.	131	191	263	—	—	46.4
25	(b) CO^2 present	per cent.	1.7	2.2	3.9	—	—	9.3
26	(c) Oxygen present	„	18.0	17.5	15.0	—	—	8.3
27	Heat used per B.H.P. hour (Oil = 9,810 calories per kg.) calories		—	2,719	2,135	1,932	1,850	1,889

HEAT ACCOUNT FOR 1 KG. OF FUEL.

			Calories.	%	Calories.	%	Calories.	%	Calories.	%	Calories.	%	Calories.	%
28	Heat equivalent (a) Indicated power		4,000	40.8	4,570	46.6	4,450	45.4	4,500	45.9	4,420	45.1	4,110	41.9
29	(b) Effective power		—	—	2,280	23.2	2,900	29.6	3,210	32.7	3,350	34.2	3,280	33.4
30	(c) Friction and air pump		—	—	2,290	23.4	1,550	15.8	1,290	13.2	1,070	10.9	830	8.5
31	Heat lost in cooling water, exhaust gases and radiation		5,810	59.2	5,240	53.4	5,360	54.6	5,310	54.1	5,390	54.9	5,700	58.1

TABLE V.
Results of Tests on High Speed Engine.

No. of Test.		1.	2.	3.	4.	5.	6.	7.	8.	9.	10.	11.	12.
1	Duration of test . . . hours	1·16	1·18	0·83	0·84	0·83	0·85	0·53	0·42	0·49	0·46	0·53	0·60
2	Revolutions per minute . .	256·8	306·6	402·4	493·9	497·4	498·3	501·1	247·4	400·1	488·1	400·5	508·1
3	Indicated horse power—power absorbed by air compressor H.P.	242	296	390	441	408	—	184	148	224	249	399	—
4	Output of dynamo . . K.W.	130·5	156·8	199·2	230·1	225·1	217·7	83·0	70·6	104·9	111·3	217·8	266·7
5	Efficiency of dynamo . . %	88·8	90	90·9	90·3	90·1	89·8	88·0	89·2	90·4	90·0	90·8	90·4
6	Brake horse power developed by engine . . . . B.H.P.	199·6	236·5	297·5	346·5	340·0	330·0	128·2	107·4	158·0	167·6	326·0	394·5
7	Mechanical efficiency = Line 6 / Line 3 %	82·6	79·8	76·2	78·6	83·3	—	69·5	72·6	70·5	67·2	81·8	—
8	Fuel consumption per I.H.P. hour (excluding compressor) lb.	·318	·312	·302	·316	·333	—	·28	·288	·298	·33	·32	—
9	Fuel consumption per B.H.P. hour . . . . . lb.	·415	·42	·43	·444	·448	·463	·446	·443	·477	·555	·434	·465
10	Fuel consumption per B.H.P. hour (with oil 18,000 B.Th.U.'s per pound) . . . . lb.	·419	·424	·434	·448	·452	·467	·45	·447	·481	·559	·438	·469
11	Cooling water. Quantity per B.H.P. hour . . . lb.	66·0	57·5	57·4	55·5	56·5	—	—	—	—	—	—	—
12	Cooling water. Inlet temperature . . . . °F.	55·4	55·4	55·4	55·4	55·4	—	—	—	—	—	—	—
13	Cooling water. Outlet temperature . . . . °F.	93	99·7	98·8	101·5	104	—	—	—	—	—	—	—
14	Exhaust gases. Temperature °F.	612	697	734	831	827	797	432	401	497	617	762	—
15	,, ,, Carbon dioxide %	6·8	8·3	8·4	9·7	9·4	—	4·5	4·4	4·6	4·8	9·6	—
16	,, ,, Oxygen %	8·4	—	8·0	6·2	7·0	—	13·8	14·0	13·2	12·6	8·4	—
17	Calorific value of oil per pound B.Th.U.	—	—	—	—	—	18,130	—	—	—	—	—	—
18	Heat units consumed per I.H.P. hour . . . . B.Th.U.	5,760	5,660	5,470	5,730	6,050	—	5,160	5,210	5,405	5,970	5,890	—
19	Heat units consumed per B.H.P. hour	7,520	7,610	7,800	8,040	8,120	8,370	8,190	8,000	8,650	10,050	7,850	8,410

Heat Account for 1 Pound of Fuel for 5 Tests.

	Test 1.		Test 2.		Test 3.		Test 4.		Test 5.	
	B.Th.U.	%	B.Th.U.	%	B.Th.U.	%	B.Th.U.	%	B.Th.U.	%
Heat equivalent (a) Indicated power	7,900	43.5	8,050	44.3	8,300	45.8	7,955	43.8	7,540	41.5
(b) Effective power	6,060	33.4	5,960	32.9	5,840	32.2	5,700	31.4	5,600	30.9
(c) Friction and all pumps	1,840	10.1	2,090	11.4	2,460	13.6	2,255	12.4	1,940	10.6
Heat carried away by cooling water	6,210	34.3	6,060	33.5	5,760	31.8	5,760	31.8	6,140	33.8
Heat rejected in exhaust gases	4,375	24.1	4,040	22.9	4,340	23.9	4,370	24.1	4,470	24.8
Error and radiation	−375	−1.9	−120	−0.7	−270	−1.5	+45	+0.3	−20	−0.1
Total	18,130	100	18,130	100	18,130	100	18,130	100	18,130	100

B.H.P. four-cylinder four-cycle engine, which at its normal output was designed for a speed of 400 revolutions per minute. The engine is totally enclosed and the cranks are set at 180°; a vertical two stage air compressor mounted on the end of the bed-plate and driven direct off the crank shaft serves for the air supply to all the cylinders. The four fuel pumps are arranged together in the front of the engine and are all driven off the horizontal cam shaft. Forced lubrication is of course adopted, and two small lubricating pumps are driven direct off the end of the crank shaft, the oil being cooled after passing through the bearings, etc., and used over again. Two other small pumps are also driven off the crank shaft for the circulation of the cooling water both for the cylinders and for the exhaust pipe, which was jacketed in this engine. Being intended for ship propulsion the machine is not provided with a governor, but has a safety regulator to prevent the engine running away. The weight of the engine, including the starting vessels and all pumps, was only about 10 tons, while a similar slow speed engine would weigh something over 50 tons. This is equivalent to 30 H.P. per ton weight, which is extremely high.

In the tests the engine was coupled direct to a continuous current generator, which was loaded as required on a resistance, and the power measured by a tested ammeter and voltmeter in the usual way. The engine was run at various speeds between about 250 and 500 revolutions per minute, the variation being obtained by controlling the amount of fuel entering the cylinders by means of a lever. The tests carried out were as follows :—

(1) With normal admission of fuel and speeds of 250, 300, and 500 revolutions per minute. (Tests 1 to 6 in Table V.)

(2) With half normal admission and speeds of 250, 300, 400 and 500 revolutions per minute. (Tests 7 to 10 in Table V.)

(3) With maximum admission and speeds of 400 and 500 revolutions per minute. (Tests 11 and 12 in Table V.)

The efficiency of the dynamo was carefully determined for each speed and output by running it at the various speeds at no load, whence all the losses were calculated and the efficiencies obtained. These are included in the table, but the figures from which they are deduced are omitted. The oil consumption was obtained by taking the supply direct from a vessel with a gauge glass, and at the beginning and end of each test the level of the oil in the vessel was arranged to be at the same point as indicated on the gauge glass, the consumption being made up by adding an accurately weighed

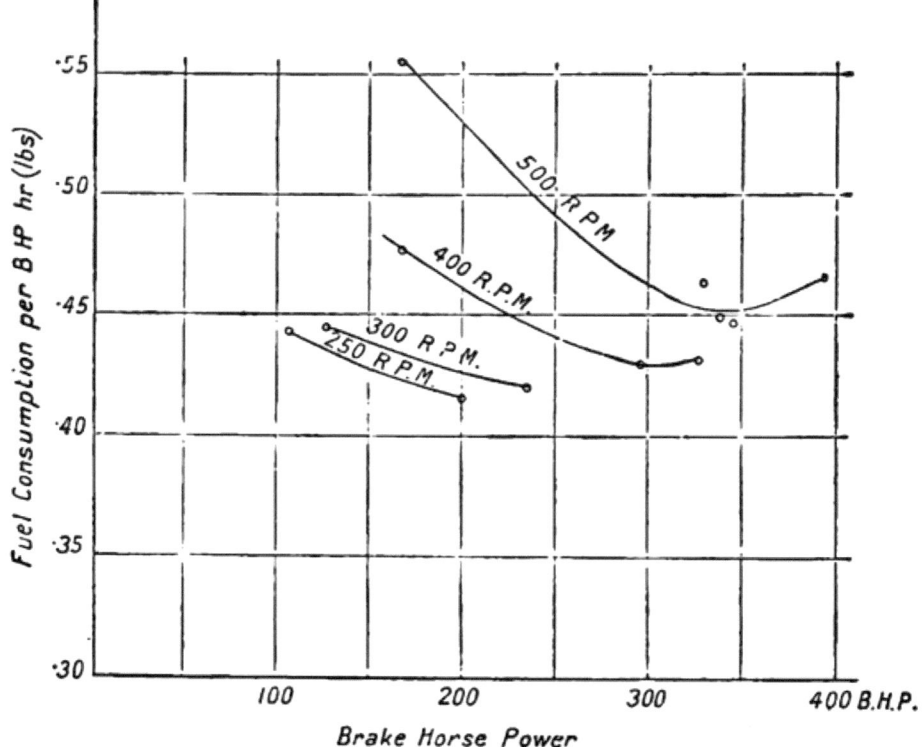

Fig. 83.—Curve showing Fuel Consumption.

amount of oil as required, and by this means intermediate check readings could be taken.

The cooling water was passed through measuring tanks and its quantity determined, and the temperatures at the inlet and outlet as well as that of the exhaust gases were registered by mercury thermometers. In *Fig.* 83 the fuel consumptions are represented graphically under all the conditions of the tests, and show remarkably constant results. At about 250 revolutions per minute the consumption was 189

Tests on 500 B.H.P. Engine.—The following is a slightly abbreviated account of a complete test carried out by Mr. Michael Longridge, on a three-cylinder slow speed four-stroke engine manufactured by Messrs. Carels, Frères, of Ghent [1] :—

The engine was a three-crank inverted vertical, with three single acting cylinders numbered 54, 55, and 56, No. 54 being above the idle end of the crank shaft. Each cylinder was 22·05 in. (560 mm.) diameter, with a piston stroke of 29·53 in. (750 mm.). The normal speed was 150 revolutions per minute.

The valves were placed in the cylinder covers as usual, and were actuated by levers driven by cams on a horizontal shaft, which in turn was driven by a vertical shaft and bevel gear from the idle end of the crank shaft. The cylinders, cylinder covers, and exhaust valves were water cooled, but the pistons were not.

The engine drove a dynamo carried upon a prolongation of the crank shaft.

The air for pulverising the oil and spraying it into the cylinders was compressed in an independent pair of three stage vertical air compressors worked by a two-throw crank shaft, belt driven by a motor receiving current from the dynamo upon the engine crank shaft. The air compressors, therefore, though essential to the working of the engine, were not in this case parts of the engine, and in calculating the mechanical efficiency of the engine from the dynamo output and the indicator diagrams this fact should not be lost sight of. Had the compressors been driven directly by the engine the difference between the work put into the dynamo, which is the brake horse-power, and the indicated horse-power would have been increased by the power required to compress the air.

The areas of the compressor pistons were :—

102·40 sq. in. (660·5 sq. cm.).
32·30 sq. in. (208·1 sq. cm.).
8·79 sq. in. (56·75 sq. cm.).

[1] Annual Report of British Engine, Boiler, and Electrical Insurance Co., Ltd.

and the stroke 7·087 in. (180 mm.), the speed, when compressing to about 64 atmospheres, being about 160 revolutions per minute.

The dynamo was twelve-pole, continuous current, shunt wound, by Lahmeyer & Co., rated to give 450 kilowatts at 550 volts when running at 150 revolutions per minute. The efficiencies given by the makers are :—

At	112 kw.	225 kw.	337 kw.	450 kw.	562 kw.
Efficiency about	·88	·925	·935	·94	·935

and these figures have been adopted in calculating the brake horse power of the engine corresponding to the measured output of the dynamo.

The power was absorbed by iron wire resistance coils, and the load regulated by appropriate switches.

The motor for driving the air compressors was six-pole, shunt wound, continuous current, by the same makers, rated to give 75 B.H.P. at 630 revolutions per minute.

The calculated efficiencies given by the makers are :—

At . .	Full load.	Three-quarter load.	Half-load.	Quarter-load.
Efficiency	90·5	89	86	76·5 m.

Four trials were made, the results of which are shown on the accompanying Tables.

The first, a preliminary trial, intended to be at full load but actually a little low, the second at full load, the third at half load, and the fourth with no external load, the engine driving the air compressors only, and, of course, the dynamo and motor which transmitted the power to them.

With respect to the figures in the Table, the following explanations should be read :—

Line 4.—The diameter of the cylinder of No. 56 engine was gauged. The diameters of the other two were taken from the drawing.

Line 6.—The revolutions were recorded by an engine counter, and the speed indicated by a tachometer.

Line 7.—The water for the jackets was supplied from the town's main, and measured through a water meter which was said to have been recently calibrated.

Line 9.—The discharge pipes from the jackets were conducted to a common pipe discharging into a drain. The same thermometer was used for measuring the temperature of inlet and discharge.

Line 11.—The temperature of the exhaust was measured close to the engine by a mercury thermometer passing through a gland in the exhaust pipe, with compressed nitrogen above the mercury to prevent the latter boiling.

All these observations were taken at intervals of ten minutes.

Line 12.—The gas samples were collected and analysed by Professor Van de Velde, of Ghent.

Line 13.—The oil used was from Galicia. There is considerable doubt about the calorific value of the oil. A sample taken at the time of the trial, and analysed by Professor Van de Velde, gave :—

Carbon	84·81 per cent.
Hydrogen	14·78 ,,
Sulphur	0·17 ,,
	99·76 per cent.

and therefore had a calorific value by calculation of :—

$$\cdot 8481 \times 14{,}540 + \cdot 1478 \times 52{,}000 + \cdot 0017 \times 4{,}000 = 20{,}049 \text{ B.T.U.}$$

As the Professor made no calorimeter test, a sample was sent over to England in March, and tested by Mr. C. I Wilson, who gave the calorific value as 10,120 calories, or 18,220 B.T.U. Owing to the great discrepancy between the two results, and to the improbably high efficiency of the engine resulting from the adoption of the latter value, another sample was sent to England in May and analysed and tested by Dr. Boverton Redwood, who gave the following figures :—

Carbon	83·17 per cent.
Hydrogen	11·56 ,,
Sulphur	0·36 ,,
Oxygen, nitrogen, etc., by difference	4·91 ,,
	100·00

TABLE VI.

No. of Trial			I.	II.	III.	IV.
1	Date	.	Feb. 13	Feb. 14	Feb. 14	Feb. 14
2	Time	.	3.55 p.m. to 5.55 p.m.	9.17 a.m. to 11-12-15	11-21-15 to 1-30-15	2-1-30 to 2-59-30
3	Duration	min.	120	115·25	129	58
4	Diameter of cylinders	. in.	22·05	22·05	22·05	22·05
5	Stroke of pistons	. ft.	2·4605	2·4605	2·4605	2·4605
6	Revolutions per minute	.	150·16	152·8	150·3	150·2
7	Jacket water per minute	.	166·8	169·85	157·85	140
8	Initial temperature of jacket water	°F.	46·3	46·3	46·3	46·3
9	Final temperature of jacket water	°F.	125	127·4	104·6	82·1
10	Temperature of outside air	°F.	48	48	48	48
11	Temperature of exhaust gases	°F.	783	806	496	275
12	Analysis of exhaust gases	CO_2	5·6	6·8	3·2	—
		N	42·9	51·3	21·5	—
		Air	51·5	41·9	75·3	—
13	Oil used	. lb.	390·3	398	221·1	44·23
14	Oil used per hour	. lb.	195·1	207·2	102·8	45·76
15	Blast pressure	Atm.	61·5	66·3	50·9	35
16	Maximum pressure shown by indicator diagrams lb. per sq. in.		510 / 515 / 525	515 / 525 / 500	490 / 480 / 505	485 / 480 / 500

TABLE VI.—Continued.

	No. of Trial		I.	II.	III.	IV.
17	M.E.P. on first piston No. 54	lb. per sq. in.	82.9	80.7	51.6	23.2
	,, on second piston No. 55.	,, ,,	92.3	93.9	52.6	20.10
	,, on third piston No. 56	,, ,,	110.0	115.6	64.8	33.9
18	Average M.E.P. in the three cylinders	,, ,,	95.05	96.7	56.33	25.4
19	Indicated horse-power		609.3	634.8	363.6	163.3
20	Oil per I.H.P. per hour	lb.	0.3202	0.3264	0.2828	0.280
21	Output of dynamo	Kw.	333	352	168.2	22.24
22	Brake horse-power of engine.	B.H.P.	475.5	502.5	245	54.6
23	Horse-power absorbed in friction		133.8	132.3	118.6	108.7
24	$\frac{B.H.P.}{I.H.P.}$		0.78	0.805	0.675	0.334
25	Oil per kilowatt hour	lb.	0.586	0.5886	0.6113	2.057
26	Oil per brake horse-power per hour	lb.	0.4103	0.4123	0.4196	0.838
27	Power absorbed by motor	Kw.	38	41	31.6	23.6
28	Horse-power given out by motor	H.P.	44.8	48.3	36.8	26.2
29	Indicated horse-power in compressor cylinders I.H.P.		36	40	28.8	18.2
30	Power absorbed in belt and compressors H.P.		8	8	8	8
31	Estimated brake horse-power of engine deducting mean of lines 28 and 29 from line 22. B.H.P		435.1	458.7	213.8	32.4
32	Estimate of mechanical efficiency of engine if pump had been driven by it		0.715	0.723	0.588	0.198
33	Oil per brake horse-power per hour.	lb.	0.444	0.451	0.481	1.415

Calorific value, 10,897 calories or 19,600 B.T.U., which is somewhat higher than that calculated from the analysis viz. :—

$$\cdot 8317 \times 14{,}540 + \cdot 1156 \times 52{,}200 + \cdot 0036 \times 4{,}000 = 18{,}144 \text{ B.T.U. per lb.}$$

As Professor Van de Velde's analysis was made from a sample taken at the trial, and it is confirmed by Dr. Redwood's test, it has been inserted in the heat account. The adoption of Mr. Wilson's value of 18,220 B.T.U. would make the thermal efficiency of the engine about 50 per cent., which is so much above the efficiency obtained with smaller engines that the writer cannot accept it without further confirmation. (The author may here remark that it is never satisfactory in estimating the efficiency of an engine to rely upon the heating value of the oil as obtained by *calculation*.)

Line 14.—To weigh the oil used, a small tank fitted with a cock near the bottom was placed on a weighing machine. The tank was first partly filled with oil from a tap in the oil main above it. It was then accurately balanced by weights in the scale pan. A single weight of 2 kilos. was then added to the weights in the scale pan and oil run into the tank till the lever of the machine floated. The 2-kilo. weight was then taken out of the scale pan and the cock at the bottom opened to allow the oil to run into a second tank which fed the engine until the lever again floated. The surface in the feed tank at the beginning of each trial was marked by its contact with a sharp-pointed gauge, and was brought to the same level before a fresh supply was run in from the weighing tank. Except at the preliminary trial on the 13th, when there was some trouble with one of the pipe connexions which required the writer's attention, the times when the surface of the oil in the measuring tank touched the point of the gauge were accurately taken so that the rates of consumption might be recorded.

The leverage of the machine (1 to 10) and the 2-kilo. weight used for weighing 20 kilos. of oil were tested with new accurate weights, and were found to be practically correct, 2 kilos. in the scale pan balancing 2,006 grammes on the machine. The writer has described the method of weighing the oil at length to remove any doubts about its accuracy which might be raised by the figures in the heat account of Trial III.[1]

Lines 17–19.—The mean effective pressures were calculated from indicator diagrams taken at intervals of 15 minutes. The indicators used were on cylinders Nos. 54 and 55, two Crosby's, and on cylinder No. 56, an Elliott Simplex. The cords connecting the indicator to the motion were only about 2 feet long. It will be seen that the mean pressures in the different cylinders differed considerably.

Line 21.—The output of the dynamo was measured by an ammeter and voltmeter belonging to Messrs. Carels, which had been calibrated before the trial. The readings of both instruments were, moreover, checked throughout by a Weston set in the circuit, which was itself checked at the Manchester Technical School before and after the trials.

To afford some check upon the dynamo efficiencies given by the makers, the C^2R losses in the armature and magnet coils and in the shunt regulator were measured. With the full load of 350 kilowatts these were as follows:—

C^2R loss in armature brushes, etc.	8·9 kw.	
,, shunt coil	3·0	,,
,, shunt regulator resistance	2·5	,,
	14·4 kw.	

Assuming the iron losses and friction (which could not be measured) to be equal to the above, the total losses would amount to about 28·8 kw., giving an efficiency of 92·4, as against 93·5 claimed by the makers.

Line 22.—The brake horse-power given in this line is at each load the measured output of the dynamo in horse-power divided by the coefficient of efficiency given by the makers for that load. As already explained, it includes the power absorbed by the motor and air compressor, and is therefore higher than it would have been had the air compressor been

[1] The heat account has been omitted.

driven by levers and links from one of the piston-rod crossheads, or by an eccentric or crank from the engine crank shaft, as under ordinary circumstances it would be.

Lines 22 and 23.—From the preceding paragraph it will be understood that the horse-power absorbed by the engine itself is less and the mechanical efficiency greater than if the air compressor had been driven directly by the engine.

Lines 27 and 28 give the kilowatts supplied to the motor which drove the air compressors and the horse-power given out by it.

Line 29.—The figure 36 H.P. in the first column was arrived at by indicating the cylinders of one of the air compressors when compressing to about 60 atmospheres and assuming that diagrams from the cylinders of the other compressor would have to be of the same areas. The difference of 8·8 H.P. between this figure and the figure 44·8 in the first column of line 28 represents the power absorbed by the driving belt and the mechanism of the compressors.

The figures in columns 2, 3, and 4 of line 29 are put down on the assumption that the fractional loss of 8·8 H.P. was constant at all loads.

Line 31.—If the compressors had been driven by the engine, the power absorbed would probably have been less than indicated by the figures in line 28 and more than shown in line 29. Assuming that it would have been half-way between the two,

Lines 31 and 32 show approximately what the brake horse-power and mechanical efficiencies of the engine would have been had the compressor formed part of the engine; and

Line 33 gives approximately the probable oil consumption per brake horse-power-hour with this arrangement.

The high percentage of heat unaccounted for on the second trial may be due to imperfect combustion, especially during the early part of the trial, when for a short time there was a little smoke from No. 56 cylinder, and the excess of heat accounted for on the third trial is most likely due to overestimation of the weight of the exhaust gases. This weight varies inversely as the percentage of CO_2 in the gases, and any leakage of air into the gas samples reduces this percentage and consequently unduly increases the calculated weight of the gases.

The conditions during the first three trials were not constant.

During the two full load trials the temperature of the exhaust and of the discharge from the jackets continued to rise for some time after commencement of each trial, while during the half-load trial both temperatures fell. The inference is that during the earlier parts of the first two trials the temperature of the cylinder walls and pistons was increasing by absorption of the heat from the gases, and during the third was falling by imparting heat to the gases. To show the effect of these exchanges of heat, heat accounts have been calculated for the periods during which the temperature conditions were fairly constant. As will be seen by these accounts, the effect upon the oil consumptions and thermal efficiencies was practically negligible.

As already explained on page 140, the line showing the rate of oil consumption in this first trial is only approximately correct, as, owing to a little difficulty in running the oil from the measuring tank into the feed tank it was not possible always to bring the level in the latter up to the point gauge before running in a fresh weighing.

The rise in temperature of the water from the jackets up to 4.45 p.m. was due to an insufficient supply. The supply was then increased.

The sudden rise in the temperature of the exhaust at 5.40 is unaccountable.

On the 14th, the engine ran with full load from 6 a.m. till breakfast time, and then with about half-load till just before the beginning of the trial. It attained its normal temperature soon after the trial began. The speed was increased soon after starting to stop the smoke from No. 56 cylinder.

As it was intended to make a half-load and no-load trial, and also to examine the valves and piston of one of the cylinders, the half-load trial was begun almost immediately the full-load trial was finished.

The last, or no-load trial, was not started till half an hour after the end of the half-load trial. No gas analysis was taken during this trial.

The engine worked well during the trials, except that there was a little smoke with the full load. The smoke came from No. 56 cylinder, which, as may be seen from the line 17 of the Table, was doing more than its fair share of the work.

After the full-load trial on the 14th, the whole of the load was suddenly thrown off. The speed increased from 153 revolutions per minute to 164 revolutions per minute, and settled to 157 revolutions per minute.

Tests on a High Speed Diesel Engine.—It is of importance to determine the extent to which the piston speed, or what is the same thing, the speed of revolution of a high speed Diesel engine, can be increased to obtain greater powers with the same diameter of cylinder. The expression for the indicated horse-power of a four-cycle single acting engine is :—

$$\text{I.H.P.} = \tfrac{1}{2} \frac{\text{P.L.A.N.}}{33000} \quad \ldots\ldots\ldots\ldots\ldots(1)$$

where P = Average indicated pressure in lb. per sq. inch.
L = Stroke of piston in feet.
A = Area of piston in sq. inches = $\frac{\pi}{4} d^2$ where
d = cylinder diameter.
N = Revolutions of engine per minute.

This formula may be expressed otherwise as :—

$$\text{I.H.P.} = \frac{\text{P.A.S.}}{2200} \quad \ldots\ldots\ldots\ldots\ldots(2)$$

where S = piston speed in feet per second.

From formula (2) it appears that with the same cylinder diameter the I.H.P. may be increased either by the employment of a higher mean pressure or by an increase of piston speed, and Dr. Seiliger made an important series of tests [1] to ascertain the limits to which these means could be carried.

[1] *Zeitschrift des Vereins doutscher Ingenicure*, 1911.

If Q = Theoretical quantity of air drawn in the cylinders per hour in cub. ft.

K = Ratio of actual quantity of air to theoretical quantity.

c = Consumption of oil per I.H.P. hour in lb.

Q_1 = Minimum quantity of air required for the combustion of 1 lb. of fuel in c.f.

Then KQ must not be less than $Q_1 c \times$ I.H.P.

$$\text{and } Q = L \times A \times \frac{N}{2} \times \frac{60}{144} \text{ cub. ft.}$$

hence $K.L.A. \dfrac{N}{2} \times \dfrac{60}{144}$ must not be less than $Q_1 c \times \frac{1}{2} \dfrac{P.L.A.N.}{33000}$

or P must not be greater than $13{,}750 \dfrac{K}{Q_1 c}$ ....(3)

From this it is seen that the mean pressure is dependent on the value K and the fuel consumption per I.H.P. hour. In the tests which were carried out on a high speed engine of 300 B.H.P. normal output it was found that both these values were in turn dependent on the piston speed, and that therefore increased power could not be obtained indefinitely in a cylinder of constant diameter by direct increase of piston speed or mean pressure. The results of the tests may be stated as follows :—

1. The fuel consumption per I.H.P. hour decreases with the speed of revolution, when the mean pressure remains constant.

2. The fuel consumption per I.H.P. hour decreases with the mean pressure when the speed of revolution remains constant.

3. The temperature of the exhaust gases decreases with the speed of revolution when the mean pressure remains constant.

4. The temperature of the exhaust gases decreases with the mean pressure when the speed of revolution remains constant.

5. The power absorbed by the air pump is directly proportional to the speed of the engine but independent of the mean pressure.

6. The power absorbed in friction, etc., increases with the speed of revolution, and also with an increase in the mean pressure.

7. The value K decreases with an increase of speed and is independent of the mean pressure.

All these important facts can be deduced theoretically and bear out the results of the tests. It will be seen from (7) that K decreases as the speed rises, i.e. K varies inversely with S, though not in the same ratio, and similarly from (1) the fuel consumption per I.H.P. hour, c rises with an increase in the piston speed. The value of the mean pressure P from formula (3) is dependent on the ratio $\frac{K}{c}$ and if the speed rises this ratio decreases and hence P falls. The product PS on which the output of the engine depends, with the same cylinder diameter, therefore tends to become constant at higher speeds, or in other words, increase of speed of revolution above a certain point will not produce a useful increase in output. This was well instanced in Seiliger's tests, as is shown in the following table.

Speed of Revolution increased r.p.m. from	to	Piston Speed increased meters per sec. from	to	Percentage Increase.	Output of engine increased. B.H.P.	Percentage Increase.
300	350	3·8	4·43	17%	41	16%
350	400	4·43	5·01	15%	10	3%
306	401	3·6	4·8	33%	76	33%
401	493	4·8	6	25%	30·5	10%

These results show clearly the distinct limitations to the output of a Diesel engine of fixed diameter of cylinder and that by mere increase of speed of revolution (or piston speed) the power developed by the motor cannot be usefully increased beyond a certain point, and that for every engine there is a value for the product of the piston speed and the mean pressure which gives most efficient results.

CHAPTER VI

DIESEL ENGINES FOR MARINE WORK

GENERAL CONSIDERATIONS—ADVANTAGES OF THE DIESEL ENGINE FOR MARINE WORK—DESIGN AND ARRANGEMENT OF DIESEL MARINE ENGINES—METHODS OF REVERSING DIESEL ENGINES—AUXILIARIES FOR DIESEL SHIPS—HORSE POWER OF MARINE DIESEL ENGINES—WEIGHTS OF MARINE DIESEL ENGINES—THE DESIGN OF LARGE ENGINES.

General Considerations.—The question of the employment of internal combustion engines for the propulsion of ships has received a large amount of attention during recent years, since, in fact, the gas engine reached its present high degree of economy and perfection. This is not remarkable in view of the much higher efficiency to be obtained by the gas engine than with the steam engine, and when the use of coal for the operation of gas engines became possible by the intermediary of gas producers, the question of driving ships with gas engines seemed likely to assume practical shape. For various reasons very little has up to the present been done in this direction, and briefly it may be said that the potential advantages to be gained by the employment of suction gas engines for ships are not sufficient to warrant the departure. In the first place the advantage of economy in the cost of operation is not very marked, since, though a large amount of work has been carried out with the object of developing a satisfactory producer working on bituminous coal, it may be taken that anthracite would have to be employed at any rate to guarantee sufficient reliability of operation for marine work. The relative prices of anthracite and the bunker coal used with steam engines at once largely minimize, if they do not entirely destroy, the economy in fuel costs with gas engines. Owing to the necessity of the producer, a gas installation saves little or nothing in space or weight, as compared with the steam plant, and firemen are required for the producer or for the boiler, though of course the same attention is not required, but in any case the reduction in the number of attendants would be small. Further a satisfactorily reversible gas engine is at present hardly an accomplished fact, and speed variation is a difficult problem; taking all matters into consideration, therefore, it is safe to say the adoption of gas engines for the propulsion of ships is not likely to make much headway in the future, although there may be one or two isolated instances in which a certain measure of success may be obtained.

It is apparent that provided an oil engine could be produced which is equal to a steam engine in reliability, it would have many points of superiority as compared with the gas engine while retaining all the general advantages of the internal combustion engine. Hence the Diesel engine, which has proved itself more efficient than, and at least as serviceable as, the gas engine for land work, seems to be eminently adapted for the propulsion of ships, but there have naturally been many difficulties to overcome before it could be in a position to compare with the steam engine, in matters which for marine work are of perhaps greater importance than mere economy. A marine engine must before everything be absolutely reliable, and with the present day perfection of the steam engine, resultant upon nearly a century of practical experience, it is easy to see that the Diesel engine had to make much progress and to pass through a long period of trial under the severest conditions of operation in practice before it could seriously be considered as a satisfactory motor for marine propulsion. After some seventeen years, during which the engine has been employed for all manner of stationary work, with a reliability now generally agreed to be equal to that of the steam engine, it may with reason be said that this probationary period has expired. At the same time, it must be admitted that marine practice is in many ways different from stationary operation, and though this point should not be exaggerated, as marine engineers are apt to make it, there is no doubt that the conditions of service at sea are, in general, much more severe than on land. It was necessary, therefore, that before the Diesel engine could hope to find ready adoption for large vessels, experience should be gained with its use on smaller boats, so that a reasonable idea as to its reliability and general suitability for ships could be obtained. There are at the present time some 500 vessels of various types propelled by Diesel engines, and many have been running for some years. Most of these are quite small boats and there are included a number of submarines, but the figure itself is sufficient to show that the introduction of the Diesel engine even in large ships cannot really be considered an innovation, but only a slight advance on an already proved arrangement. Moreover the Diesel marine engine, excepting only the type employed on submarines, where a relatively large number of cylinders is a necessity, differs but slightly from the stationary motor, since reversing and speed regulation are modifications which involve no material alterations in design, and the experience gained with the land engines is thus in a measure equivalent to that which would have had to be obtained at sea were the construction different in any marked degree.

Advantages of the Diesel Engine for Marine Work.—The advantages of the Diesel engine for marine propulsion over the steam plant are in no sense problematical but can be reduced to monetary saving in running costs, or increased earning capacity. The reduction in fuel cost must necessarily be dependent on the prices of oil and coal, and is a matter that can readily be determined by the shipowner, since the fuel that will be consumed with a Diesel motor ship, with engines of any particular power, can be guaranteed within the narrowest limits, while the coal burned in the same ship propelled by steam engines can readily be fixed in the light of past experience.

The amount of coal which is consumed in steam engine

propelled ships per H.P. naturally varies considerably with the class of vessel, and the type and power of the machinery, and also with the quality of coal burned; this latter point should be remembered in any comparison of the costs of coal and oil, since where cheap coal is used the amount is usually increased, and average figures for consumption then do not form an accurate basis. In fact the only really fair method of estimation of fuel consumption is one in which the calorific value is taken into account. An average taken over a very large number of vessels now in operation, particularly those between 3,000 and 5,000 tons displacement, of which the bulk of the world's shipping is composed, gives as the consumption of coal per I.H.P. hour, 1·55 lb., and assuming a mechanical efficiency of 85 per cent.—brake horse-power to indicated horse-power—the figure of 1·8 lb. of coal per B.H.P. is obtained. As a matter of fact an enormous number of vessels consume very much more fuel than this, 2 lb. per B.H.P. hour being a common figure for smaller vessels, but on the other hand in certain cases the consumption is less, and 1·8 may be taken as a fair average. The larger sizes of Diesel engines now being built by many firms, are usually guaranteed not to require more than 0·4 lb. of crude oil per B.H.P. hour, while the actual consumption is frequently as low as 0·37 lb. The two-cycle engine is, as previously stated, slightly less efficient than the four cycle, and for purposes of comparison it may be assumed that 0·45 lb. of fuel is required per B.H.P. hour with a marine Diesel engine.

On this basis it will be seen that in a ship propelled with Diesel engines the consumption of fuel should be approximately one-quarter of the weight of coal burned with a steam engine plant, but in reality the saving may be much greater. When running at reduced speeds the Diesel engine is relatively more efficient than the steam engine. This point is of particular importance for war vessels, which for by far the greater portion of the time, run at much below their full power and speed, while the same remark applies to trawlers and similar vessels, and even ships which make long voyages nominally at full speed, frequently have to slow down for many hours on end for various reasons. The matter need not be emphasized too strongly, but it is certainly one of the features of the Diesel engine which distinguishes it from all other prime movers which have been employed for marine propulsion, including the gas engine. With steam engines and particularly steam turbines the efficiency at low powers is undoubtedly poor, in spite of the many methods which have been devised to improve it.

There are of course no stand-by losses, which may be an important point in steamships making frequent calls at ports. The question of auxiliaries enters largely into the matter of fuel consumption, as may be well understood from the fact that the power required for the auxiliaries is some 20 to 25 per cent. of that developed by the propelling engines. Steam-driven auxiliaries are notoriously inefficient, and a considerable saving may be effected in this direction in Diesel propelled vessels, although in certain instances steam auxiliaries have been retained and a small boiler installed for them, but this is an arrangement which is not likely to be much adopted. Though it is impossible to give a figure which will apply generally, it is probable that in the majority of ships the weight of fuel if propelled by Diesel engines is approximately one-fifth of that required for a steamship, and hence the actual monetary saving in fuel costs with the former in any particular case can readily be estimated with a reasonable degree of accuracy, if the market prices of oil and coal respectively are obtained at the ports where the vessel will take in fuel. At the present time crude oil suitable for Diesel engines may be obtained at most English ports for 45s. to 50s. per ton, usually the former figure, and even better terms may be made by contract over a long period. From this it may be gauged that if the bunker coal exceeds an average price of 10s. or 11s. per ton the Diesel engine will prove more economical than the steam engine in its present stage of efficient design and construction, even assuming the less advantageous ratio of fuel in the two cases, namely, Diesel engine using one-quarter of the steam engine.

These figures assume that the same power is required whether a ship be driven by Diesel or steam engines, and this is very nearly the case, the balance being rather in favour of the former. With the employment of the Diesel engine a ship can be built with rather finer lines than a steamship, which allows a certain reduction of power with the same vessel speed. On the other hand the most suitable speed of revolution of the Diesel engine is generally speaking rather above the most economical propeller speed, and hence a slightly greater power is needed, but these two matters balance each other, at any rate near enough for all practical purposes.

The saving in the quantity of fuel used reflects itself in many other ways. For the same voyage since only one-fifth of the weight of fuel is required, a very valuable bunker space is available for general cargo space, and this is more than even the mere relative weights signify, since oil can be stored in places which would be quite unsuitable for coal, such as in the double bottom or ballast tanks.

When going into a consideration of the relative running costs of a Diesel and a steam installation, the cost of the fuel is not by any means the sole item to enter into the calculation. The amount of lubricating oil necessary is perhaps greater with a Diesel motor, but on the other hand, no fresh water has to be carried for boilers. As regards the cost of upkeep and general repairs, there is no reason to suppose that the motor ship should be at a disadvantage, and present experience rather points to the fact that the contrary is the case, which might be anticipated for the reason that there is much less machinery and fewer parts to get out of order. With a Diesel ship there are of course no stokers required and the number of attendants is much reduced, this applying to ships of all sizes and engines of all powers. In large vessels, however, the matter is a more vital one as so many firemen have to be employed, far exceeding the engine-room staff in number, as may be instanced in the extreme case of the *Mauretania*, where they were some 180 firemen as against 35 engineers. Coming to actual facts it may be as well to state that in a small vessel of 2,000 tons displacement with a Diesel engine of 500 B.H.P. the total engine-room staff consisted of four men, whilst in a vessel propelled by a Diesel motor of 1,500 B.H.P. the actual saving effected is about £300 per annum, due to the reduced number of attendants as compared with a steamship of equal power.

The saving in weight of fuel consumed per unit of work in a Diesel engine may be utilized at sea in one of two ways— the range may be increased by carrying the same amount of fuel or, with the same range, the space thus economized may be employed for extra cargo carrying capacity. The first method is of enormous value for war vessels, and at the lowest estimate the radius of action of a battleship may be increased four-fold, and in all probability allowing for the extra economy in this case owing to the average power developed being so much below the maximum, it is probable that something like seven or eight times the radius might be reckoned on in a Diesel engine battleship compared with the existing type. The value of this can hardly be too strongly emphasized, particularly in the case of countries whose accessible coaling stations are infrequent. For merchant vessels it is not as a rule of great moment to increase the range, though it may frequently be advisable on certain services owing to the fact that fuel, at many ports of call which have necessarily to be used as coaling stations, is excessive in price, and the lesser consumption of fuel therefore allows a greater choice as to where it should be taken on board, leading to an economy impossible with steamships, owing to the limitations of bunker capacity. However, most frequently the shipowner is desirous of taking full advantage of the possibility of increasing the cargo-carrying capacity of his ships and the economy of fuel consumption will generally be put to this purpose. It is easy to see how important this saving may become, especially for ships making long voyages. A vessel of 2,500 to 3,500 tons displacement propelled by a steam engine of about 1,100 or 1,200 I.H.P. would consume under working conditions some 15 tons of coal per day, while with a Diesel engine of equal or rather greater power (say 1,000 B.H.P.) would require under 4 tons of oil, showing a reduction of at least 11 tons per day, or if the vessel bunkered for 20 days, a total saving of 220 tons. Allowing for the fact that oil can be placed in a less accessible position than coal, there would be a space available for carrying cargo to the extent of nearly one-tenth of the ship's entire displacement, which reflects very considerably on the earning capacity of a cargo vessel.

In the same direction lies the economy in the space occupied by, and the weight of the machinery in a Diesel ship compared with a steamship. On this point again the question is not one of estimate but of actual fact. The average weight of machinery in vessels propelled by reciprocating engines of modern construction, including the boilers and accessories is in the neighbourhood of 1 ton for every 5 to 8 I.H.P. developed by the main engines. On larger vessels, particularly those propelled by steam turbines, the weight is somewhat less for the same power, and particularly is this so in battleships, while in destroyers and similar vessels the weight of the machinery may be reduced to 15 I.H.P. per ton. This reduction however is usually necessarily obtained by the employment of high speed engines of specially light construction, and the cases are therefore not directly comparable. The increase in speed is also accompanied by a diminution in propeller efficiency, which of course shows itself in a higher coal consumption per H.P. hour. The weight of a marine Diesel engine of the two-cycle single acting type complete with all auxiliaries and accessories varies between 10 and 15 B.H.P. per ton of total weight, with engines of the slow speed type—that is to say under 200 revolutions per minute. For high speed engines which may be employed in certain cases as much as 25 B.H.P. may be developed per ton of machinery, even with large powers, and already single engines up to 1,000 B.H.P. have been built of this weight. In certain instances, therefore, where the question of obtaining the maximum saving in weight becomes a vital one, there is some likelihood of high speed engines being adopted, with the employment of a mechanical or other gear for reducing the speed to give a high propeller efficiency, such as has already been tried in several turbine-propelled vessels. It is obvious that this arrangement will only be considered in special cases since the introduction of further gear is always to be deprecated at sea, and the higher speed engine naturally is slightly more costly in upkeep. Considering only the slow speed Diesel engine of the ordinary type as adapted for marine work (e.g. for cargo vessels), it has been found that the approximate saving in weight for a 1,500 shaft H.P. installation is somewhere in the neighbourhood of 150 tons in favour of the Diesel engine as compared with the steam equipment, and approximately the same ratio applies for larger powers. Together with the saving in weight there is also a considerable reduction in the space occupied by the machinery, since a Diesel engine requires only about the same floor area as a quadruple expansion steam engine, which permits the room taken by the boiler to be thrown open for other purposes in a Diesel ship.

Allowing for all the economies effected, namely in weight of fuel carried, weight of machinery, and in engine-room space, it may be taken as a safe estimate, that with almost any class of vessel, an extra cargo can be carried equivalent to about 15 per cent. of the displacement of the vessel. This fact makes it apparent that the question of the saving effected in the fuel bill, important though it is, should by no means be the determining factor, and from the shipowners' point of view, the increased earning capacity must be seriously considered.

The following estimates are based on figures given by Herrn Sauberlich in a paper read before the Schiffbautechnischen Gesellschaft,[1] and compare the saving to be effected in all directions by the employment of Diesel engines instead of steam engines. It is of course difficult to give any exact

[1] *Jahrbuch der Schiffbautechnischen Gesellschaft*, Berlin, 1911.

comparisons which will apply generally, since the varying services and conditions under which different vessels run, will determine the manner in which the shipowner will take advantage of the economy and convenience to be derived by the use of the oil engine, whether for instance the bunker capacity will remain the same, allowing a greater radius, or whether the range of the vessel will be only just maintained and the full economy in weight of fuel carried will be utilized to its utmost. The estimates are based on a voyage 20 days out, and 20 days home, with four round trips in the year or 160 days steaming per annum. The oil fuel carried is reckoned as sufficient for the double voyage, while the coal in the case of the steamships is sufficient for the outward journey only.

The cost of coal is taken at 15·7 marks, or say 15s. 6d. per ton, and of fuel at 35 marks, or say 35s. per ton f.o.b., the fuel consumption for the Diesel engine being 0·49 lb. per B.H.P. hour, and the coal consumption with the steam engine at about 1·25 lb. per I.H.P. hour, which rather favours the steamship.

Type of vessel		Diesel ship	Steamship
Length	feet	338	338
Beam	,,	48	48
Depth	,,	31·5	31·5
Draught	,,	21·5	21·5
Shaft horse power	B.H.P.	1,350	1,500
Gross tonnage	tons	5,550	5,400
Weight of fuel carried (double voyage in case of Diesel ship)	tons	350	480
Extra freight-carrying capacity with Diesel ship	tons	280	—
Speed	knots	10	10
Fuel consumption (·49 lb. per B.H.P. for Diesel and 1·25 lb. per I.H.P. steam engine)	tons per day	7·1	19·8
Fuel cost	per day	£12 2s. 0d.	£15 11s. 0d.
Daily saving in fuel cost with Diesel ship		£3 9s. 0d.	—
Wages and maintenance of engine-room staff	per month	£52 6s. 0d.	£72 10s. 0d.
Saving in engine-room staff with Diesel ship	per month	£20 4s. 0d.	—

The engine-room staff is reckoned as three engineers, an assistant, and six stokers in the case of the steam vessel, and three engineers, one fitter, and two greasers with the Diesel ship, or practically a reduction of four men in the latter case. The saving in a year's working may be summarized as under, taking as previously mentioned 160 steaming days.

	£	s.	d.
Increased freight of 280 tons four round trips at 8s. per ton for single voyage.	896	0	0
Saving in fuel cost at £3 9s. per day for 160 days	552	0	0
Wages and maintenance of engine-room staff	242	0	0
Total	£1,690	0	0
Extra interest and depreciation due to higher cost of Diesel plant	125	0	0
Nett saving per annum with Diesel ship	£1,565	0	0

These figures, inexact as they must necessarily be, are sufficient to show what a great economy can be effected on a vessel of this type and emphasize the point that the economy in fuel is by no means the chief item affecting comparisons between Diesel and steam ships. Were the whole of this advantage swept away and the cost of the fuel considered the same in both cases due to low price of coal or high price of oil, there would still be an economy of over £1,000 per annum which would be largely increased by adding to the cargo-carrying capacity and allowing the same weight of fuel to be carried in the two ships.

As will have been understood from previous explanations the oil used in Diesel engines is usually of the heavy bodied type with a high flash point, commonly between 150° F. and 300° F. The possibility of fire from explosion therefore need not enter, and this is of importance as, apart from the absence of danger to the engine-room staff, the question of higher insurance which might be raised were oils of a lower flash point necessary, does not arise, and it has, in fact, been decided by the insurance companies that premiums need be no higher with Diesel boats than for the most modern steamships.

The ease and cleanliness with which oil fuel may be taken on board as compared with the operation of coaling is a good point well worthy of consideration, since it is solely a matter of pumping from a reservoir through one or more pipes, and this may be carried out with great rapidity. The engine-room arrangement in a Diesel ship is comparatively simple, the absence of the complicated steam piping being particularly noticeable, and as the engine is entirely self-contained its operation is wholly controlled by the engine-room attendants, which is a point to be noted in comparison with the dependence of the running of a steam engine on the pressure of the steam from the boilers. Up to the present time many of the Diesel ships have been provided with funnels of the same type as steamships, to get rid of the exhaust gases, but this is not essential, as they could be discharged from the side of the vessel if required. With the general adoption of Diesel motors for war vessels funnels would no doubt be dispensed with, which would have an important bearing on the effective use of the guns, while the absence of any smoke is a matter of some importance in preventing the possibility of locating a ship's position by this means, since the exhaust gases are practically smokeless.

With regard to the cost of the machinery for a Diesel motor vessel, the Diesel engines at the present time are at a disadvantage. As a rough figure over a wide range of powers it may be taken that the Diesel plant is from 10 to 20 per cent. more expensive than a steam installation, including all auxiliaries in both cases. The cost of Diesel engines has, however, been falling within the last year or two and no doubt will soon be comparable with that of steam plants of the same power, but it is to be emphasized that, more than with any other machinery, price cutting is to be strongly deprecated in view of the perfection of construction required with Diesel engines, and if the reduction in cost price be carried too far it will inevitably react on the possibilities of success of the engine.

It is to be anticipated that the cost will soon be in the neighbourhood of £7 per B.H.P. for single-acting engines and £5 per B.H.P. for large double-acting motors, and there seems no reason to doubt that when more experience is gained the price of Diesel engines of very large size will not be in excess of that of steam engines, *exclusive* of boilers.

Design and Arrangement of Diesel Marine Engines.—There are several important points to be observed in the design and arrangement of ship's machinery—all so essential as to render it difficult to define any one of them as the chief. Briefly, they may be classed as follows :—

(1) The engines must be reliable, of simple construction and easy of operation.

(2) The engines must be capable of rapid and frequent reversal by a simple means.

(The question of frequent reversal, as in manœuvring, has an important bearing on the design of a Diesel ship where the engine is reversed by compressed air, inasmuch as the air reservoirs must be of ample capacity for all demands.)

(3) The engines should have a wide variation of speed both ahead and astern, which variation must be easily accomplished preferably by one handle or lever.

(4) The fuel consumption should be low, not only at maximum engine power, but within a wide variation.

(5) The weight and space occupied by the machinery should be as low as possible, but should not be sacrificed to high and generally inefficient propeller speed.

The question of the employment of two or four cycle Diesel engine for marine purposes has been discussed in Chapter II and need not be further entered into. One of the chief problems which confronts the designer is the number of cylinders of the engine for a given power, which will provide sufficient evenness of operation, and it is to be remembered that flywheels are to be avoided if possible, and in any case must be small in order to allow rapid manœuvring of the vessel. As in most other questions regarding marine engines there are two antagonistic conditions to be satisfied as far as circumstances permit, namely, that the

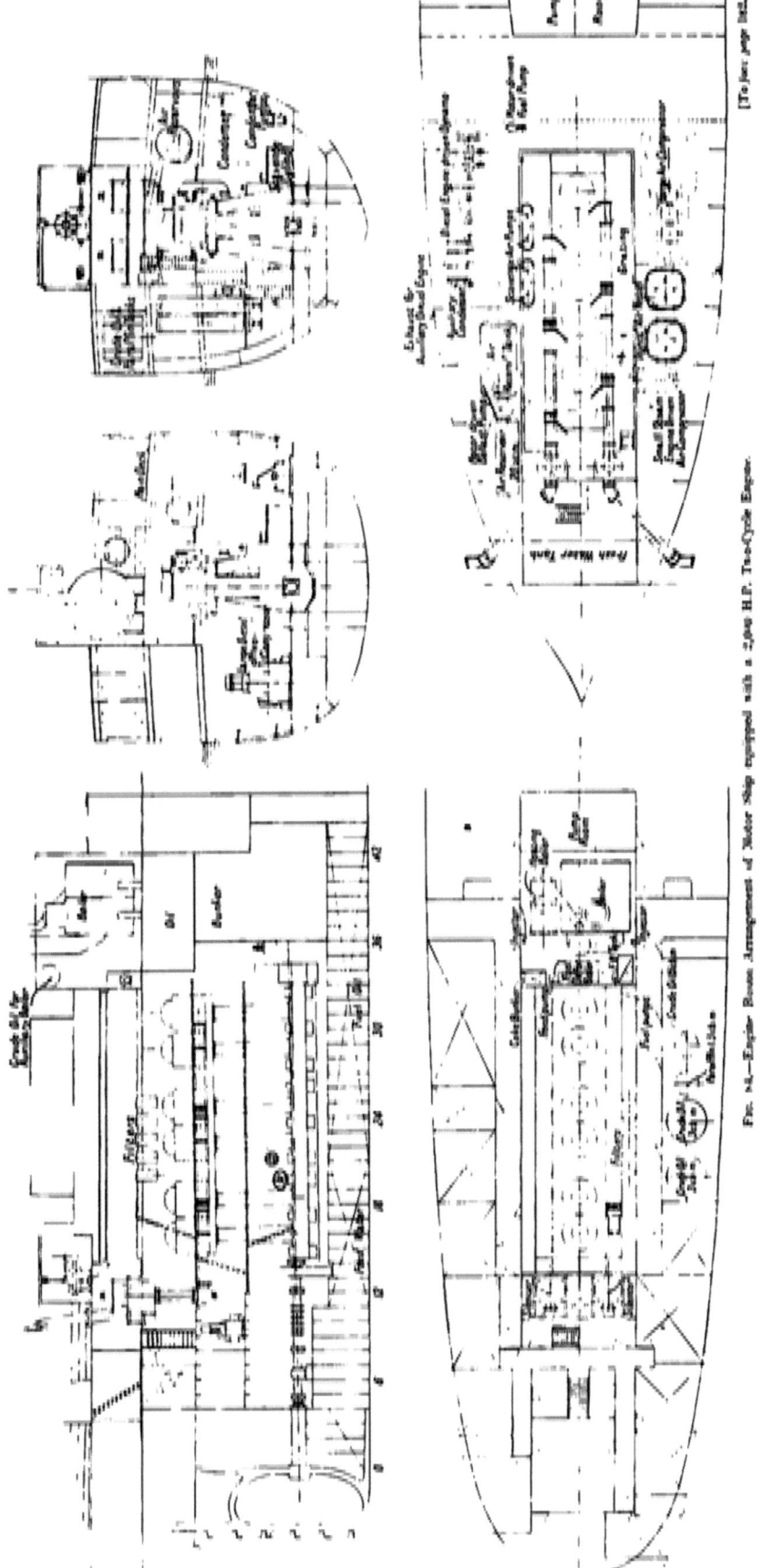

Fig. 34.—Engine Room Arrangement of Motor Ship equipped with a 2,000 H.P. Two-Cycle Engine.

engine should run smoothly, and that simplicity is essential and the number of working parts small. For the first, the higher the number of cylinders the better, while the second condition is best complied with when there is a minimum number of cylinders. In no case is it likely that an engine of less than three cylinders will be employed for marine work, and this only, of course, with the two-cycle type. In actual practice with a two-cycle single acting engine there are usually four or six cylinders, though there may possibly be more, particularly for the larger powers, and with six cylinders only a small flywheel is necessary; these two types are the standards adopted by some manufacturers —notably Messrs. Sulzer Brothers. With four-cycle engines, the least number of cylinders which is advisable is six, in order to give an even turning moment. Very frequently, however, more are employed, particularly with engines for submarines where so many other factors enter into consideration, and eight is a common number.

If three cylinders be employed for a double acting engine, no flywheel is required, but the question of balancing the engine and rendering it free from vibration is complicated by the introduction of the scavenge pumps. However, three cylinders are being adopted in most cases with engines of this type. For very large engines the question does not resolve itself merely into the advisable number of cylinders from the point of view of even turning moment and absence of vibration, but is dependent on the power which can be developed in an engine with a reasonable number of cylinders —in other words, on the maximum horse power which can be obtained from one cylinder. In any case, with very large engines, for several reasons, chief among which is the necessity for simplicity, it will probably be inadvisable to have more than eight cylinders, and hence the need will arise for twin or triple screw Diesel ships, which have much to commend them as allowing greater efficiency and giving better manœuvring facilities. Even for lower powers, twin screw Diesel vessels will probably become common, at any rate for some time ahead, until greater experience has been gained with very large engines, and this is instanced in the many twin screw boats now in service and under construction, some with engines of as much as 5,000 H.P. The largest number of cylinders which has yet been used in a Diesel engine is eight, and no doubt this will remain the limit.

It will be seen that a Diesel marine engine in general has more cylinders than a steam engine of the same power, which is in itself a disadvantage from the point of view of adding to the complication of the machinery. On the other hand, in the event of a breakdown of one or more cylinders, all the others can operate quite satisfactorily, so that the possibilities of total disablement are small in the extreme, while at any time a number of the cylinders can be shut down, giving a more economical operation of the engine at low powers. The multiplicity of cylinders has always been taken advantage of in some designs mentioned later in aiding the manoeuvring of the vessel.

For the majority of ships of between 3,000 to 5,000 tons, of which the greater portion of the world's shipping is composed, the most economical propeller speed consistent with high propeller efficiency is generally not more than 100 revolutions per minute, and as Diesel engines must adapt themselves to existing conditions (i.e. to present limitations of propeller efficiency) the greater number of Diesel marine engines have to be designed to run at about this speed or very little higher unless gearing be introduced. For battleships, submarines, and fast vessels generally a considerably higher propeller speed is allowable, but these are special cases which have to be considered separately. Stationary Diesel engines of the slow speed type thus run at a higher rate of revolution than the marine engine, the weight of which is therefore somewhat in excess of the land engine, and the space occupied is rather greater. No trouble is however experienced in the design of the slower engine, and were there any essential difficulty in the construction, or difference in the economy, it would of course be advisable to sacrifice something in the propeller efficiency and run this engine at a higher speed, but such is however not the case.

Of particular importance with marine engines is the question of rapid variation of speed between a wide range, namely between the speeds corresponding to full vessel speed and dead slow. An oil engine of the Diesel type lends itself readily to such operation since it is only a matter of regulating the quantity of fuel admitted to the cylinders, which is carried out with the utmost ease by hand. In slow speed engines running normally at about 100 to 130 revolutions per minute, 40 revolutions per minute can be obtained, which is as low as required, while with higher speed engines the minimum speed is not much above this; for instance, a 1,000 B.H.P. marine engine of the two-stroke cycle type with a top speed of about 130 revolutions per minute can be brought down by hand regulation to 30 revolutions per minute, though such a wide variation is not always attainable without special arrangements. A novel method to obtain a greater reduction of speed than is easily possible with the ordinary design of Diesel marine engine, and to give very rapid and convenient manœuvring, is that of Messrs. Cockerill, who constructed an engine of six cylinders in two sets of three, with a coupling in the middle which is capable of disconnecting one set from the other. The engine remote from the propeller shaft has coupled to it an air compressor; in the ordinary running, the two halves of the engine are coupled together and the machine runs as an ordinary six-cylinder four-cycle motor, and the speed can be varied to a large extent in the ordinary way. For very low speeds the two halves are disconnected, and the one half drives the air compressor which supplies compressed air directly to the other half of the engine, which then runs as an air motor, and the speed can, of course, be reduced to suit any requirements. When manœuvring the same arrangement is adopted and also in reversing. This type, however, is not likely to receive wide adoption, and was mainly experimental.

The Diesel engine of the land type has been developed, as far as general design and construction are concerned, somewhat on the lines of the gas engine, and hence the trunk position has been wellnigh universally adopted, although the separate crosshead design was tried by some makers and abandoned, as it necessitated shorter pistons and gave less bearing surface. With marine engines, however, the question of the employment of the separate crosshead becomes more debatable, chiefly owing to the importance justly attached by marine engineers to accessibility and ease in dismantling. For double acting engines crossheads are of course essential, but opinion is divided regarding the matter for single acting engines, both two and four cycle. The main advantage of the trunk piston is that the height of the engine is less than with a crosshead engine, while the cost is also somewhat reduced. Possibly with the ultimate design of Diesel marine engine the trunk piston will be adopted for relatively small and high speed engines, but in the early days it is advisable to conform with the practice to which marine engineers have so long been accustomed and retain the crosshead, which no doubt gives more certainty of reliability. Admittedly very little trouble has been occasioned on land with the long pistons, but marine practice is on a different footing, and excess of caution is not to be deprecated. There is of course always a slight chance of the piston seizing, with a trunk piston, and though this need not be enlarged upon, the point should not be lost sight of.

For Diesel marine engines of large power, and particularly those of the two cycle and double acting type, cooling of the pistons, valves and bearings has to be resorted to. This is not a matter of any serious difficulty, although there is divergence of opinion as to the most effective means to employ. In four-cycle engines of comparatively small size it has been found sufficient to cool the pistons by allowing the air drawn into the cylinder during the suction stroke to pass through the piston, thus serving a dual purpose of warming the air and cooling the piston. The more general method is to effect a circulation of water or oil through a cooling tank. There is no doubt of the advantage of cooling pistons and rods by oil, as with water not only may leakages detrimentally affect the lubrication, but it is also always liable to become mixed with the oil indirectly, and even get into the main bearings. For this reason some manufacturers have adopted oil cooling in preference to water cooling, though many are making attempts to run large engines without any special cooling, and this would of course be by far the best solution. As regards piston cooling the Diesel engine is more favourably placed than the explosion type of internal combustion, since there is more time for the heat to be carried away by the jacket water, and the temperature of the piston does not rise to the same extent. The exhaust valves in marine engines, which are the chief ones liable to trouble through overheating, can very conveniently be cooled by the same water as is used for the cylinder jackets. The water enters the body of the valve casing which serves as a guide for the valve rod, and passes into the valve seat, which is of a box form, and thence up through the hollow valve rod and out through the top. With regard to the cooling of bearings, if forced lubrication is employed, as is the case with some types of Diesel marine engine, the oil is passed through an oil cooler usually arranged in the bed-plate, but with the ordinary method of lubrication the bearings are water cooled by branches off the main cylinder cooling water supply pipes.

Great attention has to be paid to the arrangements for the supply of scavenge air in a two-cycle engine, and the point is of even greater importance with motors of the two-cycle double acting type. Since the scavenge pumps are such a vital detail of the engine they are now very frequently made in duplicate for marine work with the single acting two-cycle engine, while in double acting engines it is advisable to have one scavenge pump for each working cylinder, and this arrangement is likely to be frequently adopted. When two scavenge pumps are employed for the single acting engine, each is made of about 60 per cent. of the full engine capacity or rather more, so that in the event of breakdown of one pump, the disablement would not be very serious. The engine, too, is sometimes divided into two sections, that

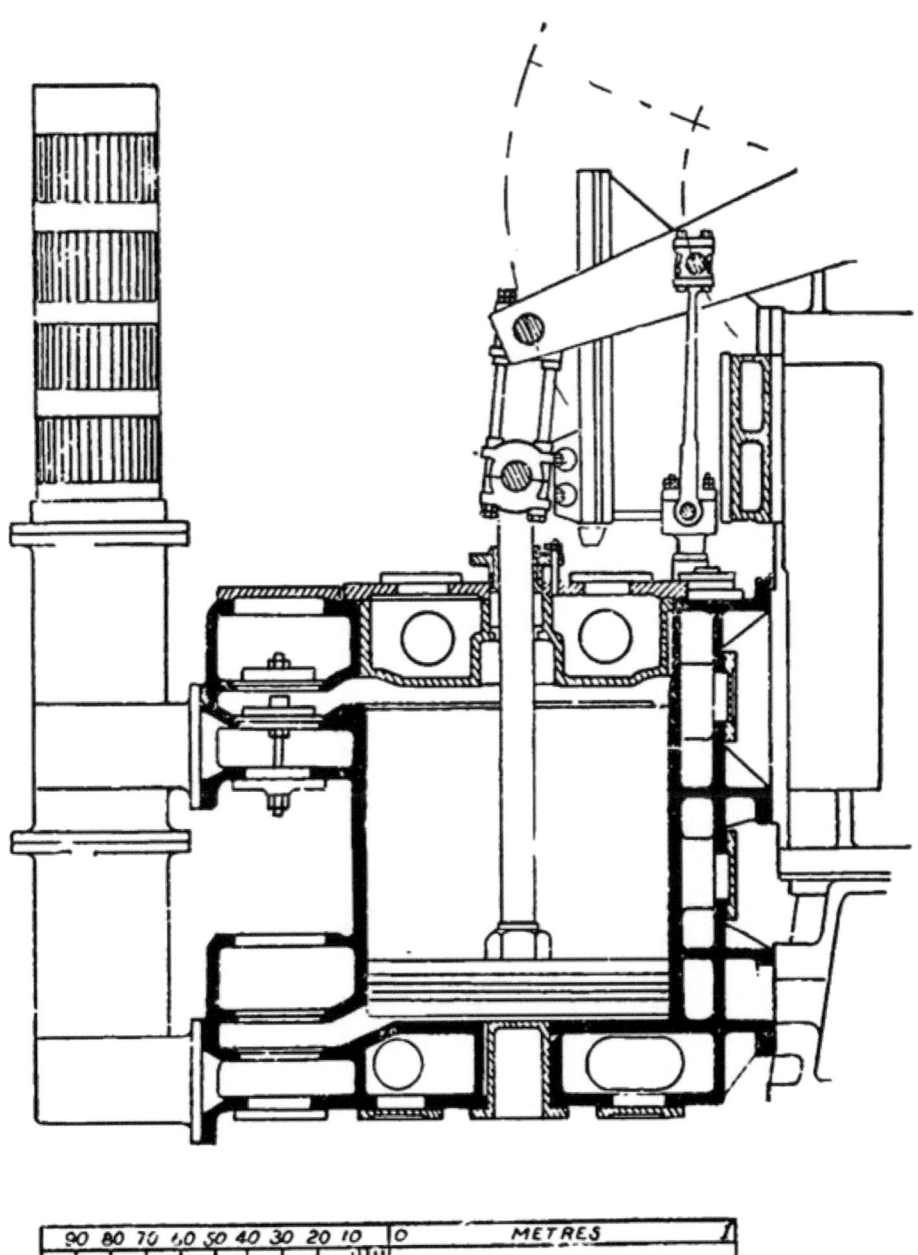

Fig. 85.—Details of one of the two Scavenge Pumps for 1,500 B.H.P. Carels' Type Marine Diesel Engine.

is to say, a 6-cylinder engine is treated as two 3-cylinder engines, and a 4-cylinder as two 2-cylinder engines, and one scavenge pump ordinarily supplies each half of the engine. The scavenge pumps with double acting engines are arranged on the crank shafting in line with the working cylinders, preferably half at each end, when a good balancing effect may be obtained by a proper disposition of the crank angles, though there are other methods adopted, described later. With single acting engines the scavenge pumps may either be on the end of the crank shaft or arranged in front of the engine and driven by levers, which has the advantage of allowing the crank shaft to be in two interchangeable halves, which would not otherwise be possible, and also makes the resemblance of the engine to a steam engine more marked, which though apparently a small matter is well worthy of consideration. It must be stated that although at least two scavenge pumps are advisable for two-stroke engines they are not essential, and in some cases of 1,000 B.H.P. single acting marine engines only one pump is employed driven off the end of the crank shaft and in a line with the working cylinders.

In the design of scavenge pumps the first point of importance is the provision of an ample supply of air, but it is difficult to say what should be the exact capacity of the pumps relative to the working cylinder volume. That it must be in excess of the latter is agreed; and for ordinary marine engines and also low speed land engines of the two-cycle type, the volume of the scavenge pump is frequently made about 25 per cent. greater than the working cylinder, but in high speed engines the difference may be as much as 50 per cent. The scavenging air does not enter the cylinders direct, but passes through a receiver, usually of small dimensions, which is desirable from the point of view of allowing the pressure to be rapidly raised and kept constant—a particularly important matter for marine engines when reversing. In most of the two-cycle engines which have hitherto been built for marine work the admission of scavenge air is carried out through valves actuated by levers in turn operated by cams on the cam shaft, just as the exhaust valves in the four-cycle engine. The arrangement adopted by some firms is shown in *Fig.* 86, two scavenge valves being employed for each cylinder, one on each side of the fuel inlet valve. In the first position in *Fig.* 86 the piston is at the top dead centre and the fuel valve is open to admit the oil, in the third position the exhaust ports are fully uncovered, the exhaust gas being expelled by the incoming air.

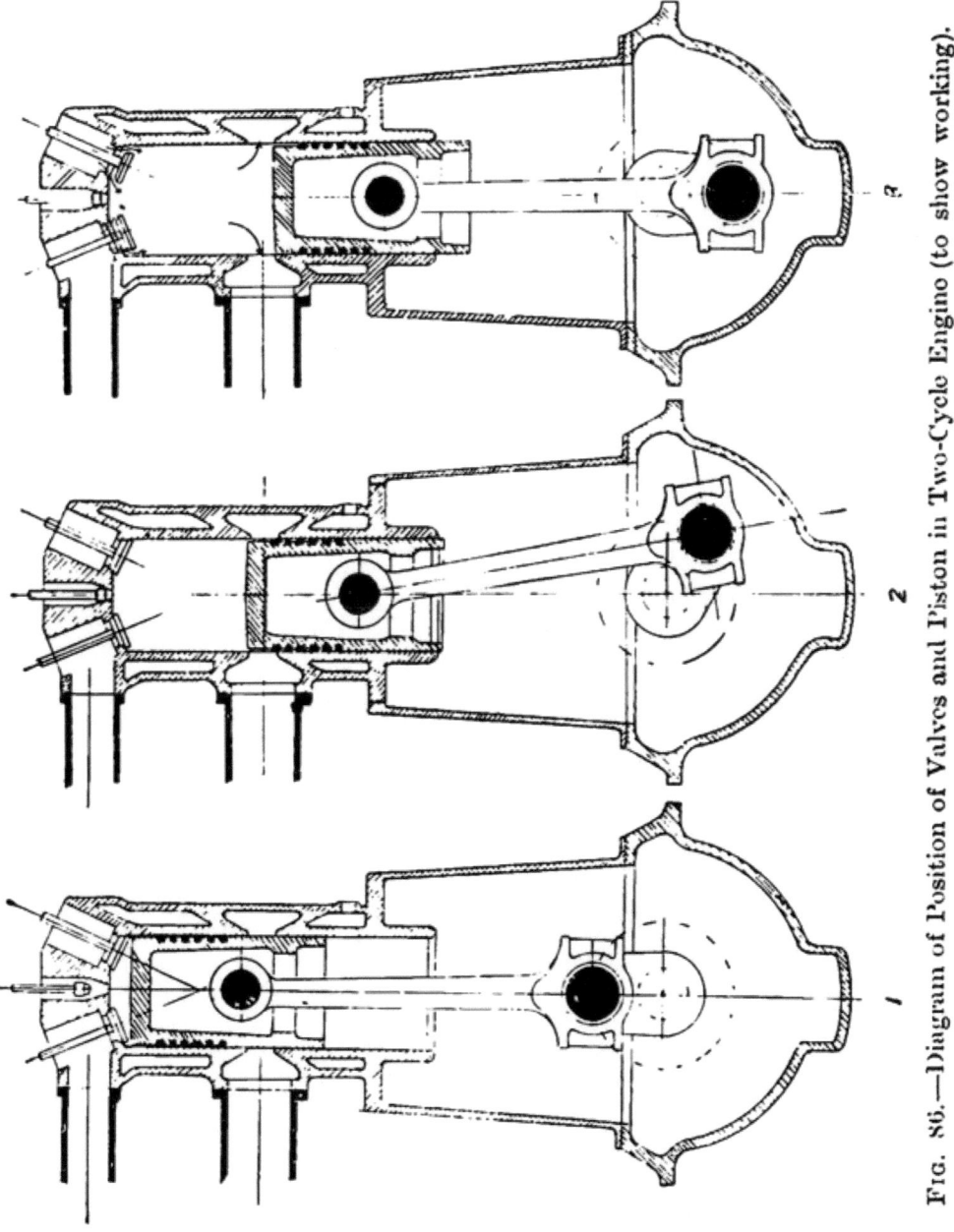

Fig. 86.—Diagram of Position of Valves and Piston in Two-Cycle Engine (to show working).

For larger engines, valves are inconvenient for the admission of the scavenge air, owing to the size necessitated to allow the requisite amount of air. For this reason ports instead of valves have recently been introduced, and with this arrangement there are two sets of ports at the bottom of the cylinder, one on each side for the exhaust and for the scavenge air. This method may be generally employed for all marine engines of the two-cycle type in the future, possessing as it does the advantage of simplicity, convenience and reliability, though there seems to be some doubt as to whether it gives so efficient a scavenging effect. There are then but two (and in some cases only one) valves for each cylinder—the fuel inlet valve and the starting valve—and this practically reduces the operation of reversing to an alternation of the position of two cams, or possibly one.

Fig. 87 shows diagrammatically the arrangement of ports adopted with this system by the A. B. Diesels Motorer of Stockholm, A being the exhaust ports, B the scavenging air pipe. The design of the piston head is such that the exhaust ports

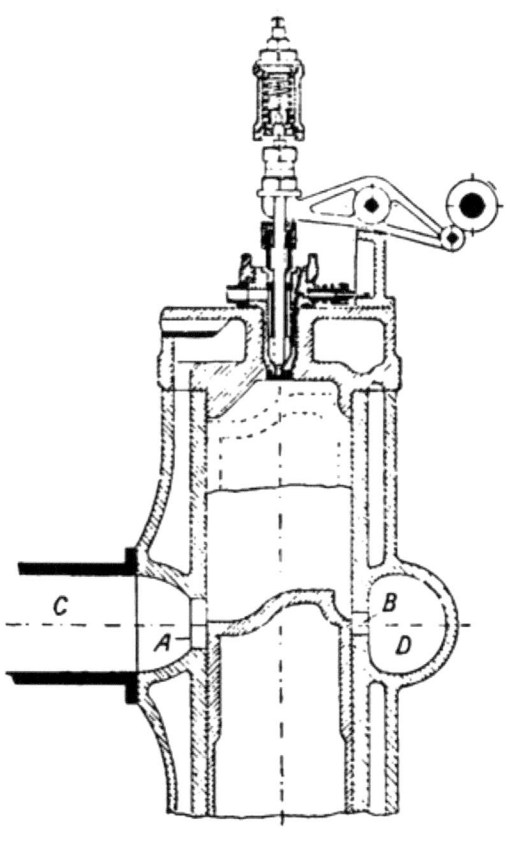

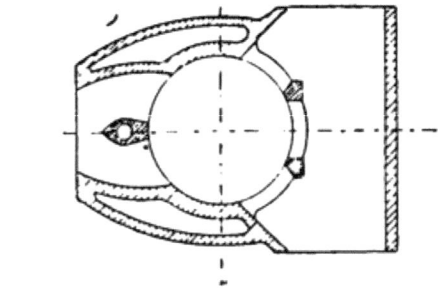

Fig. 87.—Two-Cycle Engine, with Scavenge Ports instead of Valves.

are opened on the down stroke some little time before the scavenging ports, so that part of the burnt gases may be rejected and the pressure much reduced before the air is admitted, while on the up stroke the scavenge ports, of course, are closed before the exhaust ports.

As is seen from the diagram which represents relatively the approximate length of the ports, the duration of the period for the admission of scavenging air is small and hence the velocity must be high. This seems to point to relatively large pressure of scavenging air, to give the requisite volume, but this involves more work for the pumps, while a low pressure necessitates heavier and larger cylinders, pipes and valves. A compromise has therefore to be struck, and as previously mentioned, the actual pressure is usually between 3 and 6 lb. per sq. inch, dependent on the speed of the engine.

The whole of the length of the cylinder occupied by the various ports is practically wasted from the point of view of power production, and the cylinder volume is therefore relatively larger than with a four-cycle engine, which is one of the chief reasons why it is impossible to get twice the power from a two-cycle motor compared with a four-cycle engine of the same size. Roughly, some 25 per cent. of the cylinder volume in a two-cycle ported engine is not available for useful work of power production, while for the same reason a long piston has to be adopted, though this is minimized by the employment of a crosshead and connecting rod.

A good deal of attention has been paid lately to the question of scavenging by means of ports instead of valves, and some methods adopted are described later when giving a detailed description of the particular types of marine engines. The main objection which had been urged against the employment of ports was that the scavenging effect was not so good as with valves, and that consequently incomplete combustion was obtained, giving a smoky exhaust and higher fuel consumption in an engine with scavenge ports. Careful investigation, however, which has lately been carried out, tends to show that provided special arrangements are adopted, there is no reason why the efficiency should not be equally high and the combustion practically perfect. In a long series of experiments it has been found that the results obtained with ports are within 1 per cent. of those with valves.

As has been stated, the supply of scavenge air required in a two-cycle single-acting engine may be up to 1·5 times the volume of the cylinder, or even more, depending on the pressure employed. The inlet areas, if valves be used, must therefore be very large in the case of high powered engines, and, for instance, an 1,800 H.P. motor (and even smaller engines) has four scavenge valves. This is the largest marine engine which has been built on such a principle, and the point arises as to whether the use of valves would not cause a limitation in the maximum output of a two-cycle motor. Even allowing that it would still be possible to use four valves in engines with still larger cylinders, the complication, cost, weight, and possible unreliability are all augmented—features which are much to be deprecated.

It need only be pointed out that in a six-cylinder engine of large size, twenty-four scavenge valves are necessary with a corresponding number of spares, to show what an advantage is gained by dispensing with them. It must be remembered that in scavenging with valves, the time of opening must be small (to allow sufficient compression) and the speed of scavenging high, which is not productive of the best effect. With ports the time can be longer, the part areas can be considerable, and if desired the pressure of the air can be reduced, and in some designs it is as low as $2\frac{1}{2}$ lb. per sq. in. above atmosphere.

Methods of Reversing Diesel Engines.—The problem of reversibility has never been one of serious importance with Diesel engines, since it is but a matter of detail to render an engine capable of running in either direction. The only necessity in reversing is to arrange the valve mechanism so that the valves open at a different period relative to the position of the crank or piston, and this in turn is dependent solely on the positions of the cams which operate the various valves. In a four-cycle engine the exhaust, starting, air admission, and fuel admission valves all have to open at a different time when the engine is running in the reverse direction. In a two-cycle motor with exhaust ports, only the scavenging valve, fuel inlet valve and starting valve are affected, while if scavenge ports be adopted the fuel and starting valve alone have to be operated. In some types of reversible engines, starting is effected by means of the scavenging air pump in which there is but a single valve and cam to operate in reversing the engine, and the advantage of the two-cycle engine over the four-cycle in the matter of reversing is apparent since simplicity is of such moment in marine work.

In marine engines, the ordinary type of horizontal cam shaft has to be adopted, and the arrangement of cams follows on the lines of that for stationary work. There are generally speaking two methods adopted for reversing Diesel engines, which process comprises, in effect, the alteration of the timing of the opening of the valves. There must obviously be two sets of cams, that is two cams or the equivalent for each cam lever operating a valve, and the methods hitherto employed have consisted either in having two sets of cams on the same horizontal shaft, and moving the shaft longitudinally when reversing, or else there are two distinct cam shafts, either of which may be moved so as to allow its cams to actuate the cam lever, the other shaft being then out of range of the levers. There are of course various modifications, but speaking generally the main principles described are not departed from.

Auxiliaries for Motor Ships.—In a general consideration of the question of the adoption of a new type of engine for marine propulsion, the many auxiliary appliances on ships have to be remembered, their importance being easily gauged from the fact that they usually require some 20 to 25 per cent. of the power of the main engine for their operation. For many years past there has been a tendency to replace steam-driven auxiliaries and employ electric motors for their drive, the advantage of this from the point of view of economy in operation, convenience, absence of stand-by losses, and avoidance of trouble through freezing being at once apparent. The adoption of electricity for driving all ships' auxiliaries seems therefore to be the ultimate solution in vessels of moderate and large size, and this method is to be adopted on some of the big Diesel engine vessels now being constructed. Diesel engines are employed for the dynamo drive, and the relatively great economy compared with steam engines emphasizes the total saving in fuel in the vessel, and this is particularly the case in comparison with vessels whose auxiliaries are steam driven, since the wastefulness of such machines is notorious.

With all Diesel ships it is quite essential that a second air compressor should be available apart from the one driven direct off the engine, for the supply of high pressure air, since so much is used when manœuvring, and a breakdown of the pump would render the vessel helpless if there were but one.

It is conceivable that the main engine may make a few revolutions, stop for a few minutes and then be required to reverse, and during this period it is clear that the compressor on the main engine cannot itself furnish sufficient air for this work. Indeed, it might be necessary to manœuvre the whole engine with air when going quite slowly, and for this purpose an auxiliary compressor of large capacity must be installed.

Experience will determine eventually what capacity this auxiliary machine should be, but the practice at present is to make it from half to three-quarters the capacity of the compressor on the engine itself.

When steam is provided on the vessel (see later), in order to work the cargo winches, steering gear and other auxiliary machinery, the auxiliary compressor is usually driven by a steam engine.

As a very large number of vessels that have hitherto been put in service are provided with steam-driven deck and other machinery, it is not surprising that this arrangement should have been adopted to a large extent. Without going into the question of advantages and disadvantages of the steam drive as compared with electricity or independent oil engine operation (this point is discussed elsewhere), it may be mentioned that even on some ships where steam is extensively employed, an auxiliary Diesel driven com-

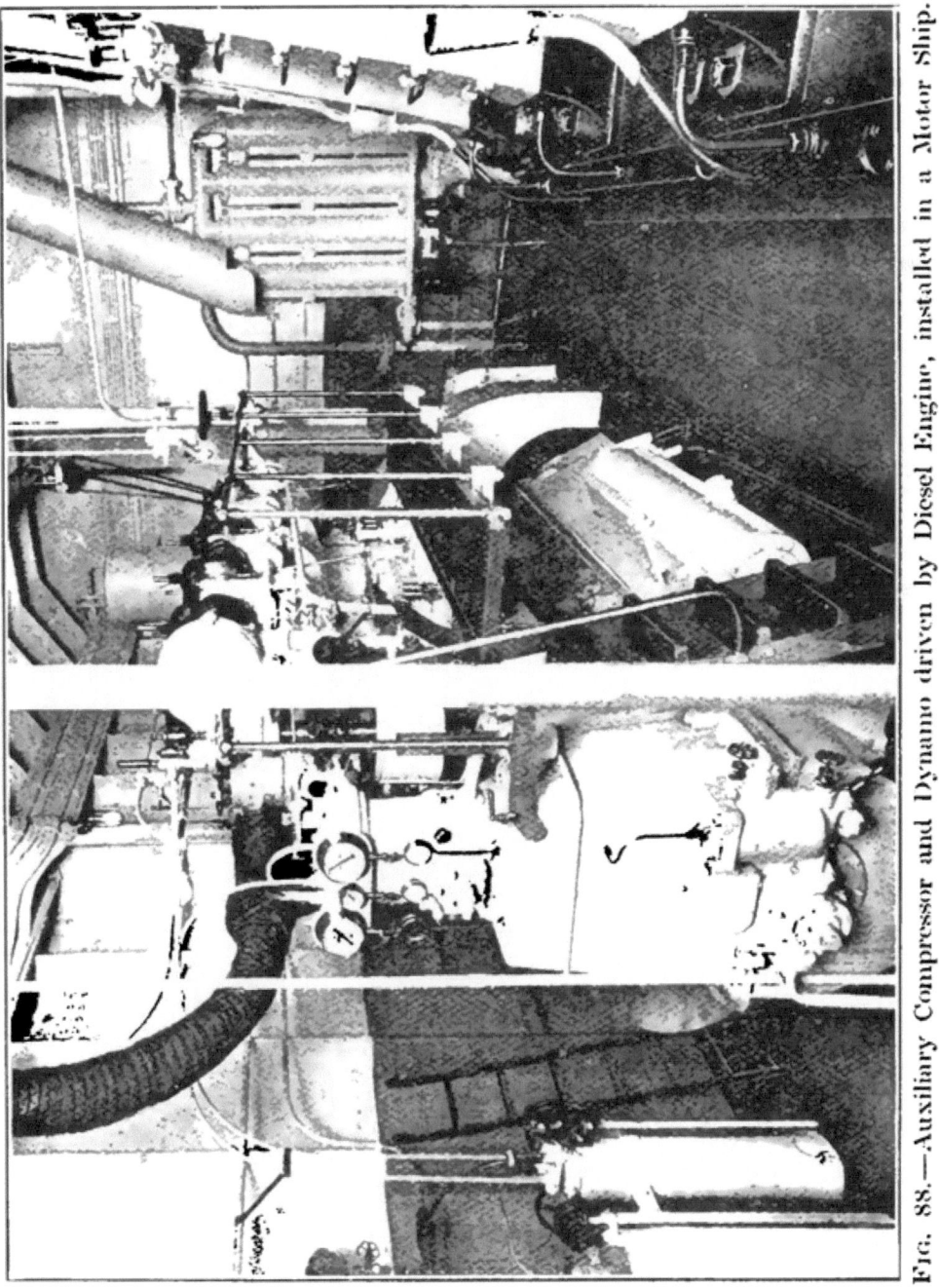

FIG. 88.—Auxiliary Compressor and Dynamo driven by Diesel Engine, installed in a Motor Ship.

pressor is installed in the engine room. When the machine is, however, coupled to a steam engine, its design naturally does not differ from ordinary practice, and both the vertical and quadruplex type have been commonly utilized for

Fig. 89.—Sulzer Auxiliary Ship's Set.

the purpose. The former is, however, gaining ground, particularly for use in conjunction with large engines.

In addition to the question of manœuvring it is desirable

to have a compressor, which can be of smaller dimensions, which is capable of supplying air for filling the starting bottles, in case the whole of the air should be lost, when the vessel is at anchor for some time, or is laid by. These smaller machines can be driven by a small steam engine, if the vessel has steam for auxiliary work, by an electric motor, or by a small oil engine.

For very large Diesel engines such as will be required in large ships in the near future, high power independent compressors will be required, and these will necessarily be driven by separate engines.

It is obvious that a very suitable arrangement for the operation of the auxiliaries in small vessels could be by compressed air, while driving such auxiliaries as can be accommodated in the engine room, direct off the reserve engine coupled to the compressor. This method has been adopted in some cases, the dynamo and some pumps being driven by the auxiliary engine, while the steering gear and other auxiliaries are driven by compressed air.

In view of the fact that so much experience has been obtained with steam-driven auxiliaries, particularly winches, windlasses and steering gear, it has been proposed that even in Diesel engine boats, such method of operation be still employed. This suggestion has, in fact, been generally adopted, and is likely to continue to find acceptance among some shipowners and engineers. The arrangement necessitates the installation of a donkey boiler to supply the steam, and this may be conveniently oil fired, though it has been proposed to utilize the exhaust gases from the main engine for the purpose. This means is, however, scarcely practicable, since, especially in two-cycle engines, the heat available is not sufficient for the work it has to accomplish, though possibly if the number of steam-driven auxiliaries be limited to the winches and windlasses it might be feasible. It has to be remembered also that some auxiliaries are required in port, particularly for loading and unloading cargo, when the main engine is standing, and hence at that time the boiler must necessarily be provided with fuel.

This arrangement of the retention of steam-driven auxiliaries and the provision of a donkey boiler is one which, although likely to find very wide adoption, may only be considered as a temporary measure employed in certain cases to avoid having too much machinery to which the marine engineer is unaccustomed.

There is moreover the objection that when the vessel has left port and begun its voyage on the open sea, the only steam required will be for the steering gear and the whistle, as any bilge pumps, etc., which are needed can be operated direct from the Diesel engines propelling the ships.

For this reason if steam auxiliaries be decided upon it is desirable that some simple means should be provided for shutting down the main engines, and for this purpose Mr. Reavell has worked out a system which is termed the "Duplex Pressure System," in which a simple compressor operated from the engine supplies air for these purposes, the air being used in the ordinary type of steam steering engine. This Duplex System provides for two pressures, the lower for ordinary work and the higher for storage purposes, and it is automatically controlled so that the compressor for storage purposes has no load thrown upon it during the whole voyage, unless some extra demand for air occurs which exceeds the normal supply. A simple form of governor is also provided for the compressor for supplying the normal air for steering, so that when the demand is less than the capacity of the compressor it is drawn out of action in a simple manner.

Such an arrangement enables the steam boiler to be shut down when the ship has left port, and steam need not be raised again until reaching harbour at the end of the voyage. All that is necessary is to close the steam valve to the deck machinery and to open the air valve from the compressor, although it is desirable perhaps to arrange for some of the exhaust gases from the main Diesel engine to be passed through the auxiliary steam boiler during the whole voyage so as to keep the water at boiling point and enable steam to be rapidly raised should an emergency arise.

There is not a single auxiliary used at sea which has not frequently been electrically driven in steamships with entire satisfaction, and hence in Diesel ships where in the ordinary way no steam is available, it is but a question of time before all auxiliaries which cannot be driven directly off the auxiliary compressor engine will be operated electrically and take their power from the main dynamo. The question as to whether the dynamo should be separately driven by another Diesel engine or off the auxiliary compressor engine depends on the size of the ship and the corresponding auxiliary power required, but as the auxiliary compressor is out of operation for long periods, reasons of economy may with safety cause the latter arrangement to be adopted even in moderately large ships.

Fuel Consumption of Motor Vessels.—Details regarding the fuel consumption of Diesel engines have been given previously for various types of motors, but it can be readily understood that the figures that are obtained on the test-bed are not exactly those met with in the course of operation in the ship. The best conditions of operation are not maintained at sea, but from the table which is given below it will be seen that the actual consumption on a commercial scale varies less from the test figures than does that of a corresponding steam engine in a steam vessel. Moreover, it has been quite clearly proved that the fuel consumption decreases to a marked extent after a Diesel engine has been in service for several months, so that this compensates almost entirely for the higher consumption which might be anticipated under the more strenuous working condition. The following table (p. 201) gives the average fuel consumptions which have been obtained with various motor ships during comparatively long periods, and whilst they cannot be taken as representing a basis of comparison between the various types of motors (since the conditions of loading vary considerably and there are other circumstances which would have to be taken into consideration), they nevertheless give a very close approximation to the consumption of oil which will be obtained with any class of motor vessels.

TABLE SHOWING CONSUMPTION OF FUEL IN MOTOR SHIPS.

Name	Boats. Type.	Length Ft.	Tonnage. D Displacement. DW Capacity.	Speed. Knots.	Engines. Type.	Builders.	Total B.H.P.	Consumption of Fuel per day (24 hours). Tons.	Remarks.
Rolandseck	General cargo	260	C. 2,700	10	Two-cycle	Tecklenborg Carels	1,500	6	Gas oil, including oil-driven dynamos and oil-fired boiler. With engines running at 100 r.p.m. and developing about 1,200-1,300 B.H.P.
Monte Penedo	General cargo	350	C. 6,500	9-10	Two-cycle	Sulzer	1,500	7·1	Gas oil S.p.G. 0·86-0·89. Lubricating oil, 350 lb. per day. Cylinder oil, 47·5 lbs. per day.
Juthlandia	General cargo and pass.	381	D. 10,000	10½-11	Four-cycle	Barclay Carels	1,900	8	1,900 B.H.P. is normal output for 10½ to 11 knots. The maximum power is about 2,000 B.H.P.
Wotan	Oil tank	104	C. 7,800	8-10	Two-cycle	Reiherstieg Carels	1,600		Full power is 1,800 B.H.P. Average speed, 75 r.p.m. Normal speed, 90 r.p.m.
Hagen	Oil tank	110	C. 7,800	11	Two-cycle	Krupp	2,300	11·1	Includes all auxiliaries.
Juno	Oil tank	258	D. 1,200	9	Four-cycle	Werkspoor	1,100	1·9	Includes donkey boiler for steering gear, dynamos and heating.
Emanuel Nobel	Oil tank	375	D. 9,700	10½	Four-cycle	Werkspoor	2,200	9·75	do. do.
Stettin	Cargo and pass.	362	C. 6,550	10½	Four-cycle	Burmeister & Wain	1,700	7·1	Includes auxiliaries, but not the heating system.

For this reason they are valuable for purposes of comparison with steam vessels doing corresponding work. In all instances the relative fuel consumption of oil and coal for motor and steam ships respectively which were given previously are well borne out, and it is probable that in most cases a corresponding steamship would consume about 4 to $4\frac{1}{2}$ times the weight of fuel as compared with a motor vessel, the one burning coal and the other using oil.

Engine-Room Staff for Motor Ships.—The staff required in the engine-room for motor vessels is considerably below that necessary for corresponding steamships, being usually in the neighbourhood of two-thirds. As, however, it is mainly the cheaper men such as the greasers who are dispensed with, it does not mean there is a reduction of one-third in the pay bill, one-quarter probably being a nearer figure. As instances of the staff required in various cases may be cited four motor vessels in which two engines each of 850 H.P. are installed, the deadweight capacity being 5,000 tons, and the length overall just over 370 feet. In these vessels the staff consists of 4 engineers, 3 assistant engineers, 3 greasers, 1 donkey man and 1 pump man. In another motor vessel 400 feet in length, having two Diesel engines capable of developing about 2,400 B.H.P., the staff consists of 4 engineers, 4 assistant engineers and 4 greasers, whereas a similar steam vessel or one to carry the same cargo, which in this case is about 7,500 tons, would require 4 engineers, 1 apprentice, 1 pump man, 1 donkey man, 3 greasers and 16 firemen and trimmers.

Weights of Marine Diesel Engines.—Though it is usually accepted that the weights of Diesel engines for marine work are below corresponding steam equipment, a few figures may be given showing the weights of actual installations. As a generalization it may be taken that for powers up to 1,000 H.P., the weight inclusive of piping, starting air bottles, manœuvring air reservoirs, with the direct driven scavenge pump and air compressor, and also the accessory circulating water and lubricating pumps, is in the neighbourhood of one ton to every 10 B.H.P. for two-cycle single-acting motors, whilst a four-cycle engine would in general be 15 to 20 per cent. heavier. The auxiliary compressor, which is practically the only auxiliary in addition to those which are necessary for a steam-driven ship, would add some 8 to 10 per cent. to the weight.

For higher powers the weight per horse power decreases unless there is a considerable reduction in speed, but not to a very large extent, and a 4,000 H.P. two-cycle single-acting marine motor, with accessories as before, weighs about 350 tons. The figures are naturally only approximate, and for moderate speed such as best suit conditions and propeller efficiency, say from about 160 revolutions per minute in the smaller engines to 120 in the larger. With double-acting motors the weights are decreased, though to what extent it is difficult at present to estimate. A 12,000 B.H.P. six-cylinder double-acting engine should, however, not weigh more than 600 to 700 tons complete.

To take a few instances, a Sulzer-Diesel marine engine of 850 B.H.P. at 160 revolutions per minute weighed 77 tons, or about 200 lb. per B.H.P., whilst another two-cycle single-acting motor of 2,000 B.H.P. weighed 170 tons or about 190 lb. per B.H.P., though at a lower speed of 130 revolutions per minute. A Krupp-Diesel motor of 1,250 B.H.P. at 140 revolutions per minute, also two-cycle single-acting, weighed 115 tons or about 210 lb. per B.H.P., whilst similar slow-speed engines of the M.A.N. type work out as follows, where it will be noticed that the 2,000 B.H.P. motor is relatively heavier than the 1,200 B.H.P.:—

B.H.P.	Revs. per Min.	Weight in Tons.	Lbs. per B.H.P.
1,200	150	91	170
1,600	120	145	200
2,000	120	178	200

The Design of Large Engines, with Particular Reference to the Motor Battleships.—In view of the probable imminence of the advent of the motor battleship, the design of very large engines, and the general arrangement of the plant which is to be anticipated, may be discussed. There is little doubt that a triple screw arrangement offers most advantages, particularly from the point of view that one or two of the engines may be shut down as desired. For the moment it may be taken that each engine should be capable of developing 20,000 H.P. in six cylinders, which is in excess of the power required on any existing battleship, excluding battle cruisers.

It is doubtful if engines of this power will be built both of the single acting and double acting type (necessarily two-cycle), and present indications point to the utilization of double-acting motors. Such large motors will probably be quite separate, and also the air compressors. With regard to the scavenge pumps, there would seem to be advantages in driving these direct off the crank shaft of the engine, although separate operation by means of Diesel engines may also be adopted. With the latter arrangement, easy regulation of the quantity of air would be possible.

By a direct drive off the crank shaft, it should not be understood that the scavenge pumps are coupled immediately to the engine shaft, as it would be preferable to arrange them some distance aft of the main engines, in separate chambers. Not only does this allow a better disposition in the engine room, but it permits of a variation in the supply of scavenge air by increasing or decreasing the pressure in the scavenge pump room.

Each engine should be provided with its own air compressor, and as these can be of such size that two are sufficient for the requirements of three engines, there is no need for an auxiliary set. There would be ample room to arrange these parallel to the main engines or at right angles, as probably the centre engine would be some distance aft of the two outer motors.

Double-acting engines require two fuel inlet valves at the bottom in any case, because of the piston rod, and no doubt there will always be two for the top, although in

Fig. 40.—2,000 H.P. Single Cylinder Two-Cycle Double Acting Diesel Engine.

single-acting engines it is quite likely that only a single valve will be employed up to 2,000 H.P. Indeed, some manufacturers take the view that immediately two valves become necessary, the limit in single-acting engines has been reached.

So far as the disposition of the machinery goes with such a design, there seems no reason to anticipate any serious difficulties either in battleships or large liners. There would be no interference with the gunnery arrangements, and the length of engine room would probably be little more than one-half of the total length of boiler and engine room combined, in the case of steam plant, whilst the weight should be 30 per cent. less.

There are apparently no unknown factors in the problem of the adoption of very large Diesel engines for battleships and the biggest merchant vessels, and there remains solely the question of application. This, however, will not rest long in abeyance, as can readily be gathered by the wonderfully rapid progress which has been made, and the now generally accepted opinion that the Diesel engine is the motor of the future for marine propulsion.

In *Fig*. 90 an illustration is given of an experimental two-cycle double-acting Diesel engine built by Messrs. Krupp, designed for 2,000 B.H.P., which gave considerably more power than this. Although this actual motor must not be taken as the prototype of the large Diesel engine, it will be found that 12,000 B.H.P. motors will embody many features of the design, one of which is the operation of the valves by means of oil under pressure.

CHAPTER VII

CONSTRUCTION OF THE DIESEL MARINE ENGINE

TWO-CYCLE ENGINE: SWISS TYPE—BELGIUM TYPES—SWEDISH TYPE—GERMAN TYPES—BRITISH TYPES—FOUR-CYCLE ENGINE: DUTCH TYPE—GERMAN TYPES—DANISH TYPE—RUSSIAN TYPES—SMALL DIESEL ENGINES

Two-Cycle Engine : Swiss Type.—At the present time the engine which is perhaps finding most general application for marine work is the two-cycle single acting type. With the marine engine there are more differences of construction than with the stationary motor, owing to the introduction in the two-cycle marine engine of a suitable reversing and regulating arrangement. The small engine of Messrs. Sulzer's construction is of the two-cycle single acting type, and it is built with four or six working cylinders—a small flywheel being provided. The cylinders are supported by pillars instead of the usual A frame, and easily removable covers enclose the crank chamber. The valves (scavenge, fuel and starting) are arranged in the cylinder head, but in each cylinder two scavenge valves are fitted, one on each side of the fuel valve, as shown in *Fig.* 91, which illustrates a typical engine of this design. By this means relatively small valves are permissible to allow the entrance of the large amount of scavenging air, and the valve bodies are lighter and more easily operated, but in the latest designs scavenge valves are omitted altogether, and ports are employed at the bottom of the cylinder.

In the engine illustrated in *Fig.* 91 there is one double acting scavenge pump in line with the working cylinders,

CONSTRUCTION OF DIESEL MARINE ENGINE 207

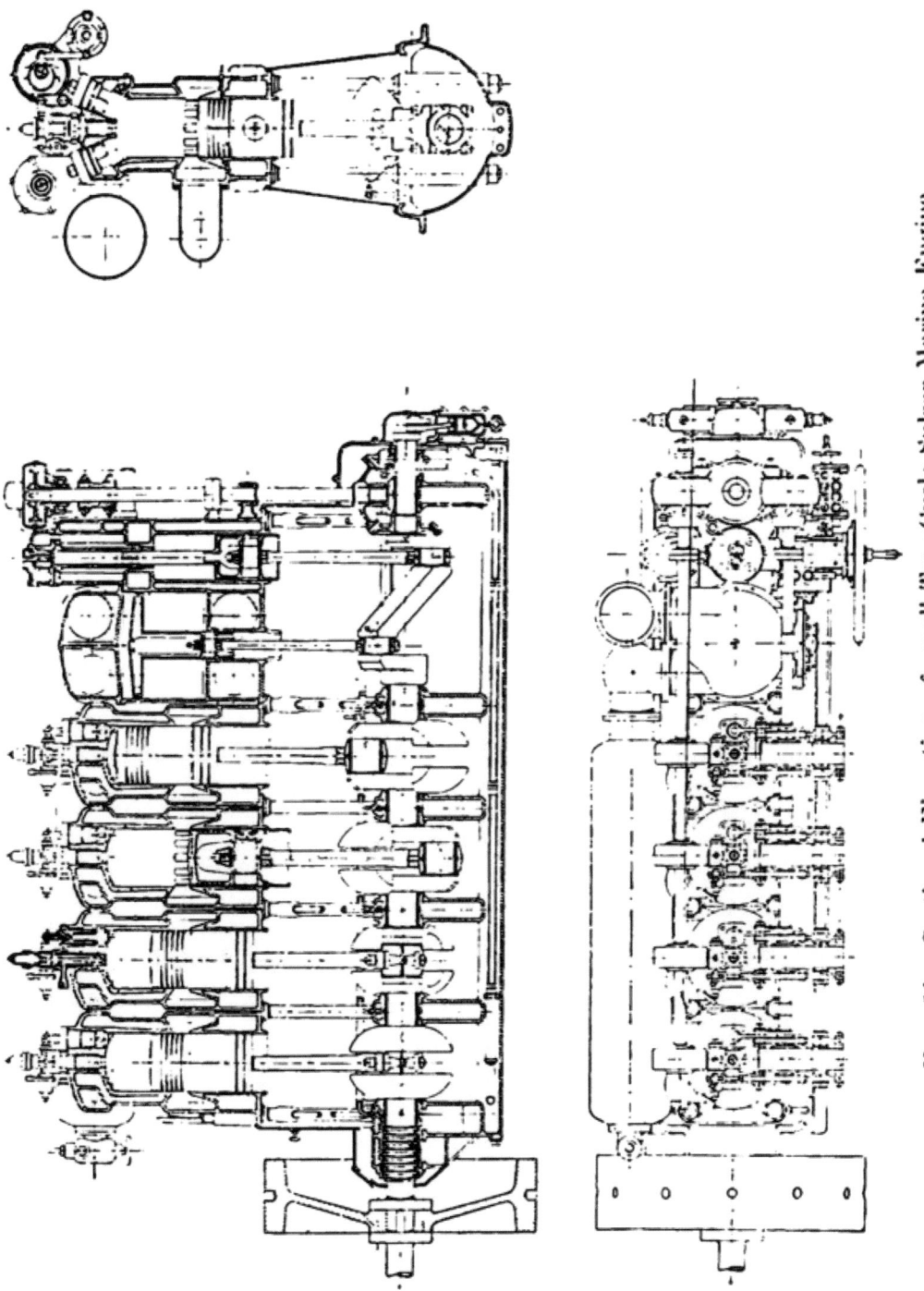

Fig. 91.—Sectional Elevation of small Two-Cycle Sulzer Marine Engine.

with a piston diameter of nearly double that of the latter. The scavenge air is delivered into the long cylindrical receiver seen at the back of the engine, and thence to the various cylinders through the valves. The burnt gaseous

G4
G5
E1
E2
E3
D2
D1
A
F1
C
H
B1
B2
B3
B4
G
F2
G1
G2
G3

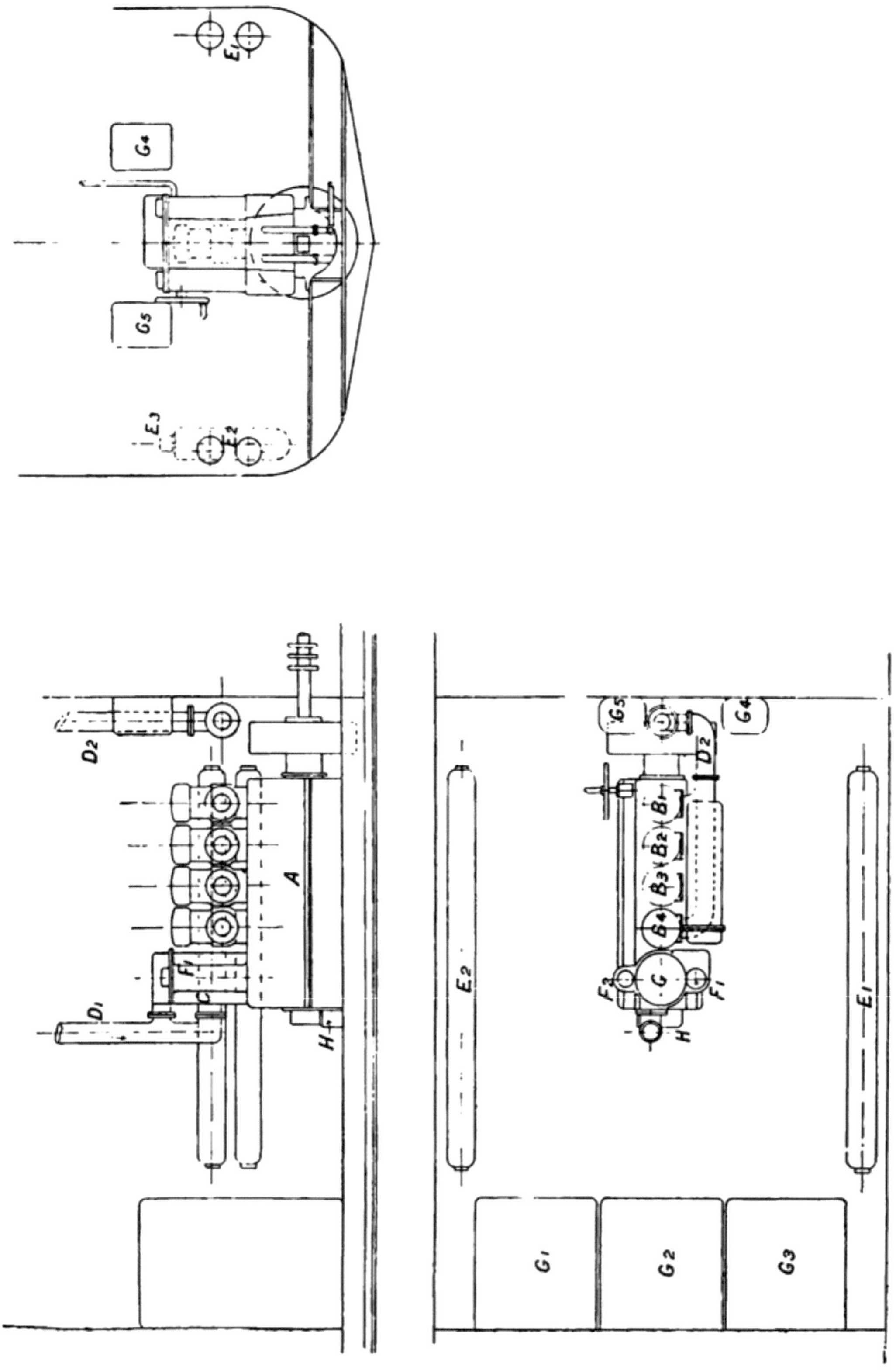

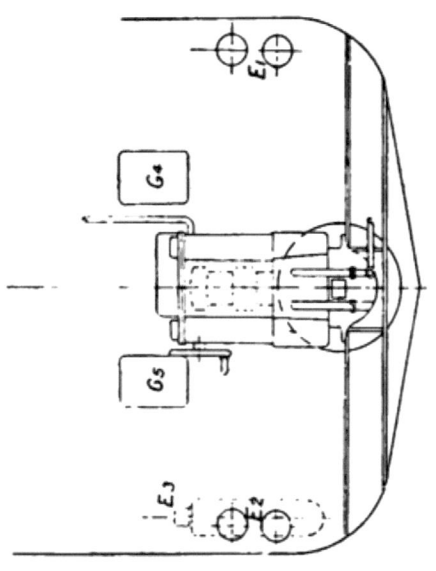

CONSTRUCTION OF DIESEL MARINE ENGINE

mixture is exhausted through longitudinal ports at the bottom of the cylinder arranged round the whole of the circumference, into a common exhaust pipe running the length of the engine and thence to the silencer. A two stage air compressor is provided arranged as shown for the supply of injection air and for filling the compressed air vesels with air required for starting and manœuvring, although this method is not always adopted, the pumps being placed in front of and behind the scavenge cylinder in some engines, being then driven by links off the scavenge pump piston rod. The pumps are water cooled, inter-

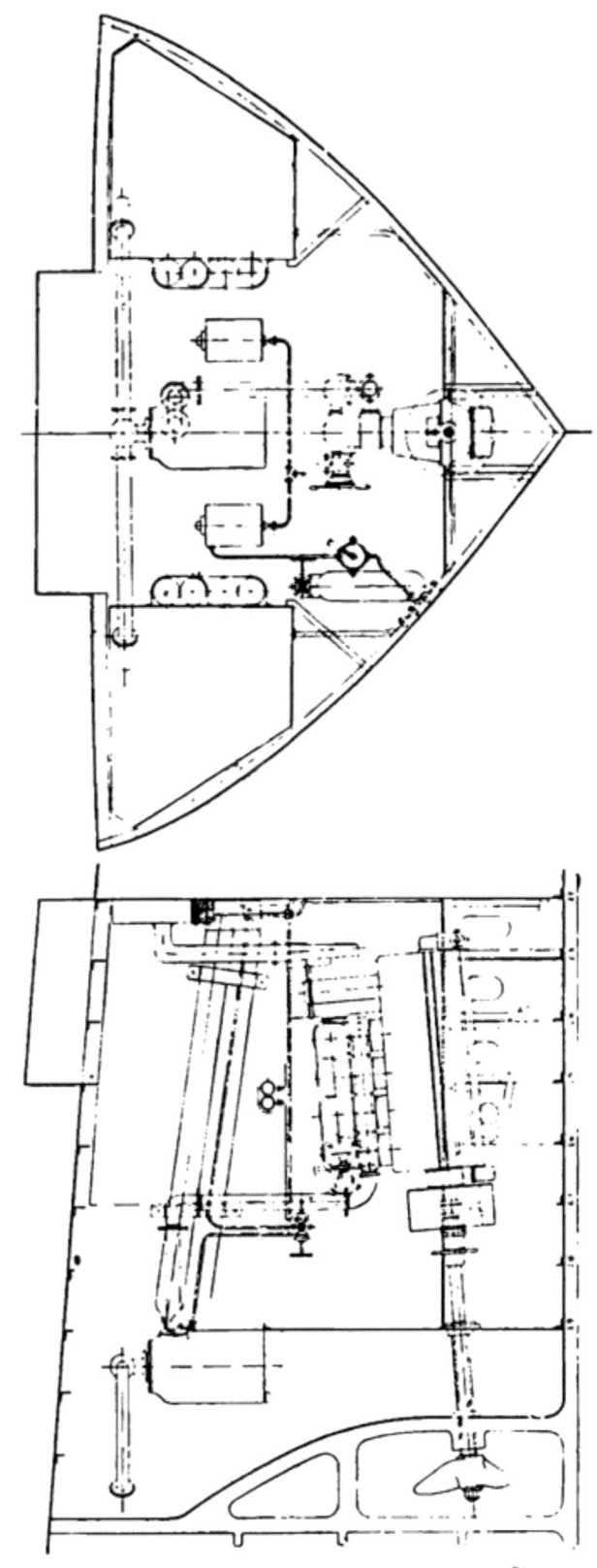

Fig. 93.—General Arrangement of small Diesel Ship, showing Auxiliaries.

mediate cooling between the stages being also arranged for.

A long trunk piston is employed, serving at the same time as a crosshead, and in the larger engines this piston is water or oil cooled. Forced lubrication is adopted for all the main bearings, the oil pumps being driven off the crank shaft at the end of the engine, and also the cooling water pump, while a thrust block is arranged on the engine itself, though for large powers it may be fixed separately on the propeller shaft as near the engine as convenient.

The operation of starting and reversing the engine is carried out by means of compressed air. The cam shaft is first put into the position in which the cams are set to operate the valve levers for ahead or astern, by turning a vertical spindle which drives this cam shaft, this operation being performed by turning the hand wheel controlling the engine. By a further rotation of the hand wheel the spindle, on which are pivoted the levers working the valves, first brings the starting valve lever into operation, thus running up the engine on compressed air, and then the fuel and scavenge valve levers, cutting out the starting valve at the same time. This is accomplished by having all the levers mounted eccentrically on the pivot spindle as shown in *Fig.* 91. The engine has an automatic arrangement for regulating the fuel and air during the reversing period, so as to assure the correct positions of the fuel inlet mechanism, and a governor is also provided to prevent the motor running beyond a determined maximum speed which, however, is only likely to occur in the event of a propeller shaft breaking or the engine racing. The actual speed is controlled by a small hand lever which regulates the amount of fuel delivered from the fuel pumps to the fuel inlet valves.

This type of motor is now seldom constructed owing to the new designs that have been brought forward, and is chiefly of interest as showing the tendencies in construction in the earlier machines of relatively small power. It was of much value, however, in affording experience in the operation of small marine motors.

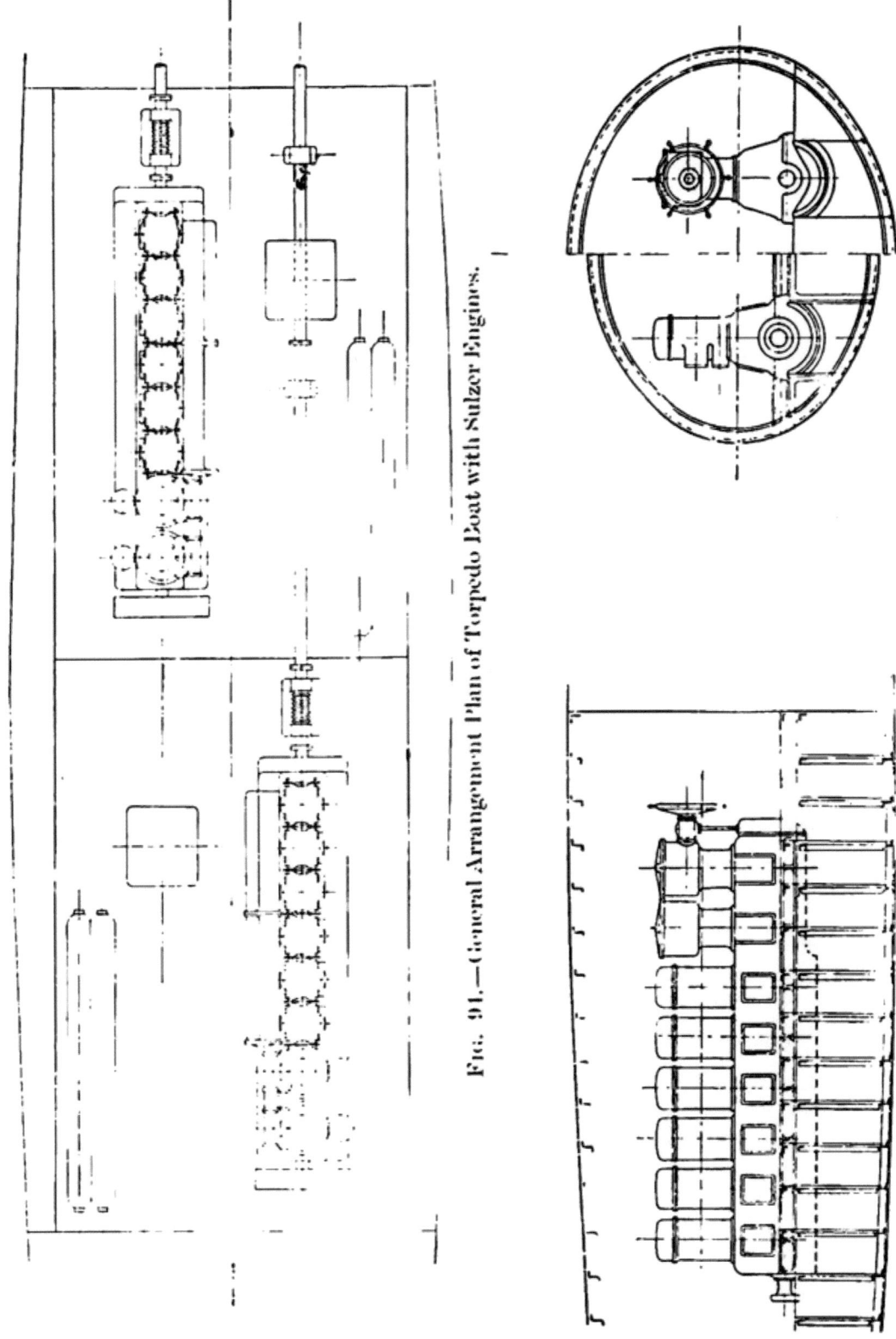

Fig. 91.—General Arrangement Plan of Torpedo Boat with Sulzer Engines.

Fig. 92 shows the general arrangement of a single engine and accessories of this type in which the references are as follows :—

A	Engine coupled direct to propeller shaft.
$B_1 B_2 B_3 B_4$	Working cylinders.
C	Scavenge pump.
D_1	Suction pipe for scavenge air.
D_2	Exhaust pipe.
E_1	Starting and manœuvring air reservoirs.
E_2	Reserve starting air reservoirs.
E_3	Ignition air reservoir.
$F_1 F_2$	Air pumps.
$G_1 G_2 G_3$	Fuel tanks.
$G_4 G_5$	Fuel reservoirs.
H	Cooling water pump.

This is a typical arrangement which has been adopted for small engines, the auxiliary air compressor being installed in any convenient position, not necessarily in the engine-room, but if desired at some portion of the vessel above the water line. *Fig.* 93 shows the general arrangement of a comparatively small Diesel engine plant, installed as an auxiliary on a sailing vessel, in which the compactness of the engine and its accessories is well seen. The various portions will be understood from the above description without further details.

The type of engine adopted by Messrs. Sulzer for submarines and torpedo boats is a six-cylinder machine with two scavenge pumps in line with the working cylinders and an air compressor for the injection and starting air in front of each scavenge cylinder. *Figs.* 94 *and* 95 show respectively the arrangement of the engines for a torpedo boat and a submarine—the engines being staggered owing to the restricted width of the engine-room.

In their most recent design of marine engine particularly adapted for large cargo vessels, Messrs. Sulzer Bros. have made several important modifications in design, and

FIG. 96.—Sulzer Direct Reversible Marine Diesel Engine; a type used for relatively small power.

Fig. 97.—Sulzer Marine Engine. Front View.

CONSTRUCTION OF DIESEL MARINE ENGINE 215

Fig. 98.—Sulzer Marine Engine. Back View

Figs. 97, 98, 102 illustrate the present construction for slow speed engines of high power. The two-cycle principle is retained, and the main point of difference lies in the abolition of all scavenge valves in the cylinder cover, the actual method of scavenging being described later.

For sizes up to 800–1,000 H.P. a four-cylinder design is employed, engines of 850 B.H.P. for a vessel of the Hamburg South American Line having a cylinder diameter of $16\frac{3}{4}$ inches and a stroke of 27 inches, the speed of revolution being 150 at maximum output. The engine is of the crosshead type, and although the crank chamber is enclosed, it is provided with covers at the back which are readily removable. The arrangement of the scavenge pump differs from that adopted by Messrs. Krupp and Messrs. Carels for similar slow speed two-cycle marine engines. Only one pump is provided for each engine, and this is driven direct off the crank shaft, being mounted on the same bed-plate at the after end. The low pressure stage of the injection air pump forms the crosshead for the scavenge pump piston, and there is a certain advantage in this arrangement in minimizing the vibration which otherwise occurs due to the heavy scavenge pump piston. The high and intermediate pressure stages of the air pump are mounted in front of the scavenge pump, and are actuated by means of a rocking lever from the connecting rod of the low pressure pump.

The method is illustrated in *Fig.* 99, in which both the high and intermediate stages of the three-stage compressor set are mounted in front of the scavenge cylinder. The drive is arranged from a crank fixed to the main crank shaft, and as is seen from the illustration, the piston of the L.P. pump forms the crosshead of the scavenge pump. The general arrangement is evident from the diagram and need not be further explained. The scavenge pump is controlled by a piston valve as seen in *Fig.* 98, and the gear on the extreme left shows the Stephenson link motion for reversing the delivery of the scavenge air when the engine is reversed.

Fig. 100 shows diagrammatically the method adopted for the supply of scavenge air to the engine cylinders. Ports are provided at the bottom for the discharge of the exhaust gases, as in all two-cycle engines, these extending only half-way round the periphery and being represented

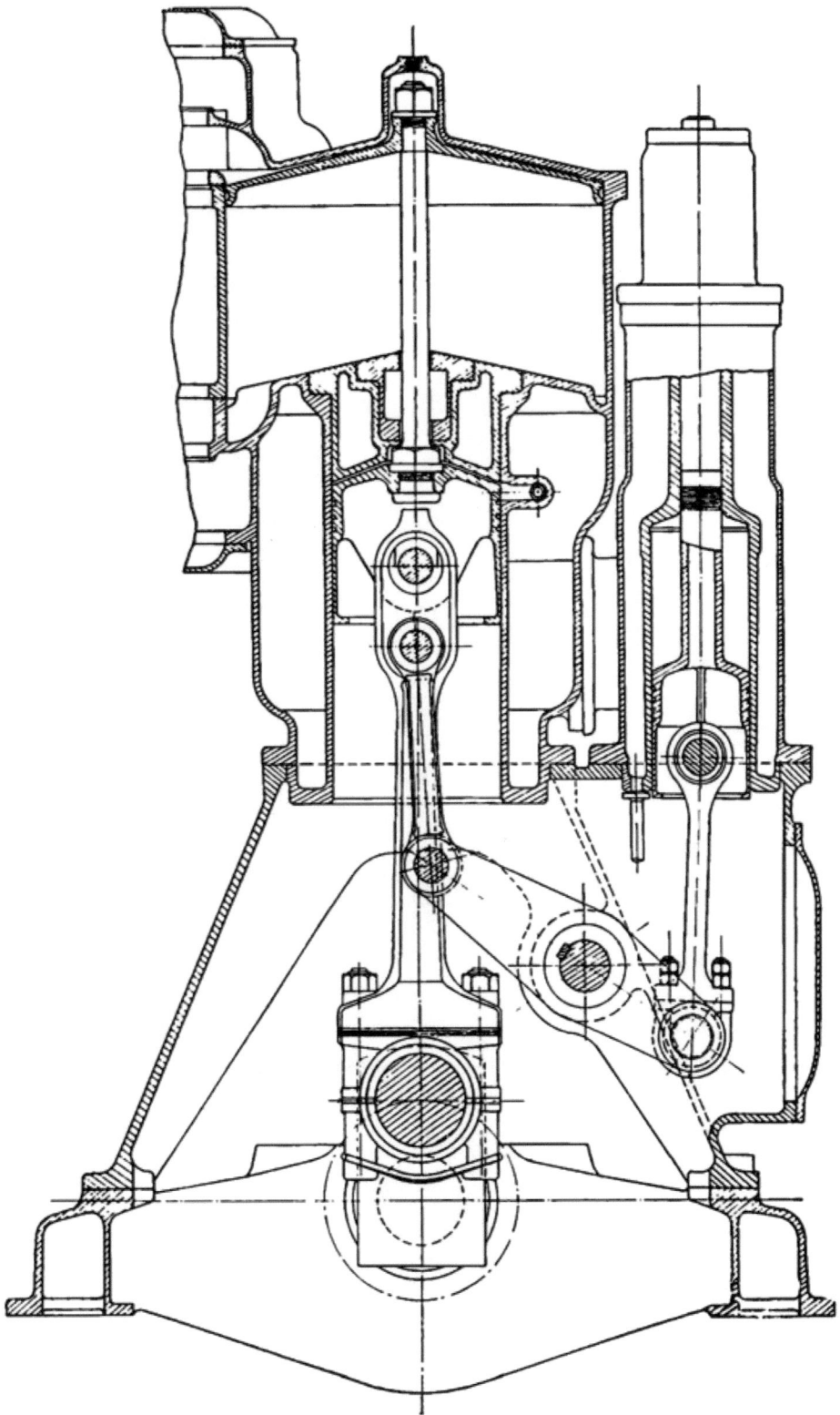

Fig. 99.—Arrangement of Scavenge Pump and Air Compressor with Sulzer Marine Engine.

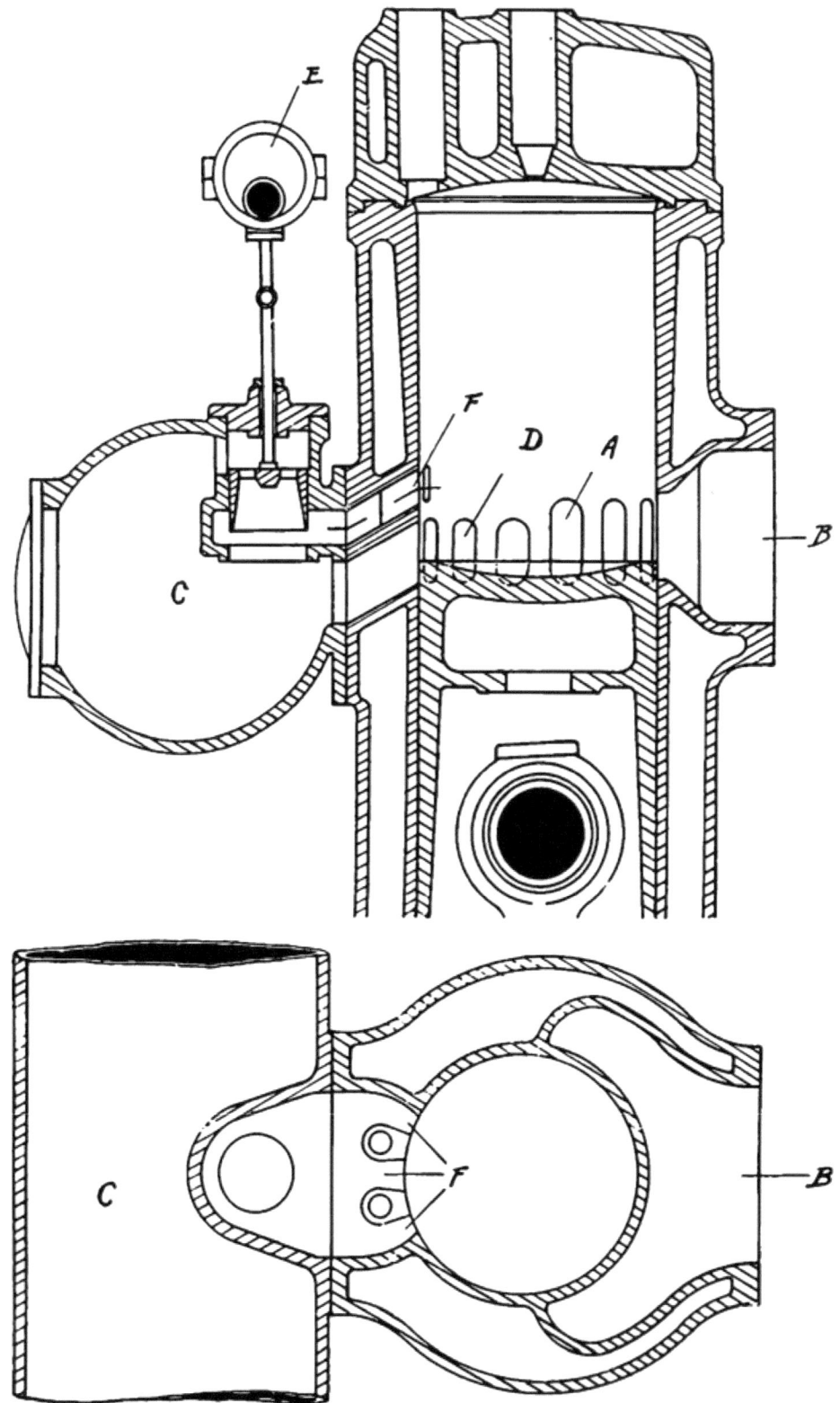

Fig. 100.—Scavenging Arrangements by means of Ports in Sulzer Engine.

in the illustration by A, the discharge into the exhaust pipe taking place through B. The scavenge air is delivered into the pipe C from the scavenge pump, and the main supply enters the cylinder through the ports D, which are spaced half-way round the periphery and are inclined so as to deflect the air upwards.

In the actual scavenge pipe itself is arranged a piston valve actuated directly from the cam shaft by means of the eccentric E. The air which passes through this valve enters the cylinder through the ports F, which extend round one-half of the circumference and are immediately above the main scavenge ports. The opening of the piston valve is so arranged that air is introduced through the slots F after the ports D have been closed by the main piston starting on its upward stroke. By this arrangement the scavenging appears to be very effective, and it is of interest to note that so many different methods of overcoming the undoubted difficulties of thoroughly efficient scavenging have been adopted in varying designs. There is, of course, the advantage that the air remaining in the cylinder after scavenging is at a pressure of about 3 lbs. per square inch instead of at atmospheric pressure.

As no valves are employed in the cylinder head for exhaust or scavenge air, there remain but the fuel inlet valve and the starting air valve. Reversing is thus simplified and is accomplished merely by turning the cam shaft through an angle relative to the crank shaft and so setting the cams operating the fuel inlet valve in a position for reverse running. This operation is carried out by raising the vertical intermediate shaft which drives the cam shaft from the crank shaft. This intermediate shaft is broken, and a sleeve coupling interposed, which permits of its being raised or lowered, and thus turning the cam shaft relative to the crank shaft. As previously mentioned, the scavenge air supply is changed on reversal by means of a Stephenson link motion.

From the illustrations of the engine, and in particular from *Fig.* 97, it can be seen that there are two hand wheels

A and B in the centre, which serve for reversing and manœuvring the engine by hand, in the event of the breakdown in the auxiliary air motors, by means of which the operations are usually carried out. The levers C and D below the wheels A and B respectively control these servo motors, the first (operated by D) being for the purpose of reversing the link motion of the ports for the scavenge pump, and also rotating the cam shaft, whilst the second (operated by C) controls the starting and fuel valve levers for starting and running.

The reversing may be followed out in stages. In the first place the scavenge pump valve has to be reversed, and the link motion previously mentioned is changed over by means of the horizontal shaft E (*Fig.* 102). A partial rotation of this shaft causes the link to reverse, and the rotation is given it by the compressed air auxiliary motor controlled by lever D on the hand wheel B. The same operation of this motor causes the cam shaft to be turned through a small angle relative to the crank shaft.

As regards the valves, there is but one cam, F, for the fuel valve, both for ahead and astern, and as in reverse running, all that is required is a change of lead from one side of the dead point to the other, it is evident that the rotation of the cam shaft is sufficient to provide this with one cam. The fuel valve cam is thus set for reverse running by the partial rotation of the cam shaft. This, however, would not set the air starting valves correctly for astern running, as the leads are different, and hence two cams are provided for each of these valves. These are fixed side by side on the cam shaft (G and H), and as there is no longitudinal motion of this shaft in reversing, as in most other engines, arrangements have to be made for bringing the starting air valve levers over the astern or ahead cam as required. This is carried out by having a vertical rod J attached to the air valve cam, at the bottom of which is the roller which is lifted by the cam. The joint of the vertical rod and the valve lever is a double one, and allows the former to move longitudinally so as to bring the roller

Fig. 101.—600 B.H.P. Sulzer High-Speed Marine Diesel Engine.

above one or other cam. The longitudinal motion is given to the shaft K from the auxiliary air motor controlled by lever C at the starting platform, the roller being coupled to this shaft K by means of a small connecting rod.

When starting up, the air valve levers (or rather the vertical rods attached to them) are brought down on the cams by a rotation of the spindle L, on which the levers are pivoted, this operation also being controlled by the auxiliary air motor from the starting platform by the lever C. The engine runs up on air, the fuel valve levers being out of action for the time being. When the engine has run up to speed after a few revolutions, the air valve levers are lifted up and the fuel valves come into operation, and the arrangement is such that the engine can run (1) with only two cylinders on air, (2) with four cylinders on air, (3) with two cylinders on air and two on fuel, and finally, (4) with four cylinders on fuel. The dial seen in the centre of the engine in *Fig.* 102 indicates how the cylinders are working in this respect. In order that this arrangement may be carried out, the spindle L on which the valve levers are pivoted is divided in two portions in the centre, so that two of the air valve levers may be down on their cams on two cylinders and two of the fuel valve levers on the remaining two cylinders.

The quantity of fuel admitted to the cylinder is controlled by means of the lever M seen in *Fig.* 100 in the centre of the engine, whilst the air injection pressure is also regulated from the starting platform, being about 60 atmospheres for full speed and 40 atmospheres for slow running. Four fuel pumps are provided at N, one for each cylinder, and the supply to each cylinder may be regulated by hand. The lever seen in front of the fuel pump chamber is for pumping up the fuel before starting. The governor O is also connected to the fuel chamber by the vertical rod P, so that when the speed exceeds the normal, the supply is reduced.

An interesting feature of the design of the engine is the control of the timing of the fuel valve at varying speeds.

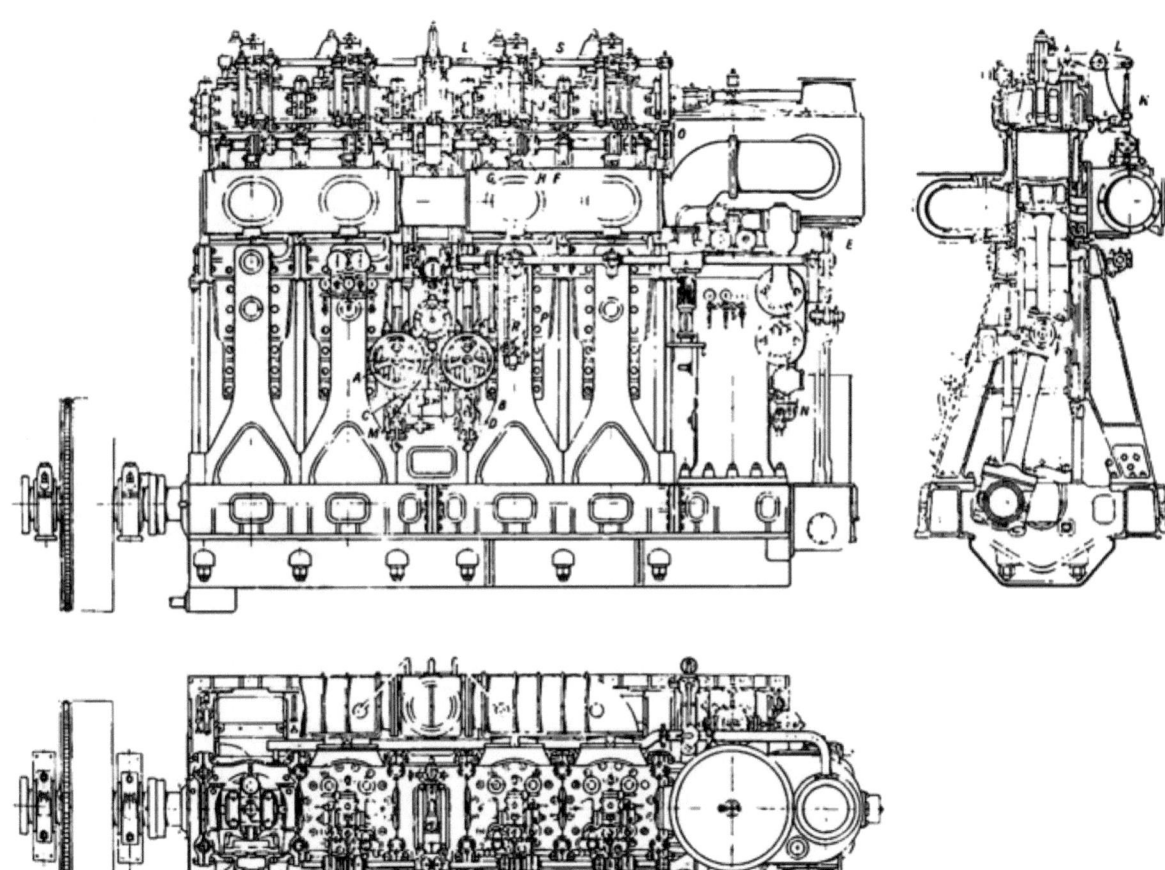

FIG. 102.—Sulzer Marine Engine.

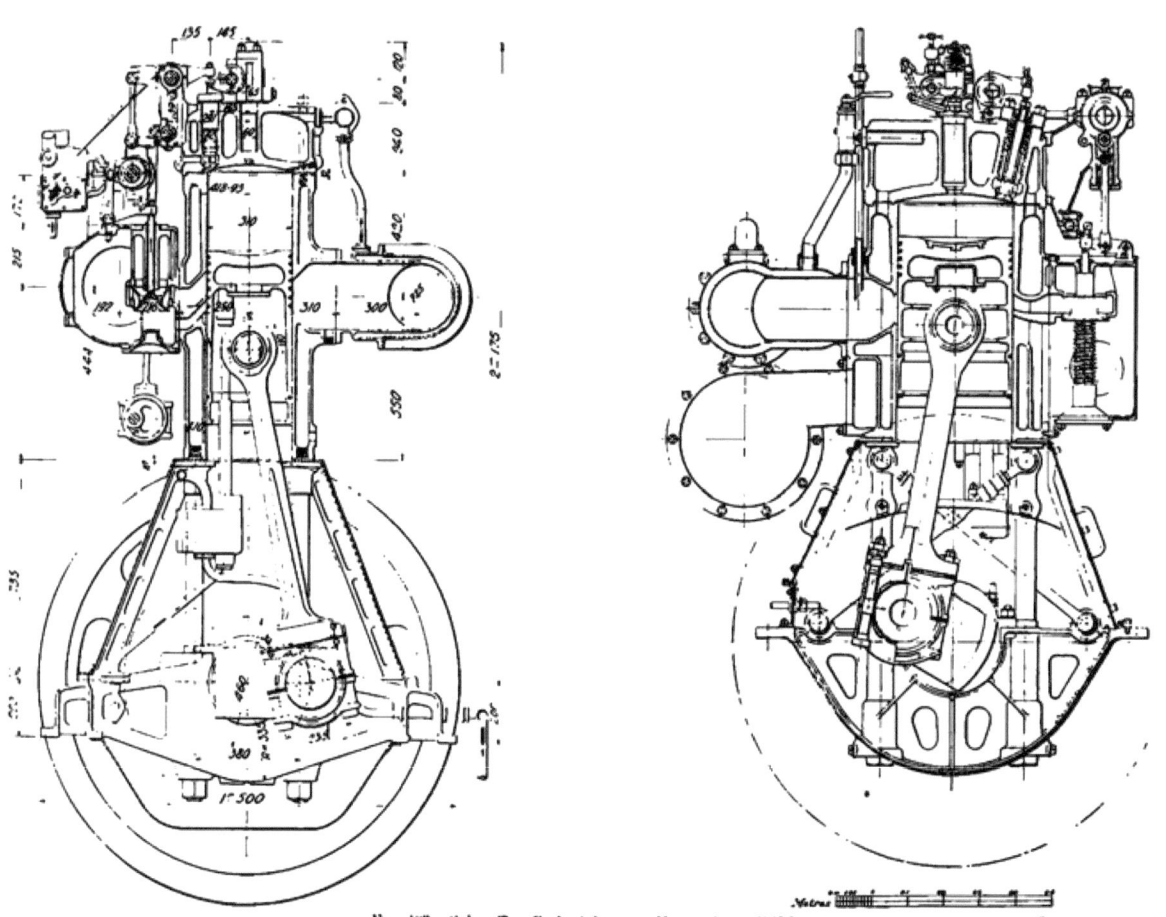

Fig. 103.—Sulzer Two-Cycle Submarine Motor of 600 B.H.P.

This is accomplished by means of the hand wheel *P*, which turns the shaft *R* and moves the vertical rod *S* connected to the fuel valve cam out of the vertical, so that the timing of its contact with the fuel valve cam is altered as required.

The various pumps seen in front of the engine are for auxiliary purposes. Forced lubrication is adopted and the oil is used continuously, being cooled in circulation. For the cylinder lubrication eight small pumps are provided, two for each cylinder, allowing four points in which the lubricating oil may enter each cylinder. The pistons are water cooled, a tube being attached to the hollow body of the piston, which dips into a water reservoir, forcing the water up into the piston. The exhaust pipe is also water cooled, and the cylinder jacket cooling is carried out in the usual way.

The fuel consumption of the engine, with all the auxiliary pumps as shown, is 0·46 lbs. per B.H.P. hour, and the weight of the engine without any auxiliaries is 55 tons. Including all pipes, air reservoirs, silencers, etc., the weight is 77 tons, and the fly-wheel weighs $9\frac{1}{2}$ tons.

Belgian Types.—In Belgium the Diesel engine has been mainly developed by Messrs. Carels of Ghent, and the original marine motor of this firm did not differ greatly from that of the earlier types of Messrs. Sulzer's, as described previously. *Fig.* 104 shows one of the first large marine engines (of 1,000 B.H.P.) of four working cylinders and one scavenge pump, this motor now being utilized for experimental work and for dynamo driving. Although containing many features which are not now considered the best practice, the engine was a remarkable achievement in that it was by far the largest directly reversible two-stroke machine built at the time.

The marine engine which has now been developed at Ghent for general ship propulsion, and which is constructed by a number of firms, is of a different type, based on the experience gained with the earlier motors. The general type is illustrated in *Fig.* 108, whilst *Fig.* 111 shows an 1,800 H.P. engine for a large oil tank vessel. Crossheads are employed and the design is of the open type with a view

Fig. 104.—1,000 H.P. Carels' Diesel Marine Engine. Early Type.

CONSTRUCTION OF DIESEL MARINE ENGINE

to conforming to the ideas of marine engineers, and to render the parts accessible. There are four or six cylinders according to the size, and generally speaking the engine is a four-cylinder one up to about 1,000 or 1,200 H.P., and six cylinders if above. Two scavenge pumps are always employed, which is a point of difference from the Sulzer motor. These scavenge pumps are arranged at the back of the engine and driven off the crossheads of two of the cylinders by means of connecting rods, in much the same way as the air pumps on some reciprocating steam engines. A Reavell compressor is arranged at the end of the engine in the same manner as in many types of stationary Diesel engines. The scavenge pumps, which are double acting, are provided with piston valves—a method which seems well adapted for the purpose.

Usually the bed-plate is divided into two or three portions, and the frame is built up by hollow box columns, on the top of which the cylinders are supported, there being two columns for each cylinder. Several of these columns (usually four) are employed for the purpose of conveying the scavenge air to the main scavenge pipe, thus reducing the complication of piping on the engine. The crank shaft is also divided, and this is of advantage in that a smaller spare length may be carried in the vessel.

In large two-cycle marine engines the question of scavenging is one of some difficulty. A big volume of air at low pressure has to be admitted, and it is impossible to accomplish this by means of one valve only, when valves are employed. In the Carels engine for large powers, four scavenge valves are fitted to each cylinder, arranged in the cover and operated by two levers and two cams. The method is somewhat expensive, and to a certain extent complicated, and largely minimizes the advantage of simplicity which the two-cycle engine might otherwise claim over the four-cycle, but it ensures very efficient scavenging.

In spite of the many valves necessitated by this arrangement, reversing is very rapidly carried out, the time taken from full speed ahead to full speed astern being about

226 DIESEL ENGINES FOR LAND AND MARINE WORK

10 seconds. The general principle of the method of reversing is to provide a separate ahead and astern cam side by side, both for the fuel valve and the starting valve, and

FIG. 105.—View of Engine Room of M.S. *France*, with two Schneider-Carels Motors of 900 B.H.P. at 230 r.p.m.

only one cam for each pair of scavenge valves. It is evident that as far as the actuation of these valves is concerned, this arrangement is sufficient if the cam shaft is turned

CONSTRUCTION OF DIESEL MARINE ENGINE 227

through a certain angle relative to the crank shaft. When the engine runs in the astern direction, the scavenge valves will be opened at the correct moment for reverse running.

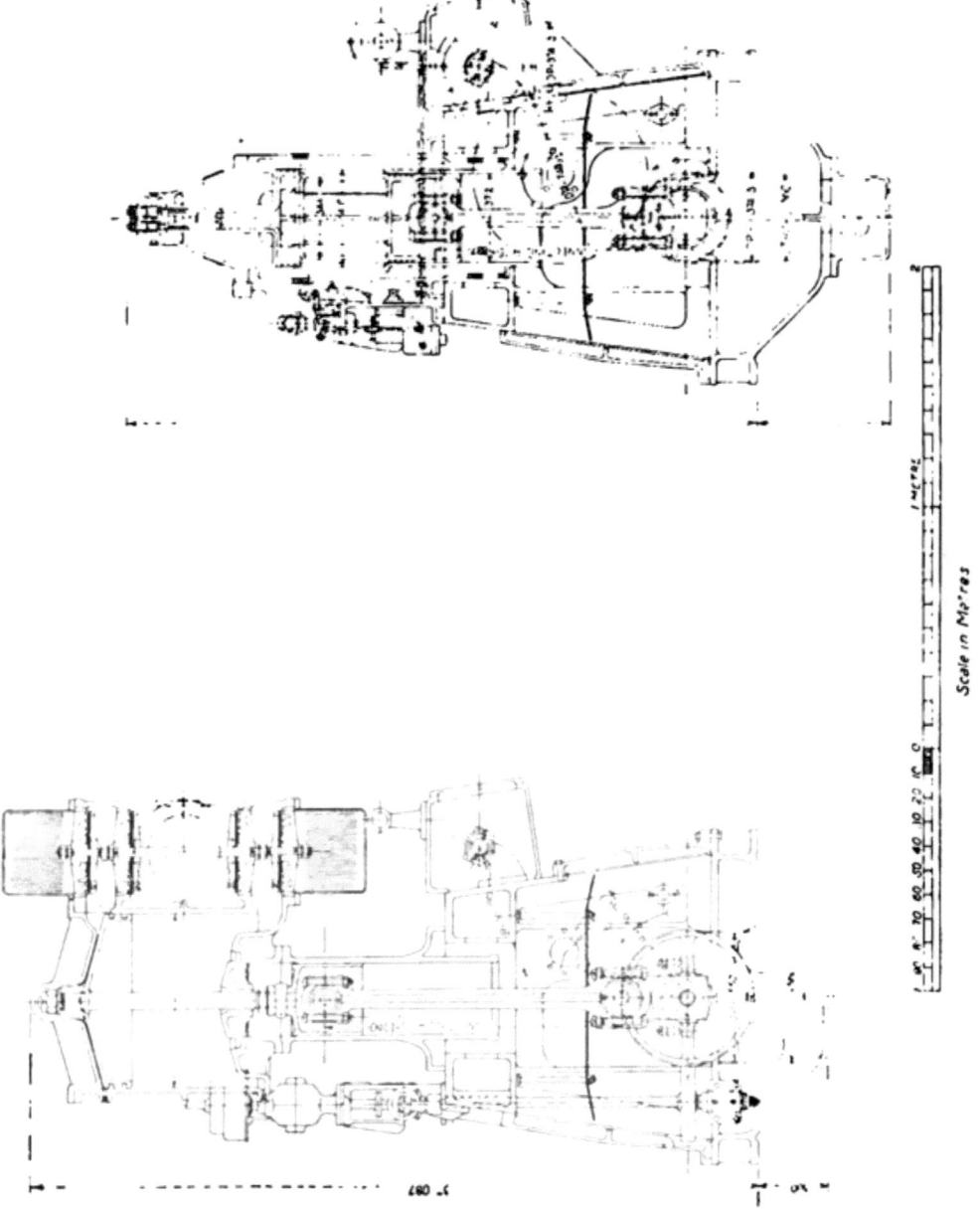

Fig. 106.—Scavenge Pump and Compressor for 900 H.P. Two-Cycle Engine at 230 r.p.m.

The turning of the cam shaft is accomplished by means of the vertical intermediate shaft seen in the centre of *Fig.* 108, by which the cam shaft is driven from the crank shaft as in stationary engines. This vertical shaft is raised either by means of the large hand wheel in the left of *Fig.* 108, or by means of a small compressed air motor. It is in two parts coupled by a sleeve, and only the upper portion is raised, thus carrying the cam shaft round through the required angle.

The operation just described sets the scavenge valve cams in their correct positions. For the fuel and starting valve cams, since the cam shaft is not capable of moving longitudinally, a secondary or manœuvring shaft is provided in front of the cam shaft. When it is desired to reverse the engine, this manœuvring shaft is moved lengthwise a distance equal to the width of one of the cams, and by this means the rollers of the levers actuating the valves are caused to come over the astern cams instead of the ahead. Before this can be done, however, the levers have all to be lifted off the cams so that the movement may be given to the manœuvring shaft. The whole of the actions for reversing or starting up the engine, except turning the cam shaft, as described previously, are accomplished by means of the handwheel seen in the centre of *Fig.* 108, which causes the manœuvring shaft to rotate. After the cams are set, the engine is started upon air, then some of the cylinders run on air and some on fuel; in the third stage all starting air is cut off, and finally all the cylinders are in operation running on fuel. The various levers and handles are interlocked, so that it is impossible for the engine to start up until the cams are in their correct positions, and no fuel can be supplied to the engine until it has run up on compressed air. The sloping handwheel seen on the right in *Fig.* 108 is for controlling the governor, which is of the centrifugal type and acts on the fuel pumps to regulate the speed of the engine.

The pistons are of cast iron and are water cooled, whilst the cylinder covers are of cast steel. The exhaust ports are at the bottom of the cylinders, and a stuffing box is fitted at the bottom to prevent leakage of exhaust gases into the engine-room.

Figs. 113 and 114 show an engine of this type of 800

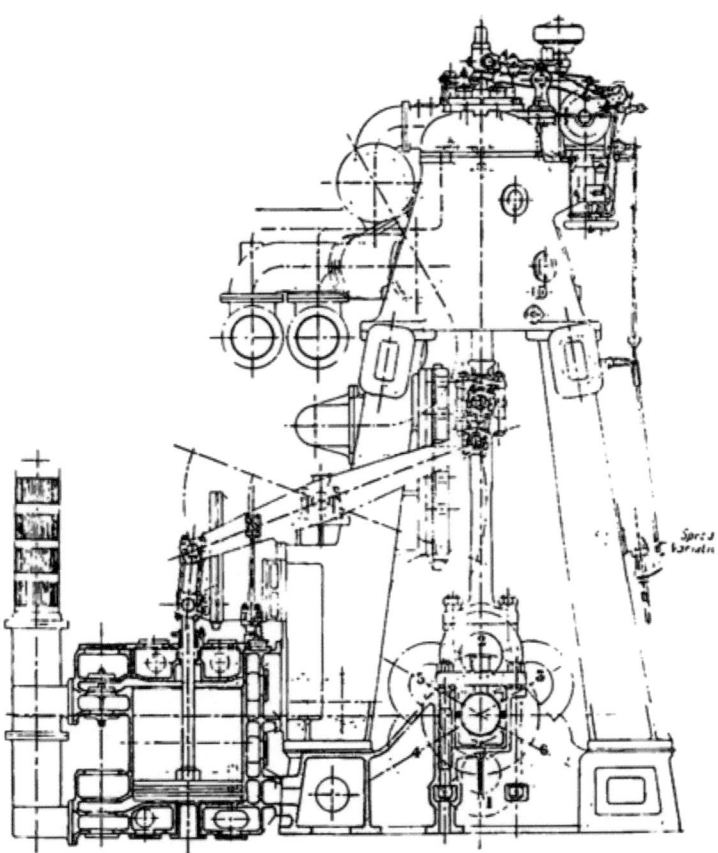

FIG. 107.—1,500 B.H.P. Carels Type Marine Motor. End View, showing Scavenge Pump.

[To face page 228.

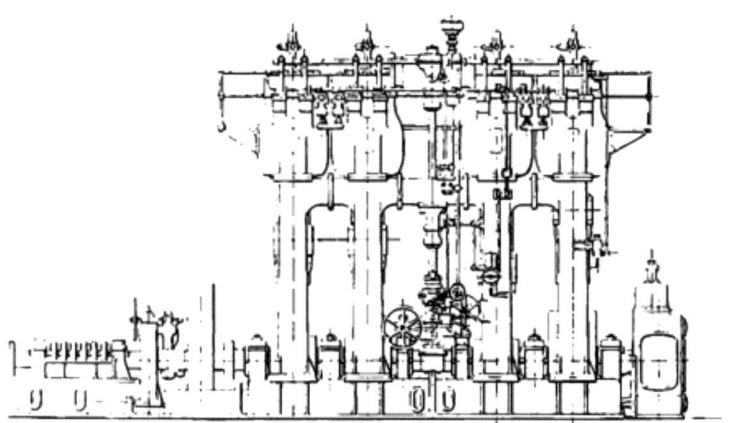
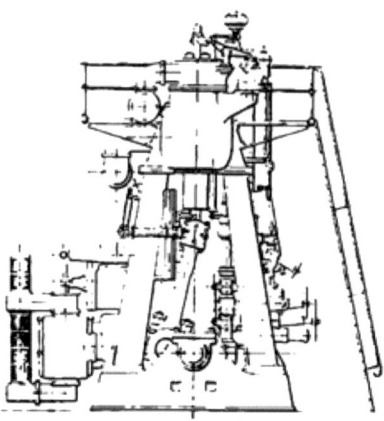

FIG. 108.—Marine Diesel Engine, Carels Type.

[To face page 228.

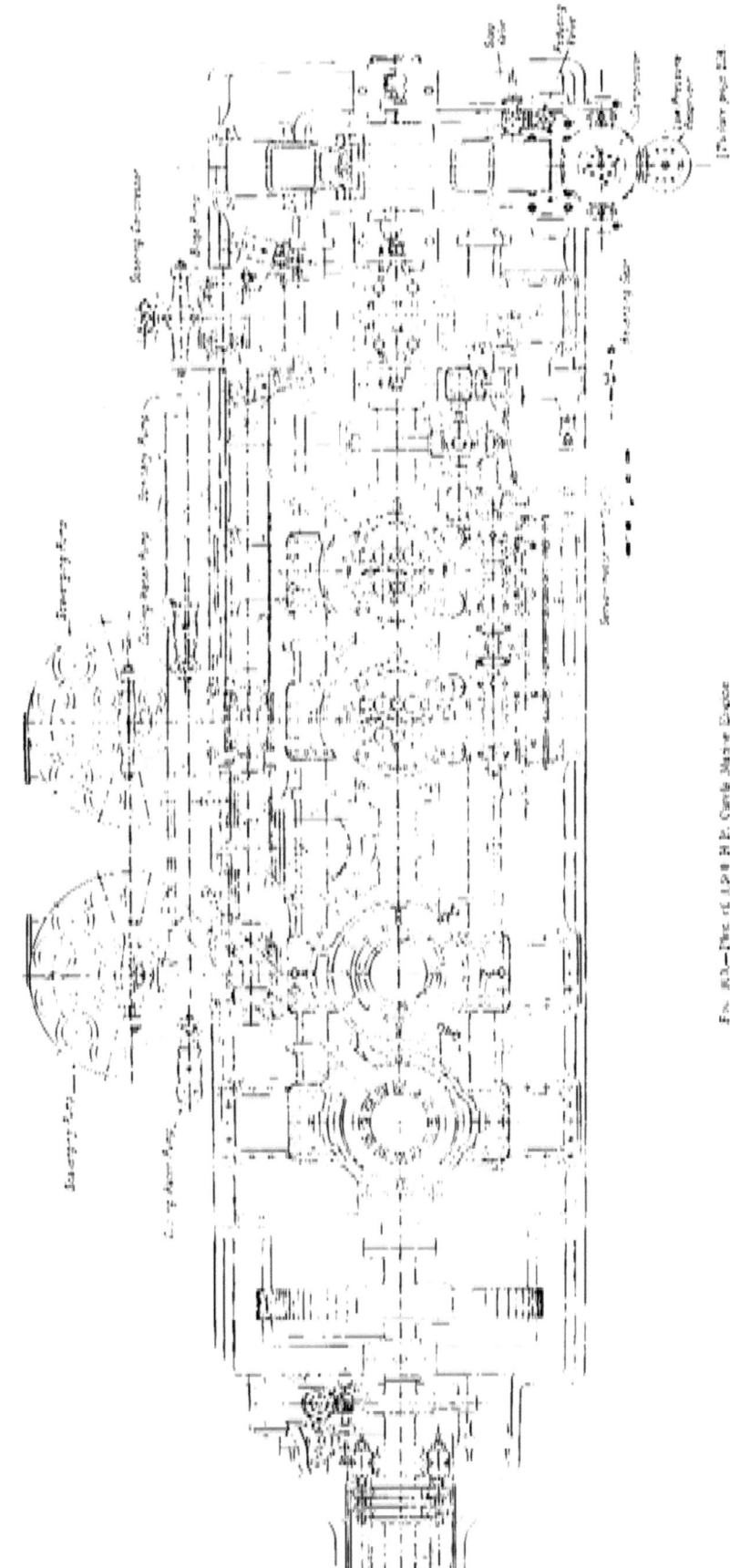

FIG. 30.—The 1,250 H.P. Curtis Marine Engine.

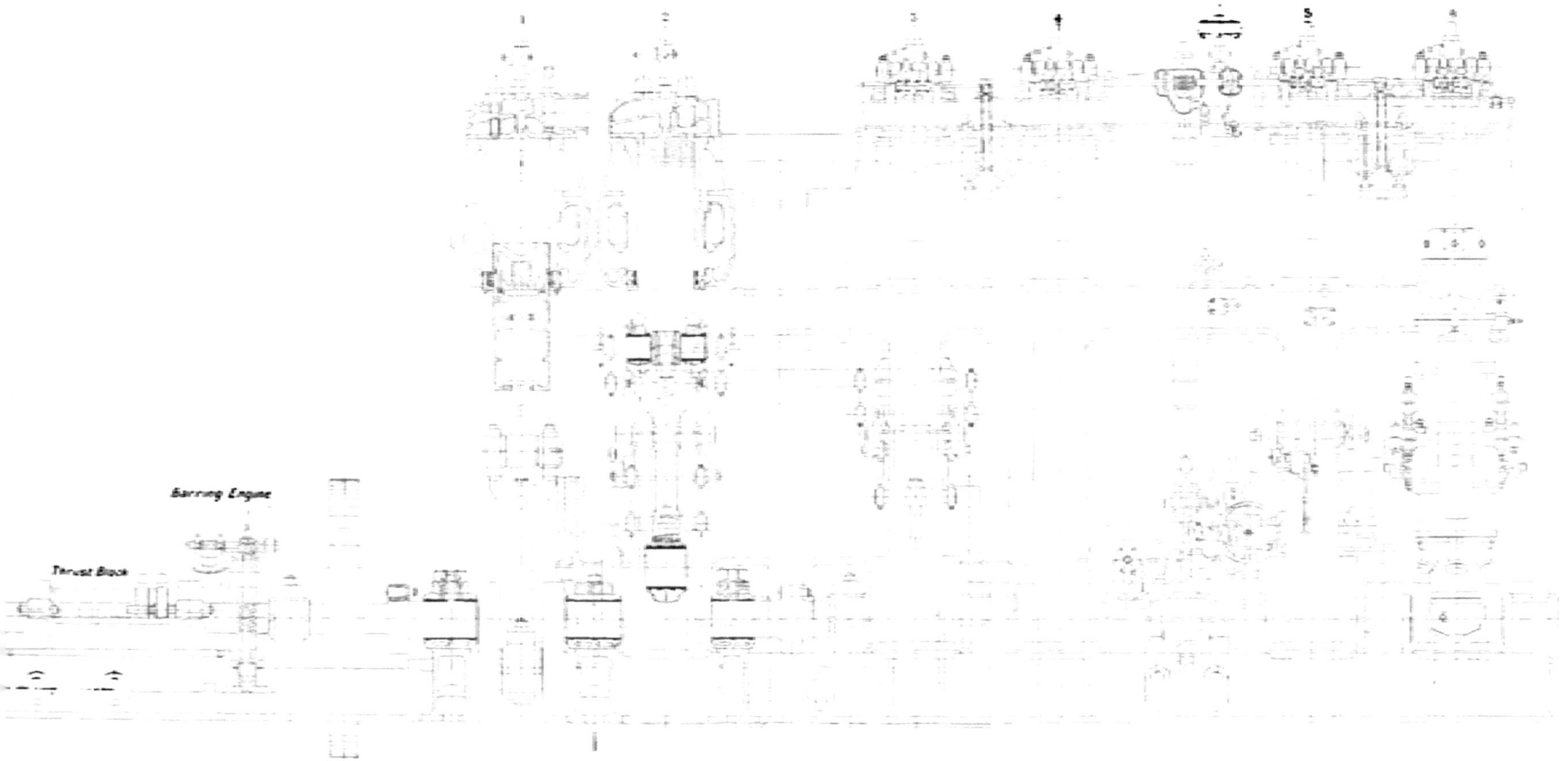

FIG. 110.—Sectional Elevation of 1,250 H.P. Quick Marine Diesel Motor (New Type).

Fig. 112.—5,000 H.P. Quadruple-Expansion Marine Engine.

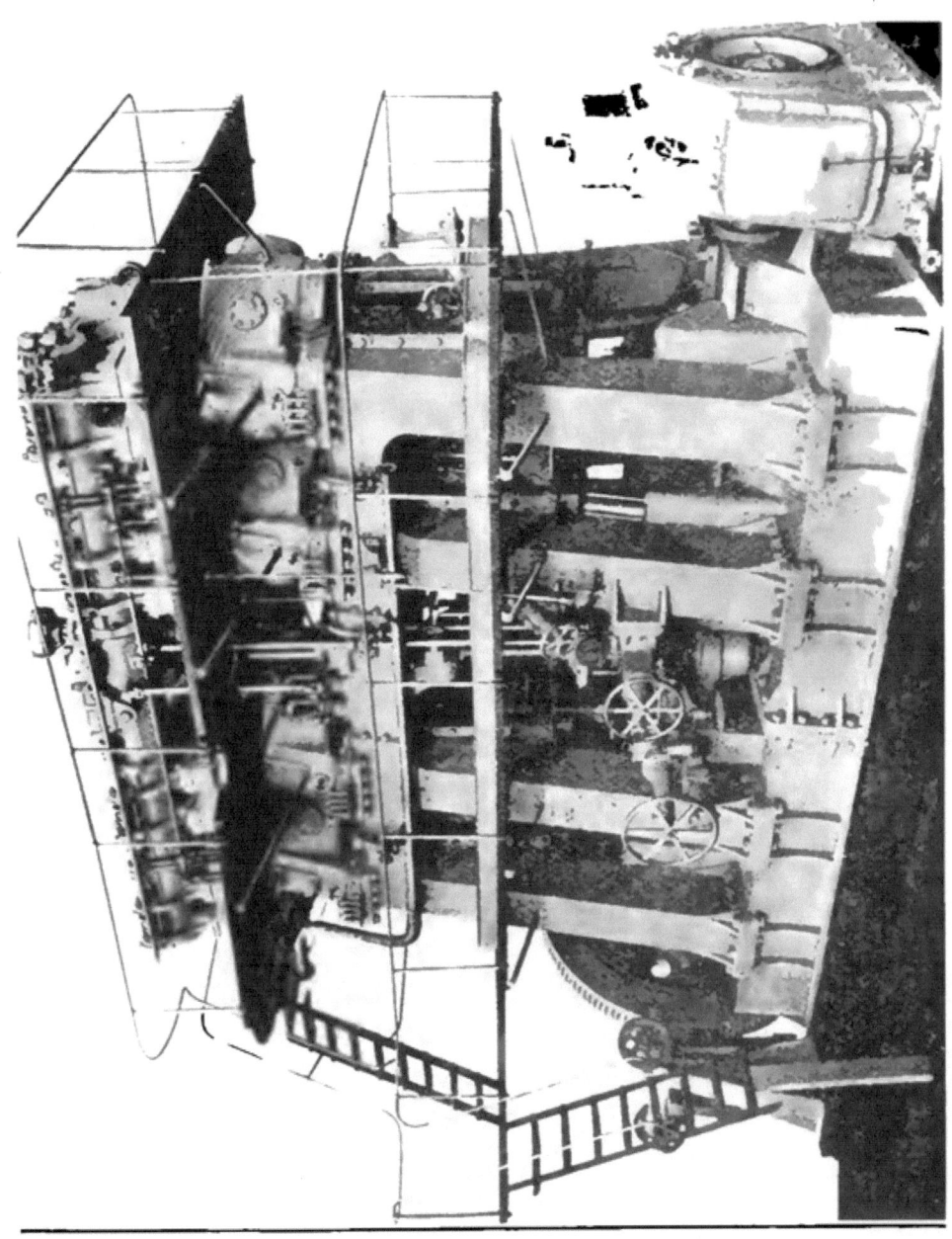

built by the Tecklenborg Co. of Bremerhaven for the motor ship *Rolandseck*.

Cockerill Engine.— In conjunction with Dr. Diesel,

Messrs. Cockerill, of Seraing, have produced a design of engine which is built in relatively large sizes, and is indeed not specially suited for smaller motors. It is of the two-cycle single-acting type, but up to the present the engines which have been constructed have been non-reversible, although directly reversible motors are now being built. The reason for the adoption of a non-reversible type was solely on account of the ship in which the engines were installed being destined for West Africa, and the consequent desirability of the absence of as many new features as possible.

In the arrangement of the motor of 650 B.H.P. at 280 revolutions per minute, there are four working cylinders with a scavenge pump at each end. Outside each of these are the high and intermediate pressure stages of the air pumps for injection and starting air, the low pressure stages being above the scavenge pumps—a method by which it is believed a smoother running may be obtained. The object is for the air pump to act as a sort of damper to the scavenge pumps, and this arrangement, or one of similar principle, has also been adopted in other designs.

The engine is of a type in which scavenging is accomplished by means of ports in the cylinder. In order to avoid the necessity either of cutting away the piston to deflect the scavenge air towards the top of the cylinder, as in the case of the Polar Diesel engine, or utilizing an auxiliary scavenging valve, as is done by Messrs. Sulzer, the scavenge ports are themselves shaped with the idea of causing the air to clear the whole of the cylinder effectively.

These ports occupy rather more than half of the circumference of the cylinder, leaving therefore less than one-half for the exhaust ports. There are two sets, one pair being arranged tangentially, so that the air entering them sweeps round the walls and rises to the top of the cylinder, whilst the other pair cause the air to rise right to the centre. By this method there is probably an economy in the quantity of air necessary to give complete scavenging.

In the cover of each cylinder there are two valves—the fuel inlet valve and the starting air valve. The motor

Fig. 114.—End View of 800 H.P. Carels' Type Two-Cycle Marine Motor.

is of the enclosed chamber type with forced lubrication, and a trunk piston is employed, which is quite suitable for powers of the motors such as have up to the present been constructed.

Swedish Type.—Some manufacturers of the two-stroke engine make use of the scavenge air cylinders for starting and reversing, with the object of doing away with the necessity of the starting valves on the cylinders. An engine of this construction, if it is provided with ports at the bottom of the cylinders for both the exhaust and the scavenge air, is thus simplified to the extent of having only one valve to be operated in the cylinder cover—namely the fuel inlet valve, and a very convenient reversing gear can be designed. The Aktiebolaget Diesels Motorer of Stockholm have developed an engine on these lines for power up to 1,000 I.H.P. It is usually constructed with four working cylinders and two scavenge air cylinders mounted on the same bed-plate, in a line with the engines. During the ordinary running of the engine the air from the two scavenge pumps is delivered into the receiver, and as the pumps are double acting and have their cranks set at 90° a very regular supply is obtained. The air, which is drawn into the cylinders from the atmosphere before compression, is delivered from the receiver into the various working cylinders as the scavenge ports are uncovered by the pistons, the pressure of the scavenge air being approximately the same as that with most other two-stroke engines, namely about 3 lb. per sq. inch above atmosphere. The scavenge or manœuvring cylinders, as they may also be called, run as compressed air engines during the periods of starting and reversing these engines, but as air is only employed for this purpose for two or three revolutions there is not a heavy call on the air receivers in which compressed air is stored for carrying out these operations. The starting and manœuvring receivers (of which there is usually one main and one auxiliary) are replenished by means of a special pump which may be situated on the top of one of the scavenge cylinders, or in any other convenient manner. The valves are arranged so that whenever the air in the receivers falls below a certain predetermined limit, the pump immediately begins to charge them until the requisite pressure is reached. The compressed air for injecting the fuel into the

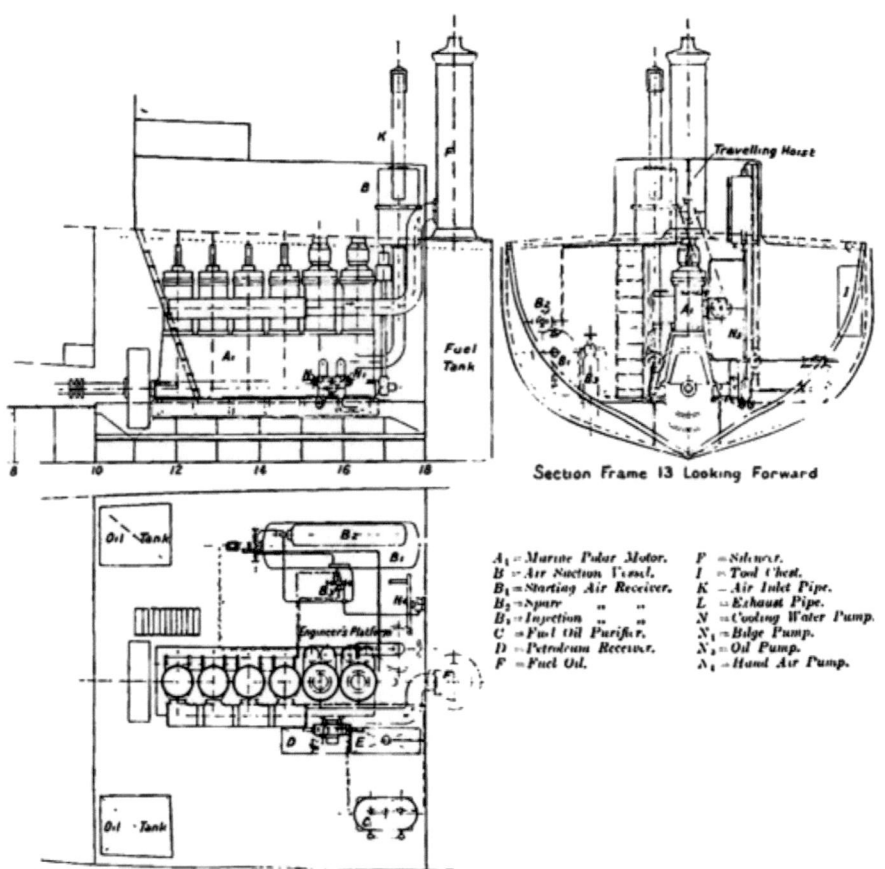

Fig. 115.—General Arrangement of Engine-room of Ship equipped with Aktiebolaget Diesels Motorer Engine.

[To face page 232.

working cylinders is provided from another compressor, and the usual type of vertical cylindrical air reservoir is employed to store this air. A separate fuel pump is fitted for each cylinder, and the type of fuel inlet valve and pulveriser described and illustrated in an earlier chapter is employed, being the same as for the stationary engine. These pumps work generally on the principle commonly adopted for Diesel engines, but as there is no governor the opening of the suction valves is not automatically controlled. The pumps are operated by links which receive their motion from the main cam shaft, and are pivoted eccentrically on a spindle which can be turned by hand, thus altering the positions of the links relative to the cam and so varying the opening of the suction valves. This in turn controls the amount of fuel admitted to the cylinder and hence the speed of the engine. For reversing, a second or reverse set of cams is provided on the cam shaft, which is moved horizontally until these cams come beneath the levers operating the fuel inlet valves, which thus open at the required point for reversing. The valves of the scavenge pumps which are worked by eccentric rods are also reversed, and their eccentrics, together with the eccentrics for driving the fuel pumps, are mounted on a separate horizontal spindle, which in reversing does not move in a longitudinal direction. When the reversing handle is put in the "astern" position the fuel pump is unable to deliver any more oil to the cylinder, and the fuel valve levers take up the positions for reverse running after the last charge of oil has been injected into the cylinders. This is arranged by the fuel valves being provided with wider cams than the regulating arrangement for the pump, so that the fuel valve opens for one revolution after the pump has been out of operation. The scavenge cylinders absorb the energy of the flywheel by running as pumps, and when the engine comes to a standstill the scavenge valves are in such positions as to allow compressed air to enter from the receiver, and the pumps then run as motors. The fuel pumps, immediately upon the engine starting, force oil up to the fuel valves, which open at the required moments, so that the engine when starting up, receives two impulses—one from the scavenge pumps operating as motors and then later from the fuel injection, which is of great value in accelerating the speed at the beginning. The scavenge pumps after one or two revolutions as air motors take up their ordinary work. One of the first British ocean-going motor vessels was the *Toiler*, a boat of 2,600 tons, built by Messrs. Swan, Hunter & Wigham Richardson, equipped with two engines of this construction, each of 180 H.P. She made a successful voyage across the Atlantic in 1911. In the *Toiler* the steering gear, windlass, and auxiliary pumps are all driven by compressed air, and a separate small Diesel engine driven compressor is provided for this work; but as at sea only the steering gear is usually required, the compressed air is then taken direct from the main engine and the auxiliary plant is shut down. Independent tests have recently been carried out on several of these engines, with a view to ascertaining the fuel consumption at full load, the results of which are most interesting in comparison with the consumption of the ordinary four-cycle engine, and from the figures obtained it appears that the difference is extremely small. Tests were made by different authorities on four separate two-cycle marine engines of standard type, after being erected in the works and before installing in the vessels for which they were built, the power being absorbed in each case by a brake of the Heenan & Froude type. In the four engines tested it was found that the fuel consumption per B.H.P. hour was respectively 211 grams., 210 grams., 201·6 grams. and 196 grams., or an average of 204·5 grams. or say ·45 lb. per B.H.P. hour, which is very much the same as for the usual four-cycle motor. All the engines were of the standard four-cylinder type, with two manœuvring cylinders in line. An illustration of a 260 H.P. engine is shown in *Fig.* 122.

For larger marine Diesel motors, that is to say anything over about 500 B.H.P., a different type of engine is built by the same firm, although many of the essential

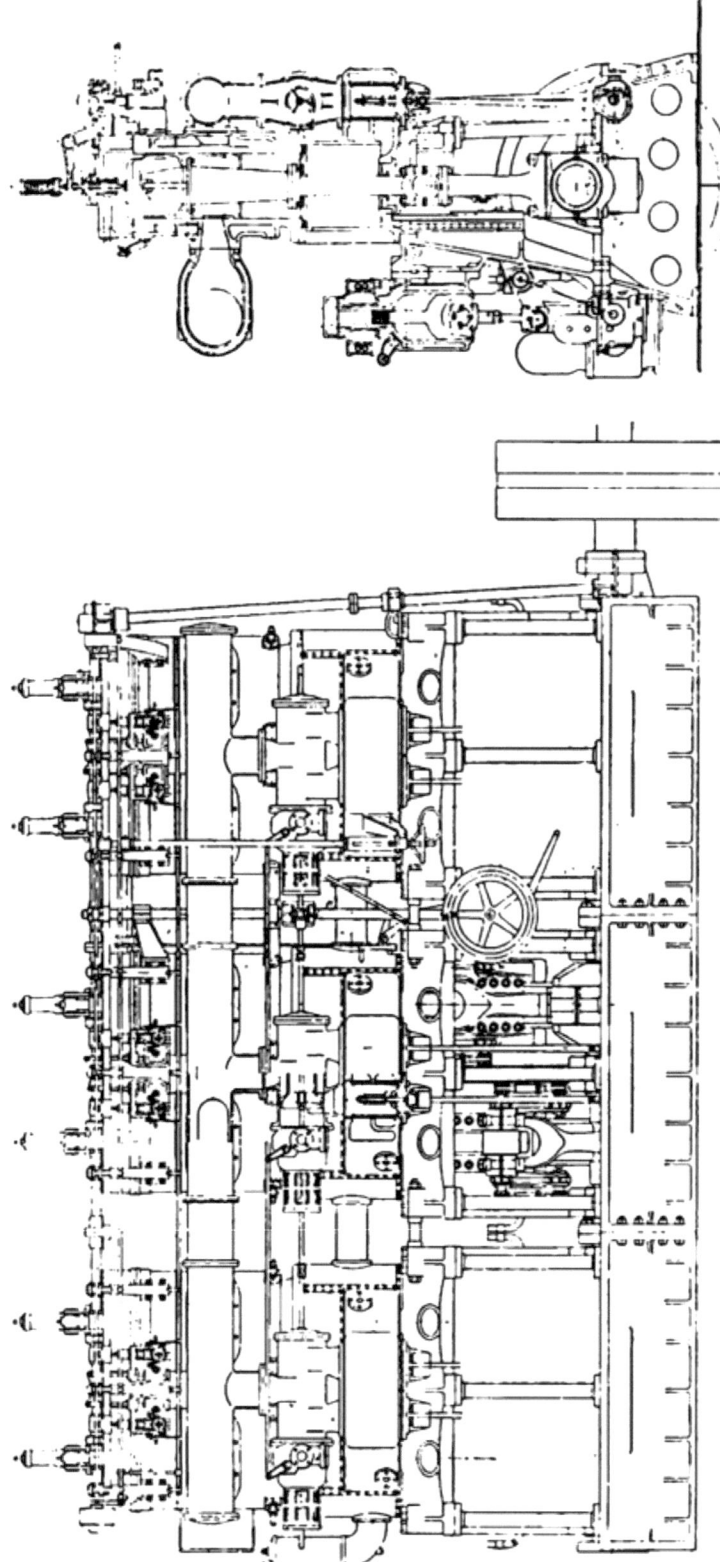

Fig. 116.—800 B.H.P. Polar Marine Engine, 135 r.p.m.

details are embodied in the larger engine. A somewhat similar design, which has, however, modifications of their own, is built by Messrs. Swan, Hunter & Wigham Richardson in this country.

As before, the motor is of the two-cycle single-acting type, but the manœuvring cylinders arranged in line with the working cylinders are abolished, and replaced by combined scavenging pumps and manœuvring cylinders below the actual working cylinders. There is thus one scavenge pump for each cylinder, but the arrangement is not exactly that adopted in many other cases and known as the stepped piston design, since the pistons of the working cylinders and the air pump are quite separate and the air is compressed by the scavenge piston on its downward and not on its upward stroke. The engine is, in many ways, an extremely simple one. Unlike practically every other type, the cylinder and liner are cast in one piece, the cylinder for the scavenge pump being quite separate. Port scavenging is employed as in the smaller motors, and as there is no auxiliary valve for the admission of scavenging air, the piston is shaped in order to deflect the air upwards and downwards so that good scavenging may be obtained. The advantage of port scavenging is shown in the construction of the cylinder cover, which contains only one valve, this being the ordinary fuel inlet valve in the centre of the cover. This valve is of the same type as that described for the smaller Polar engines.

The motor is practically of the open type, and naturally owing to the arrangement of scavenge pumps, there is an external crosshead and connecting rod. The cylinders are supported at the back by means of a cast-iron framing carrying also the guides for the crossheads, and at the front by cast-steel columns, as with some other motors, notably the Sulzer type and also the Werkspoor engine.

The important feature of using the scavenging cylinders for starting purposes is retained in this motor with the result that not only is the simplest possible design of cover obtained, but also the undesirable admission of cool air

CONSTRUCTION OF DIESEL MARINE ENGINE 237

into the heated combustion chamber during manœuvring is avoided. The method involves a certain complication in connexion with the valves for the scavenge cylinder,

FIG. 117.—Near View of Cam Shaft of 800 H.P. Polar Diesel Marine Engine.

but otherwise has much to commend it. The arrangement, however, can be reduced to comparative simplicity in operation, since when starting up there is a two-way valve which shuts off the admission of atmospheric air into the scavenge pump, and allows compressed air at a pressure of about 75 lb. per sq. inch to enter the scavenging cylinder beneath the piston, and start up the engine. The admission and discharge valves on the scavenge pumps are mechanically operated by means of eccentric rods from a horizontal spindle driven off the crank shaft. Although the pressure of the starting air in the scavenge pump only needs to be 75 lb. per sq. inch it is supplied from reservoirs at 150 lb. per sq. inch to a reducing valve to bring it down to the desired figure.

For the operation of the fuel valve in the cylinder cover there is one lever for each cylinder and two cams are arranged on the cam shaft, one for ahead and one for astern running. An interesting and useful feature, however, lies in the fact that the two cams are tapered away, so that the roller of the fuel valve lever need not be lifted when reversing as is usually the case, when ordinary flat cams are adopted. There is also a half-speed cam for slow running. With this engine the whole cam shaft is not moved longitudinally, as is common, but only a sleeve carrying the two cams for each cylinder, this movement being effected by means of a lever from the starting platform. Following a practice which is now becoming more and more usual for marine engines one fuel pump is provided for each cylinder, but instead of bunching all the pumps together, as is frequently done, each one is arranged in front of its cylinder and is driven off the cam shaft by means of an eccentric, the pump itself being only slightly below the level of the shaft. For the control of the speed of the engine the usual method of operating upon the suction valve of the fuel pump is adopted, and in order to carry this out there is a long spindle in front of the engine, attached to levers which, when the spindle is rotated, alter the stroke of the suction valve of the pump, and thus vary the speed of the engine. The movement is carried out by means of a control lever on the starting platform.

With the motors of this type which have hitherto been

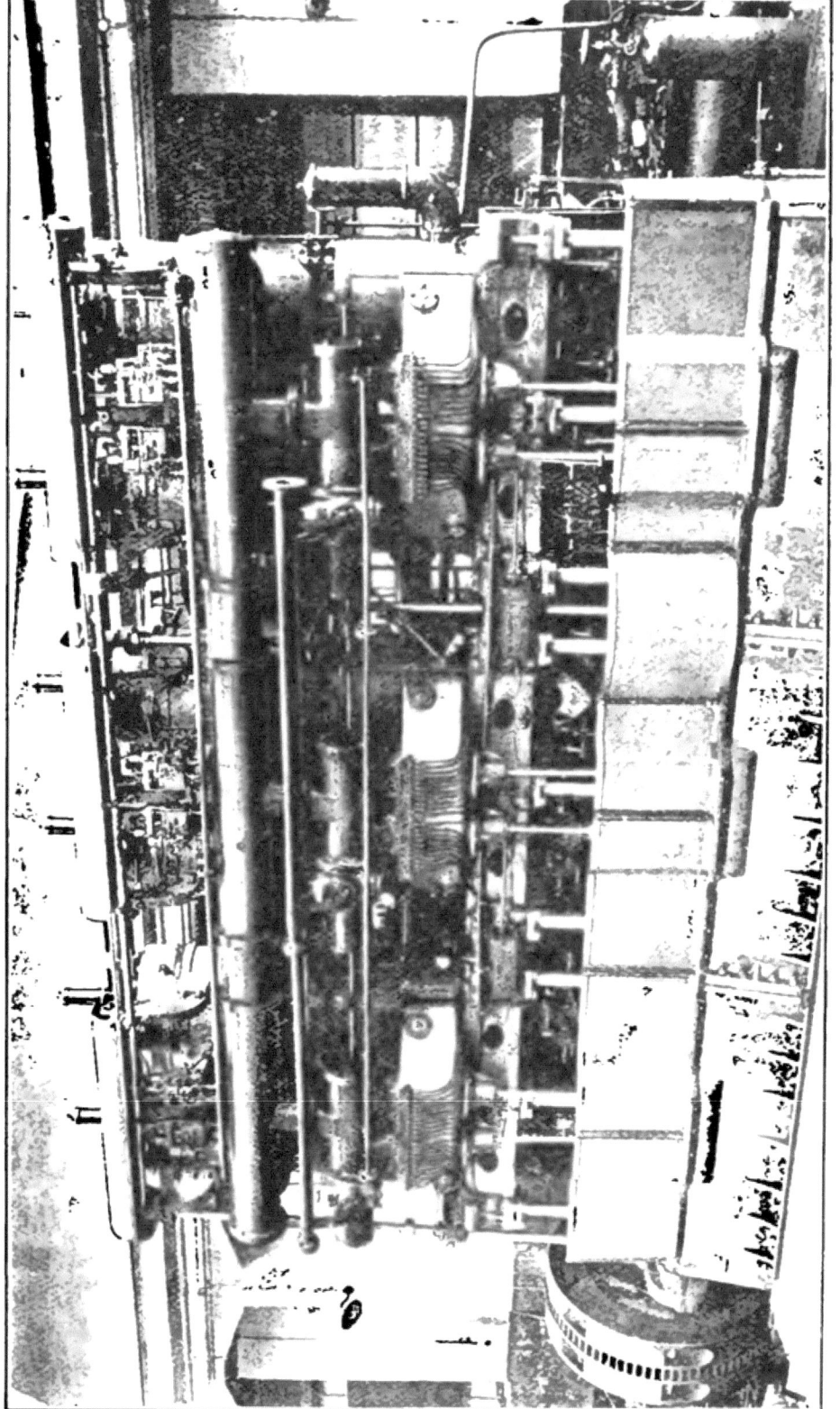

Fig. 118. 850 B.H.P. Polar Two-Cycle Reversible Marine Diesel Engine.

built, two separate two-stage compressors have been adopted, driven by means of levers from the crossheads of the two central cylinders. Probably in larger motors compressors of the three-stage type will be employed, and this has in fact been done in the Neptune engine of Messrs. Swan, Hunter & Wigham Richardson.

In reversing, apart from altering the timing of the fuel inlet valve it is necessary to operate the scavenge pump inlet and discharge valves at 180° after the ordinary timing for ahead running. This is accomplished in a comparatively simple manner by converting the inlet valves into delivery valves, and vice-versa. The cylinders are worked in pairs and it is arranged that the two inlet valves for two adjacent cylinders are one above the other, whilst there is also a delivery valve above another delivery valve for the two cylinders. Above the casing which contains the two inlet and two delivery valves is what may be termed a distribution box in which is a valve that can be moved to the right or left. On moving it to the extreme right the delivery valves become the inlet valves for the scavenge pump and the inlet valves are changed to the delivery valves, which corresponds to the operation necessary for the valves when running in the opposite direction.

For the general control and working of the engine there is one main hand-wheel which carries out all the operations necessary for reversing, and a lever which serves the purpose of admitting starting air to the scavenging cylinders for starting up. The hand-wheel moves the cam blocks longitudinally so as to bring the ahead or astern cam under the valve lever roller as required, whilst there is also an intermediate position which corresponds to the stop position on the hand-wheel. A half-speed cam is moreover provided which is brought underneath the lever roller when it is required to run at slow speed for some time.

In turning this hand-wheel the distributing valves for the admission of air to the scavenging pump are also operated at the same time, but the engine only starts up when the main starting lever on the control platform is actuated so

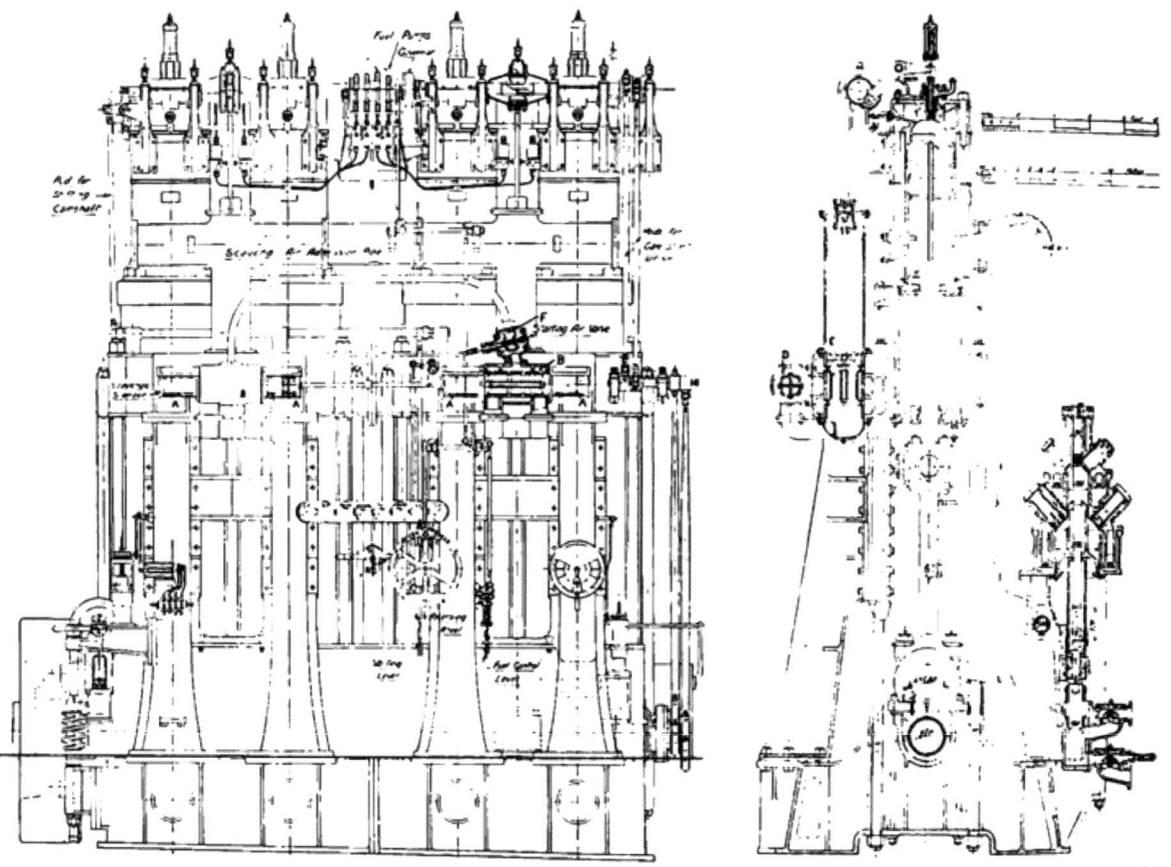

FIG. 120.—650 B.H.P. Neptune Polar Marine Engine, built by Messrs. Swan, Hunter & Wigham Richardson.

[To face page 244.

as to admit compressed air at 75 lb. per sq. inch, first to two manœuvring cylinders, then to four, and finally to six. It may incidentally be mentioned that if the engine is warm

Fig. 119. Near View of Cylinders of Polar Marine Engine as installed.

it is not usually necessary to carry the operation beyond two cylinders.

For controlling the speed of the engine in the ordinary course of running there is a ratchet wheel operated from the starting platform which controls the suction valves of

FIG. 121.—High-Speed Reversible Marine Polar Engine for Submarines and Yachts.

CONSTRUCTION OF DIESEL MARINE ENGINE 243

the various fuel pumps, the action being very much the same as is utilized in the land engines. A governor is fitted which also varies the stroke of all the suction valves of the

Fig. 122.— Polar Diesel Marine Engine.

fuel pumps at the same time, but this motion is not connected at all with the throttle control on the starting platform.

All the cylinders are provided with horizontal relief valves which may be operated from the starting platform by means of a lever if necessary. It is not usually essential for these relief valves to be opened, but if it is found that the motor is difficult to start, which may be accounted for by compressed air acting upon the bottom of the scavenge pump pistons when the engine is endeavouring to fire, then the relief valve may be opened, and at the same time compressed air is automatically cut off from the injection valves.

Fresh water is employed for the piston cooling, but for all other purposes sea water is used. The delivery into and discharge from the piston head is arranged by means of concentric pipes within the piston rod itself, the water being taken to these piston rods through the levers which operate the air injection pumps on the front of the engine.

For employment on submarines a new type of engine working on the four-cycle principle is built by the Polar firm; this is capable of running at a speed as high as 500 r.p.m. and has been adopted owing to the difficulties of scavenging and other troubles with high-speed two-cycle engines.

German Types.—A large number of two-cycle single acting engines of the Diesel type have been constructed by Messrs. Krupp of Kiel, of which several were for the German and Italian Navies, but recently four engines each of 1,250 B.H.P. running at 140 revolutions per minute have been built for the Deutsch-Amerikanische Petroleumgesellschaft for tank vessels. All engines of over 300 H.P. are made on the two-cycle principle, while those below this power are four cycle, in each case being directly reversible except for the very smallest sizes. *Fig.* 123 shows a high speed two-cycle reversible marine engine of Messrs. Krupp's construction, of 1,000 B.H.P., recently supplied to the German Admiralty, and this is typical of the general design of the two-cycle engine. There are six working cylinders divided into two sections of three each, with the air compressor in the centre and a scavenging air pump at each end, the peculiar construction of the suction chambers being well

Fig. 123. Krupp Two-Cycle high speed 1,000 B.H.P. Engine.

seen in the illustration. Each scavenging pump supplies three of the cylinders, which thus form a completely independent set, so that for low powers only one-half of working cylinders need be in operation and a greater reduction in power may thus be obtained, with corresponding increase in manœuvring facilities. For the engine exhaust, ports at the bottom of the cylinder are employed as usual with two-cycle motors, and the scavenge air is admitted through valves in the cylinder head. The crank chambers are totally enclosed, with inspection doors in front of each cylinder for examining the cranks and bearings.

The method of reversing in this engine consists in the employment of ahead and reverse cams on the same cam shaft, which is moved axially during reversing so as to bring the ahead or astern cams underneath the valve levers operating the valves as required. The valves which require an alteration in the times of opening during reversal are the fuel inlet valve, the starting valve and the scavenge valve, unless ports in the cylinder be employed instead of the latter, which is sometimes the case. The cams for the fuel and scavenge valves are arranged somewhat as shown diagrammatically in *Fig.* 124, there being a flat space between the ahead and astern cam pieces, this being the position of rest for the roller of the valve lever when the engine is stopped. For the starting valve two separate cams are provided, one for ahead and one for astern, and either of these may be put into operation according to the direction of rotation required. The action of reversing may be explained as follows. Assume the engine is running ahead,

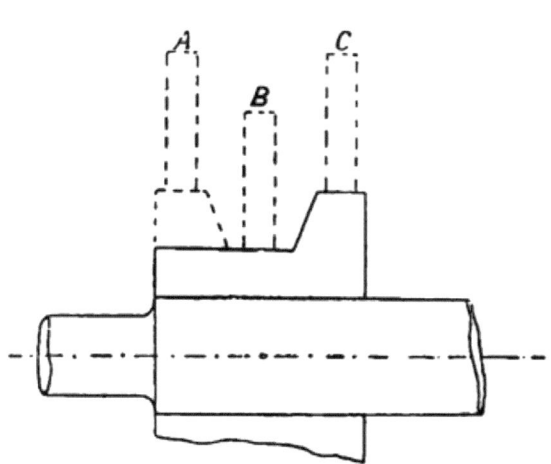

Fig. 124.—Diagram showing action of Cams for Krupp's Engine.

in which case the rollers for the scavenge air and fuel inlet valves will be in position as at A in *Fig.* 124, while both the rollers of the starting valve levers will be raised well above the cams which operate them. To bring the engine to rest the whole of the cam shaft is moved to the left, a distance equal to half the longitudinal distance between the centres of the ahead and reverse cams. The rollers operating the valve levers then rest on the flat portion of the cam sleeve as at B, *Fig.* 124, and the valves are not opened as the cam shaft rotates. This movement of the cam shaft is carried out by means of the hand-wheel seen in the centre of the engine in *Fig.* 123, which causes the motion through screw gearing. The scavenge air and fuel inlet valve levers being in the stop position the engine comes to rest, after which the starting valve lever for reverse running is brought down on its cam by means of one of the two levers seen in the centre of the engine, which give an angular motion to a shaft underneath the cam shaft and connected to it by small coupling rods. The starting valves are opened, the engine runs up as an air motor, and after two or three revolutions the starting valve levers are raised off their cam by putting the main controlling handle back to mid position, and the cam shaft is moved further to the left a distance equal to the first until the rollers of the valve levers are in the position C', *Fig.* 124, which is the astern running position. The main starting lever controlling the starting valves and the wheel controlling the position of the cam shaft are properly interlocked so that there may be no possibility of the fuel inlet valve being opened during the starting period.

For their standard engine of the slow speed type, suitable for large cargo and similar vessels, Messrs. Krupp have adopted a different design, and several of this new type have already been constructed. The two-cycle single acting principle is retained, and in some respects the engine is similar to that developed by Messrs. Carels, as previously described, being of the open crosshead type. In all sizes of motor which have at present been constructed (ranging

248 DIESEL ENGINES FOR LAND AND MARINE WORK

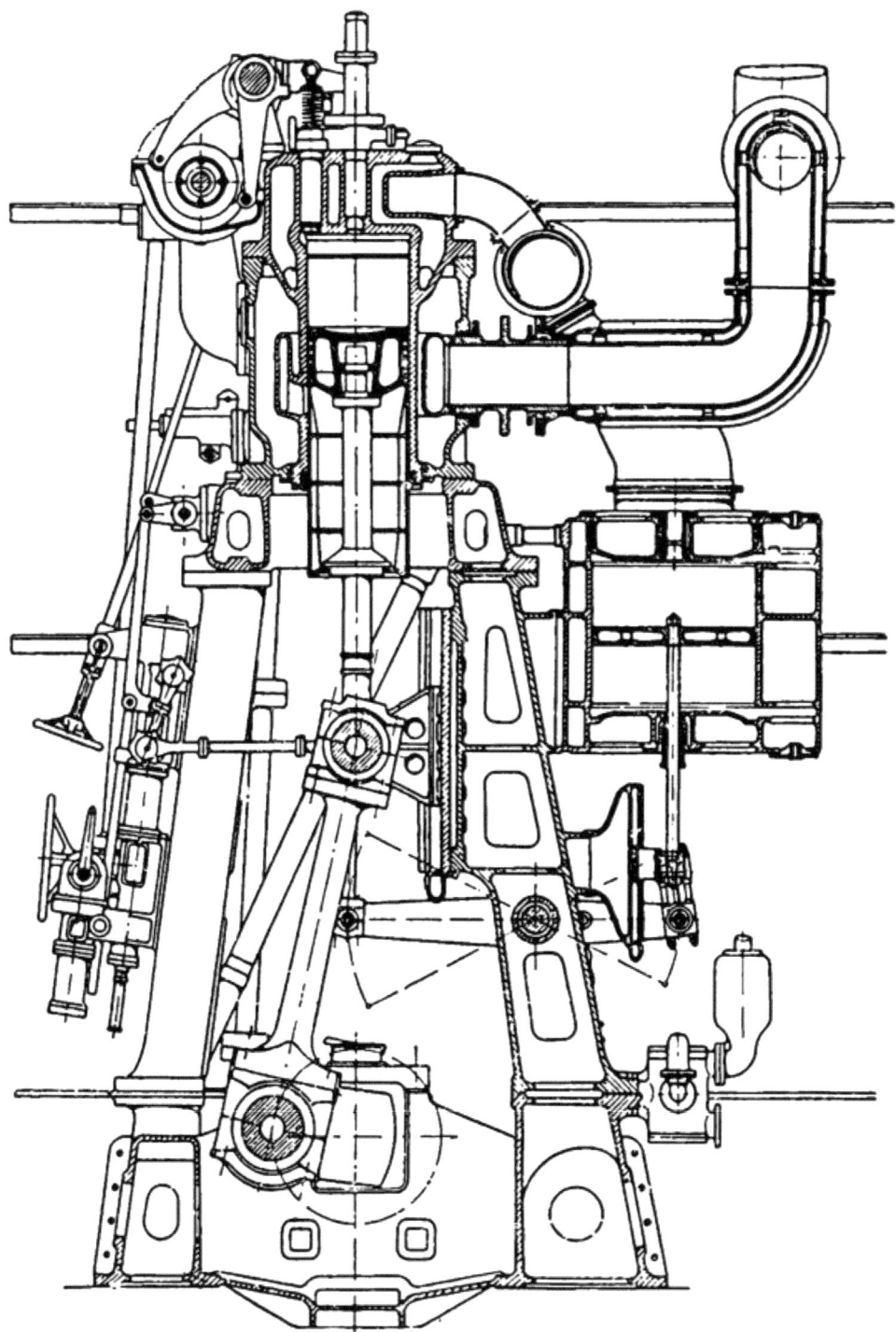

Fig. 125.—Section through Cylinder and Scavenge Pump of 1,250 B.H.P. Krupp Engine.

from 1,000 B.H.P. to 2,500 B.H.P.) six cylinders have been employed, with two scavenge cylinders arranged at the

CONSTRUCTION OF DIESEL MARINE ENGINE 249

back of the engine, driven from the crossheads of the two centre working cylinders through rocking levers.

The air compressors for the supply of starting and injection air and for manœuvring are separately driven, so

Fig. 126.—1,250 B.H.P. Krupp Diesel Engine.

that the engine itself consists only of the working cylinders and the scavenge pumps. Scavenging is effected by means of valves in the cylinder cover, there being two per cylinder, but it may be mentioned that this is not likely to be the ultimate design. As will be noticed from *Figs.* 125 *and* 126, the scavenge pumps are supported from the engine frame and raised above the engine-room floor level, thus differing from the arrangement adopted by Messrs. Carels. A stuffing

Fig. 127.—Tops of two 1,250 H.P. Krupp Two-Cycle Engines installed in Motor Ship.

box is provided at the bottom of the cylinder, to prevent the escape of exhaust gas into the engine-room.

The cylinders are supported on an "A" shaped frame formed by box columns fixed to the bed-plate, and the crosshead guide surfaces are formed on the inside of the columns and are water cooled. The arrangement and construction of the piston are seen from the illustration, which also indicates that the stroke is relatively long compared with the bore of the cylinders. It may be mentioned that the speeds of this type of engines vary from 100 to 160 r.p.m., according to the size and also the speed of the vessel in which they are installed.

The arrangements adopted for reversing follow much on the lines of those already described for the high-speed two-cycle engine of this firm. A single cam shaft is employed, on which both ahead and astern cams are mounted, and this is moved longitudinally to bring the astern or ahead cams underneath the valve levers, according to the direction of rotation required. The movement is effected either by hand or by means of a small compressed air motor, and a manœuvring hand-wheel is provided, which allows the engine to run up on compressed air, and finally brings fuel on to all the cylinders for full speed. Before moving the cam shaft longitudinally, all the valve levers are raised off the cams, in the usual manner adopted with two-cycle engines when this method of reversing is employed.

The weight of this type of engine is about 250 lb. per B.H.P., and the fuel consumption is about 0·44 lb. per B.H.P., which includes the operation of the scavenge pumps but not the air compressors. Reversing from full speed ahead to full speed astern is accomplished in about 12 seconds. An illustration of the reversing mechanism is given in *Fig*. 128.

Diesel engines for marine work are built at the Nürnberg Works of the Maschinenfabrik Augsburg-Nürnberg, of the two-stroke cycle type, but are divided into two classes—the light and the heavy weight type, the former being chiefly designed for submarines, gunboats and torpedo boats, while the latter are more suitable for tug boats and cargo vessels. The weight of the light type is from about 30–35 lb. per B.H.P. hour for large engines up to 40 lb. per B.H.P. hour for small engines, this being an inclusive weight. The engines are commonly built of six cylinders without a flywheel, or four cylinders with a flywheel, but sometimes eight cylinders are employed. The types standardized for the light weight engine are as under :—

```
150 H.P. at 550 revs. per min.
200        550
300-500  ,, 500
600        450
900        420
1,200    ,, 400
```

The approximate dimensions of some of these engines are as under :—

Horse power	150		200		300		400		500		600	
	ft.	in.	ft.	in.	ft.	in.	ft.	in.	ft.	in.	ft.	in.
Overall length	9	10⅛	11	5⅞	12	9⅝	14	5¼	14	9¼	15	9
Overall width	2	2¾	2	7½	2	11⅛	3	4½	3	7	3	11⅜
Height required for dismantling	4	4¼	4	11¼	5	7	6	3	6	6¾	6	10¾
Depth required below centre of crank shaft	1	1¾	1	2½	1	5	1	5¾	1	7	1	7¾

The usual speeds of the heavy weight engines are as follows :—

```
150-200 B.H.P. at 300-400 revs. per min.
300-330      ,, 300-330       ,,
450-550      ,, 225-275
600-750      ,, 225-275
900          ,,    260
1,200        ,,    215
```

The heavy engines are cheaper as the framework and bed-plate are of cast iron, whilst with the lighter type manganese bronze is usually employed. The speed is also less and the fuel consumption is lower with the heavy type than with the light weight motor.

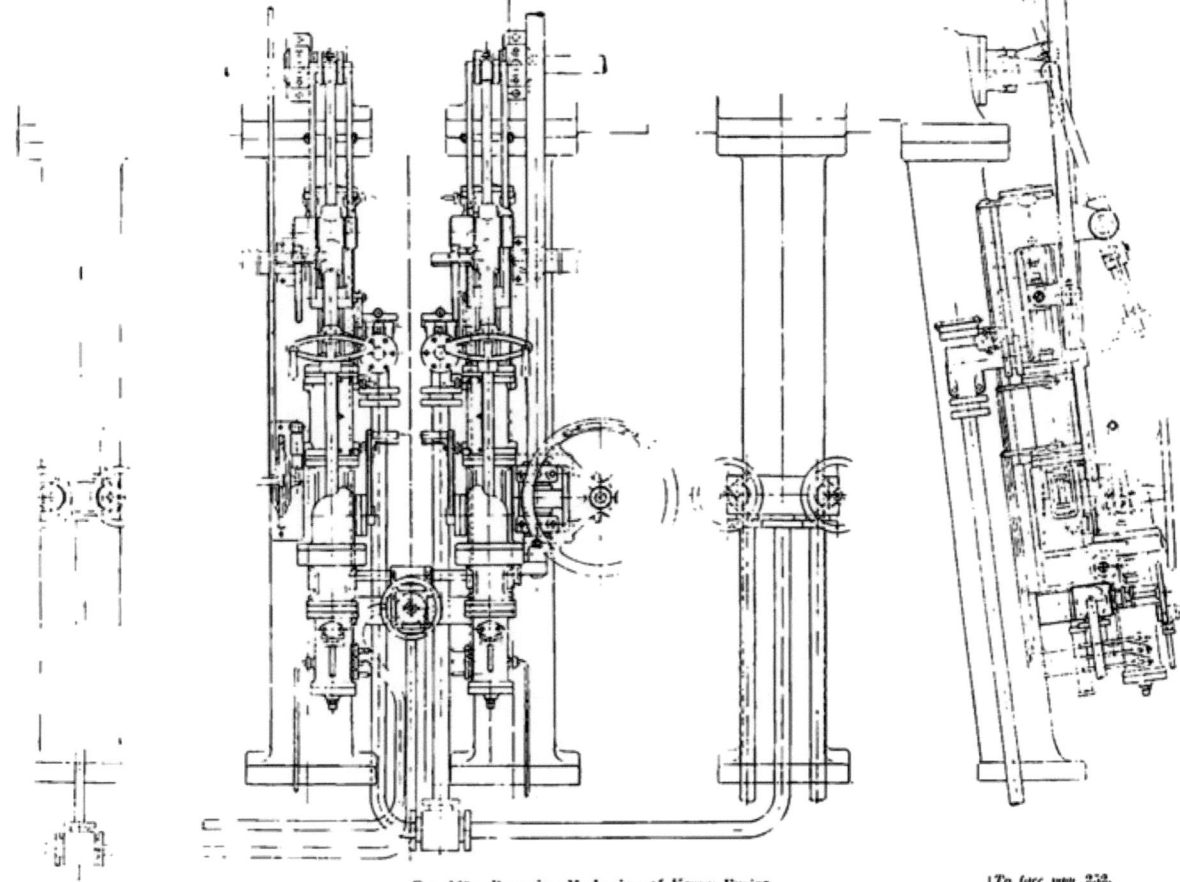

Fig. 128.—Reversing Mechanism of Krupp Engine.

FIG. 129.—1,250 B.H.P. Krupp Two-Cycle Marine Engine.

[To face page 252

CONSTRUCTION OF DIESEL MARINE ENGINE 253

Large engines are provided with two two-stage compressors for the injection and starting air, while smaller motors have but one compressor, the usual arrangement being to have it at one end of the engine. The scavenge pumps are below the working cylinders, one for each cylinder, the pistons being stepped and enlarged at the bottom to form the piston of the scavenge pump, while it also acts as the crosshead for the piston rod. The admission of the scavenge air takes place through valves in the cylinder head.

The arrangement of the working cylinder and the scavenge cylinder is shown in transverse section in *Fig.* 130, the effective sectional area of the scavenge cylinder being the difference between that of the working cylinder and the scavenge cylinder itself. As the volume of scavenge air required is usually taken as 1·2 to 1·5 times the volume swept through by the piston of the working cylinder, the diameter of the scavenge piston is from

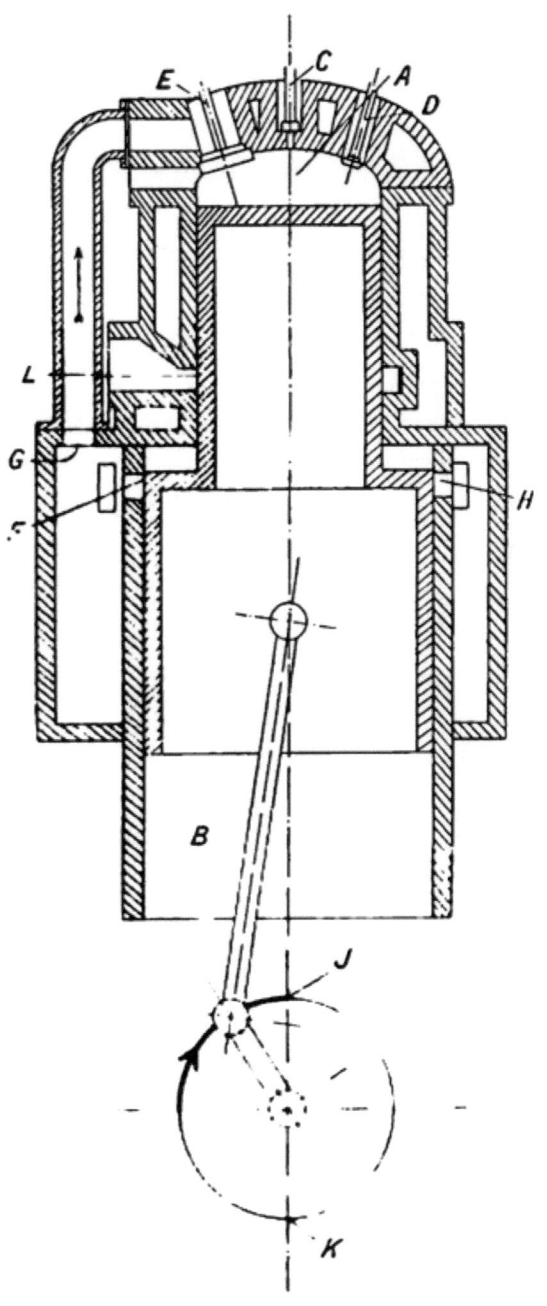

FIG. 130.—Diagrammatic Representation of Nürnberg Two-Cycle Marine Engine, showing Scavenge Arrangements.

1·4 to 1·6 times the diameter of the working piston, the latter figure being for high speed engines.

In *Fig.* 130, which is purely diagrammatic, A represents the working cylinder, B the scavenge cylinder, C the fuel admission valve, D the starting valve, and E the scavenge air admission valve. F is the outlet valve in the scavenge cylinder, through which the scavenge air passes, after being compressed to a few pounds above atmosphere, into the receiver G, whence it enters the working cylinder through E, when this latter valve opens. H is the admission valve of the scavenge cylinder through which air is drawn into the scavenge cylinder, during the suction or downward stroke of the piston. In the position shown in the figure, the working piston is just finishing the compression or upward stroke in which the air is compressed to the pressure required for combustion of the fuel. When the crank has nearly reached the top dead centre J, the fuel admission valve opens and combustion takes place, and the piston starts on its downward or working stroke, while H is also opened and air is drawn into the scavenge cylinder. Just before the crank reaches the bottom dead centre K, the valve E opens, scavenge air enters from the receiver G, and expels the exhaust gases in the working cylinder through the ports L which are then uncovered by the piston, F being closed and H open during the whole of this stroke. After the crank passes the dead centre, F opens, and H closes, while the valve remains open till just after the exhaust ports L are closed by the piston, when it closes, and during the remainder of the upward stroke F is kept open and the receiver G is charged with scavenge air from the scavenge cylinder, while the air in the working cylinder is compressed. When starting up the engine by the admission of air through the starting valve D in the usual way, this air is effectively discharged through the exhaust ports in the cylinder by admitting scavenge air through the scavenge valve E so long as these ports remain uncovered by the piston.

The working pistons are cooled with oil and the cylinder

CONSTRUCTION OF DIESEL MARINE ENGINE 255

jackets have removable covers which are useful for cleaning the jackets, rendered necessary by the employment of salt water for cooling purposes. Forced lubrication is adopted and the oil passes through a cooler and is enabled to be used over again.

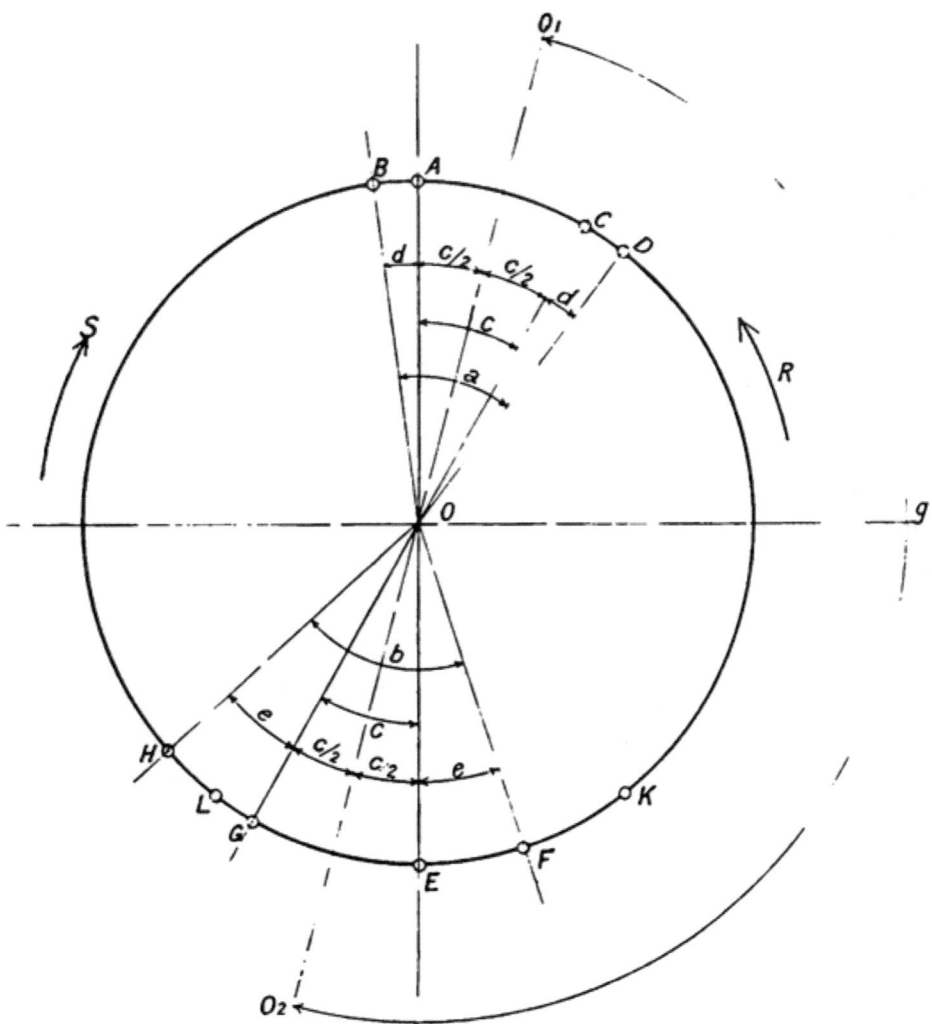

Fig. 131.—Diagram illustrating Method of Reversing Nürnberg Engine.

As is necessary in all two-cycle engines in which scavenge valves and not ports are employed, in reversing, the times of opening of three valves have to be altered; namely, the starting valve, the fuel valve, and the air inlet and scavenge valve. This is accomplished in the case of the two latter by turning the cam shaft itself through a certain angle (about 30° in the case of the Nürnberg engine) so that but one cam is needed for each scavenge valve and each fuel valve, both for ahead and reverse running. In order that the scavenge and fuel valves may be set in the reverse position together, by the same movement of the cam shaft, it is necessary that the angles of opening and preadmission of these valves should be in a certain definite ratio. This can be better explained by a reference to *Fig.* 131, which represents a crank diagram for the engine, A being the top dead centre and E the bottom. The question to be solved is, to so adjust the angle of opening (referred to the rotation of the crank shaft) of the scavenge and fuel inlet valves, that the cams operating their valve levers will have an axis of symmetry, with the result that by the same alteration of angle of the cam shaft, both the fuel valve and the scavenge valve are set for reverse running. In *Fig.* 131 B is the point of admission of the fuel, the angle of preadmission being d. The valve closes at D so that the total angle of opening is a.

K represents the point of uncovering of the exhaust ports and L of their closing, but these do not enter into the question since, of course, no alteration is necessary in reversing. At F the scavenge valve opens, the closing point being H, and the full angle of opening b. The angle of preadmission for the scavenge air is c.

The respective total angles of opening of the fuel valve (a) and the scavenge valve (b) are so adjusted that

$$a = c + 2d$$
and
$$b = c + 2e$$

or in other words the angle of opening in both cases is twice the angle of preadmission, plus a constant angle c. In the diagram if the lines $0\ 0_1$ and $0\ 0_2$ be drawn bisecting the angles a and b it is easy to show that the angle g is 180° and therefore the line $0_1\ 0_2$ is the axis of symmetry for the fuel valve and scavenge valve cams.

To explain the action of reversing consider the engine to be running in the ahead direction as indicated by the arrow

S, A and B are the top and bottom dead centres of the crank, and the angles BOA or d and FOE or e are the respective angles of preadmission for the fuel and the scavenge valves.

When the engine is started up in the reverse direction, which is accomplished by means of compressed air, as is explained later, the crank is running in the direction indicated by the arrow R, and all that is necessary to set the cams in the correct position is to move the cam shaft through an angle equal to e so that in the diagram C' and G become the respective top and bottom dead points. The angles of preadmission are then DOC' or d and GOH or e for the fuel and scavenge valves respectively, which are exactly the same as when running in the ahead direction. The cams are therefore in the correct position for reverse running and the operation is exactly the same as for the ahead rotation.

For the starting valve, if its cam were turned through an angle of only 30°, the opening of the valve would be a small period, since it would also have to be 30° plus twice the angle of preadmission, which is small. Hence an insufficient starting torque would be produced and other means have to be adopted. The arrangement used is to have two cams for each starting valve (of which there is of course one for each cylinder), one cam for ahead and the other for reverse running. These cams actuate a small valve which regulates the admission of compressed air to the starting valve, and according to which cam comes into operation the direction of rotation of the engine at starting is controlled.

A single lever controls the whole operation of reversing. In the stop position it is in the middle, while for ahead running it is moved to the right, and for astern to the left, its movement allowing the injection air to pass to the ahead or astern air valve previously mentioned. When the engine starts up in the required direction it automatically sets the cams for the fuel and scavenge valves in their right position, namely, in reverse running it turns the cam shaft through an angle of 30°. This is carried out by driving the vertical intermediate shaft operating the horizontal cam shaft by

S

means of a claw coupling, the teeth or claws of which have a clearance angle of 30° instead of the faces bearing against each other as is usual with these couplings. When the engine is running in the ahead direction the *front* faces of the claws of the half of the coupling keyed to the crank shaft bear hard against the *back* faces of the half of the coupling attached to the vertical shaft. On reversing the engine, by movement of the controlling handle and starting up on compressed air, the part of the coupling on the crank shaft runs free for an angle of 30° when the *back* faces of its teeth come against the *front* faces of claws of the half of the coupling on the vertical shaft. The coupling then drives this shaft, and hence the cam shaft in this position, the result being that the cam shaft is automatically turned through an angle of 30° relative to the crank shaft, and the cams are thus in the required position for astern running. In order that there may be no play in the coupling when the engine is running, strong springs keep the two halves of the coupling together.

The engines are of six or eight cylinders, the cranks being set at 120° or 90° in the two cases respectively. The general arrangement of this type of motor can be seen from *Fig.* 132, which represents a longitudinal section of the engine. The air pumps are fitted on the forward end of the engine, these consisting of two two-stage compressors, and the design may be compared with the submarine motors of the Krupp and similar designs. The cranks for these two pumps are set at 180°, which aids considerably in the smooth running of the machine. The cylinders may be of cast steel or cast iron, and the pistons are oil cooled—a point of more than ordinary interest. The speed can be reduced to 20 per cent. of the normal full speed of the engine.

The circulating pumps for the cooling water are driven off the engine, and the water passed through the air-pump cylinder jackets, the bearings, the oil cooler, cylinders, exhaust valves, the exhaust pipe, and thence overboard. Forced lubrication is adopted throughout, the oil pressure

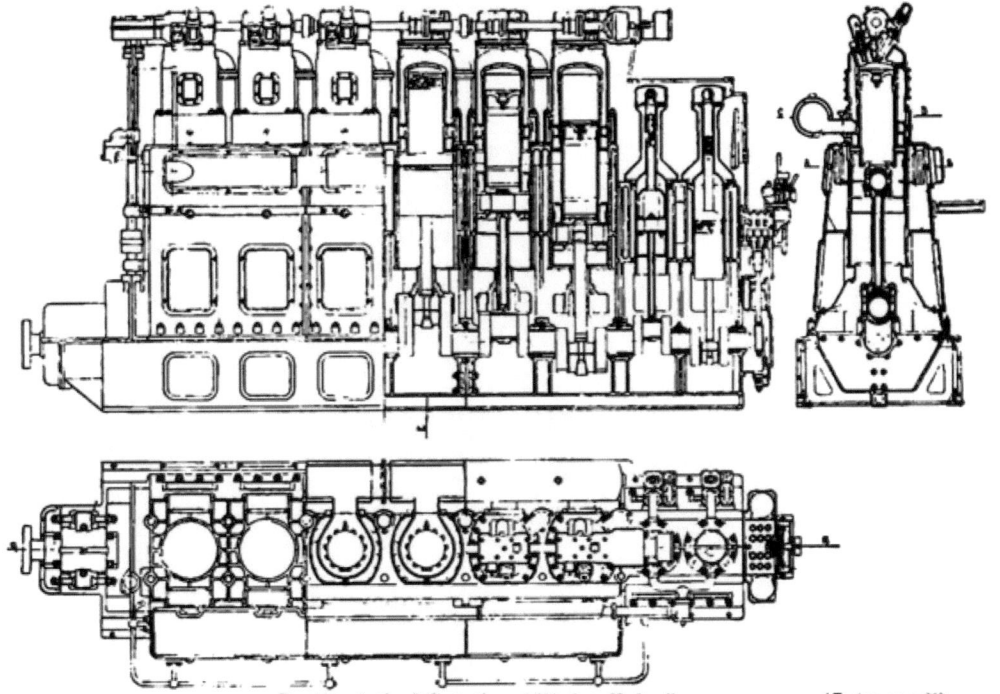

Fig. 132.—Sectional Illustrations of Nürnberg Marine E [To face page 258.

Fig. 133.—End View of Nürnberg Marine Engine.

being from 30 to 50 lb. per sq. in. It passes through the hollow crank shaft and the gudgeon pins, and is then utilized for piston cooling.

The consumption in these motors is relatively low, being in the neighbourhood of 0·44 lb. per B.H.P. hour, which may be taken as a very fair figure for this type of engine.

An illustration of one of the heavy weight type engines (which it must be remembered is purely a relative term) is given in *Figs.* 133 *and* 135. A motor of this type of 900 H.P., running at 250 revolutions per minute, has six cylinders, each of diameter 360 mm., the stroke being 600 mm. The two-stage compressors are direct driven from the crank shaft and have cylinder diameters of 200 and 100 mm. respectively, with a stroke of 450 mm. The pistons are cooled with lubricating oil, and the cylinders, in the ordinary manner, with water. The oil pumps and cooling water pumps are fitted to the front of the main engine. The weight of this engine, calculated on its rated power of 900 B.H.P., is about 120 lb. per B.H.P., and as an indication of the overloads which Diesel engines will take, it may be mentioned that the engine can be speeded up to 300 revolutions per minute and deliver 1,100 B.H.P. continuously. The minimum speed at which the motor runs is 50 revolutions per minute, i.e. 20 per cent. of full speed, which is quite sufficient for all purposes of manœuvring, and this is accomplished by cutting out three cylinders entirely. The fuel consumption is about 0·47 lb. per B.H.P. hour, and in this respect is slightly inferior to the best open type slow-speed marine Diesel engines, which usually have a consumption of 0·42 to 0·44 lb. per B.H.P. hour.

For larger powers an intermediate type of motor is constructed by the M.A.N., resembling in many ways those of the Krupp and Carels designs. It is an open type engine for powers of 1,000 to 2,000 H.P., and is naturally much heavier than the relatively light motors already described, its weight being between 180 and 220 lb. per B.H.P., according to the size and circumstances, whilst the speed varies between 100 and 150 revolutions per minute.

CONSTRUCTION OF DIESEL MARINE ENGINE 261

Fig. 134.—M.A.N. 900 H.P. Submarine Engine.

The scavenge pumps are situated at the side of the main engine and driven by rocking levers off the crossheads, the stepped piston arrangement on this type naturally being abandoned. The compressors are driven direct off the crank shaft at the forward end of the engine in the usual manner.

Engines of the two-cycle double acting type are now being built by the Maschinenfabrik Augsburg-Nürnberg, and apart from the principle of action there are various points in the construction differing from the single acting type. The engines have three working cylinders, and the scavenge cylinders are separate, though there still remains one for each working cylinder. These scavenge pumps may either be mounted in line with the main cylinders and driven direct off the crank shaft, or arranged in front of the engine, and driven by levers from the crossheads. Fuel and starting valves are provided at both ends of the cylinders, and are worked from separate cam shafts in front of the engines, the means employed for reversing being similar to that already described for the single acting engine, but the reversing gear operates both cam shafts. As previously mentioned in discussing this type of engine, two fuel valves are fitted in the bottom of each cylinder on account of the stuffing box, which is of the same type as used for double acting gas engines. For running at low speeds the fuel valves at the bottom may be put out of operation, when the engine works single acting.

The scavenge air is usually arranged to enter at both sides, and there are exhaust pipes both at the back and the front of the engine.

The following are the standard sizes to be adopted; engines of 1,000 H.P. are already running, while two of 1,500 H.P. each have also been built :—

Output B.H.P.	Revs. per minute.
750–1,100	100–140
1,100–1,900	100–140
1,700–2,700	100–140
2,400–3,800	100–140
3,100–4,900	100–140
4,100–5,200	100–120

Fig. 135. Standard High Speed Nuremberg Marine Engine. [To face page 262.

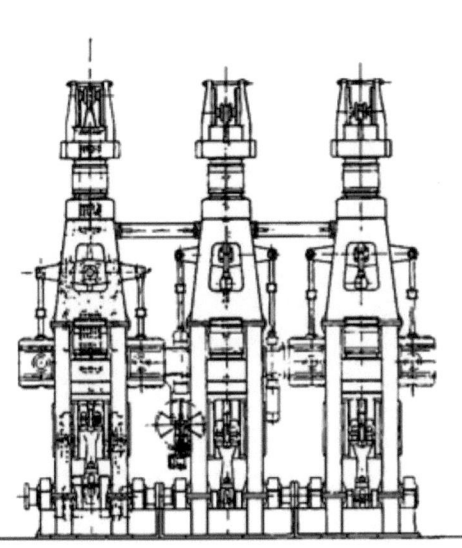
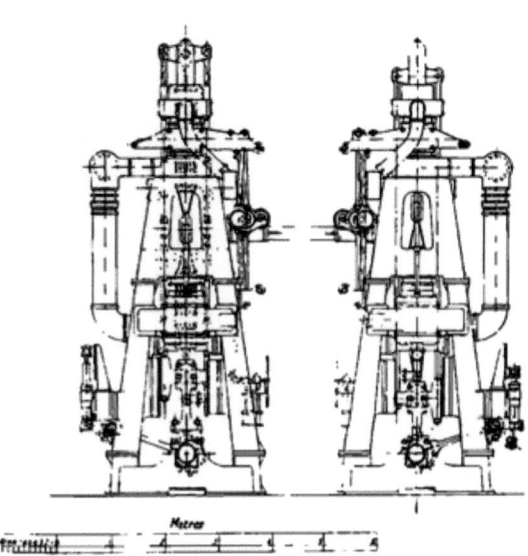
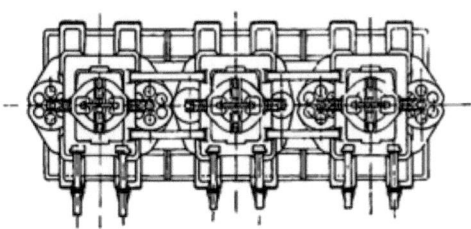

Fig. 136.—850 B.H.P. Weser-Junkers Marine Diesel Engine.

[To face page 262.

Fig. 137.—850 B.H.P. Weser-Junkers Marine Engine. [To face page 262.

One of the most distinct departures from standard practice in the design of Diesel engines is that of Professor Junkers, although in his arrangement he has brought some well-known applications from gas-engine construction into force.

Two pistons are employed in each cylinder, moving outward from, and inward to, the centre of the cylinder at the same time. The bottom piston drives the crank shaft in the usual manner through a connecting rod, whilst the upper one is attached by means of a beam lever to two long side rods outside the cylinder coupled to connecting rods driving cranks on the crank shaft.

Both top and bottom of the cylinder are open and the only valves required are one or two fuel inlet valves in the centre of the cylinder, these being of course horizontal, and injecting oil between the two pistons as they reach the centre of the cylinder. With the Junkers engine scavenging can be very effectively carried out, the arrangement of ports being that those for scavenging are disposed right at the bottom of the cylinder whilst the exhaust ports are at the top, and these can be of more liberal dimensions than usual owing to the greater available area. As the pistons reach the outer end of their stroke, air enters the scavenge ports and sweeps right through the cylinder upwards, passing out through the exhaust ports at the top. There is little doubt that this method is a very satisfactory one, and particularly so from the fact that the scavenging air is quite cold, which is not the case with most other types of scavenging gear. Usually two double-acting scavenge pumps are mounted on the end of the engine driven direct off the crank shaft, and these are provided with automatic valves. These pumps can, if desired, owing to exigencies of space, be arranged at right angles to the engine driven off the crossheads, as in the case of the Carels and other motors.

In the usual design a fuel pump is provided for each cylinder, and the governor controls the admission of fuel by means of the suction valve of the pump. The method of reversing is relatively simple, owing to the small number of valves, and consists in altering the angular position of the cam shaft in respect to the crank shaft. Starting is effected by compressed air, and the compressor is usually separately driven.

These motors have been built in as small sizes as 100 B.H.P. and up to 1,200 B.H.P.

British Types.—There are two interesting designs of marine Diesel engines which have been developed in this country, and which, although they are not likely to be produced commercially on an extensive scale, offer some points of interest, especially as they show the trend of thought in Diesel engine design of those who take up the question independently.

The Tanner-Diesel motor, illustrated in *Fig.* 138, is the one which perhaps shows most marked deviation from ordinary practice, and an experimental engine of this type was built by Messrs. Workman, Clark & Co. It is of the two-cycle, single-acting design, and in view of the desire to render it particularly suitable for large powers, certain peculiar points have been incorporated which render it of special interest.

As far as possible, valves are dispensed with, and at the present stage of Diesel engine development, there seems no doubt that this will find general favour. The scavenge ports at the bottom of the cylinder do not call for any special comment, no auxiliary valve being employed, as in the Sulzer type. The ports occupy one-half of the circumference, the other half being utilized for the exhaust ports. Instead of having a scavenge pump driven separately or directly off the crank shaft, a turbo-blower is employed, the advantage of which is its comparatively high efficiency and the ease with which the supply of air may be regulated. It would seem that this arrangement possesses some advantages in the case of large units, although for small powers it is somewhat of a detriment to add to the number of auxiliaries to which attention has to be given. The pressure of the scavenging air is about $2\frac{1}{2}$ lb. per sq. in., which is rather lower than the ordinary.

In this design, the aim has apparently been to render it suitable for a double-acting engine with as little alteration

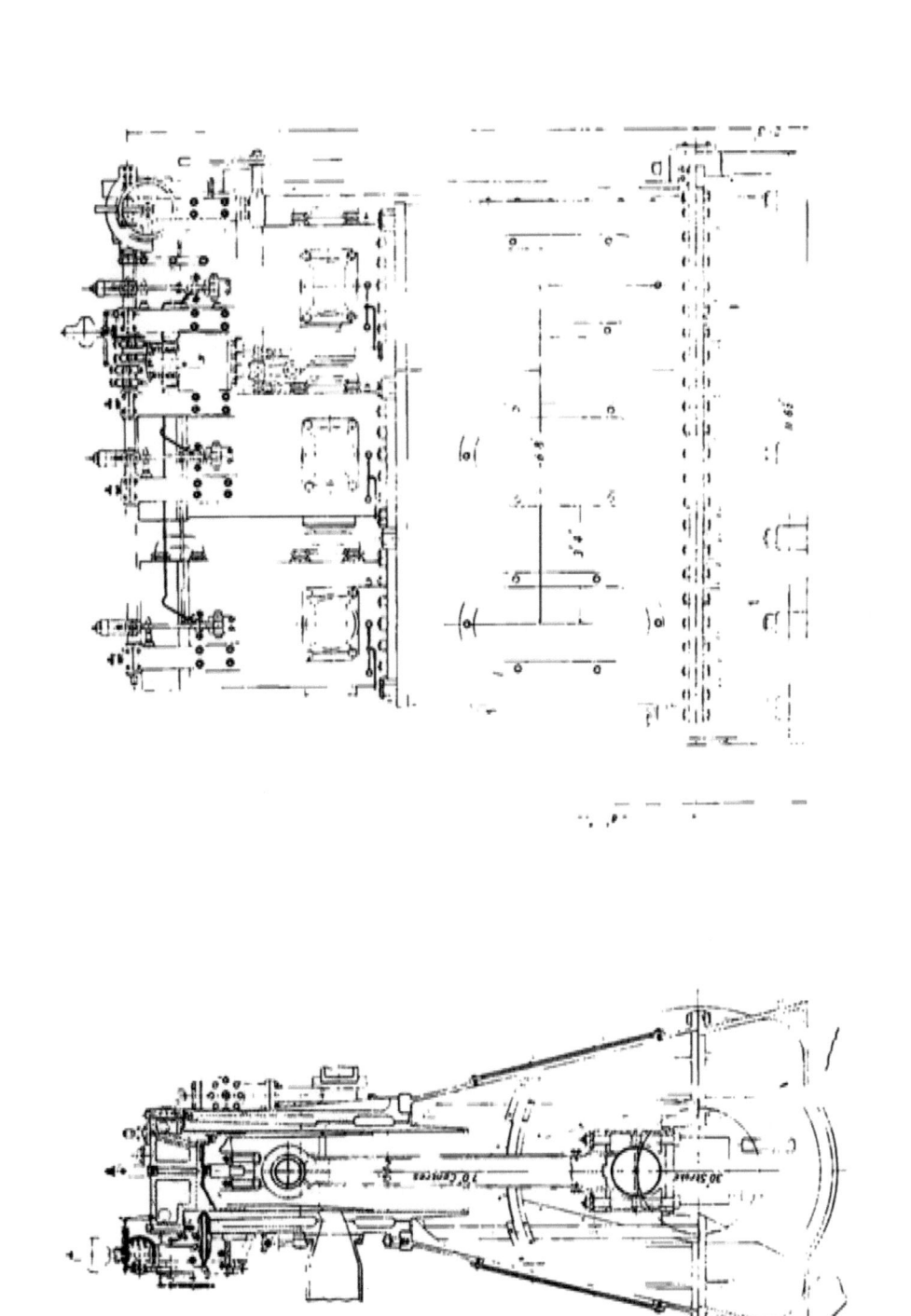

as possible, and the cover has been kept completely free of valves, except for a non-return safety valve to prevent excessive compression. Both the fuel inlet valve and the starting valve are arranged horizontally, which is quite a novel construction.

The motor is of the enclosed type and has a trunk piston—a design which will, however, not prove final, especially for the larger sizes, although even in a so-called enclosed type the parts can be made readily accessible by removing the light covers in front of the crank chamber. The cylinders are supported by steel columns in a somewhat similar manner to the Sulzer marine engine.

The pistons of the motor, contrary to usual practice, are not provided with special cooling, and in order to prevent the metal becoming overheated, shield plates are fitted, which protect the body from the greatest temperature; but this arrangement may have to be modified. Reversing is simplified by the absence of valves, and for each fuel valve three cams are provided, one for ahead, one for astern, and the third for half injection, this latter being a novel feature. The actual operation of reversing is carried out by means of a large hand-wheel, which can be seen in *Fig.* 138, representing a Tanner-Diesel motor. This wheel controls a distributing valve, which passes over three ports in a three-cylinder engine, and thus admits starting air to the cylinders one after the other. The direction of rotation of the engine on starting up depends on whether the large hand-wheel is turned to the left or right, the movement causing one of two valves to open and admit air to the distributing valve as desired. In the normal position of the hand-wheel, the air supply is cut off. In order to set the fuel cams in the correct position, the cam shaft is automatically turned through an angle of $36°$, in a similar manner to that adopted in the M.A.N. engines already described.

The first experimental cylinder built to Tanner's designs was of 19 in. diameter by 30 in. stroke, and at 150 revolutions per minute developed 250-300 I.H.P.

Fig. 139.—Experimental Doxford Diesel Engine.

In order to make the engine of the double-acting type, another cylinder would be arranged above the first, with a piston rod connecting the two pistons.

The Doxford Diesel engine, as built by Messrs. Doxford & Sons, resembles in some respects motors of Continental design. It is of the two-cycle single-acting type, provided with scavenge valve and an overhead cam shaft. The single-cylinder engine illustrated in *Fig.* 139 is of $19\frac{1}{2}$ in. diameter and 37 in. stroke, and develops about 250 B.H.P. at 130 revolutions per minute.

Reversing is accomplished by turning the cam shaft through an angle of $38°$ relative to the crank shaft, and as is usual in this class of engine in which four scavenge valves are used per cylinder, these are operated in pairs from two cams on the cam shaft. As reversing is carried out by turning the cam shaft, two separate cams and rollers are provided side by side for operating the starting air valve, since the angle turned through to set the fuel valve cams is insufficient for the air valves. The construction of this type of motor has now been abandoned.

Four-Cycle Single Acting Engine : Dutch Type.— As has been explained, the four-cycle engine is unlikely to be the ultimate solution of the problem of the Diesel engine for marine work, but it has been adopted by some makers as being the easiest step from stationary to marine work. The marine engine constructed by the Nederlandsche Fabriek of Amsterdam is of this type, and a six-cylinder Werkspoor motor of 500 B.H.P. was installed by this firm in the *Vulcanus*, which was the first large ocean-going Diesel engine propelled vessel, being 196 feet in length and having a displacement of 1,960 tons. This engine is illustrated in *Fig.* 140, while *Fig.* 141 shows a cross-section of the engine-room of the vessel. There are, as is almost universal with four-cycle marine engines, four valves for each cylinder operated in the usual way by levers actuated by cams on the horizontal cam shaft. The arrangement for reversing in this case consists of having two perfectly independent cam shafts A, B (*Figs.* 140 *and* 141) of which one (A) has on it the cams set in the positions for operating the various valves when going ahead, and the other (B) carries the reverse cams. These two shafts are supported in forked end pieces to which the spindle C in front of the engine is fixed. This spindle may be turned by the hand-wheel D, which by the link motion seen in *Fig.* 141 rotates the forked arms around the spindle C' and so brings either the ahead or astern cam shaft in the position to operate the valve levers. The rotation of the cam shaft is obtained from the shaft E, which carries a small spur wheel, which gears into a spur wheel on each of the cam shafts, and thus drives both of them continually when the engine is running. This might be considered somewhat of a disadvantage, but the power required to drive the cam shaft which is running idle is practically negligible and entails no trouble. The shaft E is itself driven direct off the crank shaft of the engine from eccentrics by means of the two long connecting rods which operate the shaft E by means of two small cranks, as is seen in *Fig.* 140. For the supply of fuel to the fuel valves two small horizontal oil pumps F are used driven off a connecting rod, but only one of them is in operation in the ordinary way. This design is contrary to the means usually adopted, since the most common method is to have a separate pump for each cylinder. The pressure of the oil pumped into the valve is regulated automatically by the arrangement G, which operates on the suction valve of the oil pump, much in the same way as the governor lever in the stationary engine, no governor being fitted to this engine. The air compressor for the injection and starting air is of the three-stage type, and is driven off the crossheads, the first stage forming a separate pump, but the second and third stage are combined. The pumps are arranged at the back of the engine, the high pressure cylinder being seen in *Fig.* 141; water cooling is adopted between all the stages. Crossheads and connecting rods are adopted for this engine; hence the piston rod is short, but the engine is relatively higher than ordinary motors of the four-stroke type. An auxiliary compressor is installed driven by a stationary type two-

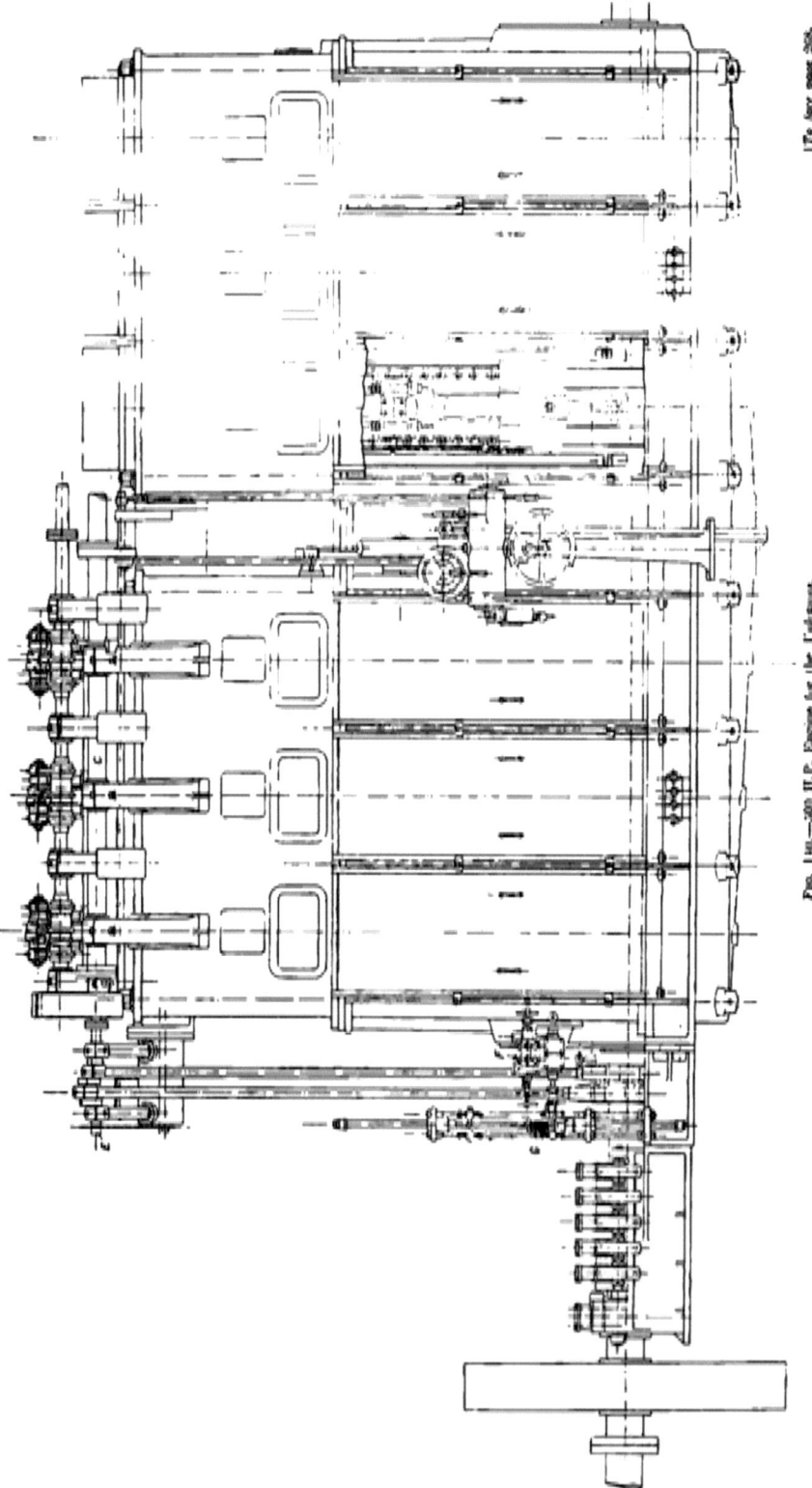

Fig. 140.—500 H.P. Engine for the Colosseum.

CONSTRUCTION OF DIESEL MARINE ENGINE 269

cylinder Diesel engine of 50 H.P. for the supply of starting and manœuvring air, and also the air which is used for auxiliary purposes. Two auxiliary pumps are driven direct

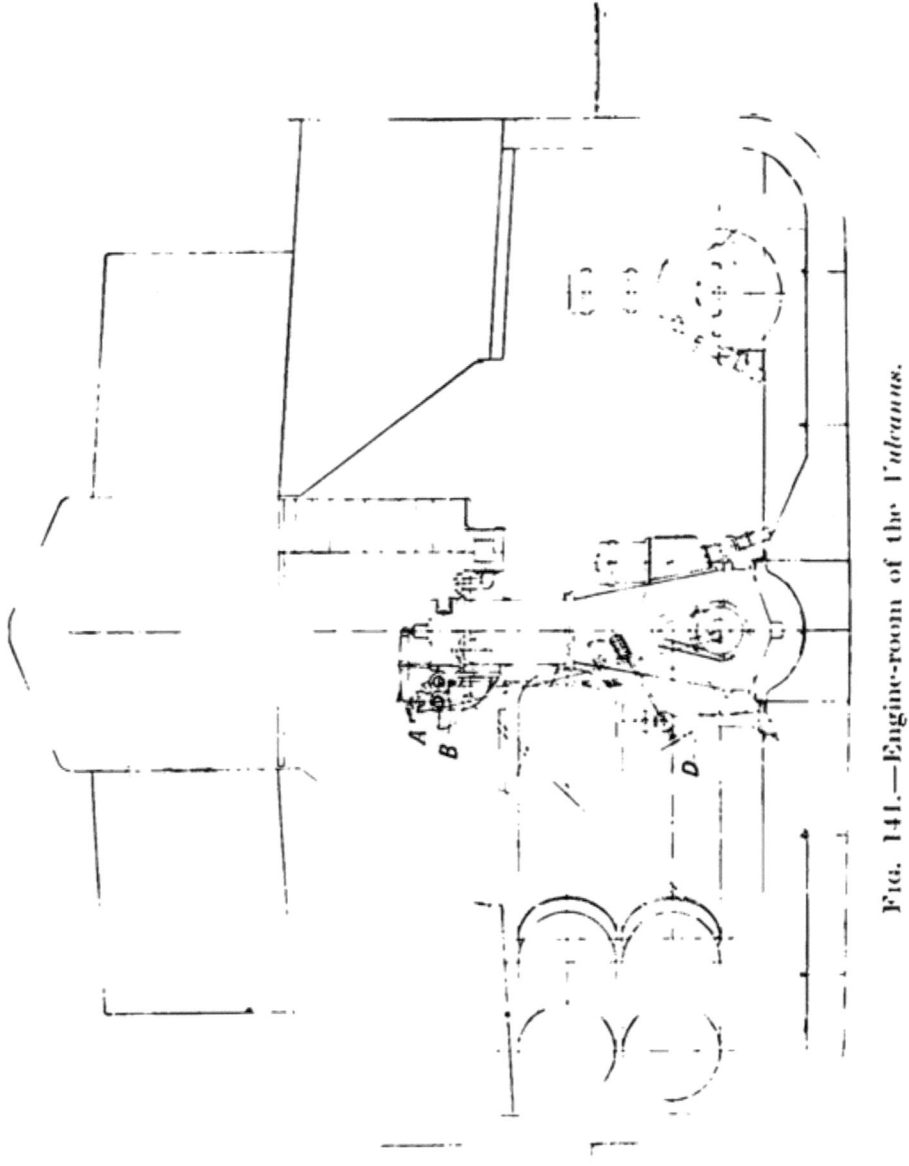

Fig. 141.—Engine-room of the *Vulcanus*.

off the engine, these being the jacket cooling water and the bilge pumps, while a second centrifugal oil pump for unloading the oil in the tanks is driven off the auxiliary engine

CONSTRUCTION OF DIESEL MARINE ENGINE 271

mainly for the purpose of taking the thrust due to the connecting rod. The advantage of this design lies in the fact that the strength of the columns is known exactly, whereas cast-iron framing is always to a certain extent an unknown quantity. Moreover, the bed-plate can be made lighter since the supporting columns are closer together, and the

Fig. 142.—250 H.P. Werkspoor Engine.

bending moment is less. The front of the engine is then quite open, only light and easily removable covers being fitted, and the arrangement is well seen in *Fig.* 142, which is an illustration of the three-cylinder 250 H.P. engine of the same type fitted in the *Sembilan*, and in *Figs.* 143 *and* 144, which show a 1,100 B.H.P. motor.

The arrangement of valves is as usual in a four-cycle

engine, there being four in the cover of each cylinder. The fuel inlet valve which is in the centre is of a novel construc-

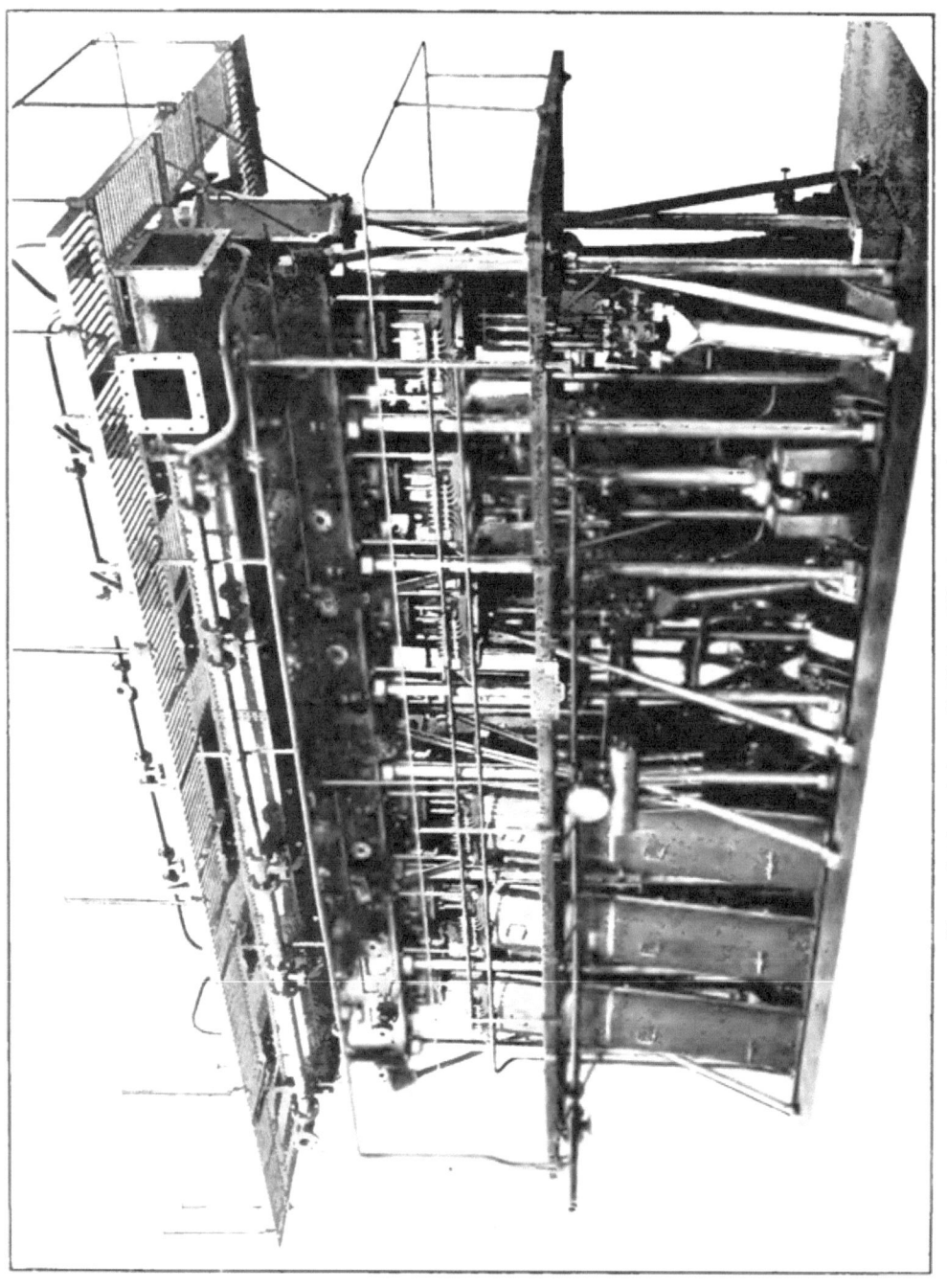

Fig. 144.—1,100 B.H.P. Werkspoor Engine.

tion. Instead of the spring holding it on its seat being immediately above the valve, the valve lever is continued

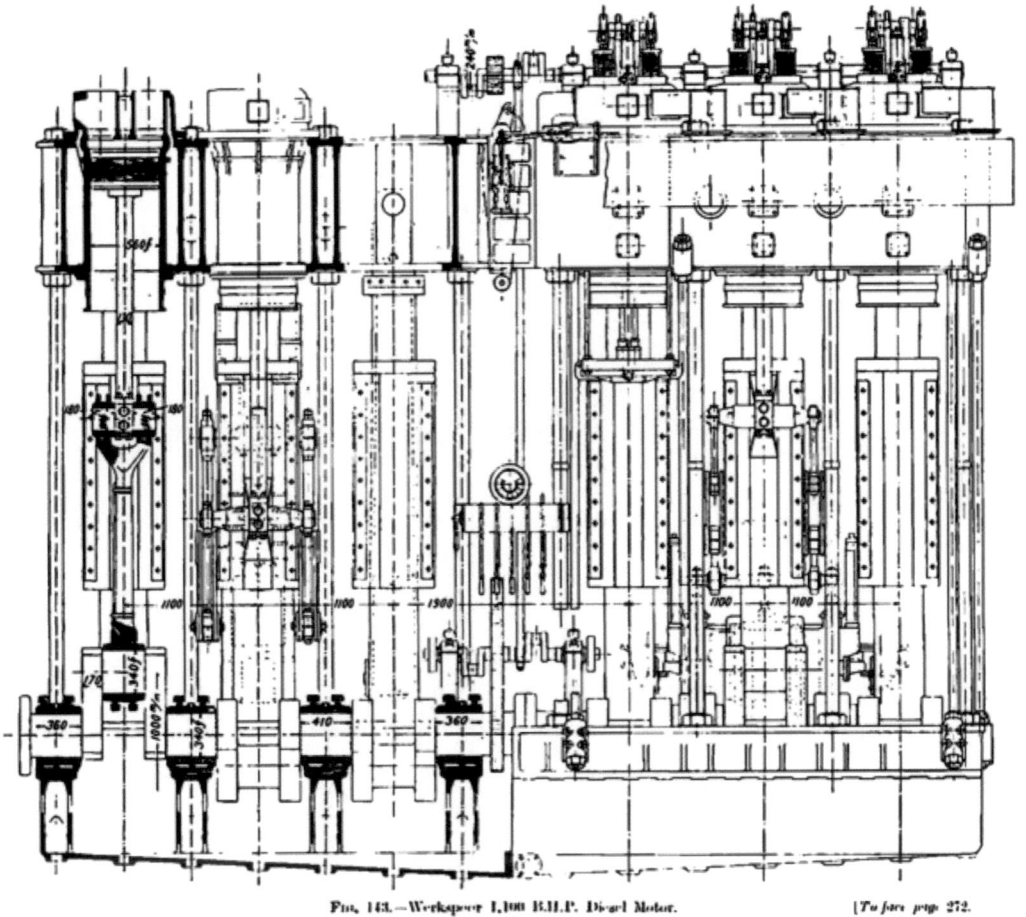

Fig. 143.—Werkspoor 1,100 B.H.P. Diesel Motor. [To face page 272.

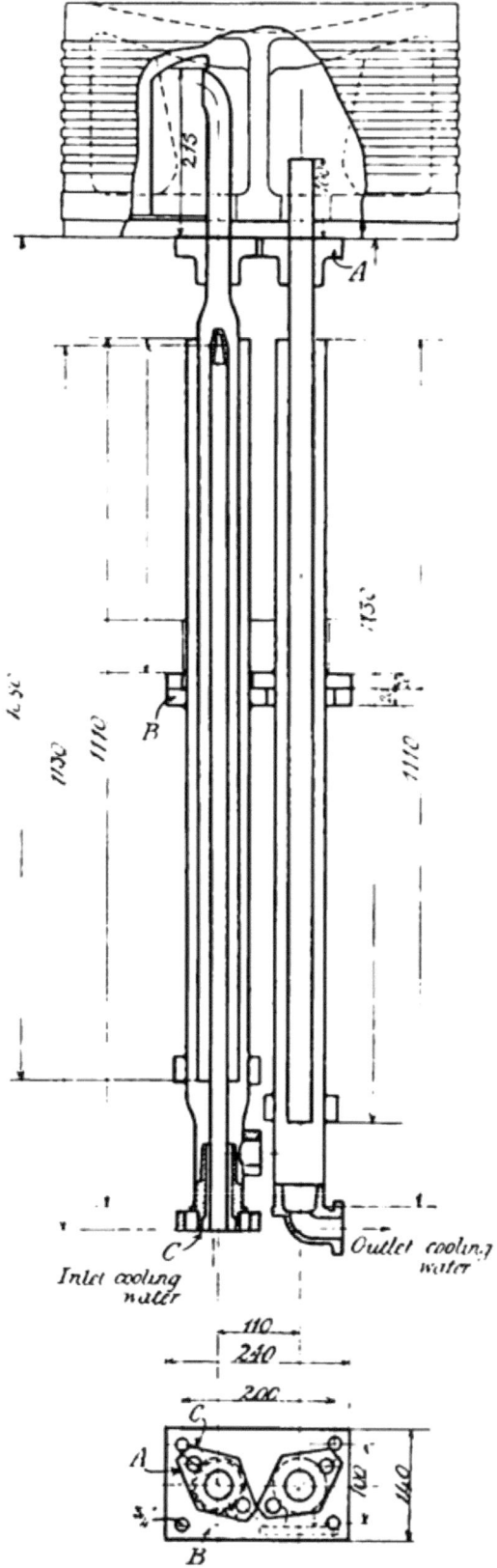

Fig. 145. Arrangement of Piston Cooling in Werkspoor 1,100 B.H.P. Marine Motor.

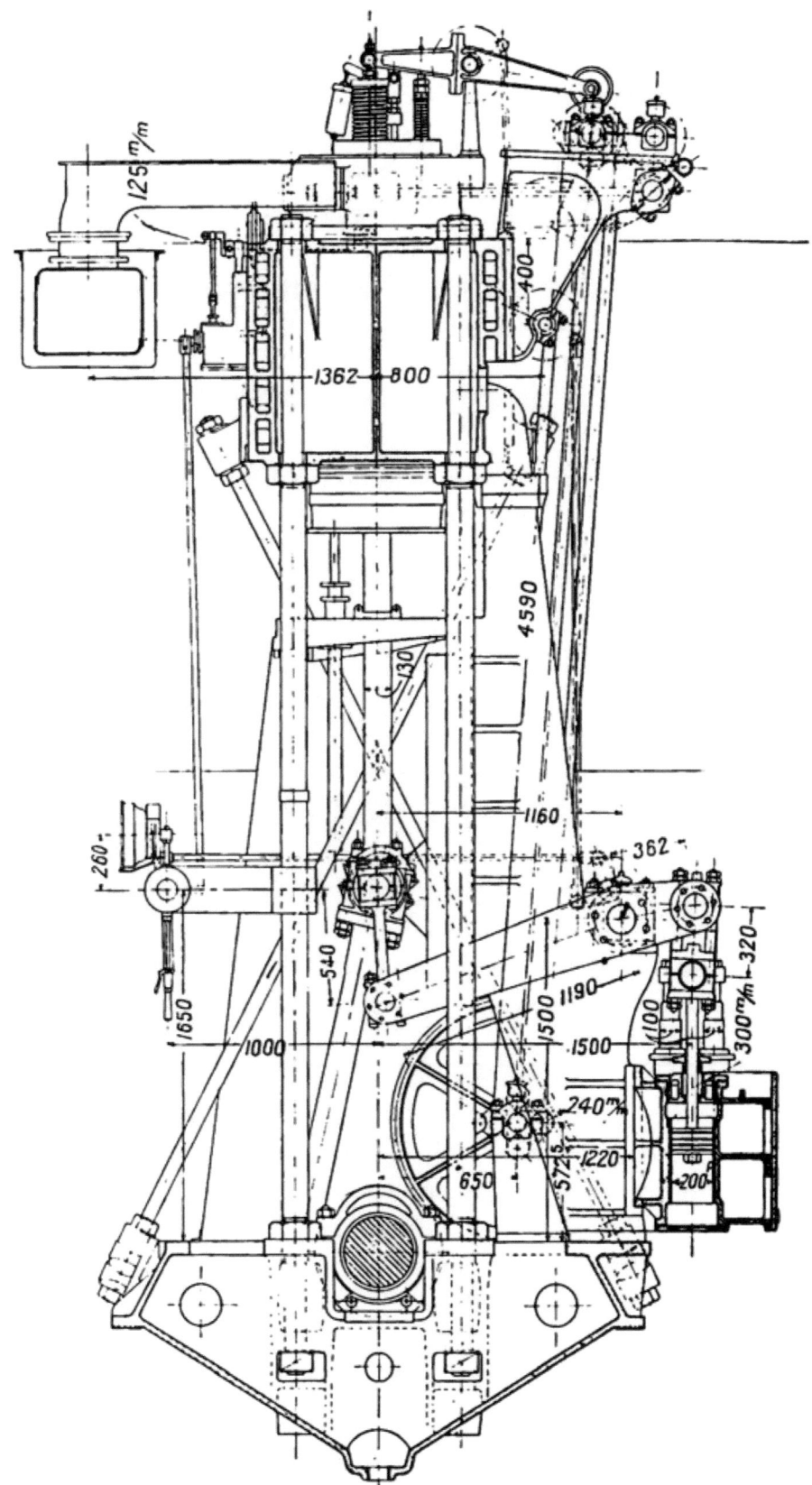

Fig. 146.—Section of Werkspoor 1,100 B.H.P. Four-Cycle Marine Motor.

beyond the valve, so that the valve serves as a sort of fulcrum, the spring exerting its pressure at one end and acting against the force of the cam, causing the lever to be depressed at the other end. The object of this design is to render the removal or examination of the fuel valve more easy.

In principle, the reversing arrangements are the same as those of the engine already described, but the detailed method of operation is quite different. All the gear is arranged in the centre of the engine, but the same method of driving the ahead cam shaft is employed, three long connecting rods coupled to eccentrics fitted on the crank shaft being used. There are two separate cam shafts, one carrying the ahead cams and one the astern; these are at the same level and are a fixed distance apart, but are connected together with gear wheels, so that, although the ahead cam shaft is alone driven direct from the crank shaft, the astern cam shaft is always rotating. The bearings for the two cam shafts are supported on flat guide bases and can move bodily towards or away from the engine, carrying the cam shafts with them. The various pairs of bearings are cast together, so that they must move at the same time, and the relative positions of the cam shafts never vary. The bearings in the centre of the engine are fixed to an auxiliary horizontal spindle behind and just below the cam shafts, and if this spindle rotates, the bearings and cam shafts are thus moved backwards or forwards, according to the direction of rotation. This rotation is effected from the starting platform in front of the engine by means of a screw and link motion, either operated by a small air-engine or by hand, as required. It was originally intended to use a small steam engine, but this was found to be inadvisable.

The reversing is carried out quite simply by means of this arrangement in about twelve seconds from full speed ahead to full speed astern. The levers are lifted clear of the cams, the cam shafts move back or forward as the case may be, the levers dropped down again, and the engine is then ready for running in the opposite direction.

Fig. 147.—Top View of two 1,100 B.H.P. Werkspoor Four-Cycle Engines in the Motor Ship *Emanuel Nobel*.

In other details the engine does not present many points of difference from the *Vulcanus* motor. The lower part of the cylinder is bolted on to the main casting so as to be readily removable in order to examine and dismantle the pistons, and this means is certainly an advantage for marine work. The pistons are water cooled, and the exhaust pipe consists of a channel of large rectangular section, which enables a silencer to be dispensed with. It was desired to use exhaust gases for heating a donkey boiler, which provides steam for various auxiliaries, but this evidently requires some modification in the boiler.

The Gusto Motor.—This is an engine of the two-cycle single-acting type hitherto built in relatively small sizes, that is to say, in powers of 350 H.P. and below. It is mainly of interest in that it is one of the few Diesel engines of the two-cycle type in which scavenging by means of ports is employed instead of the utilization of valves. In the type which is designed for powers of 200 H.P. or below, the construction is of the stepped piston type, with the scavenge pump arranged below each working cylinder as in the M.A.N. engine, but in the larger motors, the method illustrated in *Fig.* 149 is adopted. In this, although the scavenge pump is below each working cylinder, they are separated by means of a distance framing, which has the advantage that the working piston can be drawn out from below the heat cylinder with comparative ease.

As no scavenge valves are required, there is only the starting valve and fuel valve in each cylinder, and in this motor a special construction of cylinder is adopted in which the jacket and liner are cast in one piece, and no actual cylinder cover is fitted. This method, although suitable for the engine under discussion, of relatively small type, would probably be undesirable in larger motors.

Referring to the illustration, 1 represents the working cylinder in which the specially shaped top can be noticed corresponding to the shaping of the piston. This is necessary in order that the scavenge air which enters through the port 10, from the reservoir 7, formed in the framing,

Fig. 148.—Gusto Two-Cycle Marine Motor.

may be deflected upwards, so as to scavenge out the whole of the contents of the cylinder, which are exhausted through port 11. 3 represents the cylinder of the scavenge pump, and 4 its piston, whilst 8 is a piston valve controlling the

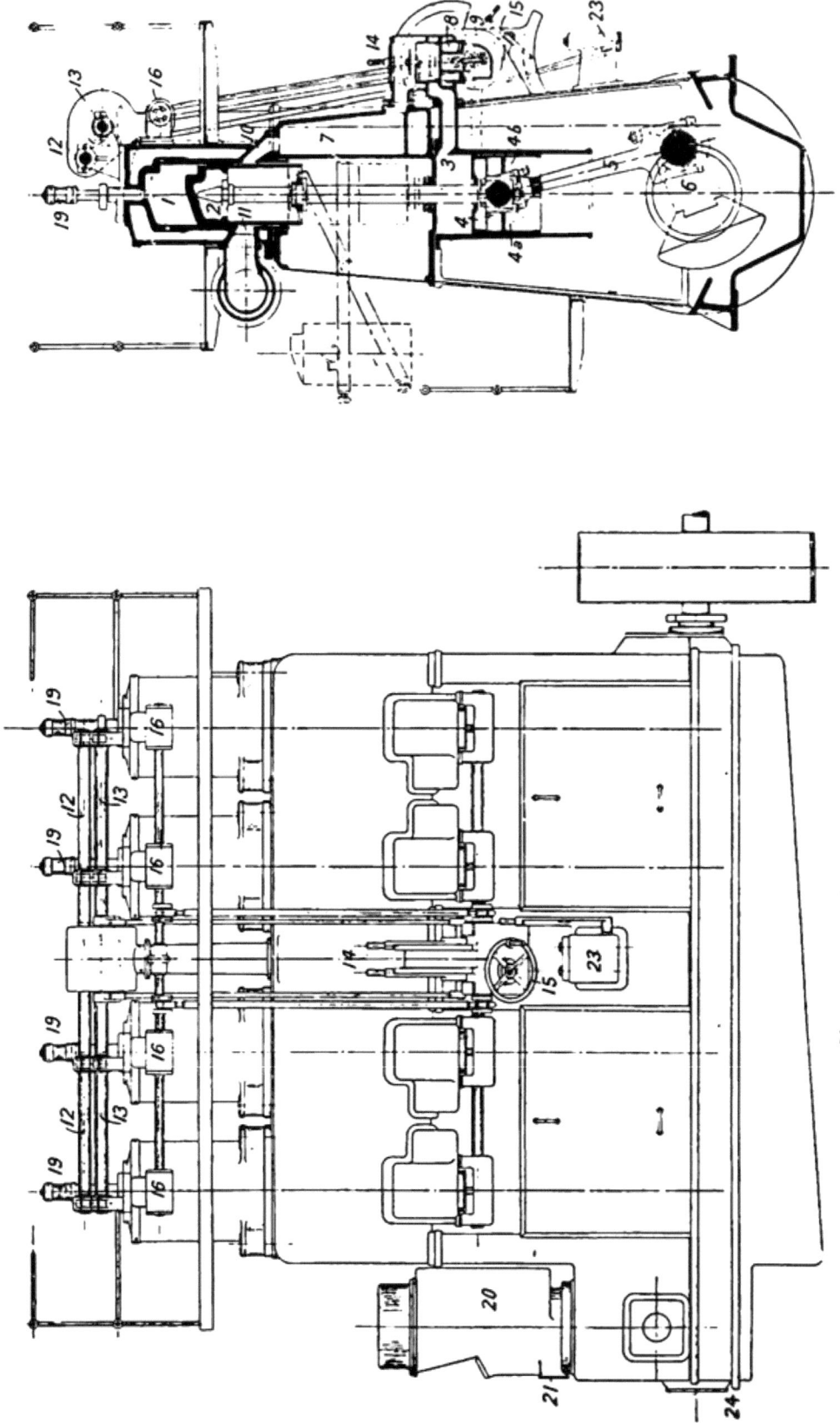

Fig. 149.—Elevation and Section of Gusto Diesel Motor.

admission of scavenge air into the reservoir 7, and thence into the cylinder. The air from the atmosphere is drawn in through this piston valve to the scavenge cylinder, after which it is compressed and the port then allows it to enter the reservoir 7. This piston valve 8 is driven by means of a small crank 9, operated from an auxiliary horizontal shaft which also drives the cam shaft 13, through the auxiliary shaft 16.

In order to reverse (for the motor is directly reversible) the cam shaft is moved eccentrically in its bearing, bringing the cam in the correct position for astern running. The hand-wheel 15 has the function of setting the piston valve of the scavenge pump in the correct position according to the direction of rotation of the engine, whilst 23 represents the fuel pump which may be controlled by means of the lever seen close to it, thus varying the speed of the engine and shutting off fuel altogether when required. A two-stage compressor is employed driven direct from the end of the crank shaft, and the connecting rod 5 and the crank 6 are of the usual steam-engine design. The motor is of the enclosed type, as forced lubrication is adopted, but there are wide doors which are readily removable by hand.

The engine has been adopted for a number of relatively small commercial vessels such as tug boats and motor coasting vessels, and it runs at a relatively high speed, usually between 220 and 300 r.p.m. Naturally its fuel consumption is not so satisfactory as that of small four-cycle motors and the construction is not suitable for high powers, but for its purpose it appears to be well adapted.

German Types.—Several firms manufacture a four-cycle engine for marine work for lower powers, and almost invariably employ a high speed engine, which differs slightly from the stationary type of high speed motor which has already been described. Four or six cylinders are employed, and if six, the engines will start up on the working cylinders in any position of the crank shaft, while if there be only four cylinders, the air pump must be arranged to be used as a fifth cylinder for starting purposes when required.

At the Augsburg works of the Maschinenfabrik Augsburg-Nürnberg, four-cycle engines are constructed up to 1,000 B.H.P. usually of four cylinders with two compressors on the end of the bed-plate, driven direct off the crank shaft. An engine of 1,000 H.P., running at 465 revolutions per minute, has a weight of only about 45 lb. per B.H.P. and a fuel consumption of about ·42 lb. per B.H.P. hour. With the high speed engines, it is customary to fit a safety governor to come into operation in case of emergency, as, for instance, in the event of the propeller shaft breaking, and so prevent the engine running away, the arrangement adopted being that the governor acts on the suction valve of the fuel pump much in the same way as with a stationary engine.

In the Augsburg engine the method of reversing which has been employed differs somewhat materially from the means generally used. There is a single cam shaft provided with separate cams for the forward and reverse running, for each of the four valves on all the cylinders, but these cams do not actuate the valve levers direct, as is customary. Instead of this, the nose of the cam lifts a small roller, of which there is one for each cam, and the valve lever thus receives its up and down motion indirectly from the cam through the roller. Considering any single valve, there is a forward and reverse roller, both of which are attached to a drum concentric with the cam shaft and capable of being turned by means of a hand lever, and of width equal to the combined widths of the two cams. In the position of the forward running the " forward " roller is down on its cam and the " reverse " roller raised out of range of its cam and the valve lever, which thus receives its motion from the forward cam. To reverse the engine the hand lever previously mentioned is moved to the right or to the left, thus turning the drum carrying the rollers through a certain angle, with the result that the " forward " roller is lifted away from its cam, whilst the " reverse " roller falls on to the reverse cam and actuates the valve lever, so as to give the valve its proper timing for reverse running. *Fig.* 150 shows a four-cycle engine of the Augsburg type of 850 H.P. at 400 r. p.m.,

FIG. 150.—High-speed M.A.N. Four-Cycle Marine Engine of 850 B.H.P.

this being designed specially for submarine work, and motors similar to this type have been fitted to submarines for the German Navy.

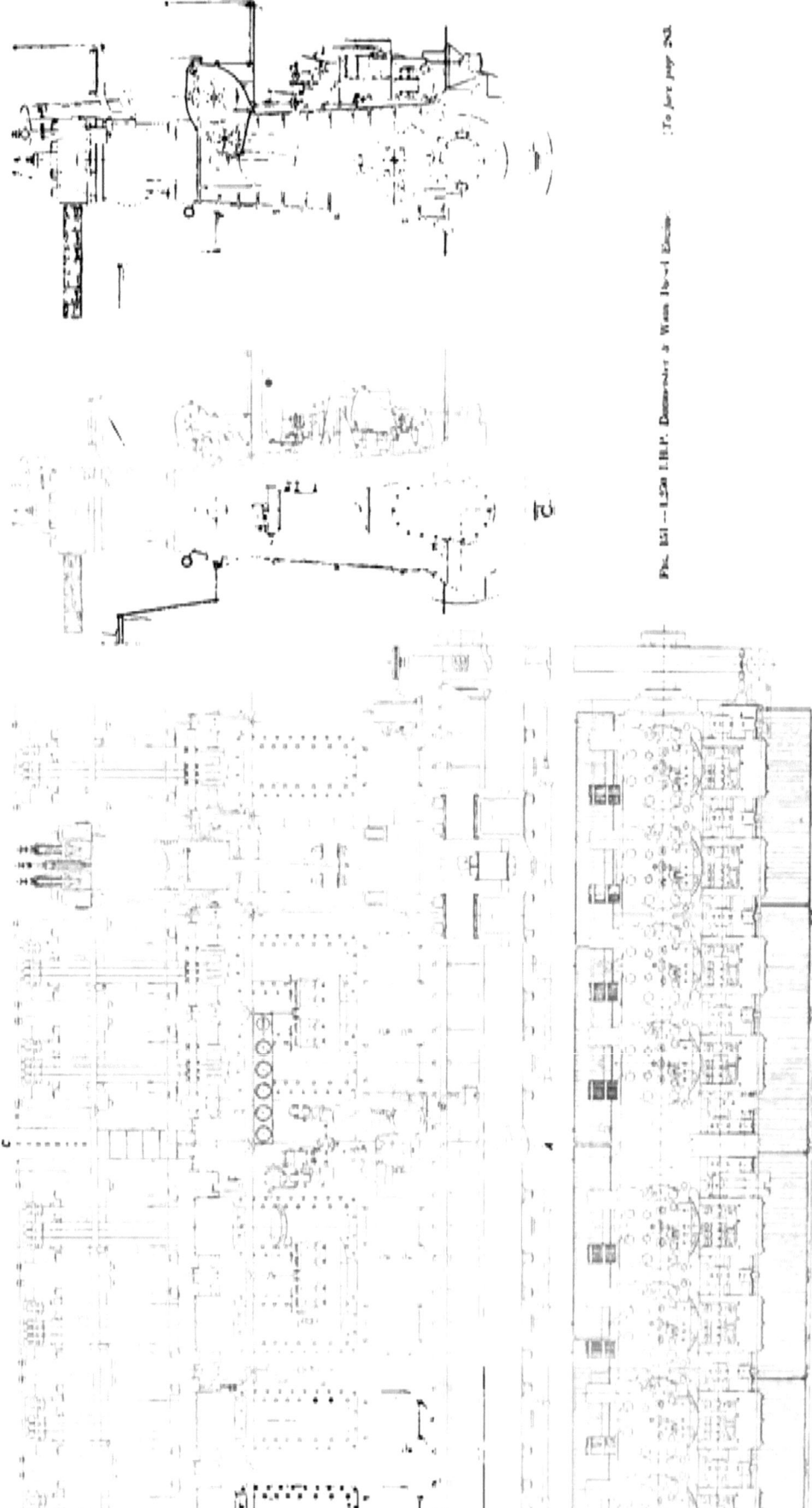

Fig. 151.—1,520 I.H.P. Decauville & Watt Bowl Engine.

For powers up to 300 B.H.P. Messrs. Krupp build a four-cycle engine usually of six cylinders with the compressor mounted on the end of the motor, driven direct off the crank shaft, but as there are six working cylinders it is unnecessary to use the compressor as a motor when starting up. The engine is of the totally enclosed high speed type, very similar to that adopted for stationary work, the speed for powers between about 150 and 300 B.H.P. being usually in the neighbourhood of 400 revolutions per minute, while the weight per B.H.P. varies from about 65 to 90 lb. per B.H.P. Reversing is carried out in much the same way as described for the two-cycle engines of this firm, except that of course an exhaust valve is used and this has also to be reversed. By an ingenious arrangement in which, during the period of running on compressed air when starting up, the exhaust cam is provided with two more nose pieces, the engine may work as a two-cycle air motor and hence the torque at starting is considerable, and the manœuvring qualities correspondingly improved.

Danish Type.—A four-cycle single acting engine which has been developed and constructed by Messrs. Burmeister & Wain, of Copenhagen, is illustrated in *Fig.* 151, this engine being of 1,250–1,500 I.H.P., installed in the *Selandia*, which is a vessel of 10,000 tons. There are eight cylinders, each having a diameter of $20\frac{7}{8}$ inches and a stroke of $28\frac{3}{4}$ inches, the normal speed of revolution being 130–140 revolutions per minute. The engine is of the crosshead type and is totally enclosed with crank chamber doors, which can be readily removed for inspection. The general design does not otherwise present many marked peculiarities, beyond that the cylinders are divided into two sets of four, which is found to be a convenient design, and allows the reversing gear to be arranged in the centre, so as to be readily operated. A further difference from the ordinary construction is in the position of the cam shaft, which is on a level with the bottom of the cylinders instead of the top, which is usually the case. This prevents the four valves in the cover being operated directly from the cams by means of

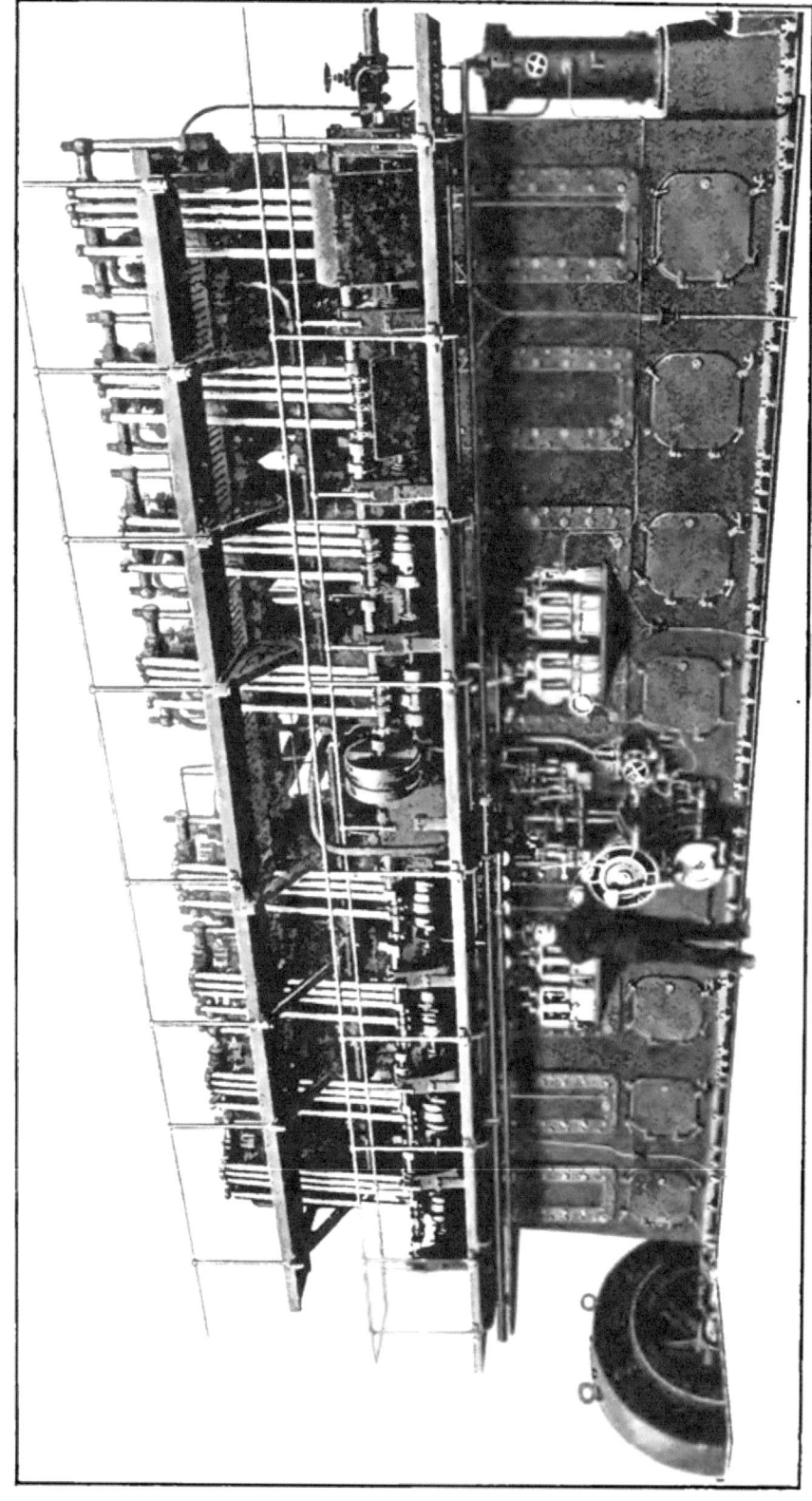

Fig. 152.—1,000 B.H.P. Burmeister & Wain Marine Diesel Engine.

CONSTRUCTION OF DIESEL MARINE ENGINE 285

short levers, and necessitates the employment of the long vertical (or nearly vertical) hollow connecting rods seen in the

Fig. 153.—Interior of Engine Room of Motor Ship with two Burmeister & Wain Diesel Engines.

illustration. It may be mentioned that this method has been adopted by some other manufacturers in their four-cycle engines, and notably Messrs. Krupp, who do not, however, build large engines of this type. When this design is employed, it is of the utmost importance that the connecting rods should be rigid, as their motion is so slight for opening the valves that any small amount of play is most undesirable and will lead to some trouble. Lack of attention to this point has already been the cause of much difficulty in some engines.

From the illustrations it can be seen how the short horizontal valve levers are arranged for operating the valves, and it will be noticed that all the valves open downward, this being exceptional for the fuel inlet valve, which usually opens upwards. The former method somewhat simplifies the construction and apparently gives good results as regards efficiency.

In the earlier pages, the general means of reversing Diesel engines were described, and the arrangement employed by Messrs. Burmeister & Wain is one which was mentioned as being common—namely, by providing side by side a separate ahead and astern cam for each valve on the cam shaft, which is moved in a longitudinal direction when reversing the engine, so as to bring the rollers at the bottom of the long connecting rods above the astern cams. The distance which the cam shaft has to be moved is, therefore, equal to the width of the cams, and the motion is carried out in a novel way. As seen in the front elevation in *Fig.* 151, slightly to the left of the centre of the engine, there is a wide disc mounted on an auxiliary shaft, in which a slot is cut about one-third of the width of the disc. This slot slopes from the top from right to left, and another disc, nearly equal in width to that of the slot and fixed on to the cam shaft, fits into the slot.

The auxiliary shaft can be turned either by hand or by means of a compressed air motor, and in turning it causes the disc on the cam shaft to move to the right or left, according to the direction of rotation, and hence the cam shaft itself is likewise moved until the reverse cams are in the required position. Before this operation is carried out, the rollers which the cams lift are raised above the cams, and are

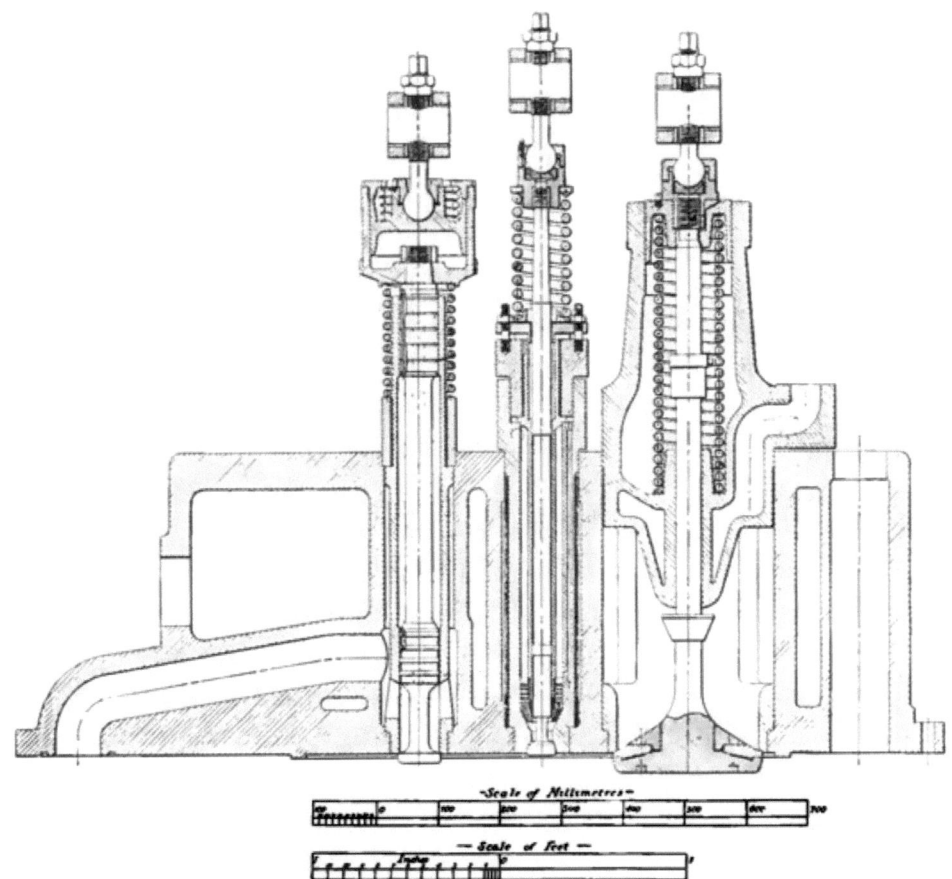

Fig. 154.—Starting, Inlet, and Fuel Valves of 2,000 I.H.P. Burmeister & Wain Marine Diesel Engine.

[To face page 286.

brought down again when the cam shaft has been moved. The lifting of the rollers is accomplished through the medium of the same auxiliary shaft, which, in the first period of its rotation, actuates eccentrics fixed to it. These are connected by short connecting rods and levers to the bottom of the long, vertical rods, which transmit the motion of the rollers to the horizontal valve rods.

Only the high pressure stage of the compressor for the provision of injection air is mounted on the engine, this compressing the air from about 300 lb. per square inch up to 800–900 lb. The low pressure compressor is direct driven from an auxiliary stationary type Diesel engine, which has also coupled to it a dynamo for the provision of electric power for lighting and auxiliaries. This low pressure compressor supplies air at about 300 lb. per square inch to the high pressure stage on the engine, and also provides the air for manœuvring purposes. In a twin-screw vessel, as the *Selandia*, two auxiliary sets are provided, one for each engine, and there is also usually a further steam-driven compressor working up to 800–900 lb. per square inch.

The exhaust from all the cylinders of the engine delivers into a common ∪ shaped pipe and thence to a silencer, whilst the atmospheric air is drawn into the cylinders through horizontal inlet slotted pipes, as seen in the illustration, this being a slight modification from usual practice where vertical inlet pipes are employed.

This is the general design adopted for motors up to about 1,500 I.H.P., but in some recent engines of 2,000 I.H.P. many modifications have been carried out. Engines of this power are made with six cylinders, having a bore of 740 mm. (29 inches) and a stroke of 1,100 mm. (43·4 inches), and run at a normal speed of 100 r.p.m. The main point of difference lies in the method of supporting the cylinders, for in the larger engines instead of having a continuous framing, made of four pieces and bolted together, there is an A frame of very heavy construction over each bearing, and the cylinder jackets of the six cylinders are cast in pairs of three each with feet which are bolted direct

to the top of the A framing. In the front of the engine, light doors are fitted between the standards which are oil-tight (since forced lubrication is adopted as with the other motors), but are readily removable so that the engine, when they are taken away, is practically of the open type. Between the upper portions of the standards, however, stiffening pieces are bolted to which the crossheads guides are fixed, and, moreover, there are steel columns running right through from the bottom of the bed-plate to the cylinder covers through the cylinder jackets, which serve to support the cylinder head. On the top of the A standard a light cover is fitted to the cylinder through which the piston rod passes by means of a suitable gland. There is a tray fixed in this cover so that any lubricating oil dropping from the piston does not mix with the oil circulating in the crank-chamber, but can be carried away and filtered and used over again. With this design of cylinder and framing a more accessible construction of cylinder is obtained.

Instead of having only the high pressure stage of the air compressor driven direct from the engine as in the motors previously described, in the larger type all three stages are directly driven. An auxiliary compressor is of course provided in a ship if equipped with this arrangement. Starting is accomplished, however, in the same way at a lower pressure than that ordinarily adopted, 360 lb. per sq. inch being the usual pressure employed. Instead of having a single fuel pump for all the cylinders there is a separate one for each cylinder in the larger motor, and this is naturally an improvement in design, especially from the point of view of safeguarding against breakdowns, or a considerable loss of power.

A new type of bed-plate is also employed very similar to the bed-plate of a marine steam engine, and is open at the bottom instead of enclosed as with the smaller engines. To it, however, throughout the whole of its length is bolted a tray in order to collect the oil. In the smaller engines oil is used for cooling the piston, this being recooled itself by a circulation of sea water around the oil cooler; but in the larger motors, owing to excessive amount of oil which is required and the difficulty of cooling such a large quantity, sea water alone is employed, being pumped directly into the piston which it reaches by means of a telescopic pipe.

The methods of operating the valves and the reversing

Fig. 156.—2,000 I.H.P. Burmeister & Wain Marine Diesel Engine, showing intermediate shaft and push rods for operating the Valves.

system are practically unaltered, the cam shaft as before being low down so that long tappet rods are necessary. There are also two sets of cams for every valve, one for ahead and one for astern, and the cam shaft is moved lengthways to the engine so as to bring the correct cams underneath the tappet rods. The cam shaft, however, is not driven by connecting rods, but by means of two spur wheels which seems to be a more accurate and reliable method.

This motor is of special interest owing to its dimensions, which are very large for a four-cycle engine, and also for the low speed, namely 100 r.p.m., which is naturally very desirable in order to obtain an efficient propeller.

No difficulties appear to have been encountered in the operation of these engines, and it is possible that even larger sizes may be built, although probably the limit in economy of construction has almost been reached with motors of this power.

Russian Types.—Owing to the abundance of oil in Russia some considerable progress has been made in the employment of Diesel engines for all purposes. For several years boats have been running in Russian waters equipped with Diesel engines. However, in most cases, ordinary stationary motors have been supplied and some type of reversing mechanism employed, either mechanical or electrical.

Two firms are now engaged in the construction of the engine, Messrs. Nobel Bros. and the Kolomna Co. In both cases the greatest attention has been paid to the four-cycle engine, although the two-cycle motor is now being developed. Up to the present, the engines built by Nobels have mostly been of the high speed type, varying from 400 B.H.P. and 250 revolutions per minute to 120 B.H.P. and 450 revolutions per minute, although there is a type of 400 or 500 B.H.P. and 310 revolutions per minute.

The motor is of the enclosed type, the chambers being mounted on a crank chamber, and, unlike some other designs of four-cycle engines, the cam shaft is overhead. Engines up to 1,000 H.P. are built of the four-cycle type.

The method of reversing adopted for this engine is somewhat different from that employed in all other 4-cycle motors.

There are two cams for each valve as usual, but instead of sliding the cam shaft along in order to bring the cams under the valve lever roller, this lever is provided with two rollers. When the hand-wheel is turned to bring about the reversing

of the motor, the roller of the valve lever immediately above the astern cam is brought down on to this cam, whilst the ahead cam is kept well out of range. In some motors, however, built by Nobels, the ordinary methods of reversing is adopted by moving the cam shaft longitudinally. This method is mostly employed for the smaller engines, as in the larger sizes the shifting of the cam shaft by hand becomes too difficult a matter.

The engines built by the Kolomna Company are also of the four-cycle type, and have been constructed up to 1,000 H.P., the engines illustrated in *Figs*. 157 *and* 158 being respectively of 250 and 600 B.H.P. These engines are of relatively high speed, and in some ways resemble the Nobel construction.

The method of reversing is a novel one. Above the cam shaft are two separate spindles on which are pivoted the various levers for operating the valves. When it is desired to reverse the motor, the levers seen in the illustration at the front of the engine are turned to an angle of 45°, which operation rises the fuel-valve lever of the cam and puts the fuel pumps out of operation, so that no fuel can be admitted to the cylinders. The same action admits air into two small air cylinders seen above each of the working cylinders, these being fitted just over the air inlet and exhaust valves in each cylinder. These cylinders act as air motors, in which the piston, being forced downwards by the admission of air, causes the valve levers of the exhaust valve and fuel inlet valve to be raised off their cams. This having been done, the cam shaft is then able to move longitudinally, and the reverse cams are brought underneath the various valve rod levers. The rollers of the levers are then once more brought down on to their cam and the engine is in a position for reverse running. The motor is started up by compressed air, before the fuel valve lever is dropped down on to its cam and fuel admitted into the cylinders. In the larger engines all these operations are carried out by compressed air in the usual way, but in the smaller type it is thought better to effect the various movements by hand.

Small Diesel Marine Engines.—At the present time it may be said that the minimum limit for Diesel engines from a commercial point of view for land work is about 50

Fig. 159.—100 H.P. Daimler Diesel Four-Cycle Reversible Marine Engine.

B.H.P., below which power it is generally found advisable to employ a motor of lower first cost even though the fuel consumption is higher. There are one or two exceptions to this such as small horizontal motors which are made in such large numbers as to reduce the cost of construction and put the engines on a par from the point of view of cost with other types such as the hot bulb engine.

For marine work it has generally been thought that the Diesel engine is hardly particularly applicable below powers of about 200 H.P., mainly again owing to the first cost, and also because of the greater simplicity of other types. There are, however, many engines of 100 H.P. and upwards designed to be specially suitable for installation in craft requiring about this power for their propulsion. These need not be discussed at length as they have none of them received wide application and have in fact only been adopted in special instances where they have particular advantages. It must, however, be remembered that this type of motor will probably make much more headway in the future, particularly if it be designed as simply as possible so that it may be operated by unskilled men, and may be considered equally reliable with other engines which are commonly installed in moderate size motor craft.

These small Diesel motors have been built both of the four and two-cycle type, and in spite of the higher fuel consumption it is probable that the latter design will find most favour owing to the greater simplicity which is perhaps the essential point in the construction of an engine working on this principle.

One of the four-cycle engines which has been manufactured on a fairly large scale is the Daimler type, which is constructed largely of bronze in order to reduce the weight, for heaviness is usually one of the disadvantages of the small Diesel engine. The four-cylinder set shown in *Fig.* 159 has a cylinder diameter of 200 mm., a stroke 230 mm., and when running at 530 r.p.m. develops about 100 B.H.P. It is made directly reversible, and weighs only about 45 cwt. complete, which appears to be about the limit in lightness for a Diesel motor of the four-cycle type of this power. There is nothing peculiar in the design apart from the fact that the cylinder covers are cast in pairs, and that there is an extra valve to each cover for reversing,

Fig. 160. Krupp Four-Cycle Marine Motor.

298 DIESEL ENGINES FOR LAND AND MARINE WORK

which of course is carried out by means of compressed air. Reversing is accomplished by sliding the cam shaft longitudinally in the usual manner, this shaft being provided with two cams for each valve, one of which operates the valve

Fig. 161.—Junkers 100 H.P. Marine Motor.

lever when going ahead and the other when running astern.

In *Fig.* 160 is illustrated another four-cycle motor also of 100 B.H.P. in six cylinders, this being of the Krupp design. It has a speed of revolution of 500 r.p.m., but is not quite so light a construction as the motor previously described.

Fig. 162. 150 H.P. Two Cycle American Diesel Marine Engine.

It is not, however, directly reversible, and its only peculiar feature lies in the method of operating the valves, the cam shaft being low down and the valve rockers actuated through the intermediary of long vertical push rods.

Among the small two-cycle engines constructed is one of the Junkers design illustrated in *Fig.* 161. This is a two-cylinder motor of 100 B.H.P. running at about 300 r.p.m., the third vertical cylinder being the scavenge pump. The principle of operation of this motor is the same as that described earlier in connexion with the Junkers large engine, there being two opposed pistons in each cylinder with the fuel inlet valve horizontal in the middle of the cylinder. This engine is said to give the particularly low fuel consumption of about 0·41 lb. per B.H.P. hour.

Fig. 162 shows a four-cylinder two-cycle motor which has recently been developed in America by the Gas Engine & Power Co. In this case the motor is of somewhat slightly larger size than those previously described; the dimensions of the cylinders are 9 inches bore by 12 inches stroke, the speed of rotation being 250 to 300 r.p.m., whilst the power is about 150 to 175 B.H.P. The motor is directly reversible, and reversing is provided for by having two cams for each valve, one for ahead and one for astern as in the previous cases. It will be noticed also with this engine that long push rods are employed with a low cam shaft. In each cylinder cover are two scavenge valves besides the usual starting valve, fuel valve and relief valve. There is a single scavenge pump driven direct off the end of the crank shaft, and the two-stage air compressor is driven by means of a lever from the crosshead of this scavenge pump.

Another two-cycle reversible motor which has been employed to a certain extent in fishing vessels and small commercial craft is the Kind engine, a six-cylinder design being shown in *Fig.* 163. This motor is one of 150 B.H.P. running at about 300 to 350 r.p.m. It is arranged with the scavenge pumps directly below the working piston, the usual stepped piston being adopted as with other high-speed engines such as the M.A.N. and the F.I.A.T. submarine motors. There is a single scavenging valve in the cylinder

FIG. 163.—150 H.P. Kind Two-Cycle Marine Diesel Engine.

cover besides the fuel valve and starting valve, no relief valves being provided with this engine.

CHAPTER VIII

THE DESIGN OF DIESEL ENGINES

CYLINDERS AND CYLINDER COVERS—PISTONS—CYLINDER DIMENSIONS—CRANK SHAFTS—AIR COMPRESSORS—SCAVENGING PUMPS

It is quite impossible to develop the design of Diesel engines along such lines as would apply generally, owing to the fact that the many different types vary considerably in important matters of construction, and not only in detail. In the first place, of course, four-cycle and two-cycle engines must be treated separately, and in each essential type we have differing methods of driving the air compressors, different arrangements for the scavenge pump, and other variations, so that the efficiencies in the several types are by no means the same. These facts must be borne in mind when using the formulæ and rules given later for calculation, and allowance made for the peculiarities presented by any special type of engine.

Cylinders and Cylinder Covers.—The cylinder covers and liners of a Diesel engine form perhaps the most vulnerable portions of the motor. They are now practically invariably constructed of close grained cast iron, although in several marine engines of the two-cycle type cast steel was employed for the covers, but this in practice was found to be unsuitable and to give rise to cracks. It has therefore been almost entirely discarded, and will probably not be employed in the future, although there is a possibility that it may be utilized for very large motors in which a totally different design from the ordinary is adopted. In motors for submarines, steel has also been brought into use.

It might be thought that the first essential reason for cylinders designed for great strength in Diesel engines would be owing to the high pressure of compression and combustion in the cylinder itself. Probably, however, the most important point is the rapid fluctuation of heat through the cylinder liner, and the consequent stresses which are set up in it. These stresses naturally increase as the diameter of the cylinder increases, and it is easy to see that owing to the great heat on the inside of the liner, expansion takes place, whilst the outside is cooled by the cooling water, so that excessive stress may result.

When it is considered that in a two-cycle engine with a cylinder of say 30 inches in diameter, the thickness of the liner has to be about 3 to $3\frac{1}{2}$ inches, it is not difficult to understand that trouble may result, and this is indeed one of the points which increase the difficulty of the design of very large Diesel engines. Apart, however, from the question of the regularly alternating stresses, owing to the high temperature to which the material of the cylinders is continuously exposed, there is a possibility of what is commonly called " growth " of the cast iron which is of course a well-known factor in other directions, particularly in regard to steam turbine.

In a two-cycle engine, the fluctuation of heat is twice as rapid as in a four-cycle motor, and indeed in the latter type comparatively little trouble has been experienced in the matter of cracked cylinder liners or cracked covers, which, however, is not the case with two-cycle engines. The following remarks therefore apply more particularly to the two-stroke type of Diesel engine.

No matter what the design may be, it is impossible to avoid very severe stresses in covers and liners of two-cycle motors, and the designer has therefore only to aim at diminishing these stresses so far as possible, by a careful examination of the causes which give rise to them. Even from the very earliest experiments which Dr. Diesel made on his first engines it was apparent that the shape of the combustion chamber had an important effect upon the reliability of the Diesel motor. Later experience has more clearly shown that it is essential for the combustion chamber, so far as

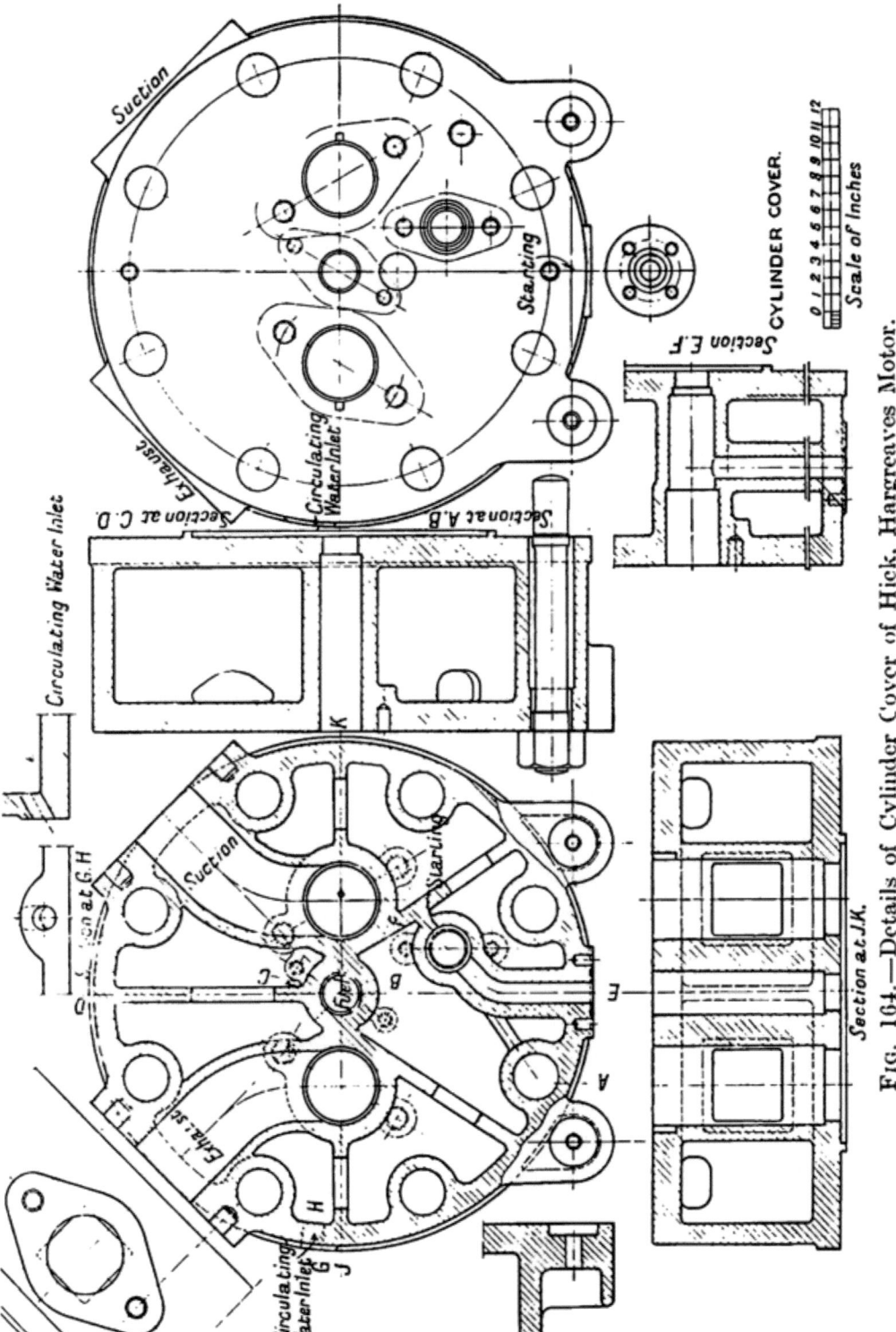

Fig. 164.—Details of Cylinder Cover of Hick, Hargreaves Motor.

possible, to be enclosed by plane surfaces and that all pockets and projections should be avoided. Moreover, the ratio between the cooling surface enclosing the combustion chamber to the total volume of the chamber should be as large as possible in order to maintain good cooling effect. This point has been overlooked in some designs which otherwise showed great possibilities.

The stresses caused in the cylinder cover are greatest nearest the point where combustion is at its maximum, and therefore it is desirable to arrange the necessary valves in the cover as remote from this point of maximum combustion as is possible and practicable; for the points where the casting is weakest are naturally those where it has been pierced in order to accommodate the various valves. It is obviously desirable, therefore, to space these valves as far apart as possible, and above all to limit their number to the absolute minimum. This naturally points to the great superiority of an engine in which a number of the usual valves are dispensed with, and in this category may be placed the two-cycle motor in which scavenge ports are employed instead of scavenge valves. Experience has already shown that where such a design is adopted the danger of the cracking of the cylinder cover and cylinder liner is not so marked as with the valve scavenging engine. This question is further discussed later. Apart from the stresses which are produced both by the pressure in the working cylinder, and also the stresses due to the heating, there are those arising in the ordinary way during the casting, but by modern methods these can be kept within a reasonable margin.

It is not possible to calculate theoretically the thickness of a cylinder liner which is necessary in a Diesel engine owing to the fact that the chief stress (which as mentioned above is that due to heat and not to pressure) cannot be precisely determined. If the liner is made too thick the stresses due to heat which increase with the thickness of the liner beyond a certain point, may be so augmented as actually to counter-balance the diminution of stress due to pressure, so that the resultant stress is greater by an increase of thickness. This does not apply to relatively small engines, but it is not difficult to see that it might be the case in regard to very large motors. In fact it would seem that when we come to engines which have to develop say 1,500 H.P. per cylinder or more it might be desirable to adopt a totally different design of cylinder liner, and to have an inner liner which is relatively thin (say one inch in thickness) so as to allow the rapid transference of the heat from the interior to the exterior of these walls. Outside of the first liner another barrel with web could be shrunk on, and take the stresses due to the pressure. An arrangement of this sort was proposed to the author by Mr. Thunholm and seems to offer great possibilities, although there are various methods by which the same principle could be carried out.

Pistons.—Owing to the high compression in a Diesel engine cylinder and the obvious necessity for the absolute prevention of any leakage with the consequent loss of compression, the piston rings have to be made with special care. There are usually five to seven of these, generally of cast iron, and perhaps the best construction is that commonly adopted for all rings which have to preserve tightness against a heavy pressure. With the old method of hammering it is difficult to prevent some eccentricity in the ring, which naturally may cause unequal wear on the cylinder walls. In the design referred to, the ring after being cut (having then no spring) is fixed in a die which is slowly rotated, and is struck on the inner side by a light chisel-pointed hammer. The strength of the blow is varied automatically, being maximum at the side of the ring remote from the cut and minimum near the cut. The width of the face of the hammer is slightly less than the depth of the ring. After the process, the ring is found to have sufficient elasticity for the purpose, is perfectly round and certainly gives excellent results in operation.

The piston is a detail of the Diesel engine which requires special attention in its design and construction mainly

THE DESIGN OF DIESEL ENGINES

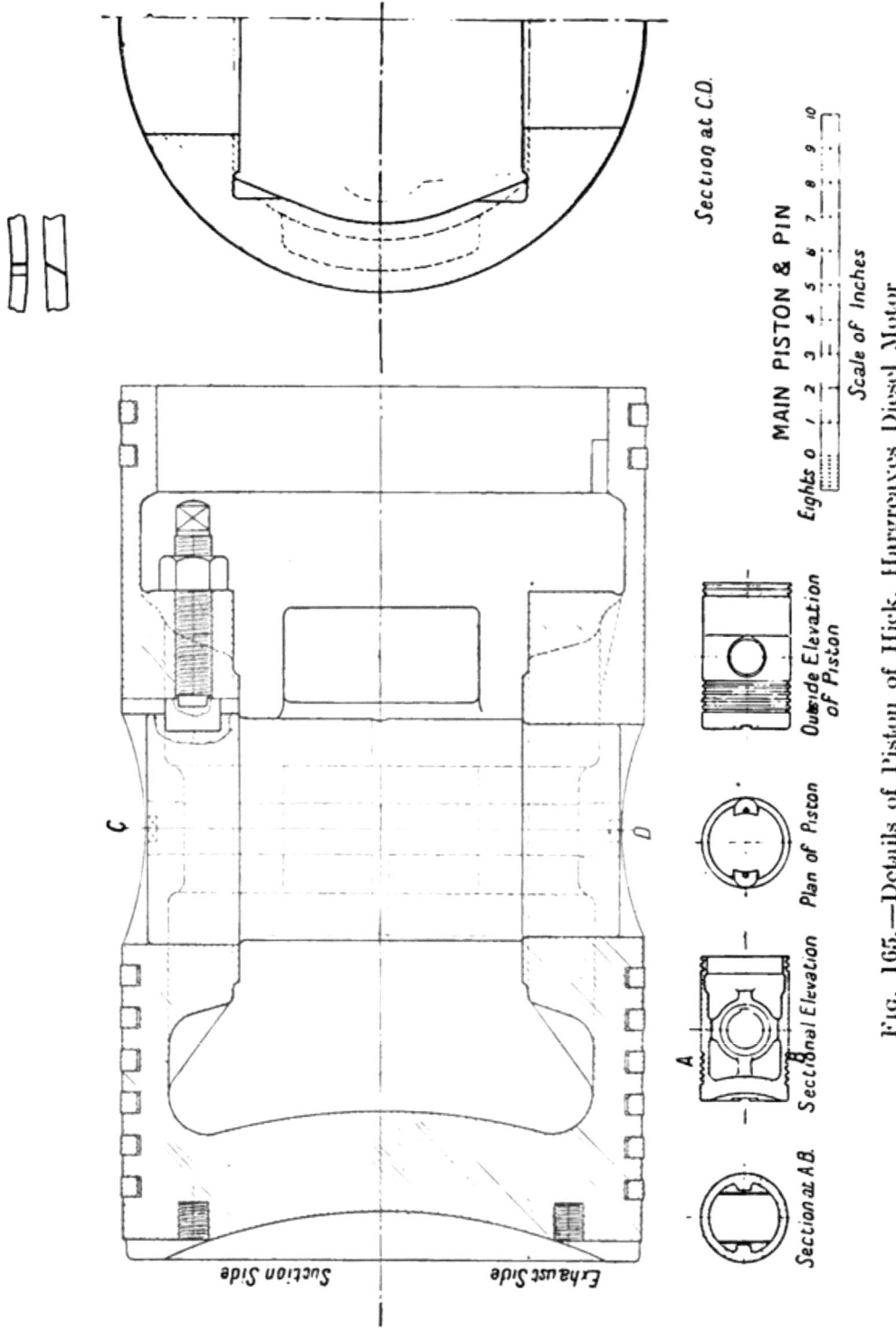

Fig. 165.—Details of Piston of Hick, Hargreaves Diesel Motor

owing to the high temperatures in the cylinder and also because of the excessive pressures involved. It is usually made to taper slightly from the top, and is of course always of cast iron. A good clearance is allowed around the portion where the gudgeon pin enters, and where there is necessarily an extra thickness of metal, in order that the greater expansion may not cause it to bend on the cylinder walls. The gudgeon pin is made a tight fit, is keyed and often locked by means of a set screw, the pin having a hole through the centre to allow the passage of lubricating oil from the cylinder walls. It is desirable that the gudgeon pin be placed as low as possible so as to be away from the zone of greatest heat.

The lubrication of the piston is carried out by admitting oil from sight feed lubricators or other means through two or more connexions passing right through the cylinder jacket. For small cylinders (up to about 15 inches in diameter) two are satisfactory, but above this size there should be four and for large cylinders six or even eight. For marine engines it is very desirable that each pair should be supplied by separate plunger pumps so that any failure should not cut off all the lubricating oil to a cylinder.

As a general rule it may be taken that the thickness of the liner for a Diesel engine of the four-cycle type varies between 0·085 and 0·10 of the cylinder diameter, whilst in a two-stroke engine it is between 0·10 and 0·125 of the diameter. The exact ratio depends to a large extent upon the experience which each particular firm has had in the construction of such parts and the maximum intensity of stress which in consequence they feel justified in allowing. Up to the present in the very large two-cycle engines which have been employed for sea-going work, the cylinder liners have been generally rather thicker than necessary, and the highest figure given, namely 0·125, has been frequently adopted. In four-cycle engines the thickness increases as a rule with the diameter (that is to say the ratio of liner thickness to the cylinder diameter), but the variation is not very marked, largely owing to the experience which has been gained with four-cycle motors in the past.

It has been found that in order to diminish the stresses

resulting from the transference of heat, an extremely desirable feature in an engine is that this heat shall be rapidly conducted to other remote parts of the machine. From this point of view the cylinder cover as ordinarily designed is of course very badly placed, and one of the advantages of a design adopted by Messrs. Krupp for large two-cycle marine engines and the Werkspoor firm for four-cycle engines in which the cover is in one piece with a liner, lies in this fact. It has obvious corresponding disadvantages, since the whole cover and liner must be replaced if one part is cracked, and the question of the relative value of the methods is no doubt largely one of personal preference.

Needless to say the penetration of the liner in order to accommodate valves is quite as detrimental as carrying out the same purpose by utilizing valves in the cylinder cover, and this is one of the unsatisfactory features of engines which, like the Junkers type, have fuel and other valves entering into the liner. It is also an argument against the horizontal fuel injection valve which has been adopted in one or two designs.

Cylinder Dimensions.—A good deal of latitude is allowed the designer in calculating the cylinder dimensions for a Diesel engine. Taking the ordinary four-cycle Diesel engine, the following formula applies for the calculation of the indicated horse-power:—

$$1 \text{ H.P.} = \frac{\frac{\pi}{4} D^2 \times \frac{L}{12} \times N \times p \times n}{33000}$$

in which D = diameter of cylinder in inches
L = length of stroke in inches
N = r.p.m.
p = mean effective pressure (lbs. per sq. inch).
n = no. of cylinders.

For two-cycle single acting engines.

$$1 \text{ H.P.} = \frac{\frac{\pi}{4} d \times \frac{L}{12} \times N \times p \times n}{33000} \times 2$$

The variables upon which the output of the motor depends are therefore the diameter of the cylinder, the length of the stroke, the speed of revolution, the mean effective pressure and the number of cylinders. Of these, the number of cylinders and the speed of revolution are usually determined beforehand from the various considerations, and the mean effective pressure which it is desirable to employ in a Diesel engine is now a fairly definite quantity for the various types of motor. The following table gives the values commonly adopted :—

TABLE SHOWING MEAN EFFECTIVE PRESSURE IN DIESEL ENGINES.

Type of Engine.	Lb. per sq. inch.
Four-cycle slow speed	95–105
,, high	90–100
Two-cycle slow	85–100
,, high	70–85

In marine engines some firms have a smaller figure for continuous operation. For instance, in four-cycle motors of the Burmeister and Wain type the mean effective pressure allowed is about 90 lb. for marine work and 103–105 for land motors. The maximum allowable for this type of engine is about 120 lb. per sq. inch. In the Werkspoor four-cycle engine the usual mean effective pressure is 95 lb. per sq. inch.

It is probable, as more experience is gained with the two-cycle motor, that a slightly higher mean effective pressure will be allowed for in the design, possibly by increasing the pressure of the scavenging air and augmenting the quantity of fuel injected. Naturally an increase in mean effective pressure brings with it an increase in the heat generated and so adds to the difficulties in connexion with the stresses in the cylinder covers and cylinder liners. Even in recent designs, pressures as high as 120 lb. per sq. inch have been obtained with two-cycle engines, but it cannot be said that the result is satisfactory on the whole, particularly for marine work.

Having fixed upon the speed of revolution of the engine, the length of stroke is naturally dependent upon the piston speed which it is permissible to employ in the engine. Although engines are sometimes constructed in which the piston speeds are not within the limits given in the table below, it may be taken as generally representative of the best practice, and any variations would only be made if necessitated by special conditions. It will be noticed that while in the ordinary four-cycle land engine the speed usually adopted is 750 to 800 feet per minute, it may rise to as much as 1,000 feet per minute in the high-speed engine, the highest figure being that adopted in the very high-speed motors employed for submarine propulsion.

TABLE OF PISTON SPEEDS IN DIESEL ENGINES.

Type of Engine.	Land or Marine.	Piston Speed.	
		Ft. per Min.	Metres per Sec.
Four-cycle slow speed	Land	750 to 800	3·75 to 4
,, high	,,	800 to 900	4 to 4·5
,, slow	Marine	650 to 800	3·25 to 4
,, high	,,	850 to 1,000	4·25 to 5
Two-cycle slow	Land or Marine	700 to 800	3·5 to 4
,, high	,, ,,	850 to 1,000	4·25 to 5

It is probable that in larger four-cycle engines than have hitherto been built, say 350 B.H.P. per cylinder and upwards, higher piston speeds would be permissible, but 900–950 ft. per minute may be taken as an absolute maximum limit according to present ideas.

For any desired indicated horse-power all the variables can thus be determined from the tables, except the diameter, which can then be calculated. The length of the stroke is, of course, calculated from the piston speed from the equation—

$$L = \frac{6S}{N}$$

in which S equals the piston speed in feet per minute.

Usually, however, it is a definite brake horse-power which is aimed for and not indicated horse-power, which involves the question of the mechanical efficiency of the motor. In other words,

$$B.H.P. = e \times I.H.P.$$

in which e equals the mechanical efficiency of the engine. The following table gives the efficiency usually obtained with Diesel engines of ordinary construction of the various types named:—

MECHANICAL EFFICIENCIES OF DIESEL ENGINES.

Type of Engine.	Efficiency = e.
Four-cycle slow speed	75–79
,, high	69–72
Two-cycle slow	69–73
high	65–70

The question of efficiency, however, is apt to be very delusive, and whilst with a given type of motor constructed on usual lines the mechanical efficiency may not vary as much as $\frac{1}{2}$ per cent., in some cases differences of as high as 10 per cent. may be noticed in different four-cycle slow-speed engines. This is due mainly to the manner in which the accessories are driven. The figures given apply to what may be termed the ordinary design of Diesel engine in which the air compressor for injecting air and, in the case of the two-cycle engine, the scavenge pump are driven directly off the engine. If, however, the air compressor is separately driven, as, for instance, in the case of some Krupp marine motors of the two-cycle type, the efficiency may rise to about 0·78 as against the usual 0·70. Again, in the smaller of the Burmeister and Wain four-cycle marine engine only the high-pressure stage is driven directly off the motor, the low and intermediate pressure stages being operated from another engine and the efficiency of the motor is as much as 0·84 to 0·85. Various other questions may complicate the issue, such, for instance, as the method of driving auxiliary pumps for cooling and lubricating oil, as well (in the case of marine engines) as the operation of accessory pumps such as bilge pumps, etc. When there are any marked variations in efficiency, therefore, these matters should be kept well to the front, otherwise a totally erroneous idea of the actual efficiency of a certain motor may be gained.

Taking all the factors into consideration, and assuming an average mean pressure and a mechanical efficiency as given above, the output of a Diesel motor of the two-cycle single-acting slow-speed type may be expressed approximately as

$$\text{B.H.P.} = 0\cdot00014 \ D^2 \ L \ N \ n$$

As a matter of fact, this may be taken as a very fair figure for the engines as at present constructed of speeds say between 90 and 150 r.p.m., and for powers of 500 H.P. upwards. The actual figure may vary between such limits as

$$\text{B.H.P.} = 0\cdot000125 \ D^2 \ L \ N \ n$$

and

$$\text{B.H.P.} = 0\cdot000155 \ D^2 \ L \ N \ n$$

In four-cycle motors the horse-power is, generally speaking, represented by

$$\text{B.H.P.} = 0\cdot00008 \ D^2 \ L \ N \ n$$

though, here again, a substantial deviation is possible.

In order to see that the design conforms to ordinary practice various checks may be made upon the dimensions obtained in the manner given above. The ratio of stroke to bore in various types of Diesel engines is fairly definite, although there are marked deviations among different firms according to their peculiarities in design. In fact, the actual ratio varies from unity to just over 2, as will be seen from the tabulated list of dimensions of various engines given later. The last-mentioned figure is, however, an exception, whilst the ratio of unity is that which is adopted on very high-speed engines, such as those of the submarine type, for obvious reasons, since it is necessary to keep down the piston speed to a reasonable amount.

For four-cycle slow-speed engines of the ordinary stationary type, where practice has become much more standardized than with other motors, the usual ratio of stroke to bore which is adopted is 1·4 to 1·5, whilst in the case of very high-speed motors, say those running at 350 r.p.m. and above, the ratio hardly varies from between unity to 1·1, according to the speed and power of the motor. For two-cycle slow-speed engines, particularly those of the marine type, 1·4 to 1·5 is quite a common figure, although many engines have the ratio 1·8 to 1·9 and even above.

Although there is no absolute line of demarcation Diesel engines are generally divided into two classes, known as the high-speed and slow-speed type. The average figures are given in the following table :—

Speeds of Rotation of Diesel Engines.

Type of Engine.	Land or Marine.	Revs. per Minute.
Four-cycle slow speed	Land	140–190
,, high ,,	,,	200–400
,, slow	Marine	100–160
,, high	,,	300–500
Two-cycle slow	Land or Marine	90–150
high	,,	300–450

The volume swept through by the piston of a Diesel engine per B.H.P. per minute is a fairly constant quantity for a particular type of engine, and this fact may be used as a check upon the values which are obtained for the stroke and bore of a motor, by the rules and formulæ given previously. The table below gives a fair idea of the various volumes for the different type of engines, although the figures are naturally dependent upon several varying factors, and above all upon the mean effective pressure which is employed in the motor. It may be taken that the ordinary engine will come within the limits given in the table unless there are some exceptional conditions imposed.

PISTON VOLUME SWEPT THROUGH PER B.H.P. IN VARIOUS ENGINES.

Type of Engine.	Piston Volume swept through per B.H.P.	
	Cubic Metres per Min.	Cubic ft. per Min.
Four-cycle slow speed	0·34 to 0·38	120 to 134
,, high	0·30 to 0·38	106 to 134
Two-cycle slow	0·17 to 0·20	60 to 70
,, high	0·18 to 0·22	63 to 77

As was stated earlier in the volume (see page 23) the clearance space in an ordinary Diesel motor of the four-cycle slow-speed type is so designed that the volume is approximately one-fifteenth of the volume swept through by the piston. This may of course be varied, depending on the maximum pressure of compression which takes place within the cylinder, and moreover the fact must be remembered that in general the piston is dished, so that there is less than one-fifteenth of the length of the stroke between the top of the piston and the bottom of the cylinder cover at the sides. The clearance volume may be calculated by following out the law of the compression of the air during the compression of the stroke. From the ordinary formulæ, the following equation as usual holds good:—

$$P_1 V_1^n = P_2 V_2^n$$

Referring to *Fig.* 6, page 21, it will be seen that

$$V_2 = \text{clearance volume}$$
$$V_1 = \text{clearance volume} + V_c$$

where V_c = volume swept through by piston

$$P_1 = \text{Pressure before compression}$$
$$P_2 = \text{Pressure after compression}$$

In another form

$$P_2 V_2^n = P_1 (V_2 + V_c)^n$$

$$\text{or } \left(\frac{V_2 + V_c}{V_2}\right)^n = \frac{P_2}{P_1}$$

$$\text{or } \log \frac{P_2}{P_1} = n \log \left(1 + \frac{V_c}{V_2}\right)$$

In general $n = 1\cdot 25$ to $1\cdot 3$ say $1\cdot 25$

Taking the ratio $\frac{P_2}{P_1} = 31$ as an example $\left(\frac{500}{16}\right)$

we have $1\cdot 25 \log \left(1 + \frac{V_c}{V_2}\right) = \log 31$

$$\text{or } \log \left(1 + \frac{V_c}{V_2}\right) = \frac{1\cdot 4914}{1\cdot 25}$$

$$= 1\cdot 1933$$
$$= \log 16$$

$$\text{Or } \frac{V_c}{V_2} = 15$$

TABULATED LIST OF DIMENSIONS OF VARIOUS TYPES OF DIESEL ENGINES.

Builder.	Marine or Land.	Type.	B.H.P.	No. of Cyls.	R.P.M.	Bore mm.	Stroke.	Piston Speed Metre per Sec.	Piston Speed Feet per Min.	Ratio Stroke to Bore.
Sulzer	Land	4-cycle slow speed	50	1	190	340	510	3.2	630	1.5
Tosi	,,	,, ,,	450	4	180	450	670	4.02	790	1.48
Hick, Hargreaves	,,	,, ,,	300	3	175	460	660	3.85	760	1.44
,, ,,	,,	,, ,,	450	3	150	570	790	3.95	775	1.38
Sulzer	,,	4-cycle high speed	300	4	300	380	420	4.2	825	1.1
Krupp	,,	,, ,,	275	4	300	380	450	4.5	885	1.18
M.A.N.	,,	,, ,,	18	1	250	215	340	2.84	560	1.58
Hick, Hargreaves	,,	4-cycle slow speed	200	3	250	408	482	4.0	789	1.18
Burmeister & Wain	Marine	,, ,,	1,000	8	140	530	730	3.4	670	1.38
,, ,,	,,	,, ,,	1,300	8	125	590	800	3.35	660	1.36
Werkspoor	,,	,, ,,	1,650	6	100	740	1,100	3.67	724	1.49
,,	,,	,, ,,	1,100	6	125	560	1,000	4.17	820	1.78
Krupp	,,	4-cycle high speed	850	6	125	520	900	3.75	740	1.73
A.B. Diesels Motorer	,,	,, ,,	300	4	400	330	330	4.4	865	1
,, ,,	,,	,, ,,	350	6	500	290	300	5.0	985	1.04
,, ,,	,,	,, ,,	450	6	400	350	350	4.67	915	1
M.A.N. Augsburg	,,	,, ,,	850	6	450	400	400	6.0	1,180	1
Sulzer	Land	2-cycle slow speed	4,000	6	132	750	1,000	4.4	865	1.33
Carels-Reiberstied	Marine	,, ,,	1,800	6	100	600	1,100	3.67	722	1.83
Carels-Tecklenburg	,,	,, ,,	1,500	6	125	500	900	3.75	739	1.8
Sulzer	,,	,, ,,	850	1	150	470	680	3.65	720	1.45
Krupp	,,	,, ,,	1,150	6	130	440	800	3.8	749	1.83
A.B. Diesels Motorer	,,	,, ,,	2,000	6	90	625	1,200	3.6	710	1.92
Swan Hunter (Polar Type)	,,	,, ,,	800	4	165	450	540	2.98	588	1.20
Weser Co. (Junkers Type)	,,	,, ,,	600	4	135	410	850	3.85	760	2.06
Carels-Schneider	,,	2-cycle high speed	850	3	120	400	400	1.6	315	1
M.A.N.	,,	,, ,,	900	4	230	450	560	4.3	846	1.25
D.A.G. (Berlin)	,,	,, ,,	950	8	450	300	340	5.1	1,003	1.13
Körting	,,	,, ,,	480	6	425	190	280	3.95	776	1.38
Krupp	,,	,, ,,	850	6	425	350	350	4.95	975	1
M.A.N.	,,	2-cycle double acting	350	6	150	250	300	4.5	886	1.2
	,,		1,000	3	125	470	630	2.7	531	1.2

Crank Shafts.—Making allowances for the special characteristics of the engine, the diameter of the crank shaft for a Diesel motor can be calculated *ab initio* from the known rules which are applied in steam engine practice. The calculations are based on the equivalent twisting moment, deduced from the combination of the twisting and bending moment of the crank shaft, considering the shaft as a beam supported from two fixed points, namely the centres of two adjacent bearings.

As, however, the maximum pressure exerted on the pistons in Diesel engines is fairly constant, and as the distance between the bearings generally has a definite relation to the diameter and stroke of the cylinder, it is possible to obtain a simple and accurate formula for a crank shaft diameter in terms of the diameter and stroke of the cylinder. In the formula given below the assumption has been made that the distance between the centre of two adjacent bearings is approximately 1·3 times the stroke of the engine, and about twice the diameter of the cylinder. Even, however, when this is not correct the formula holds true within a very close margin.

If D = diameter of cylinder in inches
L = stroke of piston ,, ,,
d = diameter of crank shaft ,,

then $d = K \sqrt[3]{D^2 L}$

where K = a constant.

The value of K is given in the following table for various types of engines.

TABLE OF CONSTANTS FOR DETERMINATION OF CRANK SHAFT DIAMETER.

Number of Cylinders.			Constant K.
Four-cycle Engine.	Two-cycle Single Acting.	Two-cycle Double Acting.	
6 or under	3	—	·525
8	4	2	·53
	6	3	·539
	8	4	·555

THE DESIGN OF DIESEL ENGINES

The diameter of the crank shaft in a Diesel engine varies from 0·55 to 0·65 of the cylinder diameter, the former figure being common in ordinary four-cycle land engines of the slow-speed type, increasing to about 0·58 for high-speed four-cycle engines, to 0·6 for four-cycle marine engines and 0·62 up to 0·65 for two-cycle marine engines in which, however, the margin of safety appears to be somewhat large.

For marine engines, although no regulations have yet been issued by Lloyd's, the Germanischer Lloyd have published the following rules for the calculation of crank shafts. The result, however, gives practically the same figure in every case as that when applying the formulæ given above.

The rule is that the diameter of the shaft shall be calculated from the following formula :—

$$d = \sqrt[3]{D^2 A}$$

in which d = the diameter of the crank shaft in centimetres.

D = cylinder diameter in centimetres.

A = a constant determined from the following table.

H = stroke of piston in centimetres.

L = distance between the centres of two adjacent bearings in centimetres.

No. of Cylinders.	A.
1, 2, and 3	$0·09H + 0·035L$
4	$0·10H + 0·035L$
5	$0·11H + 0·035L$
6	$0·13H + 0·035L$

The above table applies only to two-cycle single-acting engines. For four-cycle engines the number of cylinders in the engine should be divided by two when arriving at the constants given above.

For two-cycle double-acting engines the number of cylinders in the engine should be multiplied by two in order to arrive at the constants.

In determining the diameter of the crank shaft by the above-mentioned rules the maximum stress which is allowed is about 7,500 lb. per sq. inch.

The crank pin is almost invariably made of the same diameter as that of the crank shaft. The length of the crank pin is kept as low as possible, being generally about 1·3 times the diameter of the crank pin and often below this figure. The length of the journal is also kept within reasonable limits, and the bearing pressure on the crosshead pin and the crank pin bearing is not allowed to exceed 2,000 lb. per sq. inch, although this figure is quite a common one in modern Diesel engine practice.

In those engines in which the compression pressure in the cylinder is kept down to a figure below that ordinarily adopted, for instance in the case of Werkspoor motor, a correspondingly diminishing pressure on the crank pin is allowed for, and its diameter is made about 5 per cent. less than that actually calculated from the formula given above. The practice, however, is hardly one to be generally recommended in view of the uncertainty as to the exact pressures which come on the crank shaft.

The rules given above for the calculation of the diameter of the crank shafts are those for ordinary Diesel engines in which the air compressor for injection and starting air is driven directly off the engine. If this compressor, however, is separately driven, as is sometimes the case with large marine installations, a very slight allowance, say about 5 per cent., of the diameter may be deducted from the figures obtained from same by the rules given.

Having obtained the diameter of the crank shaft, the cranks may be designed from the ordinary known rule which applies equally in the case of a steam engine. With marine engines in calculating the diameter of the tunnel shaft the same relations between this and the diameter of the crank shaft holds as is applied in steam engines, namely that the diameter of the tunnel shaft is about 5 per cent. less than that of the crank shaft.

In most Diesel engines of the ordinary four-cycle land

type, with trunk pistons the length of the connecting rod is approximately 2½ times that of the stroke of the pistons, but as a rule this is diminished when crossheads are employed. In many four-cycle marine engines of large size the length of the connecting rod is twice that of the stroke, whilst in two-cycle and marine engines the figure is about 2¼ times.

For large engines, particularly for marine work, it is desirable to have built up crank shafts, and this is one of the reasons for the employment of a fairly long stroke in engines of this type.

SIZE OF CRANK SHAFTS.

(All dimensions are in millimetres.)

Type of Engine.	Four or Two Cycle.	B.H.P.	No. of Cylinders.	Dia.	Stroke	R.P.M.	Crank Shaft dia.	Crank Pin dia.	Ratio of Crank Shaft to cylinder dia.
Krupp	4-cycle land	300	4	380	450	300	220	220	·58
Werkspoor	4-cycle land	600	4	500	640	215	270	280	·54
Carels	4-cycle land	700	4	570	780	150	320	325	·56
Werkspoor	4-cycle marine	1,100	6	560	1,000	125	340	340	·60
Schneider	2-cycle marine	900	4	450	560	230	260	260	·58
Tecklenborg	2-cycle marine	1,500	6	510	920	120	330	330	·64
Reiherstieg	2-cycle marine	1,800	6	600	1,100	90	100	390	400	·65

Air Compressors.—In view of what has already been said in regard to the difficulties that exist in connexion with the exact determination of the cylinder dimensions of a Diesel engine, it will readily be understood that the calculations relating to air compressors are even more subject to variation. The exact quantity of air required for injection has not been accurately determined; moreover, since it varies with different fuels, and the compressor has also to provide air for starting purposes, most builders prefer to allow an ample margin in the design.

In four-cycle slow-speed stationary practice the many years' experience in operation which has been gained enables this margin to be reduced nearly to the minimum limit, but even in this case, in any design which is a departure from the standard, a reasonable excess should be allowed. With high-speed four-cycle engines, however, the same knowledge has not yet been obtained and the variations in different designs are more marked, whilst as regards two-cycle motors there is little doubt that in most cases the capacity of the compressor has been considerably in excess of actual requirements.

At sea it is of course especially important that there should be no lack of compressed air, since not only is it used for other purposes besides injection and starting, such as the operation of servo motors for reversing, etc., and for certain auxiliaries, but the demands for manœuvring are at times excessive. This is to a certain extent counteracted by the fact that an auxiliary compressor driven by an independent engine is practically invariably installed, which is put into operation if the pressure in the receivers falls, and when much manœuvring is required, as, for instance, when in a river or harbour. It is undoubtedly preferable that an air compressor should be over designed than that it should scarcely be capable of its normal work, but the desire for safety has certainly been carried too far in some cases. For instance, it is probably sufficient to design the compressor for a two-cycle marine engine with an output of 6 litres (·21 cub. foot) per B.H.P. per min. of the main engine, whereas in some cases as much as 10 or 12 litres per B.H.P. per min. has been allowed.

In one of the most usual type of compressor constructed which is of the vertical design, driven off one end of the engine directly from the crank shaft, it is not difficult to increase the delivery volume of air should tests show that it is insufficient. This can be carried out merely by the replacement of the connecting rod by a shorter one so as to increase the length of the stroke of the compressor and thus increase the volume of air compressed. Naturally this " trial and error " method is not to be recommended and in any case would only have to be adopted on an absolutely new design.

The following table gives some data regarding the usual capacities of compressors for various types of engine, the volumes being based on the air entering the low-pressure stage of the machine. It is usual to express the amount of air in terms of the ratio of volume swept through by the piston of the low-pressure stage of the compressor to that by the pistons of the working cylinders—that is to say by as many pistons as there are cylinders.

TABLE OF CAPACITIES OF AIR COMPRESSORS.

Type of Engine.	Capacity of Compressor.		Volume Ratio of Compressor to Working Cylinders per cent.
	Litres per B.H.P. per Min.	Cub. ft. per B.H.P. per Min.	
Four-cycle slow speed	6 to 9	·21 to ·31	5·5 to 7
,, high ,,	8 to 10	·28 to ·35	9 to 8
Two-cycle slow	6 to 9	·21 to ·31	6 to 12
,, high	9 to 12	·31 to ·42	10 to 14

In reversible compressors of the marine type some designers allow an extra capacity of 10 or 12 per cent. above that for the non-reversible motors, but this is by no means general.

In many respects it is not advantageous to design a compressor in excess of requirements since in this case air has to be discharged from the delivery of the first stage or else the suction has to be throttled. This means that the ratio of compression in the H.P. stage is too high (it should not exceed 9 to 1) and too much work is put upon the H.P. stage. On the whole it may be said that the lower limits of the figures given in the above table represent the best practice.

Design of Air Compressors.—Air compressors for Diesel engines are designed to deliver air from the high-pressure stage at from 60 to 70 atmospheres, or from 900 to 1,000 lb. per sq. inch. It is obviously impossible to employ single-stage compressors for this work owing to the fact that the temperature of the air after compression would be excessive. Machines of the two-stage type are generally utilized for the smaller sizes of engine, and as the diminution in the number of stages reduces the complication, two-stage compression has much to recommend it. For engines up to 500 B.H.P. it appears quite suitable, but above this power it is common to adopt three-stage compression. With some types of compressors, however, such as the Reavell quadruplex machine, it is convenient to employ more than two stages in any case, so that even with the small engine when this type of compressor is employed three-stage compression is adopted. Inter-cooling and after-cooling are, of course, necessary with all types of compressors in order to keep the temperature of the air down to a moderate figure.

The pressure for the stages are obtained in the following manner, in a two-stage compressor—

If P = Final compression pressure (absolute) in lb. per sq. inch.

P_1 = Pressure (absolute) at end of first stage in lb. per sq. inch,

then $P_1 = \sqrt{P \cdot 14.7}$

taking atmospheric pressure as 14·7 lb. per sq. inch. If the pressure be expressed in the Continental system in atmospheres then

$$P_1 = \sqrt{P}$$

In a three-stage compressor if P_a = pressure in lb. per sq. inch at end of second stage,

$$P_1 = 14 \cdot 7 \sqrt[3]{\dfrac{P}{14 \cdot 7}}$$

$$P_a = P \sqrt[3]{\dfrac{14 \cdot 7}{P}}$$

or if the pressure again be expressed in atmospheres,

$$P_1 = \sqrt[3]{P}$$

$$P_a = \sqrt[3]{P^2}$$

From the tables given previously the approximate capacity of the compressor in terms of volume of air delivered by the low-pressure stage can be obtained. This gives the volume swept through by the low-pressure piston of the compressor, the stroke and bore of which can then be determined. The actual ratio of the stroke to the bore depends a good deal upon individual preference, for there is a wide margin allowable in the piston speed of a compressor. In most ordinary four-cycle engines of the slow-speed type it varies between 0·75 and 1·2 metres per second, or 150 to 230 feet per minute. In high-speed motors it is frequently 2 to 2·5 metres per second, or about 400 to 700 feet per minute, and this figure may also be attained in large two-cycle engines, in which, although the speed of revolution is low, the stroke has to be made of a reasonable length for general convenience.

Taking the case of a two-stage compressor, the diameter of the two cylinders can be obtained as follows :—

Let V = Vol. of L.P. cylinder as obtained from table above.
D = diameter of L.P. cylinder
D_1 = ,, ,, H.P.
S = stroke of piston of compressor
P, P_a, P_1 = the pressures (absolute) at the beginning of the L.P. stage, the end of the L.P. stage, and the end of the H.P. stage respectively.

V_a, V_1 = Volumes of air at the end of first stage and second stage compression respectively.

V_a^1 = Volume of air after intercooling between first and second stage.

$\frac{\pi}{4} D_1^2 S$ omitting clearance and losses. . . .(1)

From reference to *Fig.* 166 it will be seen that the action

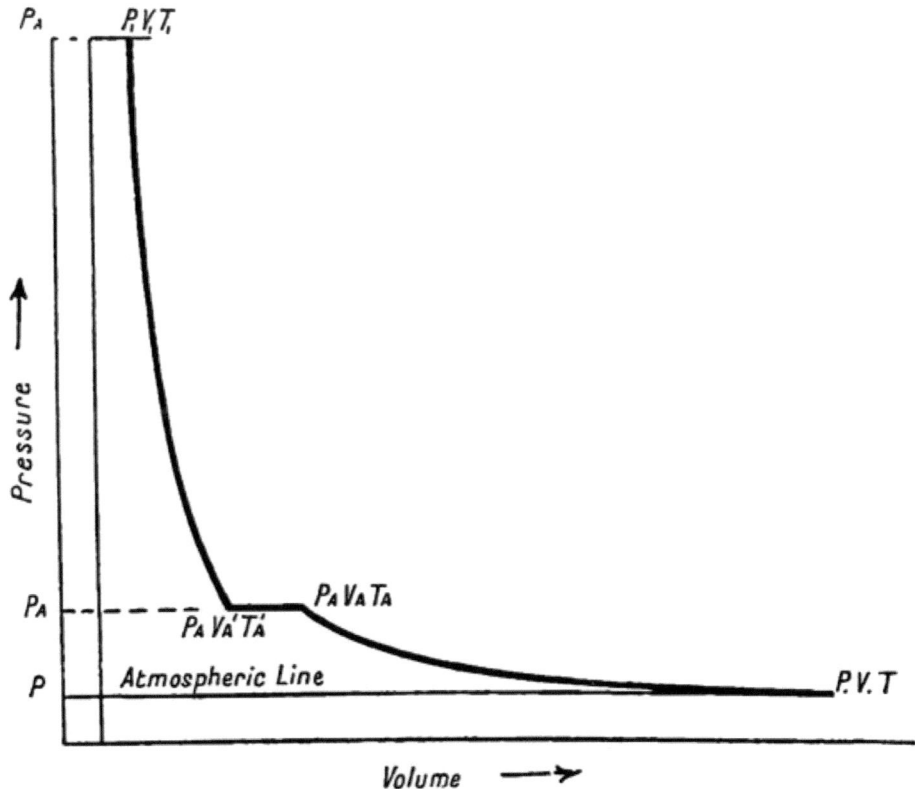

FIG. 166.—Compression Curves in Two-Stage Compressor.

of the compressor is to compress according to the equation PV^n = constant from conditions P, V, T. to conditions P_a, V_a, T_a; next to cool the gas till conditions P_a, V_a^1, T_a^1. are reached, and then compress to conditions P_1, V_1, T_1. The value of n is as follows :—

For adiabatic expansion $n = 1.41$
  ,, isothermal   ,, $n = 1.00$
In general practice $n = 1.25$

THE DESIGN OF DIESEL ENGINES

To determine V_a^1 which is first necessary, proceed as follows:—

$$P V^n = P_a V_a^n \qquad \qquad (2)$$

V is known, $P = 14.7$ lb. per sq. inch, and P_a can be determined from formulæ given above, whilst n may be taken as 1·25, hence

$$V_a^n = \frac{P V^n}{P_a} \qquad \qquad (3)$$

from which V_a can be determined.

After cooling the compressed gas (P_a, V_a, T_a) in the intercooler, its temperature becomes T_a^1 and the volume is reduced to V_a^1.

From page 11 equation (2)

$$\frac{T_a}{T} = \left(\frac{P_a}{P}\right)^{\frac{n-1}{n}} \qquad \qquad (4)$$

since in this case γ is replaced by n

$$\text{or } T_a = \left(\frac{P}{14.7}\right)^{\frac{\cdot 25}{1 \cdot 25}} \times T = \left(\frac{P_a}{14.7}\right)^{\frac{1}{5}} \times T \quad (5)$$

T may be taken as 520° F. or 288 C. absolute, hence T_a is then known.

We may now obtain V_a^1 since the pressure P_a is constant during the cooling.

$$\frac{V_a^1}{V_a} = \frac{T_a^1}{T_a} \qquad \qquad (6)$$

The temperature T_a^1 to which the air is cooled will be about 90° F., or say 32 C. Temperature must of course be absolute, therefore $T_a^1 = 460 + 90 = 550$

$$\text{hence } V_a^1 = \frac{V_a T_a^1}{T_a} \text{ can be determined } \quad (7)$$

From the above

$$D_1^2 = \frac{4 V_a^1}{\pi S} \text{ or } D = \sqrt{\frac{4 V_a^1}{\pi S}} \qquad (8)$$

which gives the value of the diameter of the H.P. stage of

the compressor. The L.P. stage diameter is then found from

$$V = \frac{\pi}{4}(D^2 - D_1^2)\ S \quad \ldots \ldots \ldots (9)$$

$$\text{or}\quad D = \sqrt{\frac{4V}{\pi S} \times D_1^2} \quad \ldots \ldots \ldots (10)$$

The calculations may be made clearer by working out an

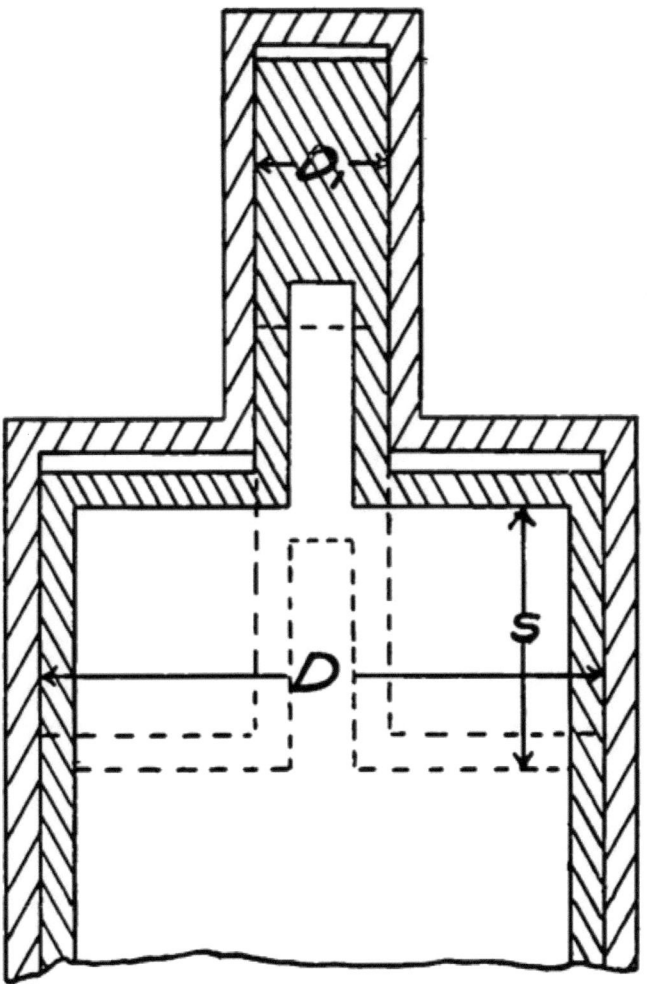

Fig. 167.—Diagrammatic Representation of Two-Stage Compressor.

example, taking a four-cycle high-speed engine capable of developing 275 B.H.P. at 300 r.p.m., having three cylinders, bore 15 inches, stroke $17\frac{3}{4}$ inches. For this the capacity of the compressor may be taken as 9 litres,

THE DESIGN OF DIESEL ENGINES

or say ·30 cub. foot per B.H.P. per min. The compressor is designed for an absolute pressure of 1,000 lb. per sq. inch, hence the absolute pressure at the end of the first stage is

$$P_a = \sqrt{14.7 \times 1000} = 121.1 \text{ lb. per sq. inch}$$
or 106·4 lb. per sq. inch gauge.

Taking the piston speed of the compressor as 425 feet per min. the stroke $S = \dfrac{425 \times 12}{300 \times 2} = 8\frac{1}{2}$ inches.

The volume swept through by the piston of the L.P. cylinder is

$$V = \frac{\cdot 30 \times 275}{300} = \cdot 275 \text{ cub. foot}$$
$$= 486 \text{ cub. inches.}$$

From equation (3)
$$V_a^{1\cdot 25} = \frac{14\cdot 7}{121\cdot 1} \; 486^{1\cdot 25}$$

hence $V_a = 89\cdot 2$ cub. inches.

From equation (5)
$$T_a = \left(\frac{121\cdot 1}{14\cdot 7}\right)^{1\cdot 5} 520$$
$$= 788° \text{ F. absolute.}$$

From equation (7)
$$V_a{}^1 = \frac{89\cdot 2 \times 550}{788}$$
$$= 62\cdot 5 \text{ cub. inches.}$$

From (8) the diameter of the H.P. cylinder is

$$D_1 = \sqrt{\frac{4}{\pi} \times \frac{62\cdot 5}{8\cdot 5}}$$
$$= 3\cdot 06, \text{ say 3 inches.}$$

To determine the diameter of the L.P. cylinder use equation (H) from which

$$D = \sqrt{\frac{4 \times 486}{\pi \times 8\cdot 5} + 3^2}$$
$$= 9\cdot 05 \text{ say } 9 \text{ inches.}$$

The compressor would therefore be made with a stroke of $8\frac{1}{2}$ inches, the diameter of the H.P. cylinder being 3 inches and of the L.P. cylinder 9 inches.

Scavenging Pumps.—The question of scavenging in two-cycle Diesel engines has an important influence upon the design, an influence which will become more and more marked with the development of the larger type of engine particularly for marine work. Whilst, as explained previously, the port scavenging engine has enormous advantages, in the matter of simplicity, and reducing the risks of cracks in the cylinder cover to a minimum, the design of engines employing this method is naturally not without its own difficulties. In order to bring these out more clearly reference may be made to *Figs.* 168 *and* 169, which illustrate the cycles of the valve and port scavenging engine respectively.

Following the indicator diagram in *Fig.* 168 fuel injection commences at c and continues at more or less constant pressure to b when the supply is cut off and expansion proceeds along the line b, a, until at a the exhaust ports are uncovered by the piston in its outward stroke. From a to e the pressure drops rapidly, reaching approximately atmospheric at e when the scavenge valve in the cylinder cover opens, and the cylinder is filled with scavenging air along ef and then back along fe, the scavenging valve closing approximately at the same time (usually just before) as the exhaust ports are covered. Compression then follows from d to c and the cycle recommences.

It will therefore be seen from this diagram that what may be termed the useful stroke is from m to d or x, whilst the total stroke is represented by mf or y. In ordinary

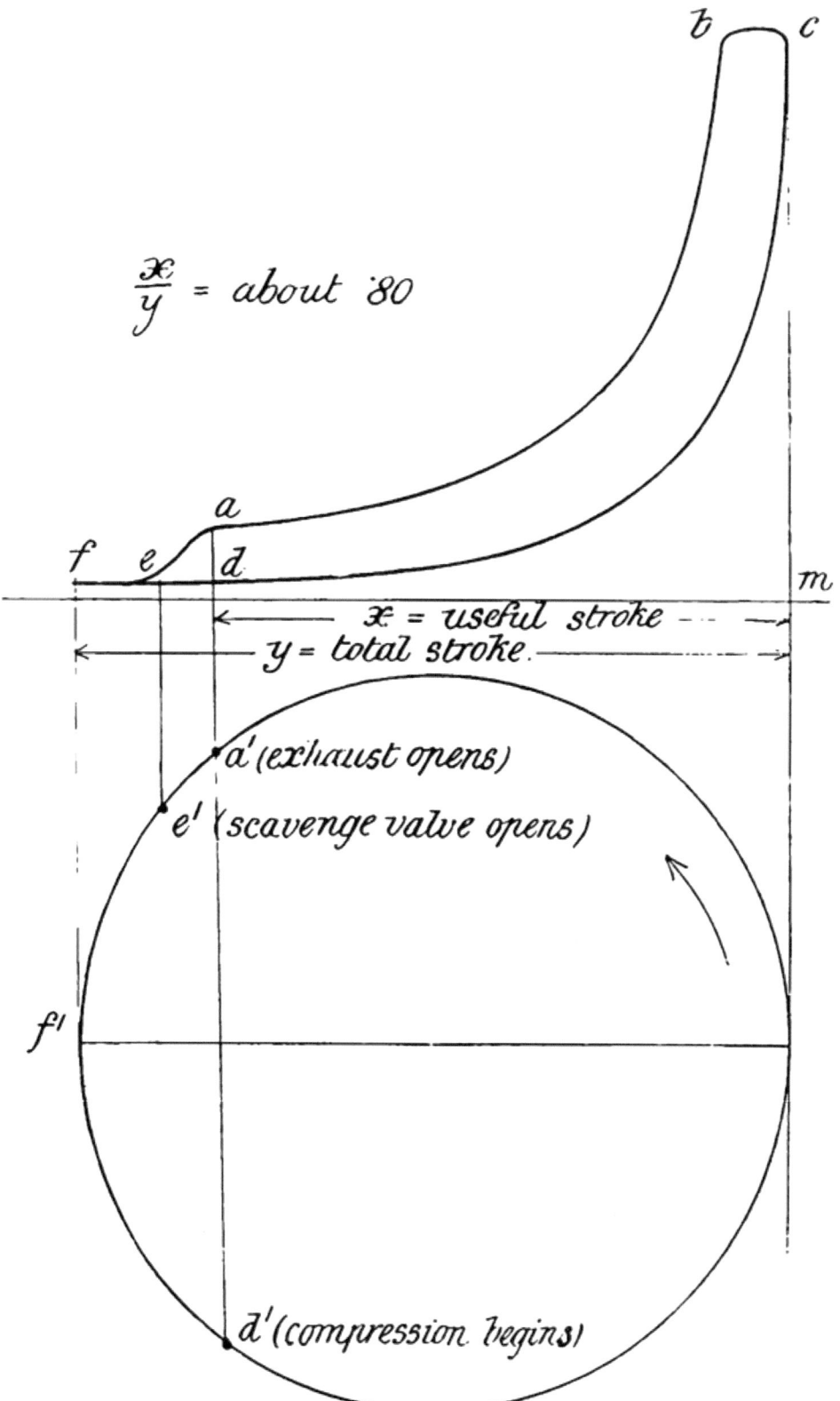

Fig. 168.—Diesel Engine Indicator Diagram with Valve Scavenging.

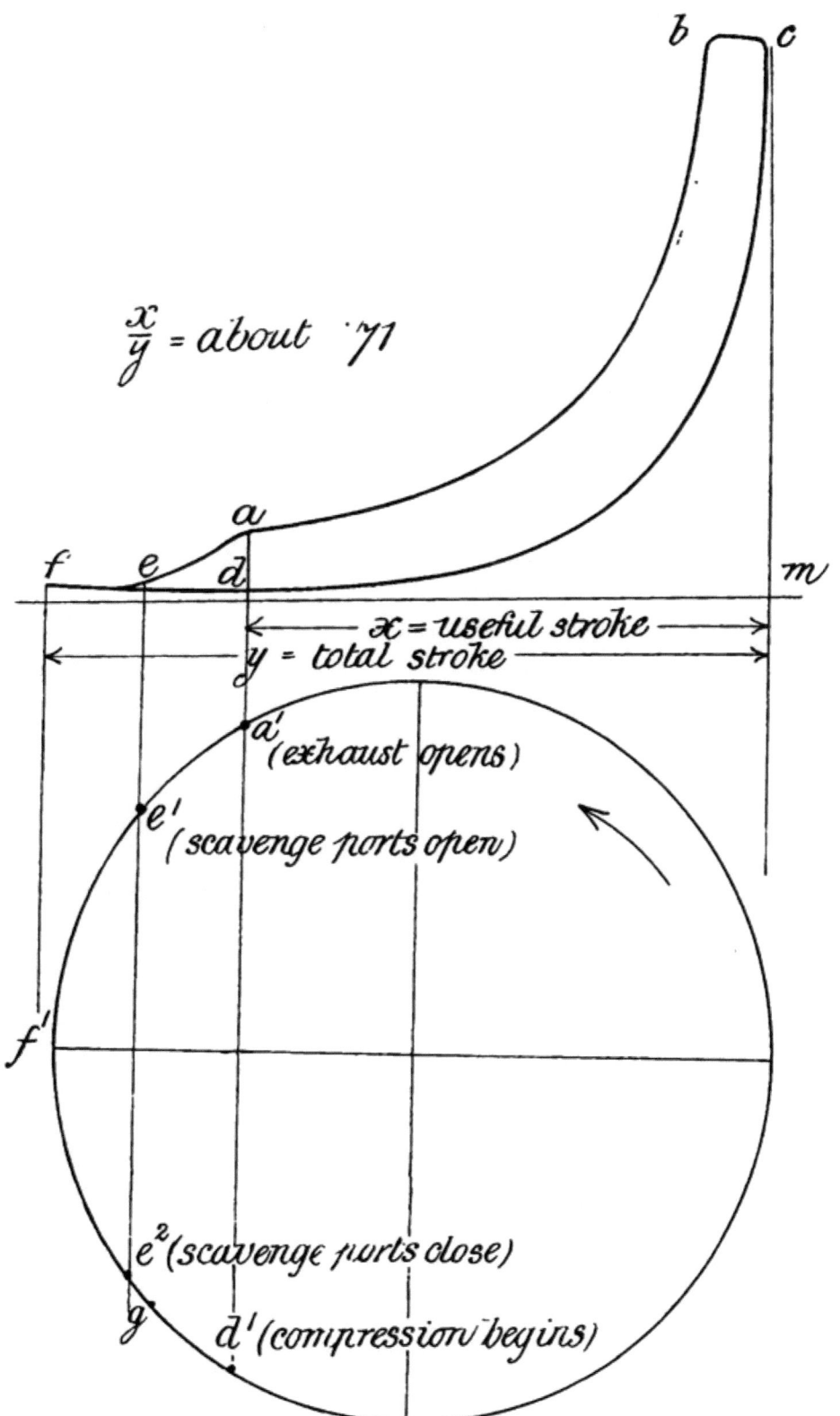

Fig. 169.—Diagram of Engine with Port Scavenging.

engines, up to say 300 or 400 B.H.P. per cylinder, this ratio with valve scavenging at the motors is about 0·8, although it decreases in larger motors.

Turning now to *Fig.* 169, which represents an engine in which port scavenging is adopted, as before fuel is injected at c and combustion takes place along cb, expansion following along ba down to a; the piston then uncovers the exhaust ports and allows the pressure of the exhaust gases to drop until e, when the scavenging air enters through the ports in the other half of the cylinder now being uncovered by the piston. In order to avoid any back pressure and consequent flowing back of the exhaust gases into the scavenge pipe it is necessary that the pressure of the exhaust gases should drop in this way, although it is found that the scavenge ports may open whilst the pressure in the cylinder is still about 2 lb. per sq. inch above atmospheric. From e to f and back again from f to e the cylinder is being charged with scavenging air, but on the return stroke at e the scavenge ports are once more closed, the exhaust ports remaining open until d, when compression commences and takes place as before along the line db.

In this case it will be seen that the effective length of the stroke is again md or x and the whole stroke y, but it is apparent from the diagram that the ratio of x to y must be very much less than before, and in fact even in moderate size engines is between ·7 and ·72. In larger engines this figure is decreased.

It is quite obvious in engines employing port scavenging, since half the belt of the cylinder at the bottom has to be occupied with the ports for the inlet of the air, and only the other half for the exhaust ports, that the latter must be considerably longer in the port scavenging engine than with valve scavenging. The action of the port scavenging engine as described is that of one in which one set of ports only are employed, but it can readily be seen that if more scavenging air can be pumped into the cylinder after the exhaust ports have closed an advantage will accrue. This is the method which has been adopted in the Sulzer engine and in other types, but this has no effect on the length of the exhaust ports.

The calculation of the dimensions of the exhaust and scavenging ports in a Diesel engine of this type is too involved to be based on theoretical consideration entirely since the size is dependent upon many factors which cannot be accurately calculated, being themselves in many cases inter-dependent. With a scavenging air pressure of from 3 to 5 lb. per sq. inch above atmosphere, the usual velocity of the scavenging air is somewhere in the neighbourhood of 320 to 350 feet per minute. The scavenging pump for a port scavenging engine should be capable of delivering from 1·5 to two times the volume of the cylinder with an allowance of about 1·3 to 1·5 times the quantity of scavenging air entering the cylinder as compared with the actual volume displacement of the piston.

There should usually be 7 to 8 ports both for the admission of scavenge air and the exit of the exhaust gases, and the combined width of these is in a neighbourhood of ·45 to ·55 times the cylinder's circumference, being equally divided between the scavenge ports and exhaust ports. In other words the total width of the scavenging port should be from ·225 to ·275 of the periphery of the cylinder.

The length of the exhaust port in a vertical direction with plain port scavenging, is between 2 and 2·2 times the vertical length of the scavenging port.

The following formula for the dimensions of the exhaust and scavenging ports will be found fairly accurate, although they are in general somewhat on the small side.

$$A = \cdot 0065 \ S^3 \ \sqrt[3]{D^2 n^2}$$

$$B = \cdot 0013 \ S^3 \ \sqrt[3]{D^2 n^2}$$

where A = Length of inlet port in inches
B = Length of exhaust port in inches
D = Diameter of cylinder in inches
n = revolutions per minute
S = Stroke of piston in inches.

This presupposes the conditions mentioned above, but it may incidentally be mentioned that in most two-cycle engines with port scavenging in which the ports for the scavenging and the exhaust are of the same width, the exhaust ports have a length of some 22 to 30 per cent. of the total stroke and the scavenging ports have a length of some 11 to 15 per cent. They may each exceed this figure and in larger motors may become as much as 35 per cent. for the exhaust port.

As regards the relative length of the main and auxiliary ports where there are auxiliary ports for admission of scavenging air after the exhaust ports have closed, in engines of moderate size up to 200 or 300 B.H.P. per cylinder, these may be made approximately equal, but in very large engines it will be found desirable to have the main ports, which are below, comparatively small, whilst the auxiliary ports are very much larger. The ports are in any case made to slope upwards so that the scavenging air may not pass directly over the top of the piston to the exhaust ports.

In order to obtain the same outputs from a port scavenging engine with cylinders of the same dimensions as those of a valve scavenging motor, it is essential that a higher mean effective pressure be employed, and as a matter of fact, this is frequently done with certain motors using this principle. For instance in the Sulzer two-cycle engine, both of the marine and land type, it is common to run the engine up to 100 to 110 lb. per sq. inch as a mean effective pressure or slightly over, and the indicator cards given in *Fig.* 8 illustrate this fact. In this case, with a four-cylinder engine, the mean effective pressures taken from the various cylinders range between 108 to 112 lb. per sq. inch, the mean for all four being 111 per sq. inch, giving a B.H.P. power of 795 B.H.P. and an indicated power of 1,135, or an efficiency of about 70 per cent., which is normal for a two-stroke motor.

CHAPTER IX

THE FUTURE OF THE DIESEL ENGINE

THE possibilities which open out in the future for engines of the Diesel or similar type, are so wide that it is necessary to restrain a natural tendency to fall into immoderate language when touching upon this point. As regards the applications of the engine for land work, but little is left to the imagination, so thoroughly has it taken root in all spheres of engineering industry. Each year has seen engines of larger size put into successful operation, and at the time when the limit seemed to have been approached in output for the four-cycle engine, the development of the two-cycle motor reached a commercial stage, with the result that land engines for driving dynamos are now at work, of the two-cycle type, in powers up to 2,500 B.H.P., and manufacturers are prepared to take orders for much larger outputs. The future then of the Diesel engine of the stationary type for ordinary work is no longer a matter of speculation and can only be a record of continued progress following on the success already attained.

There are however one or two fields in which the Diesel engine has at present not entered to any large extent, and it is here that the more interesting developments may be looked for in the course of the next few years. The two most important of these have reference to the adoption of the Diesel motor for locomotives, and for motor traction generally—motor cars and buses, and tramcars.

A large amount of work has already been put on the question of the manufacture of a locomotive driven by Diesel engines and one has, in fact, actually been constructed by

Messrs. Sulzer Bros. It is evident that the saving which could be effected, were all the practical difficulties overcome, would be enormous, and has been estimated by the companies who have carefully gone into the matter at about 75 per cent. of the present fuel running costs.

Though it is too wide a statement to say that a direct driven Diesel locomotive is impracticable, it is highly probable that before such a stage is reached on a commercial scale, another means will first be adopted, which involves less radical difference from the existing methods of employment of the Diesel engine. At the present time it is hardly unfair to say that the Diesel motor is too delicate an engine to stand the great strain which would be put upon it, under working conditions, when used for locomotive driving, and that its method of operation should, as far as possible, be the same as with ordinary engines. This, apart from other considerations, such as greater starting torque, and more easy and economical variation in speed of running, brings us naturally to the question of the employment of electricity as an intermediary between the engine and the driving wheels of the locomotive, and it is upon these lines that we may expect more immediate development. With this arrangement a non-reversible Diesel engine may be coupled direct to a dynamo, delivering its power to motors which drive the driving-wheels, among the advantages being the employment only of machinery of standard type (in which a very large amount of experience has been gained), great adhesion, and good starting torque. Something in this direction has already been done with petrol motors, and petrol electric locomotives are now comparatively common on the Continent for use on branch lines, and it is obvious that if there is an economy with petrol engines, the saving with Diesel engines will be very much greater. A steam turbo-electric locomotive for main line traffic has also been constructed in this country, so that no radically new departure is involved. Up to the present, however, direct current dynamos and motors have been employed, which is not by any means a satisfactory method, and it is probable that the

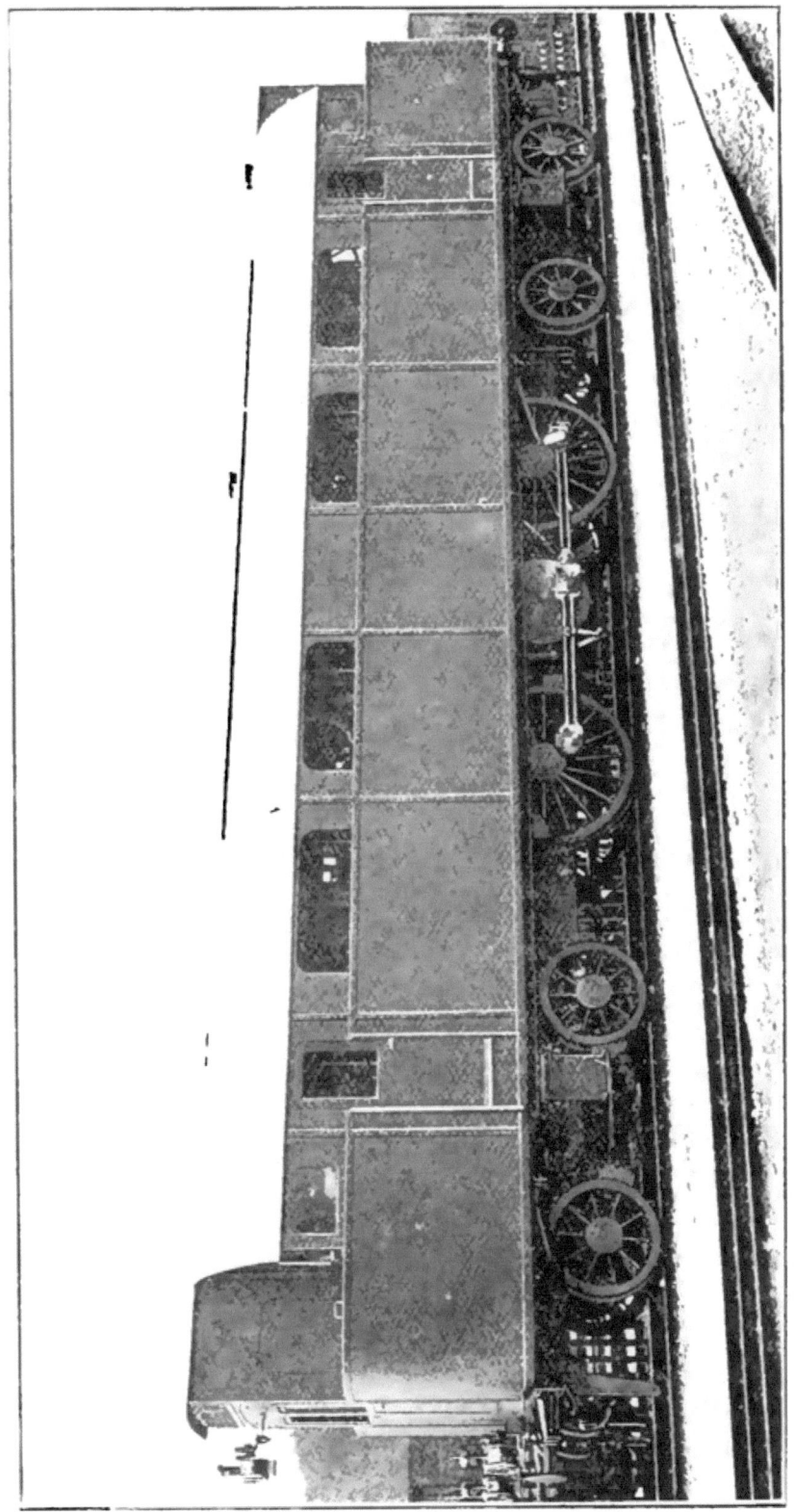

FIG. 170.—Sulzer Diesel Locomotive built for the Prussian State Railways.

THE FUTURE OF THE DIESEL ENGINE

Diesel electric locomotive, of which much may be expected in the future, will be a type in which alternating current dynamos and motors will be employed, working on one of the many systems which have been proposed.

The problem of the construction of a Diesel-driven locomotive is perhaps of greater complexity than any other in connexion with this motor, and certainly the difficulties encountered are far in excess of those connected with the application to marine work.

Although it must at present be considered only in an experimental aspect, a large locomotive has been constructed by Messrs. Sulzer Bros., driven by a Diesel engine. A

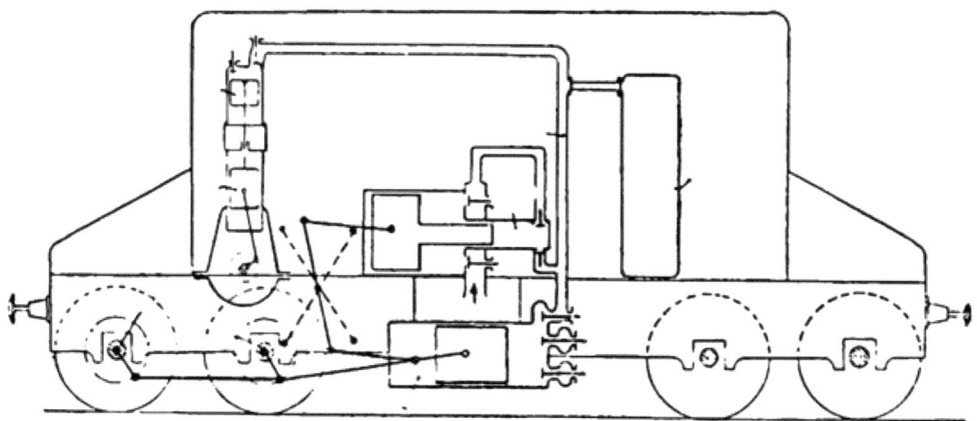

Fig. 171.—Diagram illustrating Arrangement of Sulzer Diesel Locomotive.

four-cylinder two-cycle single-acting motor is employed, the arrangement adopted being to have the engine with cylinders coupled in pairs at an angle of 90°, driving on to an intermediate crank shaft between the two driving shafts. The cranks are at 180°, and it is stated that good balancing is obtained. The scavenge pumps, of which there are two, are separate from the engine cylinders and are driven by levers from the connecting rods; they are placed between the two pairs of cylinders, being vertical and arranged longitudinally.

In order to provide a good starting torque and to help the engine up gradients, an auxiliary air-compressor is provided, driven by a vertical two-cylinder two-cycle Diesel engine, the compressor consisting of two horizontal cylinders. When greater power is required compressed air from this compressor and more fuel are supplied to the working cylinders, with the result that greater power is obtained for a short time, the auxiliary plant being out of action in the ordinary way.

A very large reserve of compressed air is carried, many air-bottles being fitted behind the engines, whilst there is also an arrangement for cooling and circulating water, so that the consumption of water is infinitesimal when compared with a steam locomotive. The power developed is about 1,200 B.H.P., and the entire locomotive, including fuel and water, weighs about 85 tons. A small boiler is provided for heating the train.

It cannot be long also before very serious attention will be given to the use of Diesel engines for road vehicles, both motor cars and buses and tramcars, and here again, at any rate in the first instance, it is probable that electricity may be employed in the same way. The final development, however, is difficult to forecast, and it is significant to note that one of the largest firms in Germany is now engaged on the perfection of a small Diesel motor suitable for direct driving of motor vehicles.

With regard to the aspect of the marine engine, so great are the possibilities offered that it is easy to be too optimistic. There does not seem any reason to suppose that, after experience has been gained, there should be any doubt as to the construction of engines of any power that may be required for the largest battleships and the fastest liners. A few years' thorough experience is, however, necessary before such a definite revolution can be effected, but as so much time and money is being expended in the matter, and as moreover the most essential difficulties seem to have been overcome, the ultimate result is hardly in doubt. When it is remembered that the adoption of oil engines at sea on a large scale is probably the most revolutionary step which has been taken in the history of marine engineering, exceeding in its importance and effect the introduction of the steam turbine, it will be seen that a too rapid culmination is not to be reached, particularly in view of the many conflicting interests in-

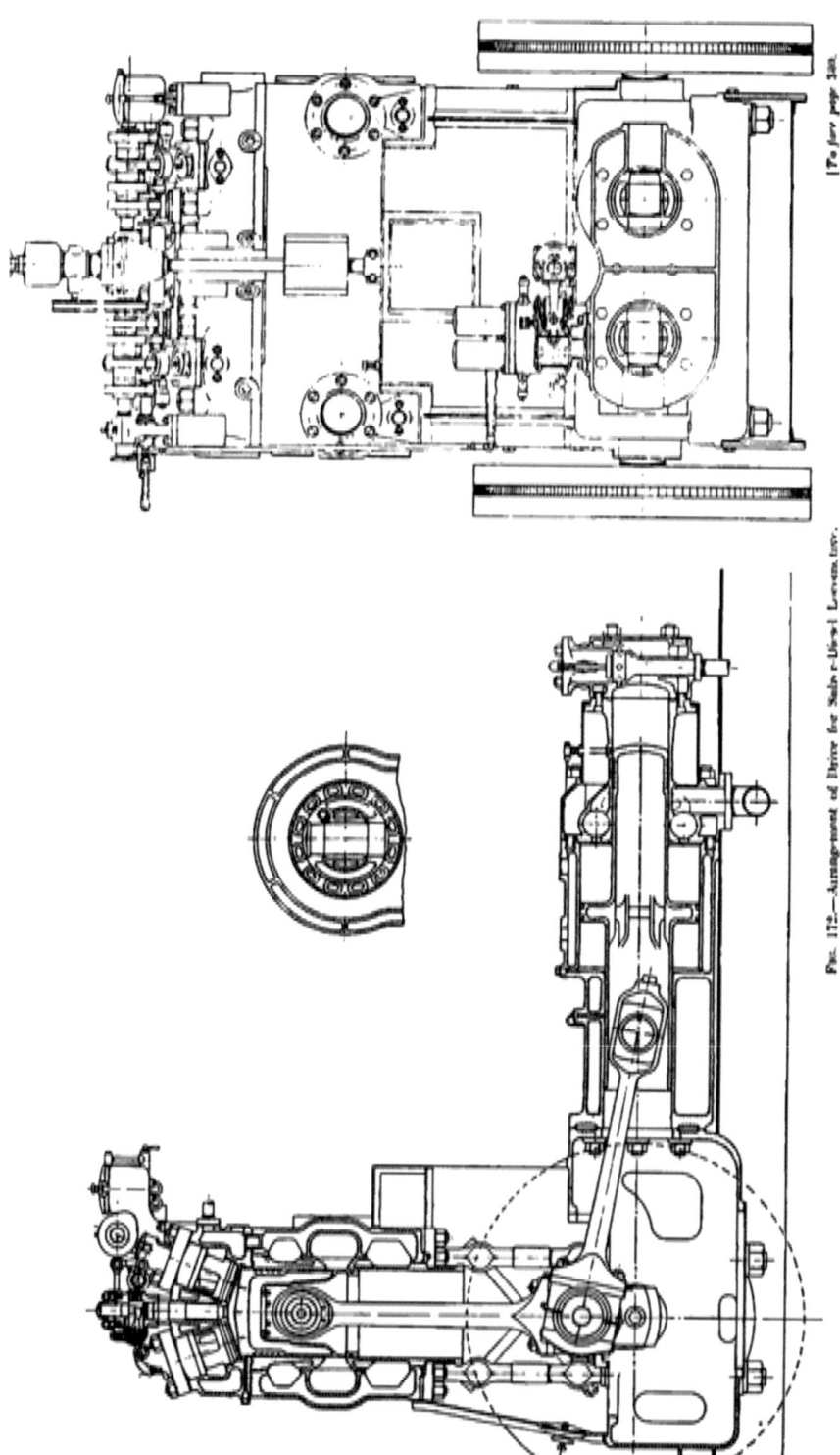

FIG. 172.—Arrangement of Drive for Sulzer-Diesel Locomotive.

volved. Most of the Admiralties are exercising a commendable spirit of caution and endeavouring to carry out experiments on a large scale, the effect of which would not be disastrous even in the event of failure. This is well instanced in the case of the British Admiralty, which has designs for a twin-screw cruiser with a Diesel engine (of 6,000 H.P.) on one shaft, whilst the other is driven by a steam set in the usual way. In the case of another twin-screw vessel each shaft is to have a steam turbine and a Diesel engine, with a clutch between so that the engine drives the shaft through the turbine, which is only in operation at high speeds.

Results are now available, after nearly three years' working of a 10,000 ton motor ship, the *Selandia*, in which the power is some 2,800 H.P. These indicate conclusively that the economies and advantages which have been shown earlier in this volume are fully confirmed. The consumption of fuel oil for all purposes, including the auxiliaries, is, on an average over the whole period of working, some $9\frac{1}{2}$ to 10 tons per day, as against 40–45 tons of coal which would be required for a similar steamship. The cost of lubricating oil is not appreciably more than in a steamship, and the attendance is considerably less. During the first eight months it was in commission the vessel travelled over 40,000 miles, and the engines have required no renewals or repairs of importance, other than the replacement of the liner in one cylinder, which cracked owing to the cooling water passage becoming choked.

The largest power in a single engine yet installed in a vessel is the Reiherstieg engine, illustrated earlier in this volume, this being a motor of about 2,000 B.H.P. It may be said at once, therefore, that, as regards vessels up to 10,000 tons or slightly over, the employment of the Diesel engine for propulsion is a matter of accomplished fact, and that success has been achieved in every direction. Builders of two-cycle single-acting engines are quite prepared to construct motors up to 6,000 B.H.P., and those of four-cycle engines up to 2,000 B.H.P., so that no difficulty may be anticipated for vessels up to 18,000 B.H.P. for single-acting engines—a figure that will be exceeded in a year or two. Incidentally, it may be mentioned that two-cycle Diesel engines for land work similar to the marine type are now on order for 4,000 B.H.P.

The possibilities of the Diesel motor for the propulsion of battleships has, perhaps more than any other factor, led to great attention being devoted to the double-acting, two-cycle engine, with a view to constructing in very large powers. Messrs. Krupp have now built a motor of this type with six cylinders, nominally of 12,000 B.H.P., but probably capable of developing 15,000 B.H.P. The motor battleship thus becomes a feasible proposition almost at once, since, although a triple screw arrangement giving 45,000 H.P. is not quite sufficient for the most modern battle cruisers, it is not likely to be a very difficult matter to further develop the engines until they give the necessary power. In all probability motors of 4,000 B.H.P. per cylinder will be built shortly, and the present limit may be assumed at 5,000 B.H.P. per cylinder.

The relatively high cost of Diesel engines compared with steam plant has been urged against their general adoption, although it has been shown in Chapter VI how quickly this extra capital expenditure is cleared off in a very short time, owing to the economies effected. Whilst it has with reason been repeatedly stated earlier in this book that Diesel engines cannot successfully be constructed very cheaply, the cost will gradually become less, and will not greatly exceed a steam installation in a few years. At the present time, it must be remembered that most large motors which are constructed are built to special designs, since improvements in detail are continually being effected, as experience is gained at sea. The result is that no general standardization can be maintained, even by a particular firm, and it is only by standardization that material cheapness of production can be attained. This state of affairs must continue for a year or two longer, but at the present time the cost of Diesel engines of the two-cycle single-acting type can be brought down to £8 per B.H.P., which is not so very considerably in excess of steam plant.

The future of the Diesel engine, both for land and marine work, is, to a very large extent, bound up with the question of the oil supply. This matter, in so far as it affects Great Britain, has been discussed by Dr. Diesel in his introduction, and it has been taken up by the British Admiralty, who appointed a Royal Commission to investigate it. That there is sufficient oil for all requirements for some time to come is undoubted, and the main difficulties to be encountered are transport and storage. So far as merchant vessels are concerned, this is not generally a very important matter, since their trade is often such that they can conveniently take oil on board at ports comparatively near the oil-fields, where the cost is relatively low. For naval purposes, however, and those vessels which find it necessary to take their fuel supply either in Europe or some distance from any oil fields, the outlook is somewhat different. If the cost of transport is to remain such as will cause the price of the oil to permit of little or no economy in fuel being obtained, as compared with the use of coal in steamships, this might to some extent retard the employment of Diesel motors in such cases. Even then it would not be a serious set-back, as even without fuel economy the other advantages of the oil engine are so great as to warrant its employment.

It is, however, to be anticipated that difficulties regarding transport or storage will be overcome almost immediately, as the shortage of oil-tank ships will soon be at an end, and storage facilities are now increasing. The question of obtaining fuel oil direct from coal, as outlined by Dr. Diesel, has not yet been considered on a large scale in this country; but no doubt this matter will receive some attention, which it undoubtedly merits, in the near future

APPENDIX

LLOYD'S RULES FOR INTERNAL COMBUSTION MARINE ENGINES—DIESEL'S ORIGINAL PATENT

THE following rules have been formulated by Lloyd's Registry of British and Foreign Shipping to govern the application of internal combustion engines to marine propulsion. The rules however are not in all cases applicable to Diesel engines and other similar motors working with high initial pressures, and for such machines special regulations will shortly be issued.

LLOYD'S RULES FOR THE SURVEY OF INTERNAL COMBUSTION ENGINES FOR MARINE PURPOSES

GENERAL

Section 1. In vessels propelled by internal combustion engines, the rules as regards Machinery will be the same as those relating to steam engines so far as regards the testing of material used in their construction and the fitting of sea connexions, discharge pipes, shafting, stern tubes and propellers.

CONSTRUCTION

Section 2. (1) The following points should be observed in connexion with the design of the engines.

(2) The shaft bearings, connecting rod brasses, the valve gear, the inlet and exhaust valves must be easily accessible.

(3) The reversing gear and clutch must be strongly constructed and easily accessible for examination and adjustment.

(4) In engines of above 60 B.H.P. which are not reversible and which are manœuvred by clutch, a governor or other arrangement must be fitted to prevent racing of the engine when de-clutched.

(5) Efficient positive means of lubrication (preferably sight feed) must be fitted to each part requiring continuous lubrication.

(6) If the engines are of the closed-in type, they must be so

fitted that the contained lubricating oil can be drained, and a metal or metal-lined tray must be fitted to prevent leakage of either fuel oil or of lubricating oil from saturating the wood work.

(7) Carburettors, where petrol is used, and vaporizers, where paraffin is used, should be so designed that when the engine is stopped the fuel supply is automatically shut off. If an overflow is provided in the carburettor or vaporizer, a gauze-covered tray with means of draining it must be fitted to prevent the fuel from flowing into the bilges.

Strong metallic gauze diaphragms should be fitted either between the carburettor (or vaporizer) and cylinders or at the air inlets.

(8) If the ignition is electric, either by magneto or by coil and accumulator, all electric leads must be well insulated and suitably protected from mechanical injury. The leads should be kept remote from petrol pipes, and should not be placed where they may be brought into contact with oil.

The commutator must be enclosed; and the sparking coils must not be placed where they can be exposed to explosive vapours.

(9) No exposed spark gap should be fitted.

(10) In paraffin and heavy oil engines where lamps are used for ignition or for vaporizing, these lamps should be fixed by some suitable bracket, and the flame enclosed when in use.

(11) The circulating pumps sea suction is to have a cock or valve on the vessel's skin placed on the turn of the bilge in an easily accessible position, and the circulating pipe is to be provided with an efficient strainer inside the vessel. The discharge overboard is to be fitted with a cock or valve on the vessel's skin if it is situated under or near the load line of the vessel.

(12) A bilge pump worked by engines or an independent power driven bilge pump is to be fitted, to draw from each part of the vessel. In open launches this bilge pump may be omitted provided suitable hand pumps are fitted.

(13) The cylinders are to be tested by hydraulic pressure to twice the working pressure to which they will be subjected. The water jackets of the cylinders to 50 lb. per sq. inch, and the exhaust pipes and silencer to 100 lb. per sq. inch.

(14) The exhaust pipes and silencer should be efficiently water cooled or lagged to prevent damage by heat, and if the exhaust is led overboard near the water-line, means must be arranged to prevent water being syphoned back to the engine.

APPENDIX

(15) The machinery must be tried under full working conditions, the report stating the approximate speed of vessel, the number of revolutions of the engines at full power, both ahead and astern, and the lowest number of revolutions of the engines which can be maintained for manœuvring purposes.

Rules for Determining Sizes of Shafts

Section 3. The crank, intermediate, and other shafts if of ordinary mild steel are to be of not less diameters than as given in the following table. When special steel is used, the sizes are to be submitted for consideration.

(1) For petrol or paraffin engines for smooth water services:—

Diameter of crank shaft in inches $= C \sqrt[3]{D S}$

where D = diameter of cylinder in inches.

S = stroke of piston in inches.

Four Stroke Cycle.	Two Stroke Cycle.	Bearing between each Crank.	Two Cranks between the Bearings.
For 1, 2, 3 or 4 Cyls.	1 or 2 Cyls.	$C = \cdot 34$	$C = \cdot 38$
„ 6 Cyls.	3 „	$C = \cdot 36$	$C = \cdot 40$
„ 8 „	4 „	$C = \cdot 38$	$C = \cdot 425$
„ 12 „	6 „	$C = \cdot 44$	$C = \cdot 49$

For open seas service add $\cdot 02$ to C.

Diameter of intermediate and screw shafts in inches $= C \sqrt[3]{D S (n \cdot 3)}$

where D = diameter of cylinder in inches.

S = stroke of piston in inches.

n = number of cylinders.

For smooth water services—

$C = \cdot 155$ for intermediate shafts.

$C = \cdot 170$ for screw shafts fitted with continuous liners.

$C = \cdot 180$ for screw shafts fitted with separate liners or with no liners.

For open seas services—

$C = \cdot 165$.

$C = \cdot 180$.

$C = \cdot 190$.

In engines of two-stroke cycle, n is to be taken as twice the number of cylinders.

(2) When ordinary deep thrust collars are used the diameter of the shaft between the collars is to be at least $\frac{21}{20}$ths of that of the intermediate shaft.

(3) In the cases of DIESEL and other Engines in which very high initial pressures are employed, particulars should be submitted for special consideration.

Fuel Tanks and Connexions

Section 4. (1) Separate fuel tanks are to be tested with all fittings to a head of at least 15 ft. of water. If pressure feed tanks are employed, they are to be tested to twice the working pressure which will come on them but at least to a head of 15 feet of water. If the tanks are made of iron or steel they should be galvanised.

(2) Strong and readily removable metallic gauze diaphragms should be fitted at all openings on petrol tanks.

(3) Paraffin or heavy oil tanks, not used under pressure, are to be fitted with air pipes leading above deck. Pressure-feed tanks and tanks containing petrol, should be provided with escape valves discharging into pipes leading to the atmosphere above deck. The upper ends of all air pipes are to be turned down and pipes above 1 inch diameter are to be provided with gauze diaphragms at the end.

(4) No glass gauges are to be fitted to fuel tanks containing either petrol, paraffin or heavy oil.

(5) Filling pipes are to be carried through the deck so that the gas displaced from the tanks has free escape to the atmosphere.

(6) Separate fuel tanks should be provided with metal-lined trays to prevent any possible leakage from them flowing into the bilges, or saturating woodwork. Arrangements are to be provided for emptying the tanks and draining the trays beneath them. For petrol tanks the trays must have drains leading overboard where possible or they should be gauze-covered trays with means for draining them.

(7) All fuel pipes are to be of annealed seamless copper with flexible bends. Their joints are to be conical, metal to metal. A cock or valve is to be fitted at each end of the pipe conveying the fuel from the tank to the carburettor or vaporizer. The fuel pipes should be led in positions where they are protected

APPENDIX

from mechanical injury and can be exposed to view throughout their whole length.

(8) The engine-room, and the compartment in which the fuel tanks are situated, are to be efficiently ventilated.

(9) An approved fire-extinguishing apparatus must be supplied.

Periodical Surveys

Section 5. (1) The machinery is to be submitted to survey annually. At these surveys the cylinders, pistons, connecting rods, crank and other shafts, inlet and exhaust valves and gear, clutches, reversing gear, propeller, sea connexions, and pumps are to be examined. The electric ignition is to be examined and the electric leads tested. The fuel tanks and all connexions are to be examined, and if deemed necessary by the Surveyor, to be tested to the same pressure as required when new. If practicable, the engines should be tested under working conditions.

(2) The screw shaft is to be drawn at intervals of not more than two years.

THE FOLLOWING IS A COPY OF DR. DIESEL'S ORIGINAL SPECIFICATION, DATED AUGUST 27, 1892 [1]

COMPLETE SPECIFICATION

A Process for Producing Motive Work from the Combustion of Fuel

The working process of the hitherto known motor engines using the combustion heat of fuels directly in the cylinder for performing work is characterized by the theoretical indicator diagram shown in *Fig.* 1 of the accompanying drawing.

On the curve 1, 2, a mixture of air and fuel is compressed, at point 2 the combustible mixture is ignited; by the now following combustion a sudden increase of pressure from 2 to 3 is produced which is accompanied by a very considerable increase of temperature; the explosion like combustion is such a quick one, that the stroke of the piston during the combustion is nearly zero. At point 3 the combustion is essentially finished. From 3 to 1

---

[1] Published by permission of the Comptroller of the Patent Office.

an expansion takes place in performing work, whereby pressure and temperature of the combustion gases decrease again.

In all hitherto known combustion processes, the combustion process is left to itself as soon as the ignition takes place, the pressure and the temperature of the same are not regulated or controlled during the proper proceeding of combustion in proportion to the then existing volume of the body of air.

From this wrong proportion between pressure, temperature and volume result in all these processes the following inconveniences.

(1) The temperature produced by the combustion is always so high, that the attainment of such a mean temperature of the contents of the cylinder that will render possible the maintaining the parts tight, the lubrication and in general the practical working of the machine, can be obtained only by energetically cooling the cylinders or furnace-walls respectively, wherefrom will result a great loss of heat.

(2) The combustion gases are insufficiently cooled by the expansion and they escape while still in a very hot condition, which constitutes a second great loss of heat.

Also, those motor engines in which pure air is compressed from 1 to 2 (see *Fig.* 1) and fuel is injected suddenly in the neighbourhood of point 2 while igniting the same simultaneously, show the increase of pressure 2, 3 combined with considerable increase of temperature.

The same takes place in motor engines which drive the compression to so high a degree that the mixture is ignited spontaneously by the temperature produced by the compression. The igniting points of the most part of fuels are very low (of petroleum for instance at from 70° to 100° C.); when by the compression this temperature has been produced, which will be the case already at low pressures (in the case of petroleum at a pressure inferior to 5 atmospheres, in the case of gas at about 15 atmospheres) the ignition will take place spontaneously. The combustion following the ignition here also raises the temperature very considerably and produces the increase of pressure 2. 3 (see *Fig.* 1). The highest temperature or combustion temperature occurring during the combustion is entirely independent of the burning or igniting points, which depend only upon the physical properties of the fuel.

In practice the explosion or combustion process requires a material time, for this reason the line 2, 3 is not quite vertical,

APPENDIX

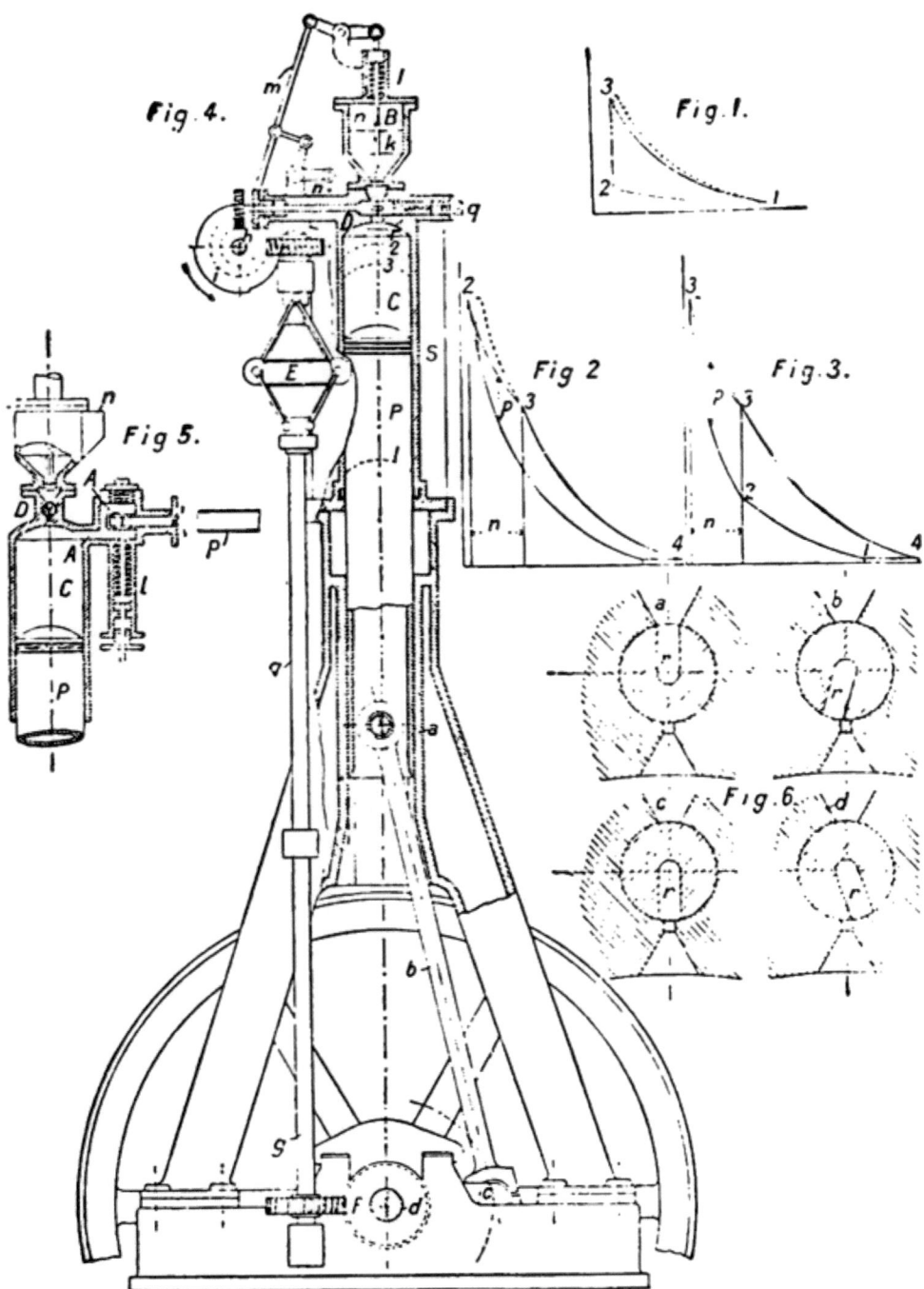

but, as shown in dotted lines, somewhat inclined with the rounded transition at 3.

The characteristic feature of all these processes remains, however:—

Increase of the pressure and of the temperature by the combustion and during the latter, and the subsequent performance of work by expansion. The process of combustion after ignition is left to itself.

The new process hereinafter described differs completely from all the other hitherto known processes. It is represented in the theoretical diagram shown in *Fig.* 2. In this process pure atmospheric air is compressed in a cylinder according to curve 1, 2 to such a degree, that by this compression from the beginning before any combustion takes place, the highest pressure of the diagram, and by this at the same time, the highest temperature is produced, that is to say the temperature at which the subsequent combustion has to take place, namely the combustion temperature (not the burning or igniting point).

If it be desired, for instance, that the later combustion shall take place at a temperature of 700° C., the pressure will be of 64 atmospheres; for 800° C. the pressure will be of 90 atmospheres, and so on.

Into this compressed body of air is then gradually introduced from outside finely divided fuel, which ignites as the air mass is heated by compression far above the temperature necessary for inflammation, simultaneously with the gradual introduction of fuel an expansion of the body of air takes place, which is regulated in such a manner that the cooling caused by the expansion destroys at each moment the heat produced by the combustion of the several introduced particles of fuel. Owing to this the combustion shows its effect not by an increase of temperature, but solely by work done; and also not by an increase of pressure, as it takes place in consequence of the simultaneous expansion at decreasing pressure.

The combustion takes place according to the curve 2, 3 (*Fig.* 2), consequently it is not a sudden one, but it takes place during an exactly prescribed period of admission of fuel during the piston stroke w, which period of admission is regulated and determined by a distributing device, and which has for its result, that the combustion proceeding after the ignition is not left to itself, but is regulated during its whole duration in such a manner that pressure, temperature and volume are in a prescribed proportion. It is the duration of this admission period which is fixed by the distributing device; the governor also influences the duration of this period, which, as with the admission period of steam engines, may be of 10 per cent. and more of the piston's stroke, but under certain circumstances may be reduced to a less percentage of the piston's stroke.

APPENDIX

If air is allowed to expand without any supply of fuel, the curve 2, 1 would be formed, i.e. the expansion would do no work, but give back simply to the piston the previously employed work of compression; but by gradually introducing fuel a pressure difference p is formed at any place between the curves 1, 2 and 2, 3, in consequence whereof the expansion work becomes greater than the compression work, and a useful effect is performed.

At point 3 of the diagram the supply of fuel ceases and the expansion of the combustion gases goes on automatically and performs work according to curve 3, 4. As the pressure at point 2 for producing the highest temperature was very high and is still very high at point 3, the expansion will produce from 3 to 4 so strong a cooling of the gas volume that in leaving the engine it will carry away only insignificant quantities of heat.

Here also the corner 2 of the diagram will not be sharply formed in practice, it will rather assume the rounded form shown in dotted lines; also in the course of the present Specification terms such as "combustion without increase of temperature" and the like must not be understood in the exact mathematical sense, as regard is to be paid to practice. I wish only to have it understood that in the new process the highest pressure and the highest temperature are produced essentially not by combustion but by mechanical compression, and that by the combustion and during the same an increase of temperature does not take place at all or only to an insignificant degree, at all events insignificant if compared to the heating by compression.

The characteristic feature of the process remains always as follows:

Increase of pressure and temperature up to about its maximum not by combustion, but prior to the combustion by mechanical compression of pure air and hereupon subsequent performance of work by gradual combustion during an exactly prescribed part of the expansion, characterized by the period of admission of fuel exactly determined by the distributing device.

According to what has been said above, the combustion itself, in opposition to all the hitherto known processes of combustion, does not produce any increase of temperature, or at least only an unessential one; the highest temperature is produced by the compression of air; it is therefore under control and will be kept correspondingly in moderate limits; as moreover the subsequent expansion cools the body of gas in a very high degree, it is obvious that no artificial cooling of the cylinder walls is necessary; that rather the mean temperature of the cylinder contents necessary for keeping the parts tight and lubricated, and in general for the practical working of the engine, is obtained solely by the process itself, whereby also it differs from all the known processes.

Fig. 3 shows a further modification of the process consisting in that the first period of the air-compression takes place under injection of water, whereby first the flatter curve 1, 2 is formed, and that then only the second part of the compression without water-injection takes place according to the steeper curve 2, 3 whereupon the combustion and expansion is conducted exactly in the same manner as in *Fig.* 2. By this means I attain considerably higher compression-pressures than in *Fig.* 2 without reaching too high temperatures which would require a cooling of the cylinder.

In consequence of the greater fall of pressure the subsequent expansion from 3 to 4 cools the body of the gas to a greater extent; the exhaust gases escape therefore in a colder condition than in *Fig.* 2 and carry away still less heat; this modification of the process gives therefore higher useful effects.

The exhaust gases may in this case be cooled even below the atmospheric temperature and be then led away to be utilized for refrigerating purposes. The result of the new process compared with all the other hitherto known processes is a considerable saving on fuel, the work done remaining the same.

Any kind of fuel in any state of aggregation is suitable for carrying out the process.

In the case of liquids or gases or vapours respectively, a jet of gas or liquid is dispersed under pressure in as divided a state as possible into the body of compressed air during the period of admission, and as long as the latter lasts. Solid fuels may be introduced in a pulverulent or dust-like condition, such solid fuels which in heating agglomerate, or are unsuitable for any other reasons for being used, are previously gasified. Liquid fuels may be converted previously into vapour and then introduced in this form. Matters inflammable with difficulty such as anthracite and the like, may be mixed with readily inflammable substances such as petroleum and the like.

The process may be carried out in a single or double acting vertical or horizontal cylinder with one or more pistons working on the same flywheel shaft and with one or more stages of compression and expansion. *Figs.* 4 *and* 5 show a motor engine with single acting cylinder C with plunger piston P, the details of

# APPENDIX

which are constructed for high pressures. Piston P is connected by the guide a, connecting rod b and crank c with the flywheel shaft d in the usual manner.

The flywheel shaft drives at f by means of hyperbolic toothed wheels the vertically upward extending shaft g carrying the governor and driving the horizontal distributing shaft h.

To the latter are secured cams i which at the right moment open the air-valve A ($Fig.$ 5) and the fuel valve k. The gear for the latter is clearly shown in $Fig.$ 4; for the valve A it is of similar construction. As soon as the cams i are out of action, the two valves are pressed down against their seats by the springs l.

The process which according to this invention takes place in the cylinder C is as follows:—

(1) Downward stroke of piston P produced by accumulated vis viva in the flywheel from the preceding working strokes. Atmospheric air is sucked in through the open valve A into the cylinder C, the lowest position of the piston is shown in dotted lines in $Fig.$ 4 and marked with 1.

(2) Upward stroke of the piston P produced also by the accumulated vis viva of the flywheel, the valve A being now closed. The air previously sucked in is compressed to such high pressures, that the temperature at which later the combustion has to take place, namely, nearly the highest temperature of the process, is produced by this compression alone.

This compression pressure is determined by the prescribed combustion temperature and it is produced by the piston P, which, in its dotted end position 2 ($Fig.$ 4) will have compressed the quantity of air drawn in to the volume corresponding to the prescribed pressure.

Such pressures cannot be obtained if from the beginning fuel is admixed, to the air such as for instance in gas and petroleum motors, as in this case already at low pressures at intermediate points of the stroke namely as soon as the igniting point of the fuel has been obtained (this temperature being in general very low) ignition would take place, and in consequence thereof interruption of the prescribed compression by combustion would ensue so that in such cases it would be impossible to carry out the prescribed process.

(3) Second downward stroke of the piston P or true working stroke.

The hopper B contains pulverised coal introduced through the lateral opening n shown in $Fig.$ 5. This hopper is shut off from the cylinder C by means of a cock D rotated by the distributing shaft by means of the hyperbolical wheels shown. The cock is shown to a larger scale in four positions at *Fig.* 6; it is provided with a lateral groove r which, when in its upper position a is charged with coal dust arriving from the hopper B; when the cock revolves, the groove turns towards the inside of the cylinder (see b); in this position the pressure between the interior of the cylinder and the groove is first equalized, as the loose powder does not offer any obstacle thereto in the other positions, one of which is shown at c; the cock allows the coal dust to fall into the compressed air; owing to the high temperature of this air the coal takes fire and produces heat, which immediately in the moment of its production is converted into work by a corresponding forward movement of the piston.

The introduction of the powder takes place gradually in a prescribed space of time in a manner similar to the sand in an hour glass, the size of the inlet slit determines the duration of the introduction during the prescribed period of admission of the fuel. The quantity of coal is determined by the size of the groove of the cock. These inner organs in combination with the outer distributing device insure that the prescribed duration of admission is complied with and that the last coal particles only pass in when the piston has arrived at the end of the period of admission.

The gradual combustion thus described consequently continues until the piston has arrived in its position 3 (dotted line in *Fig.* 4). At this moment the groove of the cock is emptied and passes in front of the inlet slit, the admission of fuel is therefore stopped. The air mixed with the combustion gases continues to expand automatically, in performing work, while the whole gas body, owing to the great fall of pressure, is cooled very considerably, and this solely by doing work and without cooling the cylinder walls, the latter being suitably insulated by a jacket s (*Fig.* 4).

(4) Second upward stroke of the piston P produced by the vis viva of the flywheel.

The gas body is driven out as by a blowpipe, through the valve A (or through a separate blow-off valve) into a pipe p (*Fig.* 5) leading it away; as the said body has been cooled already previously nearly entirely by expansion, it carries away, as a loss, only insignificant quantities of heat. The residues of the combustion are contained in very small quantity in the form of a

APPENDIX

fine dust suspended in the rapidly moving and whirling gases of combustion and are consequently also simply blown out.

After this second upward stroke the above described cycle of operations is repeated.

The motor is started by introducing through the opening r (*Fig.* 4) compressed air from a store-vessel by means of a pipe connected therewith at q. The store-vessel is kept filled with compressed air by the motor during the working. At q a special device may be arranged by means of which the motor may be started by igniting a small quantity of explosive matter.

The regulating of the machine is effected by means of the governor E of any known construction, which, when the engine runs too fast, prevents the fuel from falling from the hopper into the groove. The small coal valve k is opened at each second revolution by means of the cam i and the rod m, and allows a certain quantity of coal to fall into the groove.

When the machine works too fast the rod n connected to the governor sleeve moves the rod m so as to bring the roller attached to the lower end thereof out of the scope of the cam i; the valve k therefore remains closed and no coal falls into the cock, and in consequence also not into the cylinder, until the normal speed has been re-established.

The above described motor may also be arranged as a horizontal engine; in this case the construction of the parts is not altered but only their position. In lieu of a plunger piston a disc piston may be employed, so that the cylinder becomes a double acting one.

In the described construction the engine has, as in most of the gas motors, only a working stroke at every second revolution of the engine shaft. But two or more such single-acting cylinders may be coupled to the same flywheel shaft, whereby the working of the motor becomes more uniform. The compression of the air as well as the expansion of the combustion gases may take place by stages, as is shown by way of example in *Fig.* 7.

In this *Fig.* 7 the valves are indicated only diagrammatically, the frame, the connecting rod, the flywheel, etc., are omitted; all these parts are exactly the same as shown in *Figs.* 4 *and* 5. There are in *Fig.* 7 two cylinders C with plungers P, that is to say, two combustion cylinders, the construction, distributing devices, etc., of which are identical to those of the cylinder represented in the *Figs.* 4 *and* 5. These two cylinders C are connected by means of the controlled valves b to the two sides of a larger central cylinder B; by the two valves a which are also controlled, the two combustion cylinders are in communication with the air vessel L.

The cranks of the two cylinders C are arranged in the same

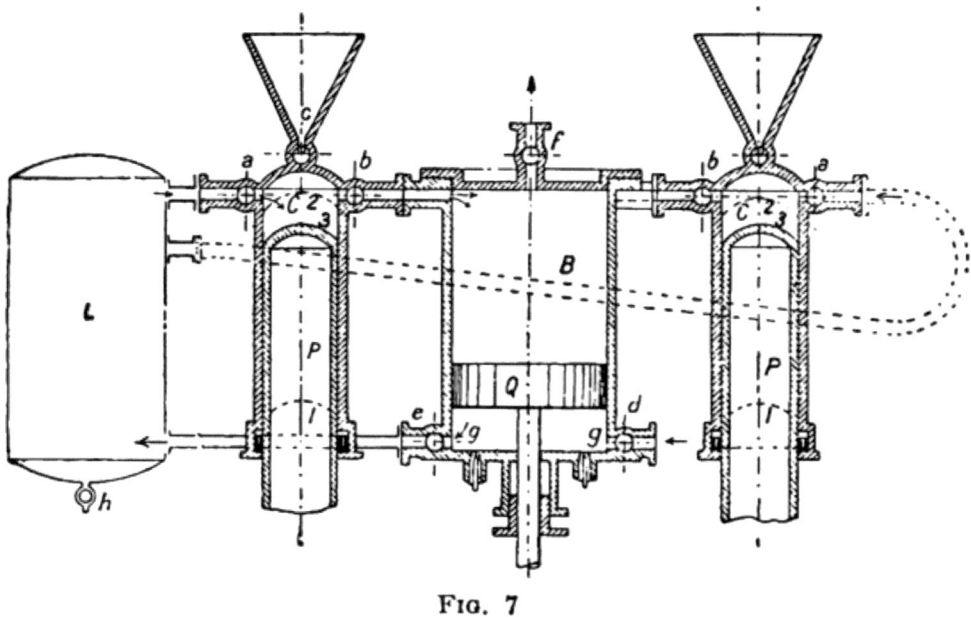

Fig. 7

position, and they form with the crank of the central cylinder B an angle of $180°$.

The working of this construction is as follows: The piston Q draws in air by its upstroke through valve d, compresses the latter by its down stroke to a certain pressure and then forces the air through valve g to the air vessel L.

The lower part of the central cylinder therefore only serves as an air pump and effects the preparatory compression of the combustion air.

This preparatory compression should go only to such an extent that the heating of the air produced by this compression remains between moderate limits.

Water nozzles are arranged still at gg through which during the preparatory compression, water may be injected at a low degree. This water is then discharged again through the cock h of the air vessel.

The process may be carried out either with or without injection of water.

The action in the cylinders C is exactly the same as has been described with reference to *Figs*. 4 *and* 5, excepting that piston P does not draw in the air from the atmosphere during its downstroke but from vessel L in which the air is already under pressure. At its upstroke piston P therefore effects the second stage of the compression up to the prescribed degree. The lower and upper end positions of the piston are shown in dotted lines and marked with 1 and 2.

Piston P now moves downward again to position 3, fuel being during this time gradually introduced and the combustion controlled, as above described. At 3 the admission of fuel ceases and the air continues to expand; when the piston has arrived in its lowest position 1, valve b opens, piston Q is at this moment just in its upper position owing to the arrangement of the cranks; piston P then moves upward and piston Q downward, and a further expansion of the combustion gases up to the volume of cylinder B takes place; hereupon valve b closes and valve f opens, so that at the following upward stroke of piston Q the combustion gases are expelled through valve f into the atmosphere, in a perfectly cooled condition, as their entire heat will have been consumed by the work done in expanding.

It has already been mentioned, that in this construction the exhaust gases can be caused to escape with a temperature which is below that of the atmosphere, so that they may still serve for cooling purposes.

As the cylinders C have a combustion period only at each second revolution I attain by arranging two such cylinders at each revolution a combustion, that is to say a working stroke as the combustion is made to take place alternately on the right and left hand. There is no obstacle to using only one combustion cylinder in place of two, or, on the other hand, more than two in which case the lower part of the cylinder B may then be used as an expansion cylinder; the air pump for the preparatory compression should then be arranged separately and force previously compressed air into the reservoir L.

The air of the reservoir L serves in this construction directly for starting the motor, as the latter may be fed during some revolutions from this reservoir with full pressure, the ignition only taking place after the flywheel has attained the necessary momentum.

The device for gradually introducing fuel is dependent on the peculiar properties of the material employed.

For solid pulverised substances, in lieu of the described revolving cock, a powder nozzle or a small pump may be used; for liquids a spray nozzle or a small pump is employed, for gases also a small pump or any other suitable device permitting the gradual introduction of the fuel, the quantity of the latter being in a definite proportion to the piston's stroke.

Figs. 8 *to* 10 show another construction of a motor in which liquid fuel is employed and at the same time the external distributing device, in particular the device for gradually introducing fuel, is of a quite different construction.

This machine consists of two entirely identical single acting cylinders provided with plunger pistons, the cranks of which are arranged on the common flywheel shaft in the same position; the frame, flywheel and distributing device are nearly exactly the same as illustrated in *Figs.* 4 *and* 5 and therefore not represented.

The combustion in the cylinders takes place alternately, so that at each revolution a working stroke is effected.

In *Fig.* 8 one of the cylinders is shown in vertical section, the other in front view with its insulating casing.

Fig. 9 is a front view of the cylinder with the distributing device, and *Fig.* 10 a plan view with a section of the distributing devices.

The process in each cylinder is the same as described with reference to *Figs.* 4 *and* 5, viz.:

Drawing in of air through valve V, then compression by one stroke up to the end position 2 of the piston shown in dotted lines; introduction of liquid fuel through nozzle D and combustion of same during the prescribed period of admission 2, 3 (*Fig.* 8), finally expansion of the body of gas and escape of the same through valve V as through a blowpipe into an outward leading pipe R.

As the drawing in follows immediately after the escape, the valve V remains open during a whole revolution, and then closed during a whole revolution. This simplest possible regulation is effected by the cam S (*Figs.* 9 *and* 10) by means of the bent lever, as shown in the drawing.

The cam S is carried by the distributing shaft W, which is driven by the shaft of the flywheel in a similar way as in *Figs.* 4 *and* 5. The nozzle D is kept closed by the needle n and serves for gradually admitting the fuel. The liquid fuel is in the inner space r of the nozzle D and is maintained there by means of a feed pump (not shown) provided with an air chamber under a pressure

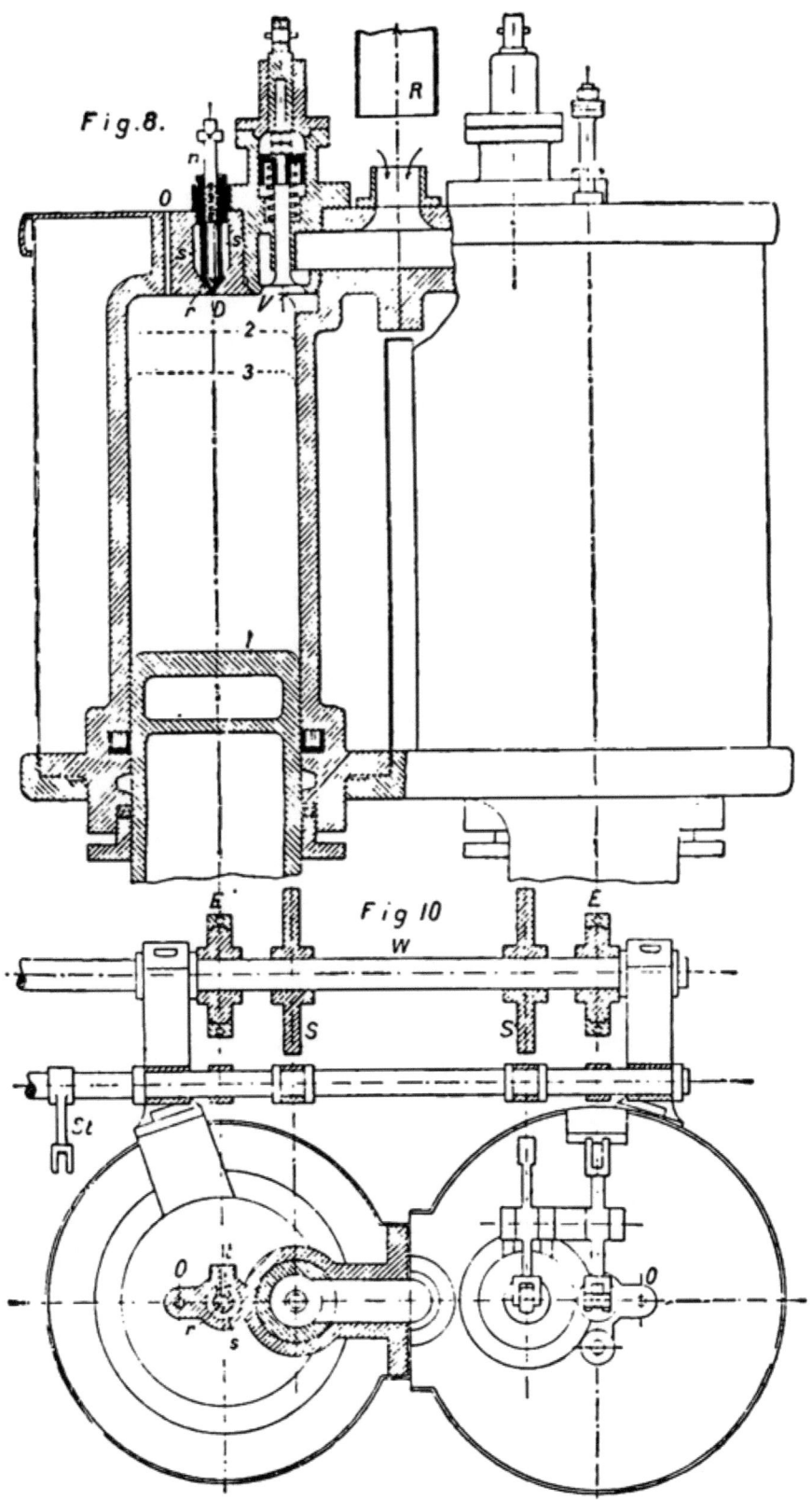

which is higher than the highest pressure of compression of the air in the cylinder.

In *Fig.* 10 is shown at t the branch pipe for the liquid fuel coming from the pump and leading to the nozzle.

At the moment of the highest compression, i.e. when the piston is in the position 2, the needle n is opened by the distributing gear and allows a sharp thin jet of liquid to enter through the very small opening D, as the liquid is under a pressure superior to the cylinder pressure. This entrance of fuel continues up to position 3 of the piston, where the distributing device cuts it off exactly, whereupon the combustion gases continue to expand automatically.

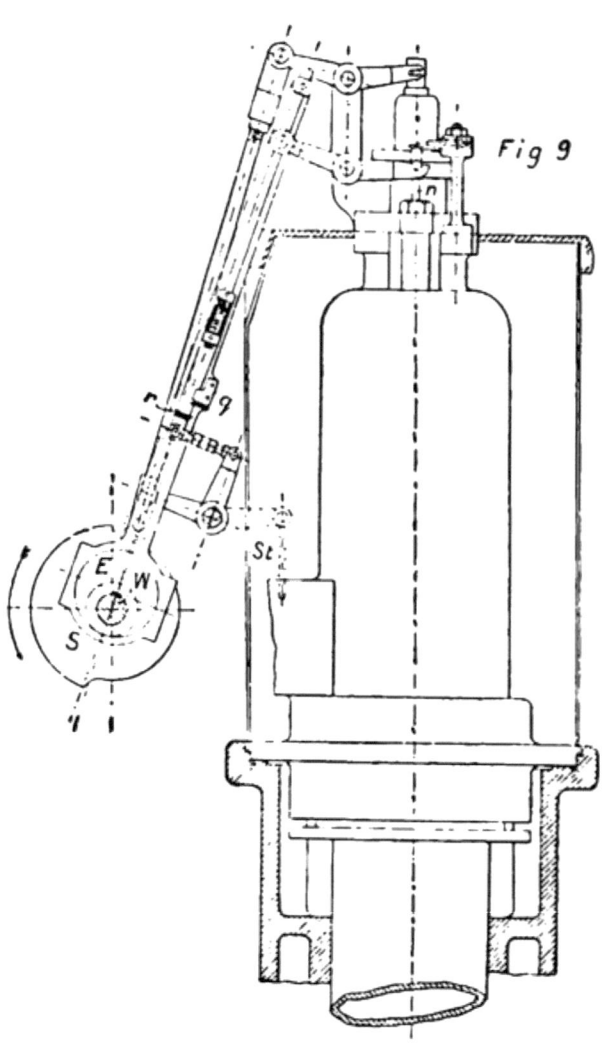

Fig 9

For regulating the jet of fuel I have provided here exactly the same construction by which in Sulzer's valve machines the period of steam admission is regulated.

An eccentric E moves the steel side piece q in an oviform curve up and down; the steel block r is attached to the rod which actuates needle n; as soon as the piece q moving downward strikes against the piece r the needle is opened and remains open until the steel piece q releases the piece r. As the piece r is adjustable from the governor by means of the rod St (see *Fig.* 9), the governor regulates simultaneously in the two cylinders the dura-

APPENDIX

tion of the period of admission of fuel, and in consequence thereof the speed of the engine.

In *Figs*. 8 *and* 10 there is formed round the nozzle D an annular space s which is in free communication with the interior of the cylinder.

When the piston moves backward under decreasing pressure the air flows from this annular space back into the cylinder and serves in this way both for dividing the jet of fuel and for producing turbulent motion for distributing the combustion heat over the whole air volume. This annular space s is only of practical importance and is not essential for the process.

There is moreover in *Figs*. 8 *and* 10 at O an opening for introducing compressed air or gases from explosive substances serving to start the motor. When in *Fig*. 8 in place of liquid, gas or vapour is compressed in the inner space r of the nozzle D the same construction may be employed. It is therefore not necessary to show a construction of engine for this application. It is especially to be remarked that the thermal results are independent of the kind of gas contained in the cylinder; it is sufficient if the quantity of air necessary for combustion is provided, the other considerable quantity of gas, which acts only as a carrier of heat, may consist of former combustion gases, added foreign gases and vapours or aqueous vapour, without in any way altering the result. It follows from the above that closed engines might be arranged so as to take up at each stroke only a small quantity of fresh air for insuring the combustion, but which retain essentially always the same body of gas, a small exhaust excepted.

Having now particularly described and ascertained the nature of my said invention and in what manner the same is to be performed, I declare that what I claim is :—

(1) The method of working combustion motors consisting in compressing in a cylinder by a working piston, pure air, or other neutral gas or vapour together with pure air, to such an extent, that the temperature hereby produced is far higher than the burning or igniting point of the fuel to be employed (curve 1–2 of the diagram in *Fig*. 2), whereupon fuel is supplied at the dead centre 50 gradually, that on account of the outward motion of the piston and the consequent expansion of the compressed air or gas the combustion takes place without essential increase of temperature and pressure (curve 2–3 of the diagram in *Fig*. 2) whereupon, after the admission of fuel has been cut off, the further expansion of the body of gas contained in the working

cylinder takes place (curve 3–4 of the diagram in *Fig.* 2) substantially as described.

(2) The mode of carrying out the process referred to in the preceding claim with multiple compression and expansion by providing the combustion cylinder on one hand with a compressing pump and reservoir and on the other hand with an expansion cylinder, or by coupling several combustion cylinders with each other or with the said compressing pump and expansion cylinder, substantially as described.

INDEX

A

A.B. Diesels Motorer engine, 74, 191, 232
Adiabatic expansion, 10
Adjustment of fuel valve, 134
Admiralty specification of fuel oil, 54
Advantages of various engines, 41
— — two-cycle engine, 44
— for marine work, 172
Air compressors, 115
— — design of, 321
American Diesel engine, 300
Analysis of fuel oil, 53
Asphalt in fuel oil, 53
Attendance of Diesel engines, 131
Augsburg engine, 281
Auxiliaries for motor ships, 174, 194, 200

B

Battleships, Diesel engines for, 203
Bolinder engine, 42
British Engine, Boiler & Insurance Co., 158
Brons engine, 42
Burmeister & Wain engine, 283

C

Cams, 65
Capacity of air compressors, 322
Carels engine, 78, 115, 223
Cargo capacity of motor ships, 176
Clearance space, 315
Cockerill engine, 229
Combustion in Diesel engine, 133
Comparison of steam and Diesel engines, 142
Comparison of steam and motor ships, 179
Compressed air for auxiliaries, 198
Constant pressure cycle, 14, 18
— — temperature cycle, 14
— volume cycle, 14, 16
Consumption of fuel in Diesel engine, 25, 140, 151, 173, 341
Cooling water for Diesel engine, 132
Cost of Diesel engines, 181
— — oil, 50, 179
— — — operation, 138
Crankshafts, 318
Crosshead engines, 186
Cycle, constant pressure, 14, 18
— — temperature, 14
— — volume, 14, 16
— thermodynamic, 13
— working, 13
— Diesel, 21
Cylinder dimensions, 309
Cylinders, design of, 303
— number of, 183

D

Daimler engine, 296
Design of Diesel engines, 182, 302
Deutche-Amerikanische Petroleum Gesellschaft, 244
Deutz engine, 73, 86, 104
Diameter of crankshafts, 318
Dimensions of Diesel engines, 357
Double-acting Diesel engine, 39, 45, 204
Doxford engine, 267
Duplex system for air compressors, 199

Diesel engine, A.B. Diesels Motorer, 74, 191, 232
— attendance of, 131
— Burmeister & Wain, 283
— Carels, 78, 115, 159, 217
— Cockerill, 229
— combustion in, 35, 133
— consumption of, 25, 140, 151, 173
— cooling water, 132
— cost of, 181
— crankshafts, 318
— cycle, 21
— Daimler, 296
— design of, 182, 302
— Deutz, 73, 86, 104
— dimensions of, 317
— Doxford, 267
— efficiency of, 1, 24, 312
— for battleships, 203
— for submarines, 211
— foundations for, 126
— four stroke type, 32, 58, 63
— fuel for, 3, 4, 5, 48
— future of, 336
— governing, 77
— Gusto, 277
— high speed, 40, 93
— horizontal, 100
— indicator cards, 26, 29, 34
— influence of, 3
— Junker's, 263, 300
— Kind, 300
— Kolomna, 291
— Krupp, 205, 244, 298
— limiting power of, 46
— locomotive, 337
— management of, 131
— M.A.N., 65, 251, 281
— Mirrlees, 80, 85, 93
— Nederlandsche Fabriek, 87, 97, 267
— Nobel, 291
— oil for, 3, 4, 5, 48
— Polar, 74, 191, 232
— port scavenging, 191, 232
— reasons for high efficiency, 24
— reversing, 193

Diesel engine, running, 61
— — scavenging in, 113, 187
— — Schneider-Carels, 226
— — solid injection, 122
— — space occupied, 126
— — speed of, 184, 252, 262, 314
— — starting up, 35, 61, 131
— — Sulzer, 99, 107, 206
— — Tanner, 264
— — testing, 146
— — two cycle, 37, 107
— — — — double-acting, 39
— — valves and cams, 65
— — valves of, 36, 65
— — valve setting of, 27, 28
— — weight of, 48, 177, 202, 251
— — Werkspoor, 87, 97, 267
— — Westgarth, 229
— — Willans, 83

E

Eberle, Chr., 150
Efficiency of Diesel engine, 1, 24, 312
Electrically driven ships' auxiliaries, 200
Emanuel Nobel, 277
Exhaust ports, dimensions of, 334
Expansion of gases, 9
— — adiabatic, 10
— — isothermal, 11

F

Foundations for Diesel engine, 126
Four-stroke cycle, 32, 58, 63
France, 226
Fuel consumption, 25, 140, 151
— — of motor ships, 201
Fuel for Diesel engines, 3, 4, 5, 49
Fuel valve, 67
— — adjustment, 134
— — for tar oil, 69
Future of Diesel engine, 337

G

Gases, expansion of, 9
Germanischer Lloyd, 319

INDEX

Governing Diesel engines, 77
Gusto engine, 277

H

Hamburg-South American Line, 216
High speed Diesel engine, 40, 93
— — — — Mirrlees, 93
— — — — Werkspoor, 97
Horizontal engine, 100
Horse-power of Diesel engines, 313

I

Indicator cards, 26, 29-31
Injection air, quantity of, 85
Instruments for testing, 147
Isothermal expansion, 11

J

Junker's engine, 263, 300

K

Kind engine, 300
Kolomna engine, 291
Krupp engine, 205, 244, 298

L

Lahmeyer, 159
Leakage past piston, 136
Lignite oil, 3
Limiting power of Diesel engines, 46, 169
Lloyd's, 319, 345
Locomotive with Diesel engine, 337
Longridge, M., 158
Loss of compression, 134
Lubrication, 137
Lubricating oil, 175

M

M.A.N. Diesel engine, 65, 251, 281
Management of Diesel engine, 131
Mauretania, 176
Mean effective pressure, 310
Mechanical efficiency, 312
Mirrlees engine, 80, 85, 93

Motor ships, auxiliaries for, 174, 194
— — cargo capacity of, 176
— — comparison with steamships, 179
— — *Emanuel Nobel*, 277
— — *France*, 226
— — fuel consumption, 200, 341
— — machinery, 183
— — power to drive, 175
— — propeller efficiency of, 177
— — *Rolandseck*, 229
— — *Selandia*, 283, 341
— — *Sembilan*, 271
— — staff of, 181, 202
— — *Vulcanus*, 267

N

Nederlandsche Fabriek, 87, 97, 267
Nobel engine, 291
Number of cylinders, 183

O

Oil, composition and analysis of, 53
— flash point, 55
— lignite, 4
— Mexico, 52
— price of, 50
— tar, 3, 51, 55
— Tarakan, 52
— Texas, 52
— Trinidad, 52
— vegetable oil, 5
Overload, 137

P

Patent, Diesel's original, 349
Piston cooling, 273
— removal, 89
— speed, 311
— volume swept through, 315
Pistons, design of, 306
Polar engine, 74, 191, 232
Port scavenging, 191, 331
Power of various engines, 43
— limiting, 46
— to drive motor ships, 175
Pressure of scavenging air, 193

Price of oil, 51, 179
Propeller efficiency of motor ships, 177

Q

Quadruplex compressor, 116
Quantity of injection air, 85

R

Reavell compressor, 116
Redwood, B., 160
Reliability, 139, 171
Reversing Diesel engines, 193, 220, 233, 240, 246, 255, 267, 275, 286, 294
Rolandseck, 229
Running Diesel engines, 61

S

Scavenge pumps, 217, 225, 232, 253
— — capacity of, 187
— — design of, 189, 320
Scavenging air, pressure of, 193
— Diesel engines, 113, 187, 219
Schneider engine, 226
Seiliger, 167
Selandia, 283, 341
Sembilan, 271
Solid injection engines, 122
Sommer, 43
Space occupied by Diesel engine, 126
Specification, Admiralty, 54
— tar oil, 55
Speed of Diesel engine, 184, 203, 252, 262, 314
Springs, 136
Staff of motor ships, 181, 202
Starting Diesel engines, 35, 61, 131
Steam engines, comparative costs, 142

Submarine Diesel engines, 211, 282
Sulzer engine, 99, 107, 206
— — indicator cards, 30
— locomotive, 339
Swan, Hunter & Wigham Richardson, 236, 240

T

Tanner engine, 264
Tar oil for Diesel engines, 3, 51, 55
Test on 200 H.P. engine, 150
— — 300 H.P. engine, 151
— — 500 H.P. engine, 158
— — high speed engine, 167
Testing Diesel engines, 146
Thermodynamic cycle, 13
Trunk piston, 186
Two-cycle Diesel engine, 37, 106

V

Valves of Diesel engine, 36
Valve setting, 27
Van de Velde, 163
Variation of speed, 185
Vegetable oil, 5
Vickers engine, 122
Vulcanus, 267

W

Weight of Diesel engines, 48, 177, 202, 251
— — ships' machinery, 177
Werkspoor engine, 87, 97, 267
Westgarth engine, 229
Wilson, 163
Willans engine, 82
Working cycle, 13

Z

Zeitschrift des Vereins deutscher Ingenieure, 167